Summary of Contents

The JavaScript Anthology
101 Essential Tips, Tricks & Hacks

by James Edwards

and Cameron Adams

The JavaScript Anthology: 101 Essential Tips, Tricks & Hacks

by James Edwards and Cameron Adams

Copyright © 2006 SitePoint Pty. Ltd.

Expert Reviewer: Bobby van der Sluis **Editor**: Georgina Laidlaw
Expert Reviewer: Derek Featherstone **Index Editor**: Bill Johncocks
Managing Editor: Simon Mackie **Cover Design**: Jess Bentley
Technical Editor: Kevin Yank **Cover Layout**: Alex Walker
Printing History: **Latest Update**: December 2006
  First Edition: February 2006

 sitepoint

Published by SitePoint Pty. Ltd.

424 Smith Street Collingwood
VIC Australia 3066.
Web: www.sitepoint.com
Email: business@sitepoint.com

ISBN 0-9752402-6-9
Printed and bound in the United States of America

About the Authors

James Edwards (aka brothercake[1]) is a freelance web developer based in the United Kingdom, specializing in advanced DHTML programming and accessible web site development. He is an outspoken advocate of standards-based development, a part-time forum moderator, and author of the Ultimate Drop Down Menu[2] system—the first commercial DHTML menu to be WCAG-compliant.

Cameron Adams has a degree in law and one in science; naturally he chose a career in web development. His business cards say, "Web Technologist" because he likes to have a hand in graphic design, JavaScript, CSS, PHP, and anything else that takes his fancy that morning. While running his own business—themaninblue.com[3]—he's consulted and worked for numerous government departments, nonprofit organizations, large corporations, and tiny startups. Cameron lives in Melbourne, Australia, where, between coding marathons, he likes to play soccer and mix some tunes for his irate neighbors.

About the Expert Reviewers

Bobby van der Sluis lives in the Netherlands and works at Blast Radius[4] in Amsterdam, where he manages the interface development department. He's a client-side web technologies and design specialist, occasionally writing about these topics on his personal web site.[5] Bobby is an evangelist of unobtrusive JavaScript, progressive enhancement, and the use of best practices, and has contributed to many notable sites, including A List Apart and CSS Zen Garden. He spends his scarce spare time with his wife Anita and newly-born daughter, Sofie.

Derek Featherstone is a well-known instructor, author, speaker, and developer with expertise in web accessibility consulting. Derek delivers technical training that is engaging, informative, and immediately applicable. A high-quality instructor, he draws on his background as a former high school teacher, plus seven years running his web development and accessibility consultancy Further Ahead.[6] Derek blogs at boxofchocolates.ca.[7]

About the Technical Editor

As Technical Director for SitePoint, Kevin Yank oversees all of its technical publications—books, articles, newsletters, and blogs. He has written over 50 articles for SitePoint, but is best known for his book, *Build Your Own Database Driven Website Using PHP &*

---

[1] http://www.brothercake.com/
[2] http://www.udm4.com/
[3] http://themaninblue.com/
[4] http://www.blastradius.com/
[5] http://www.bobbyvandersluis.com/
[6] http://www.furtherahead.com/
[7] http://boxofchocolates.ca/

MySQL. Kevin lives in Melbourne, Australia, and enjoys performing improvised comedy theatre and flying light aircraft.

About SitePoint

SitePoint specializes in publishing fun, practical, and easy-to-understand content for web professionals. Visit http://www.sitepoint.com/ to access our books, newsletters, articles and community forums.

Table of Contents

Preface

To many people, the word "JavaScript" conjures up memories of annoying popups, irritating mouse-trails, and frustrating no-right-click scripts. If you've ever been on the receiving end of such a script, you'll know how tedious they can be. Yet JavaScript is a mature, professional scripting language that's used on the majority of modern web sites, and is a key component in almost all web-based applications. Hang on! Are we talking about the same technology here?

As with so many histories, both perceptions are reasonably accurate: JavaScript does have a dubious reputation, which it earned mainly in the first dot com boom when it was used for little else than opening popups, shielding code from casual scrutiny, and adding pointless whizz-bang effects. And in recent years, as both the web development community and the world at large have become more aware of accessibility issues, JavaScript has been singled out as a cause of many problems, though in reality, it's not the technology itself that's at fault—it's the poorly planned and careless use that has given JavaScript this reputation.

Yet with the increasing popularity of remote scripting techniques (popularly referred to as "AJAX"), JavaScript is enjoying something of a renaissance. Designers, developers, and programmers from many different disciplines are becoming interested in—and impressed by—what was once the domain of specialists. Browser vendors and other technology companies are taking another look at the potential of this powerful language, as the line between the Web and the desktop becomes increasingly blurred.

JavaScript is a key component in the development of a raft of new applications, and there's never been a better time to take an interest in it.

Who Should Read this Book?

Anyone who's involved or interested in building web sites or web applications should read this book.

If you're a webmaster looking for copy-and-paste solutions to everyday needs, we have those solutions for you. If you're already an experienced JavaScript programmer, you'll find in this book scripts and discussions that sit on the bleeding edge of current practice. If you're a designer with an interest in the coding side of things, or a student who's just beginning to get into it, you'll find many rich and beautiful examples to give you insight and ideas.

Whatever your current JavaScript knowledge, we hope you'll find this book a useful and inspirational resource for modern, best practice scripting.

What's in this Book?

Chapter 1: *Getting Started With JavaScript*
This chapter, which is slightly more theoretical than the rest, provides an overview of JavaScript's capabilities and limitations, and introduces some core best practices that we'll be using through the rest of the book. It's not a beginners' tutorial, nor a ground-up summary of the language, but it focuses on finding the best ways to perform basic tasks, including practical solutions for the problems that are encountered as we try to make scripts work together.

Chapter 2: *Working with Numbers*
This chapter looks at techniques for using and processing numbers in JavaScript. It covers basic computation, number rounding, the generation and constraint of random numbers, and the use of currency values, ordinals, and other formatted numbers.

Chapter 3: *Working with Strings*
Text is the meat and drink of the Web, and processing text is one of the most common tasks in web scripting. This chapter looks at ways of manipulating strings to find information, store data, and prepare text for output, and includes a thorough introduction to regular expressions in JavaScript.

Chapter 4: *Working with Arrays*
This chapter introduces one the most powerful data-storage structures in JavaScript: the array. We'll talk about reading and writing data from an array, sorting and processing arrays, and using multidimensional arrays. We'll also discuss a similar data structure: the object literal.

Chapter 5: *Navigating the Document Object Model*
The DOM is an interface for manipulating individual parts of a document. This chapter introduces and explores the DOM, and looks at how to create and read the data from elements, attributes, and text.

Chapter 6: *Processing and Validating Forms*
In this chapter, we look at reading and writing data from different kinds of form widget, address the tasks of validating and processing form data, and discuss techniques for improving the usability of form-based interfaces.

Chapter 7: *Working with Windows and Frames*
This chapter takes a cautious look at manipulating windows and scripting across frames. These are the most controversial parts of the language, as they have the potential to create serious usability and accessibility barriers, so this chapter is centered firmly on techniques that try to avoid or alleviate these problems.

Chapter 8: *Working with Cookies*
Cookies are the simplest and most reliable method for maintaining state-persistence in JavaScript—they allow pages and applications to "remember" who you are and what you're doing. In this chapter, we introduce cookies and show you how to use them effectively.

Chapter 9: *Working with Dates and Times*
It won't win any prizes for glamour, but this chapter shows you how to get the date and time in JavaScript, how to compare and process dates and times, and how to output the final data in different formats and conventions.

Chapter 10: *Working with Images*
Images are an important part of most web designs, and this chapter explores the basic techniques involved in scripting for them. We move from simple tasks like preloading, randomly selecting, swapping, and cross-fading images, to more complex slide show, progress indicator, and image-based clock scripts.

Chapter 11: *Detecting Browser Differences*
This short chapter outlines techniques for dealing with different browsers and rendering modes. In it, we explain when and where it's appropriate to use browser detection and object detection, and how you can combine these techniques to get the most robust information.

Chapter 12: *Using JavaScript with CSS*
In this chapter, we look at how to read and write the styles from a single element or group of elements, how to read and write CSS rules to an existing or created style sheet, and how to build a style sheet switcher.

Chapter 13: *Basic Dynamic HTML*
DHTML uses HTML, the DOM, and CSS to bring static content to life, and although the term DHTML is disparaged in some quarters, we still believe it's a useful and relevant way of describing this kind of scripting. In this chapter, we cover event-handling in all its flavors, detecting the position and size of an object, tracking the mouse, and making elements appear and dis-

appear. We'll also begin to look at rearranging the DOM dynamically with a neat table-sorting script.

Chapter 14: *Time and Motion*

This chapter advances the ideas from Chapter 13 into more complex forms of scripting that use motion and animation. We'll look at timers in JavaScript, and learn how to use them for both simple and more sophisticated animations. We'll also cover drag-and-drop functionality, and put it to use selecting and sorting information, as well as creating scrollers, sliders, and transition effects.

Chapter 15: *DHTML Menus and Navigation*

This chapter enters the complex arena of DHTML menus with two major scripts—a drop-down or fly-out menu, and a folder tree or expanding menu. For each menu, we'll create a core navigation structure using clean, semantic code. Then, we'll improve on each script with usability and accessibility enhancements, including submenu indicator arrows, open and close timers, and automatic repositioning (so that a menu never runs off the page's edge). This chapter also includes solutions for the problem of menus overlapping select elements in Windows IE 5 and IE 6.

Chapter 16: *JavaScript and Accessibility*

This chapter provides an overview of the current state of play regarding JavaScript and accessibility. It's focused on ideas and techniques for making scripts accessible to the keyboard, and also touches on how scripting may impact on people with learning or cognitive disabilities. We'll also examine a range of different scripts, including AJAX applications, to see how they behave with screen readers.

Chapter 17: *Using JavaScript with Flash*

In this chapter, we look at the narrow alliance between these two technologies, learning to detect whether a user has the Flash plugin, and mastering communication between JavaScript and Flash.

Chapter 18: *Building Web Applications with JavaScript*

This chapter delves into the exciting area of online application design, including data retrieval using XMLHttpRequest, as well as the older technique of using iframes. We'll also talk about creating custom dialogs, building editable elements like rich-text entry fields, and controlling and creating text selections to generate an auto-complete search field.

Chapter 19: *Object Orientation in JavaScript*

Object oriented programming is generally considered the best approach to large-scale programming projects, and in this chapter we introduce OOP, exploring its core concepts and benefits. We'll cover the practical techniques involved in creating an object oriented or object based script, and we'll talk about scope, inheritance, and object namespacing.

Chapter 20: *Keeping up the Pace*

The final chapter looks at everyday techniques for writing faster, more efficient code that's shorter and uses less memory. We'll also cover more brutal techniques for optimizing and obfuscating production code, but with the warning that some optimizations are more trouble than they're worth!

The Book's Web Site

Located at http://www.sitepoint.com/books/jsant1, the web site supporting this book will give you access to the following facilities.

The Code Archive

As you progress through the text, you'll note a number of references to the code archive. This is a downloadable ZIP archive that contains complete code for all the examples presented in this book. You can grab it on the book's web site at http://www.sitepoint.com/books/jsant1/code.php.

Updates and Errata

The Errata page on the book's web site will always have the latest information about known typographical and code errors, and necessary updates for changes to technologies. Visit it at http://www.sitepoint.com/books/jsant1/errata.php.

The SitePoint Forums

While we've made every attempt to anticipate any questions you may have, and answer them in this book, there's no way that *any* book could teach you everything you'll ever need to know about using JavaScript in your web development projects. If you have a question about anything in this book, the best place to go for a quick answer is http://www.sitepoint.com/forums/—SitePoint's vibrant and knowledgeable community.

The SitePoint Newsletters

In addition to books like this one, SitePoint offers free email newsletters.

The SitePoint Tech Times covers the latest news, product releases, trends, tips, and techniques for all technical aspects of web development. The long-running *SitePoint Tribune* is a biweekly digest of the business and moneymaking aspects of the Web. Whether you're a freelance developer looking for tips to score that dream contract, or a marketer striving to keep abreast of changes to the major search engines, this is the newsletter for you. *The SitePoint Design View* is a monthly compilation of the best in web design. From new CSS layout methods to subtle Photoshop techniques, SitePoint's chief designer shares his years of experience in its pages.

Browse the archives or sign up to any of SitePoint's free newsletters at http://www.sitepoint.com/newsletter/.

Your Feedback

If you can't find an answer through the forums, or you wish to contact us for any other reason, the best place to write is books@sitepoint.com. We have a well-manned email support system set up to track your inquiries, and if our support staff are unable to answer your question, they send it straight to us. Suggestions for improvement, as well as notices of any mistakes you may find, are especially welcome.

Acknowledgements

I'd like to thank all those who helped and supported me while writing this book, particularly to Eddie and Debi, Jon and Kim, who provided as much encouragement as they did practical support. I'd also like to thank Dave Evans, a significant influence from my early days as a developer.

—James Edwards

1

Getting Started with JavaScript

As we hope to demonstrate in many practical solutions throughout this book, JavaScript is an amazingly useful language that offers many unique benefits. With a little consideration for how scripted functionality degrades, you can use Java-Script to bring a whole range of functional, design and usability improvements to your web sites.

Let's begin with an introduction to JavaScript, exploring what it's for, and how we can use it.

JavaScript Defined

JavaScript is a scripting language that's used to add interactivity and dynamic behaviors to web pages and applications. JavaScript can interact with other components of a web page, such as HTML and CSS, to make them change in real time, or respond to user events.

You'll undoubtedly have seen JavaScript in the source code of web pages. It might have been inline code in an HTML element, like this:

```
<a href="page.html" onclick="open('page.html'); return false;">
```

It might have appeared as a `script` element linking to another file:

```
<script type="text/javascript" src="myscript.js"></script>
```

Or it may have had code directly inside it:

```
<script type="text/javascript">
function saySomething(message)
{
  alert(message);
}
saySomething('Hello world!');
</script>
```

Don't worry about the differences between these snippets yet. There are quite a few ways—both good and bad—in which we can add JavaScript to a web page. We'll look at these approaches in detail later in this chapter.

JavaScript was developed by Netscape and implemented in Netscape 2, although it was originally called LiveScript. The growing popularity of another language, Java, prompted Netscape to change the name in an attempt to cash in on the connection, as JavaScript provided the ability to communicate between the browser and a Java applet.

But as the language was developed both by Netscape, in its original form, and by Microsoft, in the similar-but-different JScript implementation, it became clear that web scripting was too important to be left to the wolves of vendor competition. So, in 1996, development was handed over to an international standards body called ECMA, and JavaScript became ECMAScript or ECMA-262.

Most people still refer to it as JavaScript, and this can be a cause of confusion: apart from the name and similarities in syntax, Java and JavaScript are nothing alike.

JavaScript's Limitations

JavaScript is most commonly used as a **client-side language**, and in this case the "client" refers to the end-user's web browser, in which JavaScript is interpreted and run. This distinguishes it from **server-side** languages like PHP and ASP, which run on the server and send static data to the client.

Since JavaScript does not have access to the server environment, there are many tasks that, while trivial when executed in PHP, simply cannot be achieved with JavaScript: reading and writing to a database, for example, or creating text files. But since JavaScript *does* have access to the client environment, it can make decisions based on data that server-side languages simply don't have, such as the position of the mouse, or the rendered size of an element.

What About ActiveX?

If you're already quite familiar with Microsoft's JScript, you might be thinking "but JavaScript *can* do some of these things using ActiveX," and that's true—but ActiveX is not part of ECMAScript. ActiveX is a Windows-specific mechanism for allowing Internet Explorer to access COM (the Component Object Model at the heart of Windows scripting technology) and generally only runs in trusted environments, such as an intranet. There are some specific exceptions we'll come across—examples of ActiveX controls that run without special security in IE (such as the Flash plugin, and XMLHttpRequest)—but for the most part, scripting using ActiveX is outside the scope of this book.

Usually, the computer on which a client is run will not be as powerful as a server, so JavaScript is not the best tool for doing large amounts of data processing. But the immediacy of data processing on the client makes this option attractive for small amounts of processing, as a response can be received straight away; form validation, for instance, makes a good candidate for client-side processing.

But to compare server-side and client-side languages with a view to which is "better" is misguided. Neither is better—they're tools for different jobs, and the functional crossover between them is small. However, increased interactions *between* client-side and server-side scripting are giving rise to a new generation of web scripting, which uses technologies such as XMLHttpRequest to make requests for server data, run server-side scripts, and then manage the results on the client side. We'll be looking into these technologies in depth in Chapter 18.

Security Restrictions

As JavaScript operates within the realm of highly sensitive data and programs, its capabilities have been restricted to ensure that it can't be used maliciously. As such, there are many things that JavaScript simply is not allowed to do. For example, it cannot read most system settings from your computer, interact directly with your hardware, or cause programs to run.

Also, some specific interactions that would normally be allowed for a particular element are not permitted within JavaScript, because of that element's properties. For example, changing the value of a form <input> is usually no problem, but if it's a file input field (e.g., <input type="file">), writing to it is not allowed at all—a restriction that prevents malicious scripts from making users upload a file they didn't choose.

There are quite a few examples of similar security restrictions, which we'll expand on as they arise in the applications we'll cover in this book. But to summarize, here's a list of JavaScript's major limitations and security restrictions, including those we've already seen. JavaScript cannot:

- ❏ open and read files directly (except under specific circumstances, as detailed in Chapter 18).

- ❏ create or edit files on the user's computer (except cookies, which are discussed in Chapter 8).

- ❏ read HTTP POST data.

- ❏ read system settings, or any other data from the user's computer that is not made available through language or host objects.[1]

- ❏ modify the value of a file input field.

- ❏ alter the display of a document that was loaded from a different domain.

- ❏ close or modify the toolbars and other elements of a window that was not opened by script (i.e., the main browser window).

Ultimately, JavaScript might not be supported at all.

It's also worth bearing in mind that many browsers include options that allow greater precision than simply enabling or disabling JavaScript. For example, Opera includes options to disallow scripts from closing windows, moving windows, writing to the status bar, receiving right-clicks … the list goes on. There's little you can do to work around this, but mostly, you won't need to—such options have evolved to suppress "annoying" scripts (status bar scrollers, no-right-click scripts, etc.) so if you stay away from those kinds of scripts, the issue will come up only rarely.

---

[1] Host objects are things like `window` and `screen`, which are provided by the environment rather than the language itself.

JavaScript Best Practices

JavaScript best practices place a strong emphasis on the question of what you should do for people whose browsers don't support scripting, who have scripting turned off, or who are unable to interact with the script for another reason (e.g., the user makes use of an assistive technology that does not support scripting).

That final issue is the most difficult to address, and we'll be focusing on solutions to this problem in Chapter 16. In this section, I'd like to look at three core principles of good JavaScript:

progressive enhancement	providing for users who don't have JavaScript
unobtrusive scripting	separating content from behavior
consistent coding practice	using braces and semicolon terminators

The first principle ensures that we're thinking about the bigger picture whenever we use a script on our site. The second point makes for easier maintenance on our end, and better usability and **graceful degradation**[2] for the user. The third principle makes code easier to read and maintain.

Providing for Users who Don't Have JavaScript (Progressive Enhancement)

There are several reasons why users might not have JavaScript:

❑ They're using a device that doesn't support scripting at all, or supports it in a limited way.

❑ They're behind a proxy server or firewall that filters out JavaScript.

❑ They have JavaScript switched off deliberately.

The first point covers a surprisingly large and ever-growing range of devices, including small-screen devices like PDAs, mid-screen devices including WebTV

---

[2]Graceful degradation means that if JavaScript is not supported, the browser can naturally fall back on, or "degrade" to, non-scripted functionality.

and the Sony PSP, as well as legacy JavaScript browsers such as Opera 5 and Netscape 4.

The last point in the list above is arguably the least likely (apart from other developers playing devil's advocate!), but the reasons aren't all that important: some users simply don't have JavaScript, and we should accommodate them. There's no way to quantify the numbers of users who fall into this category, because detecting JavaScript support from the server is notoriously unreliable, but the figures I've seen put the proportion of users who have JavaScript switched off between 5% and 20%, depending on whether you describe search engine robots as "users."

Solution

The long-standing approach to this issue is to use the HTML `noscript` element, the contents of which are rendered by browsers that don't support the `script` element at all, and browsers that support it but have scripting turned off.

Although it's a sound idea, in practice this solution has become less useful over time, because `noscript` *cannot differentiate by capability*. A browser that offers limited JavaScript support is not going to be able to run a complicated script, but such devices *are* script-capable browsers, so they won't parse the `noscript` element either. These browsers would end up with nothing.

A better approach to this issue is to begin with static HTML, then use scripting to modify or add dynamic behaviors within that static content.

Let's look at a simple example. The preferred technique for making DHTML menus uses an unordered list as the main menu structure. We'll be devoting the whole of Chapter 15 to this subject, but this short example illustrates the point:

```
<ul id="menu">
  <li><a href="/">Home</a></li>
  <li><a href="/about/">About</a></li>
  <li><a href="/contact/">Contact</a></li>
</ul>

<script type="text/javascript" src="menu.js"></script>
```

The list of links is plain HTML, so it exists for all users, whether or not they have scripting enabled. If scripting *is* supported, our `menu.js` script can apply dynamic behaviors, but if scripting isn't supported, the content still appears. We haven't differentiated between devices explicitly—we've just provided content that's dynamic if the browser can handle it, and static if not.

This scripting approach is popularly referred to as **progressive enhancement**, and it's a methodology we'll be using throughout this book.

Discussion

The "traditional" approach to this scenario would be to generate a separate, dynamic menu in pure JavaScript, and to have fallback static content inside a no-script element:

```
<script type="text/javascript" src="menu.js"></script>

<noscript>
  <ul>
    <li><a href="/">Home</a></li>
    <li><a href="/about/">About</a></li>
    <li><a href="/contact/">Contact</a></li>
  </ul>
</noscript>
```

But, as we've already seen, a wide range of devices will fall though this net, because JavaScript support is no longer an all-or-nothing proposition. The progressive enhancement approach introduced in this solution provides default content to *all* devices, and applies scripted functionality only if it works.

Don't Ask!

Neither this technique nor the noscript element should be used to add a message that reads, "Please turn on JavaScript to continue." At best, such a message is presumptuous ("Why should I?"); at worst it may be unhelpful ("I can't!") or meaningless ("What's JavaScript?"). Just like those splash pages that say, "Please upgrade your browser," these messages are as useful to the average web user as a road sign that reads, "Please use a different car."

Occasionally, you may be faced with a situation in which equivalent functionality simply *cannot* be provided without JavaScript. In such cases, I think it's okay to have a static message that informs the user of this incompatibility (in nontechnical terms, of course). But, for the most part, try to avoid providing this kind of message unless it's literally the only way.

Separating Content from Behavior (Unobtrusive Scripting)

Separating content from behavior means keeping different aspects of a web page's construction apart. Jeffrey Zeldman famously refers to this as the "three-legged stool" of web development[3]—comprising content (HTML), presentation (CSS), and behavior (JavaScript)—which emphasizes not just the difference in each aspect's functioning, but also the fact that they should be separated from one another.

Good separation makes for sites that are easier to maintain, are more accessible, and degrade well in older or lower-spec browsers.

Solution

At one extreme, which is directly opposed to the ideal of separating content from behavior, we can write inline code directly inside attribute event handlers. This is very messy, and generally should be avoided:

```
<div id="content"
    onmouseover="this.style.borderColor='red'"
    onmouseout="this.style.borderColor='black'">
```

We can improve the situation by taking the code that does the work and abstracting it into a **function**:

```
<div id="content"
    onmouseover="changeBorder('red')"
    onmouseout="changeBorder('black')">
```

Defining a function to do the work for us lets us provide most of our code in a separate JavaScript file:

File: **separate-content-behaviors.js (excerpt)**

```
function changeBorder(element, to)
{
  element.style.borderColor = to;
}
```

---

[3]Zeldman, J. *Designing with Web Standards*. New Riders, 2003.

But a much better approach is to avoid using inline event handlers completely. Instead, we can make use of the Document Object Model (DOM) to bind the event handlers to elements in the HTML document. The DOM is a standard programming interface by which languages like JavaScript can access the contents of HTML documents, removing the need for any JavaScript code to appear in the HTML document itself. In this example, our HTML code would look like the following:

```
<div id="content">
```

Here's the scripting we'd use:

File: **separate-content-behaviors.js**

```
function changeBorder(element, to)
{
  element.style.borderColor = to;
}

var contentDiv = document.getElementById('content');

contentDiv.onmouseover = function()
{
  changeBorder('red');
};

contentDiv.onmouseout = function()
{
  changeBorder('black');
};
```

This approach allows us to add, remove, or change event handlers without having to edit the HTML, and since the document itself does not rely on or refer to the scripting at all, browsers that don't understand JavaScript will not be affected by it. This solution also provides the benefits of reusability, because we can bind the same functions to other elements as needed, without having to edit the HTML.

This solution hinges on our ability to access elements through the DOM, which we'll cover in depth in Chapter 5.

The Benefits of Separation

By practicing good separation of content and behavior, we gain not only a practical benefit in terms of smoother degradation, but also the advantage of *thinking* in terms of separation. Since we've separated the HTML and

JavaScript, instead of combining them, when we look at the HTML we're less likely to forget that its core function should be to describe the *content* of the page, independent of any scripting.

Andy Clarke refers to the **web standards trifle**,[4] which is a useful analogy, A trifle looks the way a good web site should: when you look at the bowl, you can see all the separate layers that make up the dessert. The opposite of this might be a fruit cake: when you look at the cake, you can't tell what each different ingredient is. All you can see is a mass of cake.

Discussion

It's important to note that when you bind an event handler to an element like this, you can't do it until the element actually exists. If you put the preceding script in the `head` section of a page as it is, it would report errors and fail to work, because the `content div` has not been rendered at the point at which the script is processed.

The most direct solution is to put the code inside a `load` event handler. It will always be safe there because the `load` event doesn't fire until after the document has been fully rendered:

```
window.onload = function()
{
  var contentDiv = document.getElementById('content');

    ⋮
};
```

Or more clearly, with a bit more typing:

```
window.onload = init;

function init()
{
  var contentDiv = document.getElementById('content');

    ⋮
}
```

The problem with the `load` event handler is that only one script on a page can use it; if two or more scripts attempt to install `load` event handlers, each script will override the handler of the one that came before it. The solution to this

---

[4] http://www.stuffandnonsense.co.uk/archives/web_standards_trifle.html

problem is to respond to the `load` event in a more modern way; we'll look at this shortly, in "Getting Multiple Scripts to Work on the Same Page".

Using Braces and Semicolons (Consistent Coding Practice)

In many JavaScript operations, braces and semicolons are optional, so is there any value to including them when they're not essential?

Solution

Although braces and semicolons are often optional, you should always include them. This makes code easier to read—by others, and by yourself in future—and helps you avoid problems as you reuse and reorganize the code in your scripts (which will often render an optional semicolon essential).

For example, this code is perfectly valid:

File: **semicolons-braces.js** (excerpt)

```
if (something) alert('something')
else alert('nothing')
```

This code is valid thanks to a process in the JavaScript interpreter called **semicolon insertion**. Whenever the interpreter finds two code fragments that are separated by one or more line breaks, and those fragments wouldn't make sense if they were on a single line, the interpreter treats them as though a semicolon existed between them. By a similar mechanism, the braces that normally surround the code to be executed in `if-else` statements may be inferred from the syntax, even though they're not present. Think of this process as the interpreter adding the missing code elements for you.

Even though these code elements are not always necessary, it's easier to remember to use them when they *are* required, and easier to read the resulting code, if you do use them consistently.

Our example above would be better written like this:

File: **semicolons-braces.js** (excerpt)

```
if (something) { alert('something'); }
else { alert('nothing'); }
```

This version represents the ultimate in code readability:

File: **semicolons-braces.js (excerpt)**

```
if (something)
{
  alert('something');
}
else
{
  alert('nothing');
}
```

Using Function Literals

As you become experienced with the intricacies of the JavaScript language, it will become common for you to use **function literals** to create anonymous functions as needed, and assign them to JavaScript variables and object properties. In this context, the function definition should be followed by a semicolon, which terminates the variable assignment:

```
var saySomething = function(message)
{
    ⋮
};
```

Adding a Script to a Page

Before a script can begin doing exciting things, you have to load it into a web page. There are two techniques for doing this, one of which is distinctly better than the other.

Solution

The first and most direct technique is to write code directly inside a `script` element, as we've seen before:

```
<script type="text/javascript">
function saySomething(message)
{
  alert(message);
}
```

```
saySomething('Hello world!');
</script>
```

The problem with this method is that in legacy and text-only browsers—those that don't support the `script` element at all—the contents may be rendered as literal text.

A better alternative, which avoids this problem, is always to put the script in an external JavaScript file. Here's what that looks like:

```
<script type="text/javascript" src="what-is-javascript.js"
   ></script>
```

This loads an external JavaScript file named `what-is-javascript.js`. The file should contain the code that you would otherwise put inside the `script` element, like this:

File: **what-is-javascript.js**

```
function saySomething(message)
{
  alert(message);
}

saySomething('Hello world!');
```

When you use this method, browsers that don't understand the `script` element will ignore it and render no contents (since the element is empty), but browsers that do understand it will load and process the script. This helps to keep scripting and content separate, and is far more easily maintained—you can use the same script on multiple pages without having to maintain copies of the code in multiple documents.

Discussion

You may question the recommendation of not using code directly inside the `script` element. "No problem," you might say. "I'll just put HTML comments around it." Well, I'd have to disagree with that: using HTML comments to "hide" code is a very bad habit that we should avoid falling into.

Putting HTML Comments Around Code

A validating parser is not required to read comments, much less to process them. The fact that commented JavaScript works at all is an anachronism—a throwback to an old, outdated practice that makes an assumption about the document that might not be true: it assumes that the page is served to a non-validating parser.

All the examples in this book are provided in HTML (as opposed to XHTML), so this assumption is reasonable, but if you're working with XHTML (correctly served with a MIME type of `application/xhtml+xml`), the comments in your code may be discarded by a validating XML parser before the document is processed by the browser, in which case commented scripts will no longer work *at all*. For the sake of ensuring forwards compatibility (and the associated benefits to your own coding habits as much as to individual projects), I strongly recommend that you avoid putting comments around code in this way. Your JavaScript should *always* be housed in external JavaScript files.

The `language` Attribute

The `language` attribute is no longer necessary. In the days when Netscape 4 and its contemporaries were the dominant browsers, the `<script>` tag's `language` attribute had the role of sniffing for up-level support (for example, by specifying `javascript1.3`), and impacted on small aspects of the way the script interpreter worked.

But specifying a version of JavaScript is pretty meaningless now that JavaScript is ECMAScript, and the `language` attribute has been deprecated in favor of the `type` attribute. This attribute specifies the MIME type of included files, such as scripts and style sheets, and is the only one you need to use:

```
<script type="text/javascript">
```

Technically, the value should be `text/ecmascript`, but Internet Explorer doesn't understand that. Personally, I'd be happier if it did, simply because `javascript` is (ironically) a word I have great difficulty typing—I've lost count of the number of times a script failure occurred because I'd typed `type="text/javsacript"`.

Getting Multiple Scripts to Work on the Same Page

When multiple scripts don't work together, it's almost always because the scripts want to assign event handlers for the same event on a given element. Since each element can have only one handler for each event, the scripts override one another's event handlers.

Solution

The usual suspect is the `window` object's `load` event handler, because only one script on a page can use this event; if two or more scripts are using it, the last one will override those that came before it.

We could call multiple functions from inside a single `load` handler, like this:

```
window.onload = function()
{
  firstFunction();
  secondFunction();
}
```

But, if we used this code, we'd be tied to a single piece of code from which we'd have to do everything we needed to at load time. A better solution would provide a means of adding `load` event handlers that *don't conflict with other handlers*.

When the following single function is called, it will allow us to assign *any number* of `load` event handlers, without any of them conflicting:

File: **add-load-listener.js**

```
function addLoadListener(fn)
{
  if (typeof window.addEventListener != 'undefined')
  {
    window.addEventListener('load', fn, false);
  }
  else if (typeof document.addEventListener != 'undefined')
  {
    document.addEventListener('load', fn, false);
  }
  else if (typeof window.attachEvent != 'undefined')
  {
    window.attachEvent('onload', fn);
  }
  else
  {
    var oldfn = window.onload;
    if (typeof window.onload != 'function')
    {
      window.onload = fn;
    }
    else
    {
```

```
    window.onload = function()
    {
      oldfn();
      fn();
    };
  }
 }
}
```

Once this function is in place, we can use it any number of times:

```
addLoadListener(firstFunction);
addLoadListener(secondFunction);
addLoadListener(twentyThirdFunction);
```

You get the idea!

Discussion

JavaScript includes methods for adding (and removing) **event listeners**, which operate much like event handlers, but allow multiple listeners to subscribe to a single event on an element. Unfortunately, the syntax for event listeners is completely different in Internet Explorer than it is in other browsers: where IE uses a proprietary method, others implement the W3C Standard. We'll come across this dichotomy frequently, and we'll discuss it in detail in Chapter 13.

The W3C standard method is called `addEventListener`:

```
window.addEventListener('load', firstFunction, false);
```

The IE method is called `attachEvent`:

```
window.attachEvent('onload', firstFunction);
```

As you can see, the standard construct takes the name of the event (without the "on" prefix), followed by the function that's to be called when the event occurs, and an argument that controls event bubbling (see Chapter 13 for more details on this). The IE method takes the event *handler* name (*including* the "on" prefix), followed by the name of the function.

To put these together, we need to add some tests to check for the existence of each method before we try to use it. We can do this using the JavaScript operator `typeof`, which identifies different types of data (as `"string"`, `"number"`, "boolean", "object", "array", "function", or "undefined"). A method that doesn't exist will return "undefined".

```
if (typeof window.addEventListener != 'undefined')
{
  : window.addEventListener is supported
}
```

There's one additional complication: in Opera, the load event that can trigger multiple event listeners comes from the document object, not the window. But we can't just use document because that doesn't work in older Mozilla browsers (such as Netscape 6). To plot a route through these quirks we need to test for window.addEventListener, then document.addEventListener, then window.attachEvent, in that order.

Finally, for browsers that don't support any of those methods (Mac IE 5, in practice), the fallback solution is to **chain** multiple old-style event handlers together so they'll get called in turn when the event occurs. We do this by dynamically constructing a new event handler that calls any existing handler before it calls the newly-assigned handler when the event occurs.[5]

File: **add-load-listener.js** (excerpt)

```
var oldfn = window.onload;
if (typeof window.onload != 'function')
{
  window.onload = fn;
}
else
{
  window.onload = function()
  {
    oldfn();
    fn();
  };
}
```

Don't worry if you don't understand the specifics of how this works—we'll explore the techniques involved in much greater detail in Chapter 13. There, we'll learn that event listeners are useful not just for the load event, but for *any* kind of event-driven script.

---

[5] This technique was pioneered by Simon Willison
[http://www.sitepoint.com/blogs/2004/05/26/closures-and-executing-javascript-on-page-load/].

Hiding JavaScript Source Code

If you've ever created something that you're proud of, you'll understand the desire to protect your intellectual property. But JavaScript on the Web is an open-source language by nature; it comes to the browser in its source form, so if the browser can run it, a person can read it.

There are a few applications on the Web that claim to offer source-code encryption, but in reality, there's nothing you can do to encrypt source-code that another coder couldn't decrypt in seconds. In fact, some of these programs actually cause problems: they often reformat code in such a way as to make it slower, less efficient, or just plain broken. My advice? Stay away from them like the plague.

But still, the desire to hide code remains. There is something that you can do to **obfuscate**, if not outright encrypt, the code that your users can see.

Solution

Code that has been stripped of all comments and unnecessary whitespace is very difficult to read, and as you might expect, extracting individual bits of functionality from such code is extremely difficult. The simple technique of compressing your scripts in this way can put-off all but the most determined hacker. For example, take this code:

File: **obfuscate-code.js (excerpt)**

```
var oldfn = window.onload;
if (typeof window.onload != 'function')
{
  window.onload = fn;
}
else
{
  window.onload = function()
  {
    oldfn();
    fn();
  };
}
```

We can compress that code into the following two lines simply by removing unnecessary whitespace:

File: **obfuscate-code.js (excerpt)**

```
var oldfn=window.onload;if(typeof window.onload!='function'){
window.onload=fn;}else{window.onload=function(){oldfn();fn();};}
```

However, remember that important word—unnecessary. Some whitespace is essential, such as the single spaces after `var` and `typeof`.

Discussion

This practice has advantages quite apart from the benefits of obfuscation. Scripts that are stripped of comments and unnecessary whitespace are smaller; therefore, they're faster loading, and may process more quickly.

But please do remember that the code must remain strictly formatted using semicolon line terminators and braces (as we discussed in "Using Braces and Semicolons (Consistent Coding Practice)"); otherwise, the removal of line breaks will make lines of code run together, and ultimately cause errors.

Before you start compression, remember to make a copy of the script. I know it seems obvious, but I've made this mistake plenty of times, and it's all the more galling for being so elementary! What I do these days is write and maintain scripts in their fully spaced and commented form, then run them through a bunch of search/replace expressions just before they're published. Usually, I keep two copies of a script, named `myscript.js` and `myscript-commented.js`, or something similar.

We'll come back to this subject in Chapter 20, where we'll discuss this among a range of techniques for improving the speed and efficiency of scripts, as well as reducing the amount of physical space they require.

Debugging a Script

Debugging is the process of finding and (hopefully) fixing bugs. Most browsers have some kind of bug reporting built in, and a couple of external debuggers are also worth investigating.

Understanding a Browser's Built-in Error Reporting

Opera, Mozilla browsers (such as Firefox), and Internet Explorer all have decent bug reporting functionality built in, but Opera and Mozilla's debugging tools are the most useful.

Opera

Open the JavaScript console from Tools > Advanced > JavaScript console. You can also set it to open automatically when an error occurs by going to Tools > Preferences > Advanced > Content, then clicking the JavaScript options button to open its dialog, and checking Open JavaScript console on error.

Firefox and other Mozilla browsers

Open the JavaScript console from Tools > JavaScript console.

Internet Explorer for Windows

Go to Tools > Internet Options > Advanced and uncheck the option Disable script debugging, then check the option Display a notification about every script error, to make a dialog pop up whenever an error occurs.

Internet Explorer for Mac

Go to Explorer > Preferences > Web Browser > Web Content and check the Show scripting error alerts option.

Safari doesn't include bug reporting by default, but recent versions have a "secret" Debug menu, including a JavaScript console, which you can enable by entering the following Terminal command:[6]

```
$ defaults write com.apple.safari IncludeDebugMenu -bool true
```

You can also use an extension called Safari Enhancer,[7] which includes an option to dump JavaScript messages to the Mac OS Console; however, these messages are not very helpful.

Understanding the various browsers' console messages can take a little practice, because each browser gives such different information. Here's an example of an error—a mistyped function call:

---

[6]The $ represents the command prompt, and is not to be typed.
[7] http://www.lordofthecows.com/safari_enhancer.php

```
function saySomething(message)
{
    :
  alert(message);
}
saySometing('Hello world');
```

Firefox gives a concise but very accurate report, which includes the line number at which the error occurred, and a description, as shown in Figure 1.1.

Figure 1.1. The JavaScript errors console in Firefox

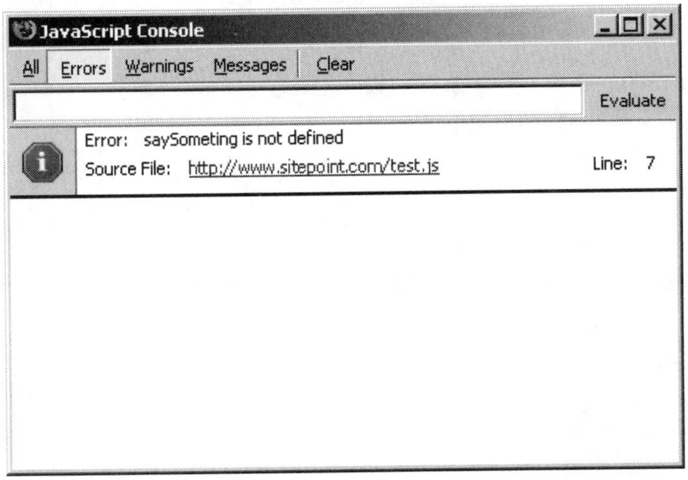

As Figure 1.2 illustrates, Opera gives an extremely verbose report, including a backtrace to the event from which the error originated, a notification of the line where it occurred, and a description.

A **backtrace** helps when an error occurs in code that was originally called by other code; for example, where an event-handler calls a function that goes on to call a second function, and it's at this point that the error occurs. Opera's console will trace this process back through each stage to its originating event or call.

Internet Explorer gives the fairly basic kind of report shown in Figure 1.3. It provides the number of the line at which the interpreter encountered the error (this may or may not be close to the true location of the actual problem),[8] plus

---

[8]Internet Explorer is particularly bad at locating errors in external JavaScript files. Often, the line number it will report as the error location will actually be the number of the line at which the script is loaded in the HTML file.

a summary of the error type, though it doesn't explain the specifics of the error itself.

Figure 1.2. The JavaScript console in Opera

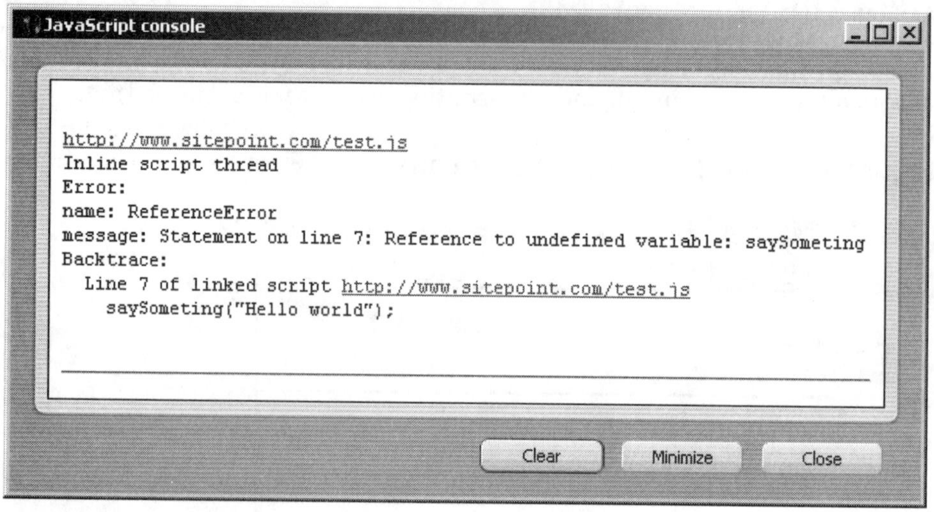

```
JavaScript console                                                _ |□| x|

    http://www.sitepoint.com/test.js
    Inline script thread
    Error:
    name: ReferenceError
    message: Statement on line 7: Reference to undefined variable: saySometing
    Backtrace:
       Line 7 of linked script http://www.sitepoint.com/test.js
          saySometing("Hello world");

                                        Clear      Minimize      Close
```

Figure 1.3. The JavaScript console in Windows IE

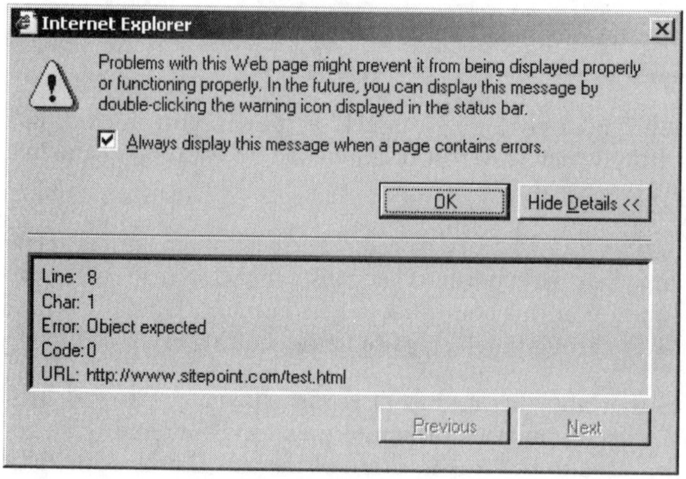

```
Internet Explorer                                              x|

 /!\   Problems with this Web page might prevent it from being displayed properly
       or functioning properly. In the future, you can display this message by
       double-clicking the warning icon displayed in the status bar.

       [✓] Always display this message when a page contains errors.

                          [    OK    ]      Hide Details <<

       Line: 8
       Char: 1
       Error: Object expected
       Code: 0
       URL: http://www.sitepoint.com/test.html

                                    Previous          Next
```

As you probably gathered, I'm not overly impressed by Internet Explorer's error reporting, but it is vastly better than nothing: at least you know that an error has occurred.

Using alert

The `alert` function is a very useful means of analyzing errors—you can use it at any point in a script to probe objects and variables to see if they contain the data you expect. For example, if you have a function that has several conditional branches, you can add an `alert` within each condition to find out which is being executed:

File: **debugging-dialogs.js**

```
function checkAge(years)
{
  if (years < 13)
  {
    alert('less than 13');

    : other scripting
  }
  else if (years >= 13 && years <= 21)
  {
    alert('13 to 21');

    : other scripting
  }
  else
  {
    alert('older');

    : other scripting
  }
}
```

Maybe the value for *years* is not coming back as a number, like it should. You could add to the start of your script an `alert` that tests the variable to see what type it is:

```
function checkAge(years)
{
  alert(typeof years);
  :
```

In theory, you can put any amount of information in an **alert** dialog, although a very long string of data could create such a wide dialog that some of the information would be clipped or outside the window. You can avoid this by formatting the output with escape characters, such as \n for a line break.

Using **try-catch**

The **try-catch** construct is an incredibly useful way to get a script just to "try something," leaving you to handle any errors that may result. The basic construct looks like this:

File: **debugging-trycatch.js** (excerpt)

```
try
{
  ⋮ some code
}
catch (err)
{
  ⋮ this gets run if the try{} block results in an error
}
```

If you're not sure where an error's coming from, you can wrap a **try-catch** around a very large block of code to trap the general failure, then tighten it around progressively smaller chunks of code within that block. For example, you could wrap a **try** brace around the first half of a function (at a convenient point in the code), then around the second half, to see where the error occurs; you could then divide the suspect half again, at a convenient point, and keep going until you've isolated the problematic line.

catch has a single argument (I've called it *err* in this case), which receives the **error object**; we can query properties of that object, such as **name** and **message**, to get details about the error.

Often, I use a **for-in** iterator to run through the entire object and find out what it says:

File: **debugging-trycatch.js** (excerpt)

```
for (var i in err)
{
  alert(i + ': ' + err[i]);
}
```

Writing to the Page or Window

If you're examining a great deal of data while debugging, or you're dealing with data that's formatted in a complicated way, it's often better to write that data directly to a page or popup window than to try to deal with lots of alert dialogs. If you're examining data in a loop, in particular, you could end up generating hundreds of dialogs, each of which you'll have to dismiss manually—a very tedious process.

In these kinds of situations, we can use an element's innerHTML property to write the data to the page. Here's an example in which we build a list using the contents of an array (data), then write it into a test div:

File: **debugging-writing.js (excerpt)**

```
var test = document.getElementById('testdiv');

test.innerHTML += '<ul>';
for (var i = 0; i < data.length; i++)
{
  test.innerHTML += '<li>' + i + '=' + data[i] + '</li>';
}
test.innerHTML += '</ul>';
```

We can also write the data into a popup, which is useful if there's no convenient place to put it on the page:

File: **debugging-writing.js (excerpt)**

```
var win = window.open('', win, 'width=320,height=240');

win.document.open();
win.document.write('<ul>');
for (var i = 0; i < data.length; i++)
{
  win.document.write('<li>' + i + '=' + data[i] + '</li>')
}
win.document.write('</ul>');
win.document.close();
```

You can format the output however you like, and use it to structure data in any way that makes it easier for you to find the error.

When you're working with smaller amounts of data, you can gain a similar advantage by writing the data to the main title element:

```
                                          File: debugging-writing.js (excerpt)
document.title = '0 = ' + data[0];
```

This final approach is most useful when tracking data that changes continually or rapidly, such as a value being processed by a `setInterval` function (an asynchronous timer we'll meet properly in Chapter 14).

Using an External Debugger

I can recommend two debuggers:

❏ **Venkman**[9] for Mozilla and Firefox

❏ **Microsoft Script Debugger**[10] for Windows Internet Explorer

External debuggers are a far more detailed way to analyze your scripts, and have much greater capabilities than their in-browser counterparts. External debuggers can do things like stopping the execution of the script at specific points, or watching particular properties so that you're informed of any change to them, however it may be caused. They also include features that allow you "step through" code line by line, in order help find errors that may occur only briefly, or are otherwise difficult to isolate.

External debuggers are complex pieces of software, and it can take time for developers to learn how to use them properly. They can be very useful for highlighting logical errors, and valuable as learning tools in their own right, but they're limited in their ability to help with browser incompatibilities: they're only useful there if the bug you're looking for is in the browser that the debugger supports!

Strict Warnings

If you open the JavaScript console in Firefox you'll see that it includes options to show Errors and Warnings. Warnings notify you of code that, though it is not erroneous per se, does rely on automatic error handling, uses deprecated syntax, or is in some other way untrue to the ECMAScript specification.[11]

For example, the variable `fruit` is defined twice in the code below:

---

[9] http://www.mozilla.org/projects/venkman/
[10] http://msdn.microsoft.com/scripting/
[11] To see these warnings, it may be necessary to enable strict reporting by typing in the address about:config and setting javascript.options.strict to `true`.

File: **strict-warnings.js** (excerpt)

```
var fruit = 'mango';

if (basket.indexOf('apple') != -1)
{
  var fruit = 'apple';
}
```

We should have omitted the second `var`, because `var` is used to declare a variable for the *first time*, which we've already done. Figure 1.4 shows how the JavaScript console will highlight our error as a warning.

Figure 1.4. The JavaScript warnings console in Firefox

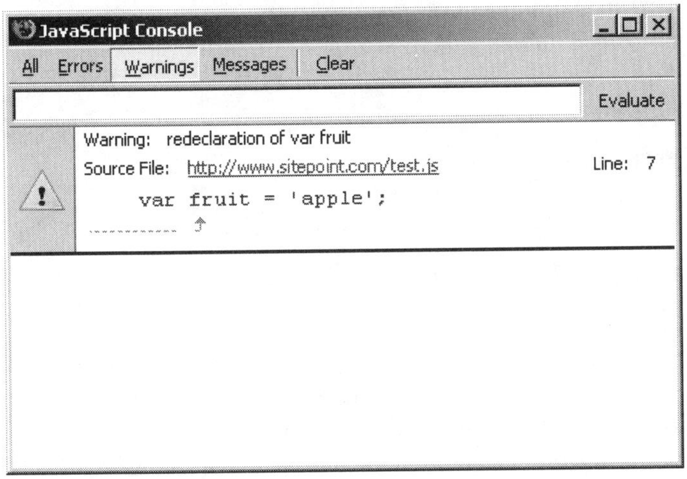

There are several coding missteps that can cause warnings like this. For example:

re-declaring a variable
> This produces the warning, "redeclaration of var *name*," as we just saw.

failing to declare a variable in the first place
> This oversight produces the warning, "assignment to undeclared variable *name*."
>
> This might arise, for example, if the first line of our code read simply `fruit = 'mango';`

assuming the existence of an object

This assumption produces the warning "reference to undefined property *name*."

For example, a test condition like if (document.getElementById) assumes the existence of the getElementById method, and banks on the fact that JavaScript's automatic error-handling capabilities will convert a nonexistent method to false in browsers in which this method doesn't exist. To achieve the same end without seeing a warning, we would be more specific, using if(typeof document.getElementById != 'undefined').

There are also some function-related warnings, and a range of other miscellaneous warnings that includes my personal favorite, "useless expression," which is produced by a statement within a function that does nothing:

File: **strict-warnings.js (excerpt)**

```
function getBasket()
{
  var fruit = 'pomegranate';
  fruit;
}
```

For a thorough rundown on the topic, I recommend Alex Vincent's article *Tackling JavaScript strict warnings*.[12]

Warnings don't *matter* in the sense that they don't prevent our scripts from working, but working to avoid warnings helps us to adopt better coding practice, which ultimately creates efficiency benefits. For instance, scripts run faster in Mozilla if there are no strict warnings, a subject we'll look at again in Chapter 20.

Type Conversion Testing

Although we shouldn't rely on type conversion to test a value that might be undefined, it's perfectly fine to do so for a value that might be null, because the ECMAScript specification requires that null evaluates to false. So, for example, having already established the existence of getElementById using the typeof operator as shown above, it's perfectly safe from then on to test for individual elements as shown below, because getElementById returns null for nonexistent elements in the DOM:

```
if (document.getElementById('something'))
{
```

---

[12] http://javascriptkit.com/javatutors/serror.shtml

```
  : the element exists
}
```

Summary

In this chapter, we've talked about best-practice approaches to scripting that will make our code easier to read and manage, and will allow it to degrade gracefully in unsupported devices. We've also begun to introduce some of the techniques we'll need to build useful scripts, including the ubiquitous `load` event listener that we'll use for almost every solution in this book!

We've covered some pretty advanced stuff already, so don't worry if some of it was difficult to take in. We'll be coming back to all the concepts and techniques we've introduced here as we progress through the remaining chapters.

Working with Numbers

Numbers and mathematics come into most scripts at some point, be it in the form of the simple arithmetic required to add up prices and work out sales tax, the process of generating and using random numbers, or the more complex mathematics involved in creating animation.

We'll investigate some of the more hard-core concepts of working with numbers in Chapter 14. In this chapter, we'll meet the basic constructs for number-crunching in JavaScript, and look at some fairly simple, but useful applications.

Doing Math with JavaScript

JavaScript provides syntax for basic arithmetic, as well as a range of properties and methods for performing more complex mathematical tasks.

Solution

There are five arithmetic operators in JavaScript, each of which is represented by a special character: multiplication (*), division (/), addition (+), subtraction (-), and modulus (%).[1]

---

[1] The modulus operator returns the remainder of a division, so **9 % 4** returns **1**. We'll use this later in the chapter to calculate ordinals.

Here are some simple examples of the operators at work:

File: **math-operators.js**

```
var s = 7, t = 2;

alert(s + t);    // 9
alert(s * t);    // 14
alert(s - t);    // 5
alert(s / t);    // 3.5
alert(s % t);    // 1
```

In addition to these basic operators, JavaScript has a built-in `Math` object that provides a range of mathematical methods and properties. The most useful methods are:

Math.ceil   rounds a number upwards, so `Math.ceil(4.2)` returns 5

Math.floor   rounds a number downwards, so `Math.floor(4.7)` returns 4

Math.round   rounds a number to the nearest integer, so `Math.round(4.2)` returns 4, while `Math.round(4.7)` returns 5

Math.pow   raises one number to the power of another, so `Math.pow(2,4)` returns 16

Math.sqrt   returns the square root of a number, so `Math.sqrt(9)` returns 3

Math.random   returns a pseudorandom number between zero and one

The properties that the `Math` object has to offer are all mathematical constants, such as `Math.E`[2] and `Math.PI`.[3] You're not likely to need these very often, but they're obviously invaluable for pure math calculations, and also for animation and vector graphics projects, where advanced mathematics may be used to calculate shapes and movement.

Discussion

Each JavaScript operator has an **operator precedence**, which controls the order of execution when two or more operators are used in a single expression. When

---

[2]This is Euler's constant, which is the base of natural logarithms [http://en.wikipedia.org/wiki/Euler's_constant].
[3]This is the ratio of the circumference of a circle to its diameter.

it comes to the arithmetic operators we've just seen, multiplication and division have the highest level of operator precedence, followed by modulus, then by addition and subtraction.[4]

Consider this expression:

```
var n = 4 / 2 + 4 * 3;
```

If we performed each calculation in the order in which it appears above, the result would be 18. However, the value that's calculated by JavaScript and assigned to n in this example is actually 14, because the results of the multiplication and division operations are calculated *before* the addition takes place. We can make this order of calculation explicit by placing **parentheses** (round brackets) around the portions of the expression that should be calculated first:

```
var n = (4 / 2) + (4 * 3);
```

Although in this example the parentheses do little more than clarify JavaScript's built-in operator precedence, parentheses can also *change* the order of evaluation. We could force left-to-right evaluation of the original expression to obtain a value of 18 by writing it like this:

```
var n = ((4 / 2) + 4) * 3;
```

Rounding a Number to x Decimal Places

In some applications, you may need to round the result to a certain number of decimal places. For instance, you may want to display temperature values in 0.1 degree increments, even though your script has access to more precise values.

Solution

We can write a function that will round to any number of places, as follows:

File: **round-number.js**

```
function roundTo(base, precision)
{
  var m = Math.pow(10, precision);
  var a = Math.round(base * m) / m;
```

---

[4]Since multiplication and division share the same precedence, these operations are evaluated left-to-right. The same goes for addition and subtraction.

```
    return a;
}
```

So, for example, if we started with a number like n = **3.942487**, we could call
roundTo(n, 0) to get 4, or roundTo(n, 3) to get **3.942**.

Discussion

The Math.round method rounds a number to the nearest integer:

```
var n = Math.round(3.942487);
```

In this example, n is assigned the value 4. If we want to round a number to *two*
decimal places, we can simply multiply it by 100, round the result, then divide
by 100 again:

```
var n = 3.942487;
n = Math.round(n * 100) / 100;
```

Now, n has the value **3.94**.

The same technique can be used to round to *any* number of decimal places, because each place equals a factor of ten. To refine this into a function, we need
one argument to round the number, and a second argument to specify the number
of decimal places to which the number will be rounded. We create our multiplier
by raising ten to the power of the number of decimal places.

In "Formatting Currency Values" in this chapter, we'll see how to format a
rounded number to a string with a specified number of digits after the decimal
point (and trailing zeroes as necessary).

To Round, or not to Round?

If you're performing financial calculations, remember that rounding is not
necessarily the right approach. The total of a shopping basket, for example,
should always be rounded *down* to the nearest penny. Depending on what
you're doing, you may want to use either Math.floor or Math.ceil (to
round downwards or upwards, respectively), instead of Math.round.

Creating and Constraining Random Numbers

Random numbers can be used as the basis for any task that needs to have a random or semi-random aspect.

Solution

We can obtain a random integer within specified limits using a combination of the Math object's random and round methods, which we saw in "Doing Math with JavaScript".

File: **random-number.js**

```
function randomBetween(min, max)
{
  return min + Math.floor(Math.random() * (max - min + 1));
}
```

So, for example, we could generate a number between four and six (inclusive) by calling randomBetween(4, 6), or a number between one and 100 by calling randomBetween(1, 100).

Discussion

Not Really Random, but Near Enough

A computer cannot generate a truly random number because computation is deterministic: it follows an unbroken chain of cause and effect in which no truly random events ever occur. Instead, it uses a set of complex algorithms to generate what's known as a **pseudorandom number**[5]—a number that gives the appearance of randomness, and is good enough for any practical purpose.

We begin with a pseudorandom number generated by Math.random:

```
return Math.random(); // a number between 0 and 1
```

---

[5] http://en.wikipedia.org/wiki/Pseudorandomness

This produces a number between zero and one (excluding either of these limits). If we multiply that by ten and use `Math.floor` to round down, we'll end up with an integer between zero and nine (inclusive):

```
return Math.floor(Math.random() * 10); // integer from 0 to 9
```

So, the number by which we multiply the output of `Math.random` determines the upper limit. If we want an integer between zero and *n* (inclusive), we must multiply by *n* + 1.

If we add five to our sample result, we'll get a number between five and 14:

```
return 5 + Math.floor(Math.random() * 10); // integer from 5 to 14
```

This final addition defines the lower limit, and shifts the range to the final upper limit.

In our `randomBetween` function, we're given the lower and upper limits we're shooting for. So, as well as adding the desired lower limit, we use *both* limits to calculate the number by which we multiply the output of `Math.random`:

File: **random-number.js** (excerpt)
```
return min + Math.floor(Math.random() * (max - min + 1));
```

Converting a Number to a String

Once you've finished a calculation, you might want to turn the output into something more readable, such as formatting a value to represent currency. To do this, we must **convert the number to a string**.

Solution

The most direct means of converting a number to a string is to use the built-in `String` constructor function:

File: **number-to-string.js** (excerpt)
```
var a = 10;
alert(typeof a);
a = String(a);
alert(typeof a);
```

In this example, the first `alert` would display "number" and the second would display "string."

You can also use the `toString` method, which is provided for every number value in JavaScript:

File: **number-to-string.js (excerpt)**

```
var a = 10;
a = a.toString();
alert(typeof a);
```

It doesn't matter which approach you use: they both give the same result.

It's a Date

If the input value to the `String` constructor is a `Date` object, the string produced will be a human-readable representation of the date. We'll learn more about this feature in Chapter 9.

Another useful technique is **string concatenation** (joining strings together), which returns a string even if some if the input values are numbers:

File: **number-to-string.js (excerpt)**

```
var a = 2468;
var s = a + ' motorway';
```

In this example, `s` has the value `"2468 motorway"`.

Less is not Always More

The succinctness of this technique has led many developers to determine that string concatenation is the most efficient means of converting a number to a string. After all, it requires the least amount of code:

```
var a = 10 + '';
```

But, since the readability of code is usually more important than a few bytes of JavaScript code, I don't recommend this approach.

Discussion

Although the result of string concatenation is always a string, the + operator will add numbers together until a string is encountered. This can produce unexpected results in an expression involving string concatenation with multiple numbers. Consider this code:

File: **number-to-string.js** (excerpt)

```
var a = 2000;
var b = 468;
var s = a + b + ' motorway';
```

This will still output `"2468 motorway"`, because a + b is evaluated first as a numeric addition. But look what happens if we change this expression:

File: **number-to-string.js** (excerpt)

```
var s = 'and its ' + a + b + ' motorway';
```

In this case, the result would be `"and its 2000468 motorway"`, because the first part of the expression that's evaluated, `'and its ' + a`, results in a string concatenation, which ensures that the remainder of the expression will continue as a series of further concatenations.

Parentheses can be used to force the numeric addition to be performed first, independent of the string concatenations:

File: **number-to-string.js** (excerpt)

```
var s = 'and its ' + (a + b) + ' motorway';
```

This gives us the desired result, `"and its 2468 motorway"`.

Formatting Currency Values

In "Rounding a Number to x Decimal Places", we saw how to round a value to a specified number of decimal places, but if you're working with currency values, you may need to format the output further, adding a decimal point and trailing zeroes as necessary.

Solution

In order to display a currency value with trailing zeroes, we must first round the value to the required number of decimal places (using the roundTo function from "Rounding a Number to x Decimal Places"). We then convert that value to a string so that we can add a decimal point, if it's needed, as well as any trailing zeroes that may be required:

File: **currency-format.js** (excerpt)

```
function formatTo(base, precision)
{
  var a = roundTo(base, precision);
  var s = a.toString();

  var decimalIndex = s.indexOf(".");
  if (precision > 0 && decimalIndex < 0)
  {
    decimalIndex = s.length;
    s += '.';
  }
  while (decimalIndex + precision + 1 > s.length)
  {
    s += '0';
  }
  return s;
}
```

So, formatTo(3.942, 2) would give us "3.94", while formatTo(4.003, 2) would give "4.00".

Discussion

After converting the rounded number to a string using the toString method described in "Converting a Number to a String", formatTo finds the position of the decimal point (if any) in the resulting string. If there is no decimal point, and one is required, a decimal point is added to the end of the string. The function then determines the number of digits that are to follow the decimal point, and adds zeroes to the end of the string until the required number of digits is produced.

Converting a String to a Number

There are many situations where a number value might be stored as a string—a value read back from a form element, for example, will always come back as a string (as we'll see in Chapter 6). In general, you can treat a JavaScript string that contains a number (and only a number) as if it *were* a number, and JavaScript will perform the string-to-number conversion for you automatically. But sometimes you need to extract a number from a string, or exercise more control over how the conversion is done.

Solution

The most direct means of converting a string to a number is to use the built-in Number constructor function:

File: **string-to-number.js (excerpt)**
```
var a = '10';
alert(typeof a);
a = Number(a);
alert(typeof a);
```

In this case, the first alert would display "string," while the second would display "number."

 Tip

Date in Milliseconds

If the input value to Number is a Date object, it returns the number of milliseconds between January 1, 1970 (UTC[6]) and the specified date/time. We'll learn more about dealing with dates and times in Chapter 9.

Another handy technique is to use the parseInt and parseFloat functions, which will attempt to find and return an integer or decimal number (respectively) at the start of a string:

File: **string-to-number.js (excerpt)**
```
var a = '24.68motorway';

var i = parseInt(a, 10);
alert(i);

var f = parseFloat(a);
alert(f);
```

Note that parseInt takes the base of the number as its second argument, while parseFloat always assumes that you're working in base ten.

The first alert will display the number 24; the second will display 24.68.

[6]For a full explanation of UTC, see Chapter 9.

Discussion

If the first character of the input is *not* a digit or some other numerical character (such as a minus sign or a decimal point), these functions will not be able to return a number. In such cases, they'll return the special value NaN (Not a Number). Consider this example:

File: **string-to-number.js** (excerpt)

```
var s = 'route66';
var n = parseInt(s, 10);
alert(n);
```

Here, the value of s cannot be converted to a number, because it starts with a non-numeric character, so n will have the value NaN.

You can test for the NaN value in your scripts using the isNaN function:

File: **test-number-conversion.js**

```
function testNumberConversion(input)
{
  var a = parseInt(input, 10);
  if (isNaN(a))
  {
    alert('"' + input + '" cannot be converted');
  }
  else
  {
    alert('"' + input + '" converts to ' + a);
  }
}
```

In fact, isNaN will return true for any value that isn't a number. The isNaN function is therefore useful whenever you need to test whether a value *is not* a number, as an alternative to using the typeof operator we saw in earlier examples (which returns "number" if the value *is* a number).

A Closer Look at parseInt

As mentioned previously, parseInt takes a second argument that specifies the base of the number to be parsed from the string. This argument is in fact optional, but I highly recommend that you always provide it.

Without this second argument, parseInt performs **automatic radix detection**; that is, it detects the base of a number by its format in the string. A number beginning with 0 is considered to be octal (base eight), a number beginning 0x or 0X is considered to be hexadecimal (base 16), and all other numbers are considered to be decimal.

So, for example, if you were to call `parseInt('08')`, the input value would be considered an octal number; but 8 is not an octal digit (because octal numbering is 0–7), so the function would return a value of zero, not eight.

To avoid any confusion, *always specify the base* when using `parseInt`.

Converting Numbers to Ordinals (-st, -nd, -rd, -th)

Ordinals define numbers as being part of an order or sequence: the words "first," "second," and "third" are all examples of ordinals. There are many examples of their use, including sports results, music charts, and dates, to name just a few.

Solution

English ordinals follow a predictable, if not beautifully simple, set of rules:

❏ "st" is appended to 1 and numbers that are one greater than a multiple of ten, except for 11 and numbers that are 11 greater than a multiple of 100.

❏ "nd" is appended to 2 and numbers that are two greater than a multiple of ten, except for 12 and numbers that are 12 greater than a multiple of 100.

❏ "rd" is appended to 3 and numbers that are three greater than a multiple of ten, except for 13 and numbers that are 13 greater than a multiple of 100.

❏ "th" is appended to everything else.

To find the appropriate ordinal for a number, we convert these rules into a set of conditions:

File: **get-ordinal.js**

```
function getOrdinal(n)
{
  var ord = 'th';

  if (n % 10 == 1 && n % 100 != 11)
  {
```

```
    ord = 'st';
  }
  else if (n % 10 == 2 && n % 100 != 12)
  {
    ord = 'nd';
  }
  else if (n % 10 == 3 && n % 100 != 13)
  {
    ord = 'rd';
  }

  return ord;
}
```

Discussion

Since most ordinals end in "th," it's simplest to assume that this is the suffix we want, unless we know otherwise.

The most valuable tool in JavaScript's arsenal for tackling this task is the modulus operator (%), which returns the remainder of a division. For example, we can find out if a number n is 12 greater than a multiple of 100 by checking if n % 100 equals 12.

The first if statement in the function, therefore, checks if n is one greater than a multiple of ten (n % 10 == 1, which includes 1 itself), but isn't 11 greater than a multiple of 100 (n % 100 != 11, which includes 11 itself), in which case it returns the "st" suffix. The remaining if statements follow the same pattern to check for the conditions under which the "nd" and "rd" suffixes should be returned.

0th?

The question of whether "th" is the correct suffix for zero is debatable. Ordinals were invented long before the concept of zero-based numbering: as with Roman numerals, they would originally have been used for counting physical things, for which you can't count zero instances!

Summary

In this chapter, we've seen how to do basic arithmetic, introduced some of the more useful methods that are available from JavaScript's Math object, and turned our hand to a few commonly-used tasks. Many of the techniques we've learned here will come in handy as we progress through the book, especially when it comes to working with dates and times (Chapter 9), and later, in our work with Dynamic HTML (Chapter 13 and Chapter 14).

3

Working with Strings

HTML is a text-based format, so if you're reading or writing data on a web page, it's inevitable that you're going to have to deal with text. Sometimes you'll create text yourself, while at other times it will be returned automatically by another function, but any time you handle text in JavaScript, it will be stored in an object called a **string**. This chapter explores the ways in which you can manipulate strings to find information, store data, and prepare text for output.

Including a Special Character in a String

The nature of the syntax that JavaScript uses to declare strings prevents us from including some characters simply by typing them literally into the code. For example, if the start and end of a string is marked with double quotes ("), you can't type a string that contains an actual quotation mark, as this special character would be misinterpreted as a string start/end marker. Other special characters mark the location of formatting devices such as tabs or new lines.

Solution

Special characters are preceded by a backslash. Whenever a backslash is included in a string, JavaScript considers the backslash itself, and the character that follows it, to be a special character sequence, and performs the necessary translation. If it helps you, think of the backslash character as indicating that the "alternative meaning" of the following character should be used. For instance, the line feed character is represented by "n," but in order to be recognized as a line feed, and not the character "n," it must be **escaped** using a backslash:

File: **special_character.js** (excerpt)

```
var a = "First line.\nSecond line.";
```

If the variable a were printed, it would appear like this:

```
First line.
Second line.
```

Discussion

Special characters can be used in a number of circumstances. Sometimes, we can turn letters of the alphabet into control characters by escaping them. At other times, characters may be used as special syntax for a function, in which case they must be escaped in order to represent their literal notation. Table 3.1 describes a few of the more common special characters.

Table 3.1. String special characters

Character	Description
\n	Line feed. This is used to indicate a new line. Different operating systems use varying combinations of \n and \r to mark the ends of lines, so you must be careful when working with strings containing new lines, such as textarea values.
\r	Carriage return.
\t	Tab space.
\'	When a string is opened with a single quote, using an escaped single quote inside the string allows that single quote to be part of the string without causing the string to close.
\"	When a string is opened with a double quote, using an escaped double quote inside the string allows that double quote to be part of the string without causing the string to close.
\\	Of course, to print an actual backslash, you have to escape its meaning as the escape character by preceding it with another backslash.

Transforming the Character Case of a String

String data is rarely presented in the form in which you want it. However, if your string is in uppercase when you need it in lowercase characters, JavaScript can help ease your worries.

Solution

JavaScript includes two string object methods that can transform strings into all lowercase or uppercase characters. To make your string all uppercase, use the `toUpperCase` method:

File: **transform_string_case.js (excerpt)**

```
var a = "very big letters";
var b = a.toUpperCase();
```

The value of the variable b will now be `"VERY BIG LETTERS"`.

To make your string all lowercase, use the `toLowerCase` method:

File: **transform_string_case.js (excerpt)**

```
var c = "VERY SMALL LETTERS";
var d = c.toLowerCase();
```

The value of the variable d will now be `"very small letters"`.

Encoding a URL

URLs reserve a number of characters for special syntax. To include these characters as part of an actual URL—particularly in the case of CGI GET parameters—you must encode them with a per cent sign (%) followed by the equivalent ASCII character code.

Solution

The `escape` function saves you from figuring out which characters to encode and what to encode them to. If you pass a string to this function, it returns a duplicate string with all sensitive characters converted to their URL-safe equivalents. As a common example, you might need to pass a URL as a parameter in the query string of another URL:

File: **encode_url.js (excerpt)**
```
var a = "http://www.sitepoint.com/directory name/?param=value";
var b = escape(a);
```

The value of the variable b will now be

```
"http%3A//www.sitepoint.com/directory%20name/%3Fparam%3Dvalue"
```

This value has a number of URL special characters that have been escaped properly, so it can be included safely in the query string of another URL.

If you wish to decode an encoded URL, escape's inverse function, unescape, can do that for you:

File: **encode_url.js (excerpt)**
```
var c = "http%3A//www.sitepoint.com/directory%20name/" +
    "%3Fparam%3Dvalue";
var d = unescape(c);
```

The value of the variable d will now be

```
"http://www.sitepoint.com/directory name/?param=value"
```

Comparing Two Strings

Checking the text in a string against a given value is one of the most common methods for determining the path a program should follow. String comparison can be used to find elements with certain attributes, to validate form fields, to parse data ... the list goes on.

Solution

We can compare two strings using the equality operator: ==. This is the same operator that's used to compare numeric values; similarly, if we place one of the two strings for comparison on either side of the operator, JavaScript will decide whether they're equal, and return an appropriate Boolean value:

File: **compare_string.js** (excerpt)

```
var a = "Cameron";
var b = "James";

if (a == b)
{
  var identity = "same";
}
else
{
  var identity = "different";
}
```

The value of the variable `identity` will now be `"different"`.

The same program could be phrased in terms of a negative comparison: are these two strings unequal? To do this, you would use the inequality operator: `!=` like so:

```
var a = "Cameron";
var b = "James";

if (a != b)
{
  var identity = "different";
}
else
{
  var identity = "same";
}
```

The value of the variable `identity` will now be `"different"`.

Discussion

The comparison operators used above are available for comparing any two data types, whether they're numbers, strings, or objects. However, the data types we use in a comparison do not have to be the same in order to be considered equal.

If a comparison is performed between two different data types, JavaScript will try to transform one of the arguments so that the pair are comparable. For instance, if one argument is a number and the other a string, the string will be transformed into a number, and a comparison made between the two numbers:

```
var a = 42;
var b = "42";

var comparison;
if (a == b)
{
  var comparison = "same";
}
else
{
  var comparison = "different";
}
```

The value of the variable `comparison` will now be `"same"`.

This is a handy shortcut in most cases, but sometimes you'll want to do a strict comparison that requires identical data types. To do this, you can use the strict equality, or identity operator: ===. When this operator is used to compare two values, no transformation is performed:

```
var a = 42;
var b = "42";

var comparison;
if (a === b)
{
  var comparison = "same";
}
else
{
  var comparison = "different";
}
```

The value of the variable `comparison` will now be `"different"`.

The identity operator is paired by the non-identity operator: !==:

```
var a = 42;
var b = "42";

if (a !== b)
{
  var comparison = "different";
}
else
{
```

```
    var comparison = "same";
}
```

The value of the variable `comparison` will now be `"different"`.

Finding a Substring within a String

Although string comparison allows you to find identical strings, it's sometimes more useful to check if a piece of text is part of a larger string, and to know exactly where that text is located within the string.

Solution

We can find a particular piece of text within a string using JavaScript's `indexOf` method. This method takes one argument—the text you want to find—and returns the index of that text:

File: **find_substring.js (excerpt)**

```
var a = "This sentence contains a substring.";
var b = a.indexOf("sentence");
```

The value of the variable **b** is now **5**.

IMPORTANT

String Index Numbering

String index numbering starts at 0, so although the text "sentence" starts on the sixth character, its index will be 5.

If the text you're searching for doesn't occur in the string, the method will return an index of -1.

Discussion

Because `indexOf` returns a unique value when it *does not* find a substring, this makes it a handy tool for testing for the existence of required data:

```
if (name.indexOf("Adams") == -1)
{
  var author = false;
}
else
{
```

```
    var author = true;
}
```

indexOf will always find the *first* occurrence of the text you specify. It is possible to find the last occurrence of text in a string using the method lastIndexOf, which operates in much the same manner:

```
var a = "First word, last word";
var b = a.lastIndexOf("word");
```

The value of the variable b is now 17.

Splitting a String into Substrings

Strings often contain more information than you need. One example is the URL of a web page. JavaScript is able to find and extract any part of a URL, whether you need the root domain name, CGI variables, or the anchor reference.

Solution

If you want to extract one continuous piece of text from within a string, the substring method can be used to obtain it. This method takes two arguments: the string index that specifies the start of the text fragment, and the string index that specifies the end of the text fragment *plus one*.

Plus One

It's important to note that the value of the second argument is actually one greater than the index of the final character of the fragment.

File: **split_string_into_substrings.js (excerpt)**

```
var a = "Bytes and bits";
var b = a.substring(10, 13);
```

The value of the variable b is now "bit".

Discussion

We rarely encounter a situation in which we know exactly the contents of the string we're operating on, and where the substring we want begins. In the following example, substring, in combination with indexOf, is able to find and extract the URL's anchor reference:

File: **split_string_into_substrings.js** (excerpt)

```
var url = "http://www.sitepoint.com/javascript.htm#chapter_3";
var hash = url.indexOf("#");
var anchor = url.substring(hash + 1, url.length);
```

The value of the variable `anchor` is now `"chapter_3"`.

Determining String Length

Tip

We can determine the length of a string by reading its `length` property. The length is the total number of characters in the string, which means that its value is one greater than the index of the last character in the string.

As previously mentioned, `indexOf` will find only the first occurrence of the text that you're searching for. If you want to find and manipulate multiple occurrences of the same text, you may be better off using regular expressions, which are explained in the next solution.

Aside from singular values, strings are also an extremely versatile and portable method of storing multiple data items. If your string is actually a list of items separated by a delimiter, JavaScript allows you to extract all of those items with just one method call. The `split` method takes one argument—the delimiter text—and divides up the string based on that delimiter. It then returns an array containing each of the items that were in the string:

File: **split_string_into_substrings.js** (excerpt)

```
var c = "Chico,Groucho,Gummo,Harpo,Zeppo";
var d = c.split(",");
```

The variable `d` is now an array, where `d[0]` is `"Chico"`, `d[1]` is `"Groucho"`, `d[2]` is `"Gummo"`, `d[3]` is `"Harpo"` and `d[4]` is `"Zeppo"`. For more information on arrays and how they store multiple data values, see Chapter 4.

Creating a Regular Expression

Regular expressions comprise a widely used search-and-replace syntax that's available across many programming languages. The popularity of regular expressions is largely due to their concise and powerful nature, and it is for this reason that they're also available in JavaScript.

Solution

We have two ways to create a regular expression in JavaScript. The first approach uses a regular expression literal, where the regular expression pattern is delimited by two forward slashes:

```
var a = /pattern.*/;
```

Escape the Forward Slash!

Tip

To include a forward slash as part of a regular expression literal, you must escape it using a preceding backslash (\ /); otherwise, it will mark the end of the pattern.

The second way to create a regular expression is to instantiate a new RegExp object by giving the pattern string to its constructor as an argument:

```
var a = new RegExp("pattern.*");
```

Regular Expressions vs the RegExp Constructor

Tip

It's easier to read regular expression literals than the code required by the RegExp constructor. They also provide better runtime performance. However, if you must construct a regular expression dynamically using string input, you'll have to use the RegExp constructor.

Mac Memory Leak

Internet Explorer 5.0 for the Mac suffers a memory leak when the RegExp constructor is used to create regular expressions. Therefore, in a complex script that involves the repeated creation of regular expressions, you may receive an "out of memory" error in this browser. It's generally safer to use regular expression literals unless you really must use the constructor method.

JavaScript regular expressions can also include three modifiers that affect the manner in which the pattern is matched:

g (global)	By default, JavaScript only matches the first occurrence of the regular expression pattern. This flag indicates that *all* occurrences of the pattern should be matched.
i (case insensitive)	By default, JavaScript matches only text that has the exact same case as the regular expres-

sion pattern. This flag allows text to be matched irrespective of its case.

m (multi-line)
This flag specifies that a string should be treated as multiple lines, where a new line is created by including either a carriage return (\r) or a line feed (\n). This means that the end of string anchor ($) and the start of string anchor (^) will also match the end and start of a line.

To include modifiers with the special regular expression definition syntax, include the flags after the closing forward slash. Multiple modifiers are written consecutively, without separation:

```
var a = /pattern.*/gim;
```

If you're instantiating a RegExp object, include the modifiers as a second argument to the constructor:

```
var a = new RegExp("pattern.*", "gim");
```

Discussion

Although—or perhaps because—regular expressions are extremely powerful, they are notoriously hard to decipher. Even after you have a handle on regular expression syntax, it's always a good idea to comment exactly what your regular expressions do (or are meant to do).

Essentially, a regular expression represents a pattern that uses ordinary characters and special characters. For instance, if you wanted a pattern that matched the string "JavaScript," your regular expression pattern could be:

```
JavaScript
```

However, by including special characters, your pattern could also be:

```
Java.*
```

Table 3.2. Regular expression special characters

Character	Description
. (dot)	This is the wildcard character. It matches any single character except line break characters (\r and \n). When the m modifier is included with the regular expression, the dot is also meant to match line break characters; however, its implementation across browsers is inconsistent, so it cannot be used reliably in this manner.
* (asterisk)	An asterisk requires that the preceding character appear zero or more times. When matching, the asterisk will be *greedy*, including as many characters as possible. For example, for the string "a word here, a word there," the pattern "a.*word" will match "a word here, a word." In order to make a minimal match, use the question mark character (explained below).
+ (plus)	This character requires that the preceding character appears one or more times. When matching, the plus will be *greedy* (see above).
? (question mark)	This character allows the preceding character to be optional. If placed after a plus, an asterisk, or another question mark, it dictates that the match for this preceding symbol will include as few characters as possible.
^ (caret)	The caret matches the start of the string. This does not include any characters—it considers merely the position itself. If the m modifier is included in the regular expression, the caret will also match the start of a line.
$ (dollar)	A dollar character matches the end of the string. This does not include any characters—it considers merely the position itself. If the m modifier is included in the regular expression, the dollar will also match the end of a line.
| (pipe)	The pipe causes the regular expression to match either the pattern on the left of the pipe, or the pattern on the right.
((round bracket)	This character starts a grouping of the characters contained between the opening round bracket and its corresponding closing round bracket. As such, you can apply a modifier like *, +, or ? to an entire group of characters by placing it after the closing bracket. You can also refer to a bracketed portion of a regular expression to obtain the portion of the string that it matched.

Character	Description
[(square bracket)	This character starts a character class. A character class matches one character out of those specified by the class. The class can include an explicit list of characters, e.g., [aqz] (which is the same as a|q|z), or a range of characters, e.g., [a-z] (which is the same as a|b|c|d|e…). A character class can also match one character that's not specified by the class, provided a caret is included after the opening square bracket (e.g., [^a] will match any character except "a").

Both the dot (.) and asterisk (*) are special characters that have a specific meaning inside a regular expression. By including them in the above pattern, that pattern matches not only the string "JavaScript," but "Javascript," "JavaHouse," "Java, the most populous island in the world," and a multitude of other possible character combinations. Table 3.2 lists some of the most commonly used regular expression special characters.

If you wish to use one of these special characters as a literal character to be matched by the regular expression pattern, escape it by placing a backslash (\) before it, as we saw when including special characters previously in this chapter.

For a more extensive listing of regular expression syntax, visit RegularExpressions.info,[1] and for more information on regular expressions in JavaScript, see Kevin Yank's SitePoint article *Regular Expressions in JavaScript*.[2]

Testing whether a String Matches a Regular Expression

Although `indexOf` allows you to test easily whether or not a string contains a literal piece of text, regular expressions offer a far more flexible range of pattern-matching capabilities, including the ability to test for the existence of multiple patterns of text in the same string.

---

[1] http://www.regularexpressions.info/
[2] http://www.sitepoint.com/article/expressions-javascript/

Solution

Once a regular expression pattern has been created, the `test` method allows a string to be compared to that pattern. This method takes a string as its argument, and returns a Boolean value that indicates whether or not the string matched the pattern. This allows `test` to be used as a condition inside control structures, such as an `if` statement:

File: **regular_expression_test.js** (excerpt)

```
var string = "Want to test a string? Use a regular expression!";
var pattern = /test.*regular/;

if (pattern.test(string))
{
  var result = "Matched";
}
else
{
  var result = "Not matched";
}
```

The value of the variable `result` is now `"Matched"`.

Testing whether a String Contains Only Numeric Data

The regular expression syntax contains special characters for detecting particular character types. Using one of these, we can determine whether a string contains only numbers.

Solution

Used in a regular expression pattern, the `\d` special character matches only digits (i.e., 0–9). We can use `\d` to create a pattern that matches both integers and floating point numbers, but nothing else:

File: **numerical_data_test.js** (excerpt)

```
var numericalString = "3.14159265";
var characterString = "3 point 1";
var pattern = /^-?\d+(\.\d+)?$/;
```

```
var a = pattern.test(numericalString);
var b = pattern.test(characterString);
```

The value of the variable `a` will now be `true`, and the value of the variable `b` will now be `false`.

Discussion

If we break down the regular expression used above, it reads something like this:

`^-?`	At the start of the string, you may have a minus sign.
`\d+`	Then, you'll have one or more digits.
`(\.\d+)?`	Then, you may optionally have a period (full stop) followed by one or more digits.
`$`	Then, the string must end.

Allowing only a minus sign, numbers, and one period in the string precludes the string from containing any non-numerical data.

Testing whether a String is a Valid Phone Number

A North American phone number can be generalized to the form (*XXX*) *XXX-XXXX*, where *X* represents a digit. Phone numbers in other countries vary slightly, but usually conform to a similar pattern. Using this pattern, we can write a regular expression that matches phone numbers.

Solution

Because the length of phone numbers varies from country to country, it is inadvisable to place any restrictions on the length of a phone number, but we can ensure it meets a generalized form:

File: **phone_number_test.js** (excerpt)

```
var telephoneString = "(03) 9555 5555";
var emailString = "bill@microsoft.com";
var pattern = /^(\(\d+\) ?)?(\d+[\- ])*\d+$/;
```

```
var a = pattern.test(telephoneString);
var b = pattern.test(emailString);
```

The value of the variable `a` will now be `true`, and the value of the variable `b` will now be `false`.

Discussion

We can dissect the regular expression used above to discern its exact meaning:

`^(\(\d+\) ?)?`   At the start of the string, you may optionally have an open round bracket, followed by one or more numbers, followed by a closed round bracket, optionally followed by a space.

`(\d+[\- ])*`   You may then have zero or more groups of one or more digits. Each of these groups must be followed by a space or a hyphen.

`\d+$`   Finally, the string must end with one or more digits.

This pattern allows for an optional area code with round brackets followed by groups of digits, each separated by a space or a hyphen. This is quite a loose pattern, but so, too, are the standards for telephone numbers around the world. If you require a specific format, you should be able tailor this pattern to your needs fairly easily.

Testing whether a String is a Valid Email Address

The technical specification for the format of an email address is quite complex, but 99.9% of email addresses can be matched by a regular expression that won't spill over onto two lines.

Solution

The first half of an email address has a greater set of possible characters than the second half, which is limited by its need to be a domain name. The two are divided by the ubiquitous "at" symbol:

File: **`email_address_test.js`** (excerpt)

```javascript
var validEmail = "anakin36@tatooine.com";
var invalidEmail = "darth@thedeathstar";
var pattern = /^[\w\.\-]+@([\w\-]+\.)+[a-zA-Z]+$/;

var a = pattern.test(validEmail);
var b = pattern.test(invalidEmail);
```

The value of the variable a will now be `true`, and the value of the variable b will be `false`.

Discussion

A few different parts go into defining this pattern:

`^[\w\.\-]+`	The \w special character indicates a "word" character, which can be any upper- or lowercase character or number. At the start of the string, you must have any combination of word characters, full stops, and hyphens.
`@`	Then you must have an "at" symbol.
`([\w\-]+\.)+`	Then you must have at least one group of word characters or hyphens, followed by a full stop (the domain and subdomain names).
`[a-zA-Z]+$`	Finally, the string must end with one or more alphabetical characters (the top-level domain).

This pattern strikes the right balance between freedom and restriction. It is possible for the only requirements to be an "@" sandwiched between two strings, but this is quite a trivial check, and ultimately unhelpful in validation.

Searching and Replacing Text using a Regular Expression

As well as matching strings with patterns, regular expressions can also be used to replace and manipulate text within a string.

Solution

JavaScript supplies another ready-made regular expression method that allows you to replace text. The string method `replace` takes two arguments: a regular expression pattern, and the replacement text for that pattern. It will then match the text inside the string with the pattern and replace the matched text with the replacement text:

File: **search_replace_regular_expression.js** (excerpt)
```
var pattern = /closures/;
var string = "JavaScript programmers love closures";
var result = string.replace(pattern, "bananas");
```

The value of the variable `result` is now `"JavaScript programmers love bananas"`.

Don't Forget the g!

Remember, if you want to search for and replace every occurrence of the pattern in a string, you must include the g modifier with the regular expression, to make it global: `/closures/g`

Discussion

In addition to the straight replacement of a literal piece of text, `replace` is also able to manipulate the matched text using **back-references** and **callback functions**.

Back-references refer to the text matched by the regular expression pattern, and allow you to use parts of that text inside the replacement string. Back-references are created using round brackets in the regular expression pattern, and are referenced using $*x*, where *x* is the number of the back-reference you want to include (the first one is "$1," and they increment left to right through the pattern):

File: **search_replace_regular_expression.js** (excerpt)
```
var pattern = /JavaScript (.*) closures/;
var string = "JavaScript programmers love closures";
var result = string.replace(pattern, "Visual Basic $1 debugging");
```

The value of the variable `result` is now `"Visual Basic programmers love debugging"`.

A further enhancement to the `replace` method is its ability to accept a callback function as its second argument. By passing a callback function as the second argument, we can have the matched text manipulated by that function, and returned as the replacement text. Several arguments are supplied to the callback function when it's invoked, including:

1. the text that matched the pattern

2. each of the back-references that were captured in the pattern, as separate arguments

3. the offset within the string where the full match occurred

4. the entire text of the string

Using this callback function you can, for example, transform the matched text to lowercase and insert it as a replacement in the original string:

File: **search_replace_regular_expression.js** (excerpt)

```
function transformToLowercase(theString)
{
  return theString.toLowerCase();
}

var string = "Element names should be LOWERCASE.";
var pattern = /LOWERCASE/;
var result = string.replace(pattern, transformToLowercase);
```

The value of the variable `result` is now `"Element names should be lowercase."`

Are Callback Functions Allowed?

Some browsers, including Safari 2.0 and Internet Explorer 5.0, do not allow callback functions to be passed to the `replace` method.

Summary

This chapter has taught you about one of the most basic data types in JavaScript: the string. The methods explained above will be used repeatedly throughout the rest of this book. As the underlying structure of a web page relies heavily on strings to store its content, this chapter has given you the foundation you need to start accessing and manipulating the HTML on your own pages.

Working with Arrays

Arrays are incredibly useful constructs; it's impossible to say too many good things about them (though I'll try)!

An array is a "group" or "list" of data. It's a more convenient way to store and structure information than is defining lots of variables with slightly different names, like this:

```
var planets0 = 'mercury';
var planets1 = 'venus';
var planets2 = 'earth';

alert(planets1);        // alerts 'venus'
```

Instead of the above, we can use an array to structure the data like this:

```
var planets = new Array('mercury', 'venus', 'earth');

alert(planets[1]);      // alerts 'venus'
```

We refer to the members of an array using a number in square brackets, starting from zero. In this example, the planet Mercury is `planets[0]`, while our own corner of the cosmos is `planets[2]`.

This convenience alone makes arrays invaluable, but they also offer considerable power for manipulating data, as we'll see in this chapter.

Using Array-literals

Solution

An array-literal is a normal array that's written in a way that's quicker to type and less code-intensive. Here's an example:

File: **array-literal.js (excerpt)**

```
var planets = ['mercury', 'venus', 'earth'];
```

This is exactly the same as the code below:

```
var planets = new Array('mercury', 'venus', 'earth');
```

This kind of shortcut syntax is provided by the language, making common constructs more convenient.

Creating an Array of Arrays

The members of an array can be anything—numbers, strings, functions, even other arrays—and, within an array, you can mix different types of data freely.

Solution

An array of arrays is known as a **matrix** or **multi-dimensional array**. As you might expect, it's constructed like this:

File: **array-of-arrays.js (excerpt)**

```
var planets = new Array(
    new Array('mercury', 'venus', 'earth'),
    new Array('uranus', 'neptune', 'pluto')
    );
```

You can also construct a multi-dimensional array using array-literal syntax, like this:

File: **array-of-arrays.js (excerpt)**

```
var planets = [
    ['mercury', 'venus', 'earth'],
    ['uranus', 'neptune', 'pluto']
    ];
```

Items in a multi-dimensional array are addressed in the same way as single arrays, but for one difference: we address each item using multiple values, starting from the outermost array. For example, the value 'pluto' is located at index 1 of the outermost array, and index 2 of the nested array, so we would refer to it as planets[1][2].

We can insert additional arrays inside those, nesting them as deeply as we like, and refer to their items using further bracketed numbers.

Discussion

A two-dimensional array is like a "grid" or "table" of data. For example, motor-racing results could be presented in a table like Table 4.1.

Table 4.1. Motor race results

1	K Raikkonen	Fin	McLaren	1:45:15.556
2	N Heidfeld	Ger	Williams	+13.8
3	M Webber	Aus	Williams	+18.4
4	F Alonso	Spa	Renault	+36.4
5	JP Montoya	Col	McLaren	+36.6

Those same results can be stored in a matrix:

File: **array-of-arrays.js** (excerpt)

```
var results = [
    [1, 'K Raikkonen', 'Fin', 'McLaren', '1:45:15.556'],
    [2, 'N Heidfeld', 'Ger', 'McLaren', '+13.8'],
    [3, 'M Webber', 'Aus', 'Williams', '+18.4'],
    [4, 'F Alonso', 'Spa', 'Renault', '+36.4'],
    [5, 'JP Montoya', 'Col', 'McLaren', '+36.6']
];
```

To iterate through a matrix, we use nested for loops:

File: **array-of-arrays.js** (excerpt)

```
for (var i = 0; i < results.length; i++)
{
  for (var j = 0; j < results[i].length; j++)
  {
    alert('results[' + i + '][' + j + '] = ' + results[i][j]);
```

```
    }
}
```

Within the innermost loop, we can identify groups of data simply by evaluating i and/or j. For example, if i is zero, we know that these are the details of the winner:

```
for (var i = 0; i < results.length; i++)
{
  for (var j = 0; j < results[i].length; j++)
  {
    if (i == 0)
    {
      alert('Winner: ' + results[i][j]);
    }
  }
}
```

If j is 1, we know that these are the drivers' names:

```
for (var i = 0; i < results.length; i++)
{
  for (var j = 0; j < results[i].length; j++)
  {
    if (j == 1)
    {
      alert('Driver: ' + results[i][j]);
    }
  }
}
```

We can use this loop/evaluation structure to identify any single item, or group of items, within a "row" or "column" (to complete the analogy, i is the "row" or outer array index, and j is the "column" or inner array index, so column three of row zero would equate to results[0][3]).

You can, of course, go deeper than this—arrays within arrays within arrays, as deep as you like—but my analogy breaks down there as I wrestle to conceive a four-dimensional table! I hoped I've made the point: you can extend multi-dimensional arrays as far as you need to!

Indexing an Array with Strings Instead of Numbers

We can index an array using strings, instead of numbers. This is often useful when we use multidimensional arrays to group related data.

Solution

To put together an array with string indexes, we can't construct and populate it in one fell swoop. We have to create the array, then index and populate it:

```
                                          File: index-with-strings.js (excerpt)
var planets = [];

planets['inner'] = ['mercury', 'venus', 'earth'];
planets['outer'] = ['uranus', 'neptune', 'pluto'];
```

Now, we could reference 'venus' as planets['inner'][1], and 'pluto' as planets['outer'][2].

Discussion

The length property does *not include* string-indexed array members, so we can't iterate through such an array using a numerical for loop. The alert dialog in the following example will never fire, because planets.length is zero:

```
var planets = [];

planets['inner'] = ['mercury', 'venus', 'earth'];
planets['outer'] = ['uranus', 'neptune', 'pluto'];

for (var i = 0; i < planets.length; i++)
{
  alert(planets[i]);
}
```

Instead, we can use an in enumerator (which we first saw in Chapter 1) to iterate through the array as if it were an object:

File: **index-with-strings.js (excerpt)**

```
for (var i in planets)
{
  alert(planets[i]);
}
```

Of course, an array *is* just another type of object, and the members of an array are just a subset of that object's properties—namely, those properties that have a numeric index. The `length` property is merely the total of that subset, which is why string-indexed members aren't included.

The `in` Enumerator

An `in` enumerator will expose *all* the custom properties and methods of an object—not necessarily just the ones you're using to store data. If, for example, you bind a new method to the `Array` object (we'll do so later in this chapter), that method will be included whenever you use an `in` enumerator on *any* array. If that's a problem, you can use the `typeof` comparator to test the data type, for example, to ignore functions:

```
for (var i in planets)
{
  if (typeof planets[i] != 'function')
  {
    : planets[i] is a value we're interested in
  }
}
```

In fact, string-indexed members of an array are literally the same as named properties of that array object. We could just as easily write them like this:

```
var planets = [];

planets.inner = ['mercury', 'venus', 'earth'];
planets.outer = ['uranus', 'neptune', 'pluto'];
```

The syntax for an **object-literal** (a new `Object` written using shortcut syntax) is very similar. Here, again, is the same data, all of which, with an object-literal, can be constructed at once:

```
var planets = {
  'inner': ['mercury', 'venus', 'earth'],
  'outer': ['uranus', 'neptune', 'pluto']
};
```

An object-literal uses curly-braces to surround the data; each property name is delimited from its value with a colon, while complete pairs are separated with a comma:

File: **index-with-strings.js** (excerpt)

```
var myData = {'name1': value1, 'name2': value2, …};
```

The quote marks around the property names are not actually required, but I usually include them anyway for visual consistency. The properties themselves can be anything—strings, numbers, functions, arrays, other objects—and you can mix data types freely here, as well.

Using objects as data structures in this way is known as **Object-based scripting**. This is not the same as object-oriented scripting; however, it's a good way to get an understanding of the principles of Object Orientation, besides being a useful technique in its own right. For more about this, see Chapter 19.

Turning an Array into a String

JavaScript provides a number of methods for processing arrays. One of the most useful is the ability to turn an array into a string.

Solution

The join method concatenates all the members of an array into a string, along with a separator. If the separator argument is omitted, a comma is used by default:

File: **array-into-string.js**

```
var planets = ['mercury', 'venus', 'earth'];

var word = planets.join('');
alert(word);

var list = planets.join();
alert(list);

var sentence = planets.join(' then ');
alert(sentence);
```

Now, word is 'mercuryvenusearth', list is 'mercury,venus,earth', and sentence is 'mercury then venus then earth'.

Discussion

Just as you can join an array into a string, you can also split a string into an array. For details see "Splitting a String into Substrings" in Chapter 3.

Adding or Removing Members from an Array

Arrays allow the addition or removal of members at any position.

Solution

IE 5.0 Support Snafu

Neither push nor splice are supported in Internet Explorer 5.0 for Windows, but don't worry—we have a cure for that in the discussion section!

The push method adds one or more new members to the *end* of an array:

File: **add-remove-members.js** (excerpt)
```
var planets = ['mercury', 'venus', 'earth'];
planets.push('mars', 'jupiter');
alert(planets);
```

Now, planets contains 'mercury', 'venus', 'earth', 'mars', and 'jupiter', in that order.

The splice method can remove members from an array. We simply need to specify the location and the number of members to remove:

File: **add-remove-members.js** (excerpt)
```
var planets = ['mercury', 'venus', 'earth', 'mars', 'jupiter'];
planets.splice(2, 2);
alert(planets);
```

This leaves us with 'mercury', 'venus', and 'jupiter'.

splice can also add any new members that are supplied as extra arguments:

File: **add-remove-members.js** (excerpt)

```
var planets = ['mercury', 'mars', 'jupiter'];
planets.splice(1, 0, 'venus', 'earth');
alert(planets);
```

This gives us `'mercury'`, `'venus'`, `'earth'`, `'mars'`, and `'jupiter'`.

This method can even remove and replace members at the same time:

File: **add-remove-members.js** (excerpt)

```
var planets = ['mercury', 'venus', 'earth', 'saturn'];
planets.splice(0, 3, 'mars', 'jupiter');
alert(planets);
```

This leaves us with `'mars'`, `'jupiter'`, and `'saturn'`.

As you can see from these examples, the first argument to `splice` is the index at which to start; the second argument identifies how many members to remove (this can be zero); further arguments are optional, and list any new members that are to be added to the array at that point.

Discussion

Neither `push` nor `splice` is natively supported in Internet Explorer 5.0 for Windows, which could be rather unfortunate, considering how useful they are.

However, we can achieve the most basic `push` functionality using the array `length` property to add one member at a time to the end of an array. The `length` of our array is one greater than the index of the final item, since numbering starts from zero. Therefore, it identifies the index of the *next* item to add:

File: **add-remove-members.js** (excerpt)

```
var planets = ['mercury', 'venus', 'earth'];
planets[planets.length] = 'mars';
alert(planets);
```

For any task more complex than this, we really do need `push` and `splice`, but in fact, we can use the same basic technique to *recreate* those methods ourselves!

Prototyping

For greatest convenience, we can bind our recreations directly to the `Array` class. (When we say `new Array`, we're creating a "new" instance of the

Array class; binding a method to that class affects all instances of it.) This is called **prototyping**, and is one of the core techniques of Object Orientation in JavaScript, but frankly, it's a bit far off-topic to warrant discussion here. See Chapter 19 to find out more about how this works.

You can copy and use these working examples as they are: simply paste this code before your other scripting, then use push and splice as normal. Although these methods will override the *existing* methods in browsers that already support them, that won't cause any problems. These are faithful reproductions that behave and return the same way:

File: **add-remove-members.js** (excerpt)

```
Array.prototype.push = function()
{
  for (var i = 0; i < arguments.length; i++)
  {
    this[this.length] = arguments[i];
  }
  return arguments[i - 1];
};
Array.prototype.splice = function(a, b)
{
  var tmp = [];
  for (var i = a + b; i < this.length; i++)
  {
    tmp[tmp.length] = this[i];
  }

  var rem = [];
  for (i = a; i < a + b; i++)
  {
    rem[rem.length] = this[i];
  }

  this.length = a;

  for (i = 2; i < arguments.length; i++)
  {
    this[this.length] = arguments[i];
  }

  for(i = 0; i < tmp.length; i++)
  {
    this[this.length] = tmp[i];
  }
```

```
  return rem;
};
```

Sorting an Array into Alphabetical or Numeric Order

Sorting by letter or number allows you to order data by particular criteria. You could order names alphabetically, or phone numbers by area code.

Solution

The `sort` method will sort an array into alphabetical order:

File: **sort-array.js (excerpt)**

```
var planets = ['mercury', 'venus', 'earth', 'mars', 'jupiter'];
planets.sort();
```

This gives us `'earth'`, `'jupiter'`, `'mars'`, `'mercury'`, and `'venus'`.

But a dictionary sort won't work with numbers, because the alphabetical order of numbers is not the same as their numeric order. For example, "10" would be sorted before "2."

Fortunately, `sort` also takes an optional argument: a reference to a comparison function that defines the sorting criteria. Using a comparison function allows for numeric sorting:

File: **sort-array.js**

```
function compare(a, b)
{
  return a - b;
}

var gravities = [0.38, 0.91, 1, 0.38, 2.54];
gravities.sort(compare);
```

The `gravities` array is now in numeric order: 0.38, 0.38, 0.91, 1, 2.54.

Discussion

The default behavior of `sort` is to sort an array lexicographically (in dictionary order). The optional argument is a reference to a function that defines the pair-sorting criteria:

```
function compare(a, b)
{
  : comparison code
}
```

If this function is specified, the array is sorted by its return value:

- ❏ If it returns less than 0, sort a before b.

- ❏ If it returns 0, leave a and b unchanged with respect to each other.

- ❏ If it returns greater than 0, sort b before a.

To sort an array numerically, we simply subtract b from a. Let's take two values, for example: a = 3 and b = 6. If we subtract b from a, the result is -3, which is less than zero, so a is sorted before b. Hence, subtracting b from a sorts an array numerically, while subtracting a from b sorts it into reverse-numeric order.

Sorting a Multi-dimensional Array

It's often useful to be able to sort a multi-dimensional array by the value of only *one* of its member indices.

Solution

If we put our planet names and gravity data together into a multi-dimensional array, we can sort it so that the planets are listed in order of gravitational pull:

File: **sort-matrix.js**

```
function compare(a, b)
{
  return a[1] - b[1];
}

var planets = [
    ['mercury', 0.38],
```

```
    ['venus', 0.91],
    ['earth', 1],
    ['mars', 0.38],
    ['jupiter', 2.54]
    ];

planets.sort(compare);
```

Here, the second item (the gravity figure) is used to sort the main array, while the first item (the planet name) merely comes along for the ride, as it were. The array is now ordered like this:

```
    ['mercury', 0.38],
    ['mars', 0.38],
    ['venus', 0.91],
    ['earth', 1],
    ['jupiter', 2.54]
```

Another use for this kind of sorting is to order sports or contest results for which you have stored names and scores in a multi-dimensional array: you can sort the data by name or score as required.

Discussion

JavaScript uses a **stable sort** algorithm, which means that the relative order of a and b does not change if a and b are equal. But in the multi-dimensional example above, the arguments being compared are *not* direct sorting criteria—we're sorting by a member of an array, not the array itself, and none of the arrays is exactly equal to another.

Therefore, we cannot guarantee a stable sort: whether the Mercury array is sorted before the Mars array is something that could vary between browsers. In fact, all browsers place Mercury first, except for Firefox and other Mozilla browsers, which sort Mars before Mercury.

Sorting an Array Randomly

Random sorting is particularly useful for gaming applications, such as mixing up contestants' names in a lottery or sweepstakes, or "shuffling" a virtual deck of cards.

Solution

We've seen how a comparison function can control the outcome of a `sort` according to whether it returns a sum greater or less than zero. If that outcome is determined randomly, the result will be a random sort:

File: **sort-randomly.js**

```
function compare(a, b)
{
  if (Math.random() * 2 > 1) { return 1; }
  else { return -1; }
}
```

In this case, our `if-else` condition has an even chance, but if necessary, we could weight the odds by adjusting the range of the random number. For more about this, see "Creating and Constraining Random Numbers" in Chapter 2.

Summary

When I first learned JavaScript, I had great difficulty getting my head around the value of arrays. I couldn't see the benefit of them, and remember saying, "Why not just use lots of variables with different names?" My brother, a far more experienced programmer than I, laughed at this and replied, "You'll learn!"

I did, and I hope I've passed on the enthusiasm I gained. Arrays are not merely convenient structures; they allow us to organize and sort data with far more power than is possible with individual variables.

5 Navigating the Document Object Model

Browsers give JavaScript programs access to the elements on a web page via the Document Object Model (DOM)—an internal representation of the headings, paragraphs, lists, styles, IDs, classes, and all the other data to be found in the HTML on your page.

The DOM can be thought of as a tree consisting of interconnected **nodes**. Each tag in an HTML document is represented by a node; any tags that are nested inside that tag are nodes that are connected to it as children, or branches in the tree. Each of these nodes is called an **element node**.[1] There are several other types of nodes; the most useful are the **document node**, **text node**, and **attribute node**. The document node represents the document itself, and is the root of the DOM tree. Text nodes represent the text contained between an element's tags. Attribute nodes represent the attributes specified inside an element's opening tag. Consider this basic HTML page structure:

```
<html>
  <head>
    <title>Stairway to the stars</title>
  </head>
  <body>
    <h1 id="top">Stairway to the stars</h1>
```

---

[1] Strictly speaking, each element node represents a *pair* of tags—the start and end tags of an element (e.g., `<p>` and `</p>`)—or a single self-closing tag (e.g., `<br>`, or `<br/>` in XHTML).

```
    <p class="introduction">For centuries, the stars have been
        more to humankind than just burning balls of gas …</p>
    </body>
</html>
```

The DOM for this page could be visualized as Figure 5.1.

Every page has a document node, but its descendents are derived from the content of the document itself. Through the use of element nodes, text nodes, and attribute nodes, every piece of information on a page is accessible via JavaScript.

The DOM isn't just restricted to HTML and JavaScript, though. Here's how the W3C DOM specification site[2] explains the matter:

> The Document Object Model is a platform- and language-neutral interface that will allow programs and scripts to dynamically access and update the content, structure and style of documents.

So, even though the mixture of JavaScript and HTML is the most common combination of technologies in which the DOM is utilized, the knowledge you gain from this chapter can be applied to a number of different programming languages and document types.

In order to make you a "master of your DOMain," this chapter will explain how to find any element you're looking for on a web page, then change it, rearrange it, or erase it completely.

---

[2] http://www.w3.org/DOM/

Figure 5.1. The DOM structure of a simple HTML page, visualized as a tree hierarchy

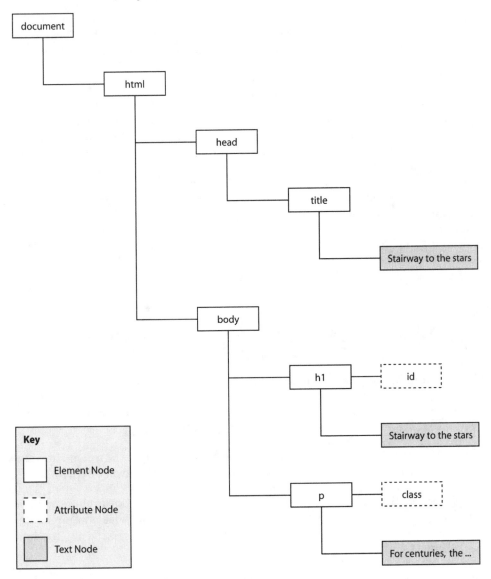

Accessing Elements

Access provides control, control is power, and you're a power programmer, right? So you need access to everything that's on a web page. Fortunately, JavaScript gives you access to any element on a page using just a few methods and properties.

Solution

Although it's possible to navigate an HTML document like a road map—starting from home and working your way towards your destination one node at a time—this is usually an inefficient way of finding an element because it requires a lot of code, and any changes in the structure of the document will usually mean that you have to rewrite your scripts. If you want to find something quickly and easily, the method that you should tattoo onto the back of your hand is `document.getElementById`.

Assuming that you have the correct markup in place, `getElementById` will allow you immediately to access any element by its unique `id` attribute value. For instance, imagine your web page contains this code:

File: **access_element.html** (excerpt)

```html
<p>
  <a id="sirius" href="sirius.html">Journey to the stars</a>
</p>
```

You can use the `a` element's `id` attribute to get direct access to the element itself:

File: **access_element.js** (excerpt)

```javascript
var elementRef = document.getElementById("sirius");
```

The value of the variable `elementRef` will now be referenced to the `a` element—any operations that you perform on `elementRef` will affect that exact hyperlink.

`getElementById` is good for working with a specific element; however, sometimes you'll want to work with a *group* of elements. In order to retrieve a group of elements on the basis of their tag names, you can use the method `getElementsByTagName`.

As can be seen from its name, `getElementsByTagName` takes a tag name and returns all elements of that type. Assume that we have this HTML code:

File: **access_element2.html (excerpt)**

```
<ul>
  <li>
    <a href="sirius.html">Sirius</a>
  </li>
  <li>
    <a href="canopus.html">Canopus</a>
  </li>
  <li>
    <a href="arcturus.html">Arcturus</a>
  </li>
  <li>
    <a href="vega.html">Vega</a>
  </li>
</ul>
```

We can retrieve a collection that contains each of the hyperlinks like so:

File: **access_element2.js (excerpt)**

```
var anchors = document.getElementsByTagName("a");
```

The value of the variable anchors will now be a **collection** of a elements. Collections are similar to arrays in that each of the items in a collection is referenced using square bracket notation, and the items are indexed numerically starting at zero. The collection returned by getElementsByTagName sorts the elements by their source order, so we can reference each of the links thus:

anchors[0]   the a element for "Sirius"

anchors[1]   the a element for "Canopus"

anchors[2]   the a element for "Arcturus"

anchors[3]   the a element for "Vega"

Using this collection you can iterate through the elements and perform an operation on them, such as assigning a class using the element nodes' className property:

File: **access_element2.js (excerpt)**

```
var anchors = document.getElementsByTagName("a");

for (var i = 0; i < anchors.length; i++)
{
```

```
  anchors[i].className = "starLink";
}
```

Unlike getElementById, which may be called on the document node only, the getElementsByTagName method is available from every single element node. You can limit the scope of the getElementsByTagName method by executing it on a particular element. getElementsByTagName will only return elements that are descendents of the element on which the method was called.

If we have two lists, but want to assign a new class to the links in one list only, we can target those a elements exclusively by calling getElementsByTagName on their parent list:

File: **access_element3.html** (excerpt)

```
<ul id="planets">
  <li>
    <a href="mercury.html">Mercury</a>
  </li>
  <li>
    <a href="venus.html">Venus</a>
  </li>
  <li>
    <a href="earth.html">Earth</a>
  </li>
  <li>
    <a href="mars.html">Mars</a>
  </li>
</ul>
<ul id="stars">
  <li>
    <a href="sirius.html">Sirius</a>
  </li>
  <li>
    <a href="canopus.html">Canopus</a>
  </li>
  <li>
    <a href="arcturus.html">Arcturus</a>
  </li>
  <li>
    <a href="vega.html">Vega</a>
  </li>
</ul>
```

To target the list of stars, we need to obtain a reference to the parent ul element, then call getElementsByTagName on it directly:

File: **access_element3.js (excerpt)**

```
var starsList = document.getElementById("stars");
var starsAnchors = starsList.getElementsByTagName("a");
```

The value of the variable `starsAnchors` will be a collection of the `a` elements inside the `stars` unordered list, instead of a collection of *all* `a` elements on the page.

Tip

DOM 0 Collections

Many "special" elements in an HTML document can be accessed by even more direct means. The `body` element of the document can be accessed as `document.body`. A collection of all the forms in a document may be found in `document.forms`. All of the images in a document may be found in `document.images`.

In fact, most of these collections have been around since before the DOM was standardized by the W3C, and are commonly referred to as **DOM 0 properties**.

Because the initial implementations of these features were not standardized, these collections have occasionally proven unreliable in browsers that are moving towards standards compliance. Early versions of some Mozilla browsers (e.g., Firefox), for example, did not support these collections on XHTML documents.

Today's browsers generally do a good job of supporting these collections; however, if you *do* run into problems, it's worth trying the more verbose `getElementsByTagName` method of accessing the relevant elements. Instead of `document.body`, for example, you could use:

```
var body = document.getElementsByTagName("body")[0];
```

Discussion

If you really need to step through the DOM hierarchy element by element, each node has several properties that enable you to access related nodes:

node.`childNodes`   a collection that contains source-order references to each of the children of the specified node, including both elements and text nodes

node.`firstChild`   the first child node of the specified node

node`.lastchild`	the last child node of the specific node
node`.parentNode`	a reference to the parent element of the specified node
node`.nextSibling`	the next node in the document that has the same parent as the specified node
node`.previousSibling`	the previous element that's on the same level as the specified node

If any of these properties do not exist for a specific node (e.g., the last node of a parent will not have a next sibling), they will have a value of `null`.

Take a look at this simple page:

File: **access_element4.html (excerpt)**

```
<div id="outerGalaxy">
  <ul id="starList">
    <li id="star1">
      Rigel
    </li>
    <li id="star2">
      Altair
    </li>
    <li id="star3">
      Betelgeuse
    </li>
  </ul>
</div>
```

The list item with ID `star2` could be referenced using any of these expressions:

```
document.getElementById("star1").nextSibling;
document.getElementById("star3").previousSibling;
document.getElementById("starList").childNodes[1];
document.getElementById("star1").parentNode.childNodes[1];
```

Whitespace Nodes

Some browsers will create **whitespace nodes** between the element nodes in any DOM structure that was interpreted from a text string (e.g., an HTML file). Whitespace nodes are text nodes that contain only whitespace (tabs, spaces, new lines) to help format the code in the way it was written in the source file.

When you're traversing the DOM node by node using the above properties, you should always allow for these whitespace nodes. Usually, this means checking that the node you've retrieved is an element node, not just a whitespace node that's separating elements.

There are two easy ways to check whether a node is an element node or a text node. The `nodeName` property of a text node will always be `"#text"`, whereas the `nodeName` of an element node will identify the element type. However, in distinguishing text nodes from element nodes, it's easier to check the `nodeType` property. Element nodes have a `nodeType` of 1, whereas text nodes have a `nodeType` of 3. You can use this knowledge as a test when retrieving elements:

File: **access_element4.js (excerpt)**

```
var star2 = document.getElementById("star1").nextSibling;

while (star2.nodeType == "3")
{
  star2 = star2.nextSibling;
}
```

Using these DOM properties, it's possible to start your journey at the root `html` element, and end up buried in the `legend` of some deeply-nested `fieldset`—it's all just a matter of following the nodes.

Creating Elements and Text Nodes

JavaScript doesn't just have the ability to modify existing elements in the DOM; it can also create new elements and place them anywhere within a page's structure.

Solution

`createElement` is the aptly named method that allows you to create new elements. It only takes one argument—the type (as a string) of the element you wish to create—and returns a reference to the newly-created element:

File: **create_elements.js (excerpt)**

```
var newAnchor = document.createElement("a");
```

The variable `newAnchor` will be a new `a` element, ready to be inserted into the page.

Specifying Namespaces in Documents with an XML MIME Type

If you're coding JavaScript for use in documents with a MIME type of `application/xhtml+xml` (or some other XML MIME type), you should use the method `createElementNS`, instead of `createElement`, to specify the namespace for which you're creating the element:

```
var newAnchor = document.createElementNS(
    "http://www.w3.org/1999/xhtml", "a");
```

This distinction applies to a number of DOM methods, such as `removeElement`/`removeElementNS` and `getAttribute`/`getAttributeNS`; however, we won't use the namespace-enhanced versions of these methods in this book.

Simon Willison provides a brief explanation of working with JavaScript and different MIME types[3] on his web site.

The text that goes inside an element is actually a child text node of the element, so it must be created separately. Text nodes are different from element nodes, so they have their own creation method, `createTextNode`:

*File: **create_elements.js** (excerpt)*

```
var anchorText = document.createTextNode("monoceros");
```

If you're modifying an existing text node, you can access the text it contains via the `nodeValue` property. This allows you to get and set the text inside a text node:

```
var textNode = document.createTextNode("monoceros");
var oldText = textNode.nodeValue;
textNode.nodeValue = "pyxis";
```

The value of the variable `oldText` is now `"monoceros"`, and the text inside `textNode` is now `"pyxis"`.

You can insert either an element node or a text node as the last child of an existing element using its `appendChild` method. This method will place the new node after all of the element's existing children.

Consider this fragment of HTML:

---

[3] http://simon.incutio.com/archive/2003/06/15/javascriptWithXML

File: **create_elements.html** (excerpt)

```
<p id="starLinks">
  <a href="sirius.html">Sirius</a>
</p>
```

We can use DOM methods to create and insert another link at the end of the paragraph:

File: **create_elements.js** (excerpt)

```
var anchorText = document.createTextNode("monoceros");

var newAnchor = document.createElement("a");
newAnchor.appendChild(anchorText);

var parent = document.getElementById("starLinks");
var newChild = parent.appendChild(newAnchor);
```

The value of the variable `newChild` will be a reference to the newly inserted element.

If we were to translate the state of the DOM after this code had executed into HTML code, it would look like this:

```
<p id="starLinks">
  <a href="sirius.htm">Sirius</a><a>monoceros</a>
</p>
```

We didn't specify any attributes for the new element, so it doesn't link anywhere at the moment. The process for specifying attributes is explained shortly in "Reading and Writing the Attributes of an Element".

Discussion

There are three basic ways by which a new element or text node can be inserted into a web page. The approach you use will depend upon the point at which you want the new node to be inserted: as the last child of an element, before another node, or as the replacement for a node. The process of appending an element as the last child was explained above. You can insert the node before an existing node using the `insertBefore` method of its parent element, and you can replace a node using the `replaceChild` method of its parent element.

In order to use `insertBefore`, you need to have references to the node you're going to insert, and to the node before which you wish to insert it. Consider this HTML code:

File: **create_elements2.html (excerpt)**

```
<p id="starLinks">
  <a id="sirius" href="sirius.html">Sirius</a>
</p>
```

We can insert a new link before the existing one by calling `insertBefore` from its parent element (the paragraph):

File: **create_elements2.js (excerpt)**

```
var anchorText = document.createTextNode("monoceros");

var newAnchor = document.createElement("a");
newAnchor.appendChild(anchorText);

var existingAnchor = document.getElementById("sirius");
var parent = existingAnchor.parentNode;
var newChild = parent.insertBefore(newAnchor, existingAnchor);
```

The value of the variable `newChild` will be a reference to the newly inserted element.

If we were to translate into HTML the state of the DOM after this operation, it would look like this:

```
<p id="starLinks">
  <a>monoceros</a><a id="sirius" href="sirius.htm">Sirius</a>
</p>
```

Instead, we could replace the existing link entirely using `replaceChild`:

File: **create_elements3.js (excerpt)**

```
var anchorText = document.createTextNode("monoceros");

var newAnchor = document.createElement("a");
newAnchor.appendChild(anchorText);

var existingAnchor = document.getElementById("sirius");
var parent = existingAnchor.parentNode;
var newChild = parent.replaceChild(newAnchor, existingAnchor);
```

The DOM would then look like this:

```
<p id="starLinks">
  <a>monoceros</a>
</p>
```

Changing the Type of an Element

Are your ordered lists feeling a bit unordered? Do your headings have paragraph envy? Using a little JavaScript knowledge, it's possible to change the type of an element entirely, while preserving the structure of its children.

Solution

There's no straightforward, simple way to change the type of an element. In order to achieve this feat you'll have to perform a bit of a juggling act.

Let's assume that we want to change this paragraph into a `div`:

File: **change_type_of_element.js** (excerpt)

```
<p id="starLinks">
  <a href="sirius.html">Sirius</a>
  <a href="achanar.html">Achanar</a>
  <a href="hadar.html">Hadar</a>
</p>
```

We need to create a new `div`, move each of the paragraph's children into it, then swap the new element for the old:

File: **change_type_of_element.js** (excerpt)

```
var div = document.createElement("div");
var paragraph = document.getElementById("starLinks");

for (var i = 0; i < paragraph.childNodes.length; i++)
{
  var clone = paragraph.childNodes[i].cloneNode(true);

  div.appendChild(clone);
}

paragraph.parentNode.replaceChild(div, paragraph);
```

The only unfamiliar line here should be the point at which a **clone** is created for each of the paragraph's children. The `cloneNode` method produces an identical copy of the node from which it's called. By passing this method the argument true, we indicate that we want all of that element's children to be copied along with the element itself. Using cloneNode, we can mirror the original element's children under the new div, then remove the paragraph once we're finished copying.

While cloning nodes is useful in some circumstances, it turns out that there's a cleaner way to approach this specific problem. We can simply move the child nodes of the existing paragraph into the new div. DOM nodes can belong only to one parent element at a time, so adding the nodes to the div also removes them from the paragraph:

File: **change_type_of_element2.js (excerpt)**

```
var div = document.createElement("div");
var paragraph = document.getElementById("starLinks");

while (paragraph.childNodes.length > 0) {
  div.appendChild(paragraph.firstChild);
}

paragraph.parentNode.replaceChild(div, paragraph);
```

Take Care Changing the Node Structure of the DOM

The elements in a collection are updated automatically whenever a change occurs in the DOM—even if you copy that collection into a variable before the change occurs. So, if you remove from the DOM an element that was contained in a collection with which you had been working, the element reference will also be removed from the collection. This will change the length of the collection as well as the indexes of any elements that appear after the removed element.

When performing operations that affect the node structure of the DOM—such as moving a node to a new parent element—you have to be careful about iterative processes. The code above uses a while loop that only accesses the first child of the paragraph, because each time a child is relocated, the length of the childNodes collection will decrease by one, and all the elements in the collection will shift along. A for loop with a counter variable would not handle all the children correctly because it would assume that the contents of the collection would remain the same throughout the loop.

Discussion

There's no easy way to copy the attributes of an element to its replacement.[4] If you want the new element to have the same id, class, href, and so on, you'll have to copy the values over manually:

File: **change_type_of_element.js** (excerpt)

```
div.id = paragraph.getAttribute("id");
div.className = paragraph.className;
```

Removing an Element or Text Node

Once an element has outlived its usefulness, it's time to give it the chop. You can use JavaScript to remove any element cleanly from the DOM.

Solution

The removeChild method removes any child node from its parent, and returns a reference to the removed object.

Let's start off with this HTML:

File: **remove_element.html** (excerpt)

```
<p>
  <a id="sirius" href="sirius.html">Sirius</a>
</p>
```

We could use removeChild to remove the hyperlink from its parent paragraph like so:

File: **remove_element.js** (excerpt)

```
var anchor = document.getElementById("sirius");
var parent = anchor.parentNode;
var removedChild = parent.removeChild(anchor);
```

The variable removedChild will be a reference to the a element, but that element will not be located anywhere in the DOM: it will simply be available in memory, much as if we had just created it using createElement. This allows us to relocate it to another position on the page, it we wish, or we can simply let the variable

---

[4]If you look at the DOM specification, it *looks* like there is. Unfortunately, Internet Explorer's support for the relevant properties and methods is just not up to the task.

disappear at the end of the script, and the reference will be lost altogether—effectively deleting it. Following the above code, the DOM will end up like this:

```
<p>
</p>
```

Of course, you don't need to assign the return value from `removeChild` to a variable. You can just execute it and forget about the element altogether:

```
var anchor = document.getElementById("sirius");
var parent = anchor.parentNode;
parent.removeChild(anchor);
```

Discussion

If the element that you're deleting has children that you wish to preserve (i.e., you just want to "unwrap" them by removing their parent), you must rescue those children to make sure they stay in the document when their parent is removed. You can achieve this using the already-mentioned `insertBefore` method, which, when used on elements that are already contained in the DOM, first removes them, then inserts them at the appropriate point.

The paragraph in the following HTML contains multiple children:

File: **remove_element2.html (excerpt)**

```
<div id="starContainer">
  <p id="starLinks">
    <a href="aldebaran.html">Aldebaran</a>
    <a href="castor.html">Castor</a>
    <a href="pollux.html">Pollux</a>
  </p>
</div>
```

We can loop through the paragraph's `childNodes` collection, and relocate each of its children individually before removing the element itself:

File: **remove_element2.js (excerpt)**

```
var parent = document.getElementById("starLinks");
var container = document.getElementById("starContainer");

while (parent.childNodes.length > 0)
{
  container.insertBefore(parent.childNodes[0], parent);
}
```

```
container.removeChild(parent);
```

The page's DOM will now look like this:

```
<div id="starContainer">
  <a href="aldebaran.htm">Aldebaran</a>
  <a href="castor.htm">Castor</a>
  <a href="pollux.htm">Pollux</a>
</div>
```

Reading and Writing the Attributes of an Element

The most frequently used parts of an HTML element are its attributes—its id, class, href, title, or any of a hundred other pieces of information that can be included in an HTML tag. JavaScript is able not only to read these values, but write them as well.

Solution

Two methods exist for reading and writing an element's attributes. getAttribute allows you to read the value of an attribute, while setAttribute allows you to write it.

Consider this HTML:

File: read_write_attributes.html (excerpt)

```
<a id="antares" href="antares.html" title="A far away place">
  Antares</a>
```

We would be able to read the attributes of the element like so:

File: read_write_attributes.js (excerpt)

```
var anchor = document.getElementById("antares");
var anchorId = anchor.getAttribute("id");
var anchorTitle = anchor.getAttribute("title");
```

The value of the variable anchorId will be "antares", and the value of the variable anchorTitle will be "A far away place".

To change the attributes of the hyperlink, we use `setAttribute`, passing it the name of the attribute to be changed, and the value we want to change it to:

File: **read_write_attributes2.js (excerpt)**

```
var anchor = document.getElementById("antares");

anchor.setAttribute("title", "Not that far away");

var newTitle = anchor.getAttribute("title");
```

The value of the variable `newTitle` will now be `"Not that far away"`.

Discussion

In its journey from the free-roaming Netscape wilderness to the more tightly defined, standards-based terrain of the modern age, the DOM standard has picked up a fair amount of extra syntax for dealing with HTML. One of the most pervasive of these extras is the mapping between DOM properties and HTML attributes.

When a document is parsed into its DOM form, special attribute nodes are created for an element's attributes. These nodes are not accessible as "children" of that element: they are accessible only via the two methods mentioned above. However, as a throwback to the original DOM implementations (called DOM 0, where the zero suggests these features came prior to standards), current DOM specs contain additional functionality that's specific to HTML. In particular, attributes are accessible directly as properties of an element. So, the `href` attribute of a hyperlink is accessible through *link*`.getAttribute("href")` as well as through *link*`.href`.

This shortcut syntax is not only cleaner and more readable: in some situations it is also *necessary*. Internet Explorer 6 and versions below will not propagate changes made via `setAttribute` to the visual display of an element. So any changes that are made to the `class`, `id`, or `style` of an element using `setAttribute` will not affect the way it's displayed. In order for those changes to take effect, they must be made via the element node's attribute-specific properties.

To further confuse matters, the values that are returned when an attribute-specific property is read vary between browsers, the most notable variations occurring in Konqueror. If an attribute doesn't exist, Konqueror will return `null` as the value of an attribute-specific property, while all other browsers will return an empty string. In a more specific case, some browsers will return *link*`.getAttribute("href")` as an absolute URL (e.g., `"http://www.example.com/ant-`

`ares.html"`), while others return the actual attribute value (e.g., `"antares.html"`). In this case, it's safer to use the dot property, as it consistently returns the absolute URL across browsers.

So, what's the general solution to these problems?

The basic rule is this: if you are certain that an attribute has been assigned a value, it's safe to use the dot property method to access it. If you're unsure whether or not an attribute has been set, you should first use one of the DOM methods to ensure that it has a value, then use the dot property to obtain its value.

For *reading* an unverified attribute, use the following:

```
var anchor = document.getElementById("sirius");

if (anchor.getAttribute("title") &&
    anchor.title == "Not the satellite radio")
{
    ⋮
}
```

This makes sure that the attribute exists, and is not `null`, before fetching its value.

For *writing to* an unverified attribute, use the following code:

```
var anchor = document.getElementById("sirius");

anchor.setAttribute("title", "");
anchor.title = "Yes, the satellite radio";
```

This code makes sure that the attribute is created correctly first, and is then set in such a way that Internet Explorer will not have problems if the attribute affects the visual display of the element.

This rule has a few exceptions for attributes whose existence you can guarantee. The most notable of these "must-have" attributes are `style` and `class`, which will always be valid for any given element; thus, you can immediately reference them as dot properties (*element*`.style` and *element*`.className` respectively).

`class` is one of two attributes that get a little tricky, because `class` is a reserved word in JavaScript. As a property, it is written *element*`.className`, but using getAttribute/setAttribute, we write *element*`.getAttribute("class")`, *except in Internet Explorer*, where we still use *element*`.getAttribute("className")`.

The other attribute that we have to watch out for is the `for` attribute of a `label`. It follows the same rules as `class`, but its property form is `htmlFor`. Using getAttribute/setAttribute, we write *element*`.getAttribute("for")`, but in Internet Explorer it's *element*`.getAttribute("htmlFor")`.

Getting all Elements with a Particular Attribute Value

The ability to find all the elements that have a particular attribute can be pretty handy when you need to modify all elements that have the same `class` or `title`, for example.

Solution

In order to find elements with a particular attribute value, we need to check every element on the page for that attribute. This is a very calculation-intensive operation, so it shouldn't be undertaken lightly. If you wanted to find all `input` elements with `type="checkbox"`, you're better off limiting your search to `input` elements first:

```
var inputs = document.getElementsByTagName("input");

for (var i = 0; i < inputs.length; i++)
{
  if (inputs.getAttribute("type") == "checkbox")
  {
    ⋮
  }
}
```

This will require less calculation than iterating through *every* element on the page and checking its `type`. However, the function presented in this solution—getElementsByAttribute—is ideal when you need to find a number of elements of *different* types that have the same attribute value.

The easiest way to check every element on a page is to loop through the collection returned by `getElementsByTagName("*")`. The only problem with this method is that Internet Explorer 5.0 and 5.5 do not support the asterisk wildcard for tag selection. Luckily, these browsers support the `document.all` property, which is an array containing all the elements on the page. getElementsByAttribute handles this issue with a simple code branch, then proceeds to check the elements for a given attribute value, adding matches to an array to be returned:

File: **get_elements_by_attribute.js** (excerpt)

```
function getElementsByAttribute(attribute, attributeValue)
{
  var elementArray = new Array();
  var matchedArray = new Array();

  if (document.all)
  {
    elementArray = document.all;
  }
  else
  {
    elementArray = document.getElementsByTagName("*");
  }

  for (var i = 0; i < elementArray.length; i++)
  {
    if (attribute == "class")
    {
      var pattern = new RegExp("(^| )" +
          attributeValue + "( |$)");

      if (pattern.test(elementArray[i].className))
      {
        matchedArray[matchedArray.length] = elementArray[i];
      }
    }
    else if (attribute == "for")
    {
      if (elementArray[i].getAttribute("htmlFor") ||
          elementArray[i].getAttribute("for"))
      {
        if (elementArray[i].htmlFor == attributeValue)
        {
          matchedArray[matchedArray.length] = elementArray[i];
        }
      }
    }
    else if (elementArray[i].getAttribute(attribute) ==
        attributeValue)
    {
```

```
        matchedArray[matchedArray.length] = elementArray[i];
    }
  }

  return matchedArray;
}
```

A lot of the code in `getElementsByAttribute` deals with the browser differences in attribute handling that were mentioned earlier in this chapter, in "Reading and Writing the Attributes of an Element". The necessary techniques are used if the required attribute is `class` or `for`. As an added bonus when checking for a match on the `class` attribute, if an element has been assigned multiple classes, the function automatically checks each of these to see whether it matches the required value.

Adding and Removing Multiple Classes to/from an Element

Combining multiple classes is a very useful CSS technique. It provides a very primitive means of inheritance by allowing a number of different styles to be combined on the one element, allowing you to mix and match different effects throughout a site. They're particularly useful in situations like highlighting elements: a class can be added that highlights an element without disturbing any of the other visual properties that may have been applied to the element by other classes. However, if you are assigning classes in JavaScript you have to be careful that you don't inadvertently overwrite previously assigned classes.

Solution

The class for any element is accessible via its `className` property. This property allows you both to read and write the classes that are currently applied to that element. Because it's just one string, the most difficult part of working with `className` is that you need to deal with the syntax it uses to represent multiple classes.

The class names in an element's `className` property are separated by spaces. The first class name is not preceded by anything, and the last class name is not followed by anything. This makes it easy to add a class to the class list naively: just concatenate a space and the new class name to the end of `className`. However, you'll want to avoid adding a class name that already exists in the list, as this will make removing the class harder. You'll also want to avoid using a space at the beginning of the `className` value, because this will cause errors in Opera 7:

File: **add_remove_classes.js (excerpt)**

```
function addClass(target, classValue)
{
  var pattern = new RegExp("(^| )" + classValue + "( |$)");

  if (!pattern.test(target.className))
  {
    if (target.className == "")
    {
      target.className = classValue;
    }
    else
    {
      target.className += " " + classValue;
    }
  }

  return true;
}
```

First, `addClass` creates a regular expression pattern containing the class to be added. It then uses this pattern to test the current `className` value. If the class name doesn't already exist, we check for an empty `className` value (in which case the class name is assigned to the property verbatim), or we append to the existing value a space and the new class name.

Separating Classes

Some regular expression examples for finding classes use the word boundary special character (\b) to separate classes. However, this will not work with all valid class names, such as those containing hyphens.

The process for removing a class uses a regular expression pattern that's identical to the one we use to add a class, but we don't need to perform as many checks:

File: **add_remove_classes.js (excerpt)**

```
function removeClass(target, classValue)
{
  var removedClass = target.className;
  var pattern = new RegExp("(^| )" + classValue + "( |$)");
```

```
    removedClass = removedClass.replace(pattern, "$1");
    removedClass = removedClass.replace(/ $/, "");

    target.className = removedClass;

    return true;
}
```

After `removeClass` has executed the replacement regular expression on a copy of the `className` property's value, it cleans up the resulting value by removing any trailing space (which is created when we remove the last class in a multiple class `className`), then assigns it back to the target's `className`.

Summary

This chapter introduced the basic but powerful tools that you'll need in order to manipulate the Document Object Model. It's important that you understand the DOM—the skeleton beneath everything you see in a browser—as you manipulate any web page. Knowing how to create, edit, and delete parts of the DOM is crucial to understanding the remainder of this book. Once you've mastered these techniques, you'll be well on your way to becoming a proficient JavaScript programmer.

6

Processing and Validating Forms

Forms are the bane of most web developers' existences. Forms defy the laws of styling, stick out like a sore thumb, and require reams of back-end code. Yet they are the only way for users to communicate vital details about themselves to your web site, which makes forms indispensable for communication, shopping, and a host of other interactive purposes.

JavaScript cannot replace the back-end logic that processes form data, but it can function as a superb usability aid. Using just a bit of client-side scripting, you can turn a five-page interrogation into a rewarding experience for your users. Whether you're helping them to discover errors in their data, or guiding them to complete the right sections, JavaScript can make tedious form entry just that little bit more bearable.

Reading and Writing the Data in a Text Field

Text fields can be used for almost any type of data: searches, names, numbers, dates—whatever you can think of. Accordingly, there are countless situations in which you'll want to manipulate the data they contain.

Solution

Before you can access the data that a text field contains, you have to *find* that exact text field. The easiest way to do this in an HTML document is to use a special DOM collection called `forms`. The `forms` collection is an array that contains "shortcuts" to each of the `form` elements on a web page. Each of these shortcuts has a sub-collection, called `elements`, which allows you to access each of the elements in a form.

Have a look at this form, which is illustrated in Figure 6.1:

File: **read_write_text_field.html** (excerpt)

```
<form id="contactForm" action="">
  <fieldset>
    <legend>Contact Details</legend>
    <label for="firstName">
      First name:
    </label>
    <input id="firstName" name="firstName" value="Arthur">
    <label for="lastName">
      Last name:
    </label>
    <input id="lastName" name="lastName" value="Dent">
  </fieldset>
</form>
```

Figure 6.1. Simple form with two text fields

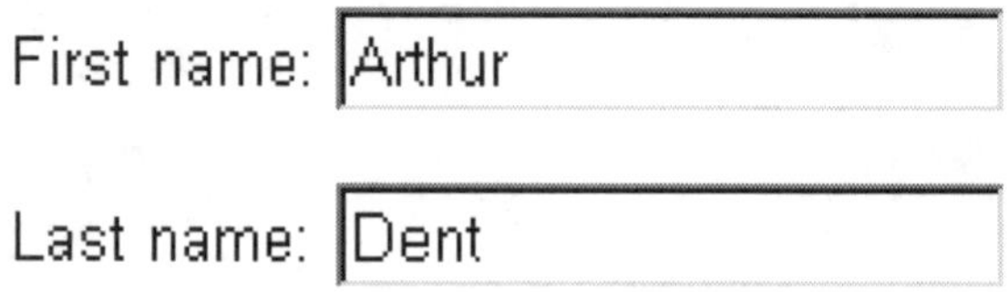

First name: Arthur

Last name: Dent

You could access the form using its source order index—because it's the first form in the document, its index will be 0—but the `forms` collection is also an associative array that automatically associates a form's `id` with the form itself. This means that you can also use the `id` of the form as an index to the `forms` collection:

File: **read_write_text_field.js (excerpt)**

```
var formByIndex = document.forms[0];
var formById = document.forms["contactForm"];
```

In the above code, both variables point to the same form element contained in the HTML document above.

Index Tip

If you have multiple forms on a page, it's safest to use the id of a form as an index to the forms collection. Otherwise, if the order of the forms changes in the document source, you will have to change any numerical indices in your JavaScript code to match it.

Avoid Accessing Forms from the document Object

Although it's possible to access a form directly from the document object (document.*formId*), this is an extremely inefficient method of locating an element, as it requires the browser to search the entire DOM tree for the corresponding node.

To access the elements contained within a form, you just access its individual elements collection either by index or name/id:

File: **read_write_text_field.js (excerpt)**

```
var firstNameElement = document.forms["contactForm"].elements[0];
var lastNameElement =
    document.forms["contactForm"].elements["lastName"];
```

You can use a shortcut to the elements collection by accessing the form as you would a two-dimensional array:

```
var firstNameElement = document.forms["contactForm"]["firstName"];
```

Once you've found the text field that you want to access, finding out what data it contains is a simple matter of reading its value property. The value is a read-writable property, so if you wish to change the data in a text field, just assign a string directly to value:

File: **read_write_text_field.js (excerpt)**

```
var contactForm = document.forms["contactForm"];
var oldValue = contactForm["firstName"].value;
contactForm["firstName"].value = "Zaphod";
```

The value of the variable `oldValue` is now `"Arthur"`; as you can see in Figure 6.2, the text field's new value is `"Zaphod"`.

Figure 6.2. Changing the first text field value

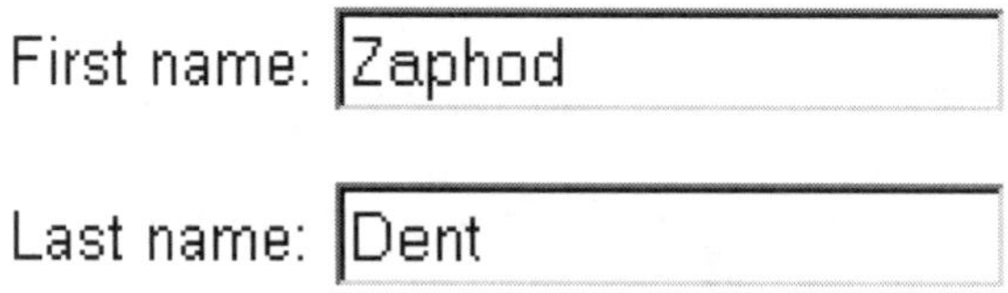

First name: Zaphod

Last name: Dent

Discussion

Although the `forms` collection is a tidy way of accessing form elements on a web page, it is a construct specific to HTML and XHTML. An alternative technique, which also works with XML documents that *aren't* XHTML, is to use the standard (DOM) methods to access the attribute values of document elements. See Chapter 5 for details on how to access elements by navigating the DOM.

Reading and Setting the State of a Checkbox

Checkboxes provide the user with an easy, one-click choice: on or off. Because they don't take any text input from the user, JavaScript handles checkbox properties differently than text fields. You have to understand these differences before you can begin to modify them.

Solution

In order to read or set whether a checkbox is checked, you need to access its `checked` property. This Boolean value determines the checked state of the specific checkbox. Consider this form:

File: **read_set_checkbox.html** (excerpt)

```html
<form id="characterForm" action="">
  <fieldset>
    <legend>Characters</legend>
    <p>
      My favorite character is:
    </p>
    <input type="checkbox" id="checkbox1" name="checkbox1"
        value="Marvin">
    <label for="checkbox1">
      Marvin
    </label>
    <input type="checkbox" id="checkbox2" name="checkbox2"
        value="Trillian">
    <label for="checkbox2">
      Trillian
    </label>
  </fieldset>
</form>
```

Let's suppose that the user manipulates the checkboxes to reflect Figure 6.3.

Figure 6.3. Two checkboxes with different checked states

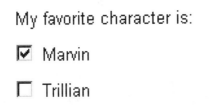

We can read the current checked state of these checkboxes like so:

File: **read_set_checkbox.js** (excerpt)

```javascript
var checkbox1 = document.forms["characterForm"]["checkbox1"];
var checkbox2 = document.forms["characterForm"]["checkbox2"];
var checkedState1 = checkbox1.checked;
var checkedState2 = checkbox2.checked;
```

The value of the variable `checkedState1` is now `true`, while the value of the variable `checkedState2` is `false`.

Changing the `checked` property of a checkbox will be reflected visually on the web page. Suppose you executed the following code:

File: **read_set_checkbox2.js** (excerpt)

```
var checkbox1 = document.forms["characterForm"]["checkbox1"];
var checkbox2 = document.forms["characterForm"]["checkbox2"];
checkbox1.checked = false;
checkbox2.checked = true;
```

The web page would change from the state above to that shown in Figure 6.4.

Figure 6.4. After the checkboxes' checked property has changed

My favorite character is:

☐ Marvin

☑ Trillian

Discussion

The *value* of a checkbox or radio button is distinctly different than whether it is checked or not. When users click on a checkbox, they're not changing the actual value of that checkbox in the same way that they change the value of a text field: they are merely changing its *state*.

Imagine that the state of the inputs is that shown in Figure 6.5.

Figure 6.5. Two checkboxes with different checked states

My favorite character is:

☑ Marvin

☐ Trillian

In this case, `checkbox1`'s value is `"Marvin"` *and* it is checked, but `checkbox2`'s value is still `"Trillian"` even though it is *not* checked. The difference between the two is that when the form is submitted, the CGI parameters sent to the server will include `checkbox1` but not `checkbox2`.

Most of the time you'll want the capacity to change a checkbox's state, as above. But if you want to read or write the value for a checkbox, it is much the same as reading or writing a text field's value:

File: **read_set_checkbox3.js** (excerpt)

```
var checkbox1 = document.forms["characterForm"]["checkbox1"];
var oldValue = checkbox1.value;
checkbox1.value = "Ford";
```

The value of the variable `oldValue` is now `"Marvin"`, and the checkbox's new value is `"Ford"`.

Reading and Setting the State of a Radio Button

Although an individual radio button offers users the same binary options as a checkbox, radio buttons differ slightly because you can group a series of them together, and only one of that group may be checked at any one time.

Solution

Radio buttons are slightly different from checkboxes. Because a radio button is really one of a *group* of buttons, only one of which can be checked at any time, these buttons are accessed as one object.

Consider this form:

File: **read_set_radio_button.html** (excerpt)
```html
<form id="characterForm" action="">
  <fieldset>
    <legend>Characters</legend>
    <p>
      My favorite character is:
    </p>
    <input type="radio" id="characterA" name="character"
        value="Marvin">
    <label for="characterA">
      Marvin
    </label>
    <input type="radio" id="characterB" name="character"
        value="Trillian">
    <label for="characterB">
      Trillian
    </label>
  </fieldset>
</form>
```

Here, each of the radio buttons that has the name attribute character will be stored under the same form element:

File: **read_set_radio_button.js** (excerpt)
```js
var characterGroup = document.forms["characterForm"]["character"];
```

The variable characterGroup is now a collection that represents the group of radio buttons with the name attribute character. So, to access the first radio button in the group, you provide its array index to the collection:

```js
var characterGroup = document.forms["characterForm"]["character"];
var character1 = characterGroup[0];
```

This is really just one extra layer of access: once you've located the particular radio button you need, it has the same value and checked properties as a checkbox:

File: **read_set_radio_button.js (excerpt)**

```
var characterGroup = document.forms["characterForm"]["character"];
var currValue = characterGroup[0].value;
var currChecked = characterGroup[0].checked;
```

One trick to remember when working with radio buttons is that you cannot determine which radio button (if any) is checked by reading just one property. You must loop through each of the radio buttons in a group, and read the checked property of each, to determine which is checked:

File: **read_set_radio_button2.js (excerpt)**

```
var characterGroup = document.forms["characterForm"]["character"];

for (var i = 0; i < characterGroup.length; i++)
{
  if (characterGroup[i].checked == true)
  {
    alert("Your favorite character is " +
        characterGroup[i].value);
  }
}
```

You needn't worry about having to do this when *writing* the checked property of a radio button, though. When you change a radio button's checked property to true, it will automatically set all others to false.

Reading and Setting the Value of a Select Box

Select boxes are similar to radio buttons in that they enable the user to select one option from a predefined set. However, the methods available for dealing with their values differ from those available to radio buttons.

Solution

Although the select box is another group of options—like a set of radio buttons—it has some shortcuts that abstract the need to access its array of options.

The value property of a select element allows you automatically to read the value of the currently selected option, and if you set value to the value of one of the options, that option will automatically be set.

Consider this form:

File: **read_set_select.html (excerpt)**

```html
<form id="characterForm" action="">
  <fieldset>
    <legend>Characters</legend>
    <label for="character">
      My favorite character is:
    </label>
    <select id="character" name="character">
      <option value="A">Marvin</option>
      <option value="B" selected="selected">Trillian</option>
      <option value="C">Slartibartfast</option>
    </select>
  </fieldset>
</form>
```

Imagine that a user selects the second option in this form, as shown in Figure 6.6.

Figure 6.6. Selecting the second option in the select box

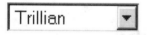

In this case, the value of the select box will correspond to the value of the second option:

File: **read_set_select.js (excerpt)**

```js
var character = document.forms["characterForm"]["character"];
var selectValue = character.value;
```

The value of the variable `selectValue` is now `"B"`.

We can also set the value of the select box to the value of the third option:

File: **read_set_select2.js (excerpt)**

```js
var character = document.forms["characterForm"]["character"];
character.value = "C";
```

Now, the select box looks like Figure 6.7.

Figure 6.7. The select box after it is changed by JavaScript

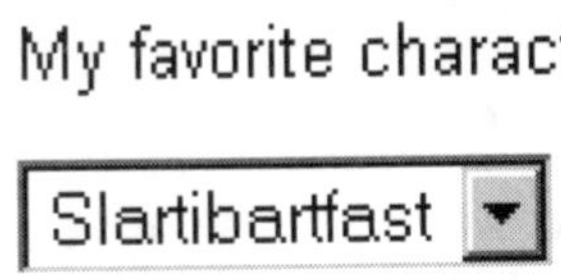

My favorite character is:

Slartibartfast ▼

Discussion

If you require direct access to each of a select box's `option` elements, this is still available through the `select`'s secondary array. In conjunction with the `selectedIndex` property, this array allows you to read and set the options of a select box using only array indices:

File: **read_set_select3.js (excerpt)**
```
var character = document.forms["characterForm"]["character"];
var oldValue = character[character.selectedIndex].value;
character.selectedIndex = 2;
```

Starting from Figure 6.6 above, this code sets the value of the variable `oldValue` to `"B"`, and selects the third option in the select box.

Validating a Mandatory Text Field

When users *have* to fill out a text field, it's best to provide them with a gentle reminder, in case they forget to complete it.

Solution

An empty text field is simply one that has no value. To detect this, you can check whether the field's `value` is equal to an empty string:

```
File: validate_mandatory_text_field.js (excerpt)
if (textField.value == "")
{
  ⋮ error…
```

Going one step further, if you wish to detect a field that may not be empty, but contains only **whitespace** (such as spaces and tabs), you can use a regular expression test, like those we saw in Chapter 3:

```
File: validate_mandatory_text_field2.js (excerpt)
if (textField.value == "" || /^\s+$/.test(textField.value))
{
  ⋮ error…
```

Validating a Numeric Field

HTML forms don't have a field type that can only contain numbers, so the best we can do is to use a text field and validate it to make sure it only contains numbers.

Solution

The value of a text field will always be a string data type, even if you only want numbers to be entered into it. Therefore, the easiest way to test that a text field contains only numbers is to use the `parseInt` function and compare it to the original string (for details of the `parseInt` function, see Chapter 2). If the text field contains any non-numeric characters, its value will be different from the integer that is returned by `parseInt`:

```
File: validate_numerical_field.js (excerpt)
if (textField.value != parseInt(textField.value, 10))
{
  ⋮ error…
```

If your field is allowed to accept floating point numbers, use the `parseFloat` function:

```
File: validate_numerical_field2.js (excerpt)
if (textField.value != parseFloat(textField.value, 10))
{
  ⋮ error…
```

Validating an Email Address Field

The hardest part of validating an email address is defining the syntax to which valid email addresses adhere.

Solution

It's easy to check a text field using the regular expression we defined in "Testing whether a String is a Valid Email Address" in Chapter 3 for testing email addresses:

File: **validate_email_field.js** (excerpt)

```
if (!/^[\w\.\-]+@([\w\-]+\.)+[a-zA-Z]+$/.test(textField.value))
{
  : error…
```

Checking for Unselected Radio Buttons

While it is easy to test whether a checkbox has been checked, it's slightly more difficult to determine whether any of the radio buttons in a group has been selected.

Solution

To detect whether a user has selected an option from a group of radio buttons, you have to check each of the radio buttons individually. If none of their checked properties is true, then the user hasn't selected an option:

File: **check_unselected_radio_buttons.js** (excerpt)

```
var characterGroup = document.forms["characterForm"]["character"];
var characterSelected = false;

for (var i = 0; i < characterGroup.length; i++)
{
  if (characterGroup[i].checked == true)
  {
    characterSelected = true;
    break;
  }
}
```

```
if (!characterSelected)
{
  : error...
```

The variable `characterSelected` keeps track of whether any of the radio buttons has been selected. If a selected radio button is not found, that variable will still be `false` when the `for` loop finishes, in which case you can execute some code to handle it.

Tip

break

The `break` command is a special instruction that tells the JavaScript program to break out of the current program loop (or `switch` statement) and pass control to the next statement beyond the loop or `switch`. In the situation above, once we find a checked radio button, we don't need to test the rest of the buttons, so we can stop the loop. While this isn't strictly necessary, it saves needless calculation and makes our program more efficient.

Stopping a Form Being Submitted Unless all its Fields are Valid

The whole point about validating a field is to make sure that invalid data doesn't reach the server. So, when a form is submitted with errors, you've got to stop that submission dead in its tracks!

Solution

When a user submits a form, it triggers an event before sending the data off to the server. This and other events are explained further in Chapter 13, but for now, the event we're interested in is `submit`. We'll use this to validate all of a form's relevant fields before it sends any data.

When the web page loads, the `onsubmit` event handler must be set to divert the form's submission to our own function:

File: **stop_form_submit.js** (excerpt)
```
document.forms[0].onsubmit = validateFields;
```

The function `validateFields` will be executed before the form is submitted; inside it, we'll check whether the data in the required fields is valid or not. If the data in all the fields is valid, the function should return `true`, allowing the submission process to continue as normal. Otherwise, the return value should be `false`, which will abort the form's submission:

File: **stop_form_submit.js (excerpt)**

```
function validateFields()
{
  var firstName = document.forms[0].elements["firstName"];

  if (firstName.value != "")
  {
    /* Continue with submission */
    return true;
  }
  else
  {
    alert("Please fill in your first name");

    /* Abort submission */
    return false;
  }
}
```

You can perform as many checks on the form data as you like before you submit the form. These checks could involve using some of the validation techniques described in the previous tip, or other checks that you want to make on the form's fields.

To alert the user to any errors in the form, it's easiest to use an `alert` dialog box, as above, but the creation of inline error messages can be far more effective, as we'll see later in this chapter.

Validating a Form with an Unknown Number of Fields

Solution

Creating a script that validates a form can be quite tedious, particularly if the form has a lot of fields that need to be checked. The solution is to have a script that automatically goes through all of a form's elements and validates them appropriately.

Using the `elements` collection of a form, it is easy enough to loop through all of a form's fields, but the validating function still has to know what to do with each field—whether it is simply required, or it must contain numeric data, an email address, and so on. The only way to get around this is to write a field's validation criteria into the HTML code.

Out of all of a field's attributes, its `class` is the most appropriate place to store the validation type. So, if a text field is a required field, you could assign it a class called `checkRequired`, like so:

File: **validate_form.html** (excerpt)

```
<input type="text" class="checkRequired" …>
```

The validating function can parse the `className` of that form field to determine which checks it should apply. For instance, assume we have HTML that includes these validation markers:

File: **validate_form.html** (excerpt)

```
<form id="contactForm">
  <fieldset>
    <legend>Contact Details</legend>
    <label for="firstName">
      First name:
    </label>
    <input type="text" id="firstName" name="firstName"
        class="checkRequired">
    <label for="lastName">
      Last name:
    </label>
    <input type="text" id="lastName" name="lastName"
        class="checkRequired">
    <label for="email">
      Email address:
    </label>
    <input type="text" id="email" name="email"
        class="checkRequired checkEmail">
    <label for="message">
      Message:
    </label>
    <textarea id="message" name="message"></textarea>
  </fieldset>
</form>
```

The validating function can handle each of the fields appropriately:

File: **validate_form.js (excerpt)**

```javascript
function validateFields()
{
  var elements = document.forms["contactForm"].elements;
  var emailPattern = /^[\w\.\-]+@([\w\-]+\.)+[a-zA-Z]+$/;

  for (var i = 0; i < elements.length; i++)
  {
    if (/(^| )checkRequired( | $)/.test(elements[i].className) &&
        elements[i].value == "")
    {
      elements[i].focus();
      alert("Please fill out this field.");
      return false;
    }

    if (/(^| )checkEmail( | $)/.test(elements[i].className) &&
        !emailPattern.test(elements[i].value))
    {
      elements[i].focus();
      alert("Please fill in a valid email address.");
      return false;
    }
  }

  return true;
}
```

If we add any more fields to the form, we don't have to modify the JavaScript: it will check them automatically!

Printing Inline Error Messages when Validating a Form

Earlier, we saw how to validate different form fields according to the types of data they required from the user. Then, we used alert boxes to inform the user of any errors, but inline messages are a more usable way of presenting errors. They provide a permanent indication of the error that the user has to correct, and they can be more proximate to the field that the user should be focused on.

Solution

Instead of printing an error message to an alert box, we can insert the same text in an appropriate place on the page. Take a look at this form:

File: **print_inline_error_messages.html** (excerpt)

```
<form id="contactForm" action="">
  <fieldset>
    <legend>Contact Details</legend>
    <label for="firstName">
      First name:
    </label>
    <input id="firstName" name="firstName">
    <label for="lastName">
      Last name:
    </label>
    <input id="lastName" name="lastName" value="Dent">
  </fieldset>
</form>
```

Error messages are best placed inside the label that's associated with the erroneous form field, like so:

File: **print_inline_error_messages.js** (excerpt)

```
var firstName = document.forms["contactForm"]["firstName"];

if (firstName.value == "")
{
  var errorSpan = document.createElement("span");
  var errorMessage = document.createTextNode(
      "Please enter a first name");

  errorSpan.appendChild(errorMessage);
  errorSpan.className = "errorMsg";

  var fieldLabel = firstName.previousSibling;

  while (fieldLabel.nodeName.toLowerCase() != "label")
  {
    fieldLabel = fieldLabel.previousSibling;
  }

  fieldLabel.appendChild(errorSpan);
}
```

Once we find that the first name field is invalid, we need to create the HTML element that will contain the error message and insert it into the correct place. The process we used to do this above is outlined in more detail in Chapter 8, but it also requires a knowledge of the markup used on the original page. Because we know that the `label` is before the text field, we can navigate to it using the `previousSibling` property of the text field, then insert the error message at the end of the label text.

With appropriate CSS styling of the `errorMsg` class, our page looks like Figure 6.8 after an error has been found.

Figure 6.8. An inline error message displayed after a user submits an invalid text field

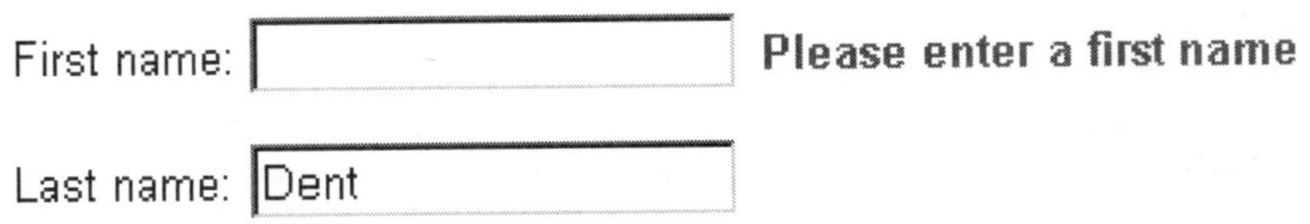

First name: [   ] **Please enter a first name**

Last name: [Dent   ]

Making Form Fields Appear or Disappear, Based on the Value of other Fields

Often, parts of a form will have to be filled out only if a user gives a particular answer to one of the previous questions. Displaying all these non-applicable sections on a page can confuse users pretty quickly, or at least tax their brains a little more than is necessary. To eliminate this confusion, it's often a good idea to display optional areas only as required.

Solution

The display of page elements is governed by their style properties, and under a development regime that separates scripting from styling, all style properties should be controlled with CSS. What does this mean when it comes to showing and hiding form elements? It means that we should not use JavaScript directly to show or hide an element. Instead, we should modify its `class`, and let the CSS decide how it should be displayed.

Let's take the example in Figure 6.9, where the answer to a radio button question requires the user to elaborate further.

Figure 6.9. A form question that depends upon a previous answer

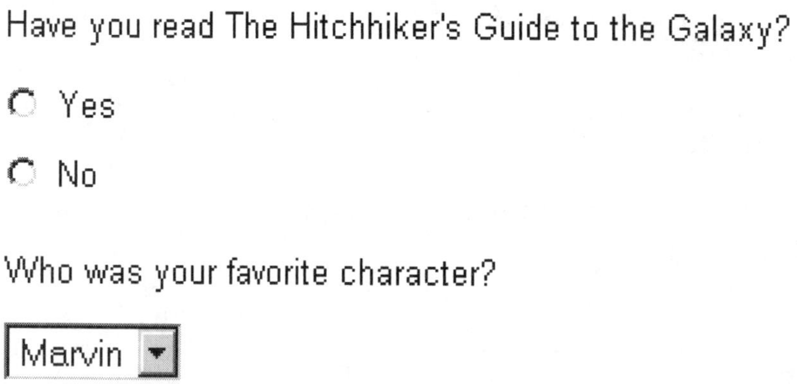

Have you read The Hitchhiker's Guide to the Galaxy?

○ Yes

○ No

Who was your favorite character?

| Marvin ▼ |

The HTML code for this form would look something like this:

File: **fields_appear_disappear.html** (excerpt)

```
<form action="">
  <fieldset>
    <legend>Characters</legend>
    <p>
      Have you read The Hitchhiker's Guide to the Galaxy?
    </p>
    <input type="radio" name="read" id="readYes" />
    <label for="readYes">
      Yes
    </label>
    <input type="radio" name="read" id="readNo" />
    <label for="readNo">
      No
    </label>
    <div id="optional">
      <label for="character">
        Who was your favorite character?
      </label>
      <select id="character" name="character">
        <option value="A">Marvin</option>
        <option value="B">Trillian</option>
        <option value="C">Ford</option>
```

```
    </select>
  </div>
 </fieldset>
</form>
```

Because we're using JavaScript to display the optional question, we should also use JavaScript to hide it initially. If the hidden content was hard-coded to make it hidden initially, users without JavaScript would never be able to see it. Instead, the hiding can be done on page load:

File: **fields_appear_disappear.js** (excerpt)

```
addLoadListener(init);

function init()
{
  var optional = document.getElementById("optional");
  optional.className = "hidden";
```

To hide the optional question, we'll locate it off the left-hand side of the screen using an appropriate CSS rule. This makes the question "invisible" to visual browsers, but still accessible to screen readers. The css-discuss Wiki has more details on this method of hiding content.[1] Here's how it's done:

File: **fields_appear_disappear.css** (excerpt)

```
.hidden
{
  position: absolute;
  left: -1500em;
}
```

The combination of class and CSS hides the optional question when the page loads, as shown in Figure 6.10.

Figure 6.10. The optional question remains hidden on page load

Have you read The Hitchhiker's Guide to the Galaxy?

○ Yes

○ No

---

[1] http://css-discuss.incutio.com/?page=ScreenreaderVisibility

To make the question visible, we need to remove the class when the user clicks Yes. In order to capture this change, we can detect when a user clicks on the Yes button using the `onclick` event handler:

File: **fields_appear_disappear.js** (excerpt)

```
function init()
{
  :
  var readYes = document.getElementById("readYes");
  readYes.onclick = showOptional;
}

function showOptional()
{
  var optional = document.getElementById("optional");
  optional.className = "";

  return true;
}
```

The optional question will now display. Of course, if a user clicks Yes, then clicks No, we want the optional question to disappear. In this case, we reverse the process:

File: **fields_appear_disappear.js** (excerpt)

```
function init()
{
  :
  var readNo = document.getElementById("readNo");
  readNo.onclick = hideOptional;

  return true;
}

function hideOptional()
{
  var optional = document.getElementById("optional");
  optional.className = "hidden";

  return true;
}
```

Using this method, you can show and hide as many form elements as you want. You could even change the CSS to disable the optional question, instead of hiding it, as depicted in Figure 6.11.

Figure 6.11. Changing the CSS can make an optional question look disabled

Have you read The Hitchhiker's Guide to the Galaxy?

○ Yes

○ No

Who was your favorite character?

Summary

Forms can be daunting for both the user and the developer, but by applying and adapting the tips I've described to you here, you'll have full access to every form element on the page. With the power to read, set, validate, show, and hide all your form elements, there's nothing stopping you from making your forms a pain-free experience.

Working with Windows and Frames

This chapter is about simple window and frame manipulation, including tasks like opening popups, communicating between frames,[1] and finding out the page's scrolling position.

Plenty of people feel that window manipulation is akin to the Dark Side. They believe that a window is part of the user's GUI, not the document, and since JavaScript is a document scripting language, it has no business manipulating windows.

I'm generally inclined to agree, yet I know that opinion is sometimes a luxury. If your clients ask for something specific, you can't necessarily change their minds, or have the freedom to turn down work on the basis of such a principle. In this chapter, we'll cover a range of practical window and frame manipulation tasks while remaining sensitive to the usability and accessibility issues that can arise from their use.

Note, though, that there are limits, and some varieties of window scripting are particularly unfriendly. We won't be dealing with aggressive tactics like closing or modifying the user's *primary* window, moving windows around the screen, or opening full-screen or "chromeless" windows. These are exactly the kinds of abuses that have given JavaScript a bad name.

---

[1] The techniques involved in reading data from an `iframe` will be covered in Chapter 18.

Through most of this chapter we'll be looking closely at the properties and methods of the `window` object. These are implemented by different browsers in a variety of ways, most of which have been in use since the days before JavaScript was standardized.

We'll have quite a few code branches to deal with, but we'll avoid the dreaded browser sniffing by careful use of **object detection**, the process of detecting an object or feature to test for compatibility, rather than detecting specific browsers.

Using Popup Windows

Should you use popup windows? The most considered answer I have is this: *not if you can help it*. Popup windows have gained a bad reputation from marketers' aggressive use of them, but even *requested* popups can be barriers to good usability.

I won't say that popups are *never* appropriate, but I will say that they're *seldom* so. Nevertheless, there are situations where popping open a new window is arguably the most appropriate solution: an online survey might be one example, as the format may make the content more approachable; DHTML games are another, as the viewport may need to be of a known size.

I'll qualify my opinion by discussing the problems that popups create, then providing a pragmatic method for using them that mitigates these problems as much as possible.

What's Wrong with Popups?

The main problem with most popup window scripts is that they don't consider the needs of the user—they address only the needs of the designer. The results? We've all seen them:

❑ popups that are generated from links, though those links do nothing when scripting is not available

❑ popup windows that don't have a status bar, so you can't necessarily tell whether the document has loaded or stalled, is still loading, etc.

❑ popups that don't give users the ability to resize the window, and popups that fail to generate scrollbars for content that might scale outside the window

❑ windows that are "chromeless," or open to the full size of the user's screen

These issues are not just questions of usability, but of accessibility as well. For example, screen-reader users may not be notified by their devices that a new window has opened. This could obviously cause confusion if they then attempted to go back in the browser history (they can't). The same thing might happen for a sighted user if a window opens at full-size: you and I may be familiar with using the taskbar to monitor open windows, but not all computer users are—they may not even realize that a new window has popped up.

If you're going to use popups, looking out for issues like these, and being generally sensitive to their impacts, will make your popups friendlier to users, and less of a strain on your conscience.

Also, bear in mind that, from a *developer's* perspective, popup windows are not guaranteed to work: most browsers now include options to suppress popup windows, and in some cases, suppression occurs even if the popup is generated in response to a user event.

You may be able to allow for this as you would for situations in which scripting was not supported: by ensuring that the underlying trigger for the popup still does something useful if the popup fails. Or you might have your code open a window and then check its own `closed` property, to see if it's actually displayed (we'll look at this technique in the next solution).

But neither of these approaches is guaranteed to work with every browser and popup blocker out there, so for this as much as the usability reasons, it's simpler and better to avoid using popups whenever you can.

How Do I Minimize the Problems?

What we need to do is establish some golden rules for the ethical use of popups:

❑ Make sure any triggering link degrades properly when scripting is not available.

❑ Always include the status bar.

❑ Always include a mechanism to overflow the content: either allow window resizing, or allow scrollbars to appear, or both.

❑ Don't open windows that are larger than 640x480 pixels.

By limiting the size of popups, you ensure that they're smaller than users' primary windows on the vast majority of monitors. This increases the likelihood that the user will realize that the popup is a new window.

Solution

Here's a generic popup function that's based on the guidelines above:

File: **make-popup.js** (excerpt)

```
function makePopup(url, width, height, overflow)
{
  if (width > 640) { width = 640; }
  if (height > 480) { height = 480; }

  if (overflow == '' || !/^(scroll|resize|both)$/.test(overflow))
  {
    overflow = 'both';
  }

  var win = window.open(url, '',
      'width=' + width + ',height=' + height
      + ',scrollbars=' + (/^(scroll|both)$/.test(overflow) ?
      'yes' : 'no')
      + ',resizable=' + (/^(resize|both)$/.test(overflow) ?
      'yes' : 'no')
      + ',status=yes,toolbar=no,menubar=no,location=no'
  );

  return win;
}
```

As well as limiting the window size, this script refuses to create a popup that doesn't have an overflow, so if you don't specify "scroll", "resize", or "both" for the *overflow* argument, the default setting of "both" will be used.

 Tip

The Ternary Operator

This script uses a shortcut expression called a **ternary operator** to evaluate each of the overflow options. The ternary operator uses ? and : characters to divide the two possible outcomes of an evaluation, and is equivalent to a single pair of if..else conditions. Consider this code:

```
if (outlook == 'optimistic') { glass = 'half-full'; }
else { glass = 'half-empty'; }
```

That code is equivalent to the markup below:

```
glass = (outlook == 'optimistic' ? 'half-full' :
    'half-empty');
```

The parentheses are not required, but you may find they make the expression easier to read.

For more about this and other useful shortcuts, see Chapter 20.

Once you have the popup function in place, you can call it in a variety of ways. For example, you could use a regular link:

File: **make-popup.html** (excerpt)
```
<a href="survey.html" id="survey_link">Online survey</a>
```

If scripting is not available, this will work just like any other link, but if scripting *is* available, the script can trigger a `click` event handler that passes its `href` to the `makePopup` function, along with the other settings. The return value of the handler depends on whether or not the window is actually opened; browsers that block the popup will follow the link as normal:

File: **make-popup.js** (excerpt)
```
document.getElementById('survey_link').onclick = function()
{
  var survey = makePopup(this.href, 640, 480, 'scroll');

  return survey.closed;
};
```

In general, if you have a script that requires that a window be generated, you can call the `makePopup` function directly with a URL:

```
var cpanel = makePopup('cpanel.html', 480, 240, 'resize');
```

If you need to close that window later in your script, you can do so by using the `close` method on the stored window reference:

```
cpanel.close();
```

Discussion

The `window.open` method can take a number of arguments—in addition to the URL and window name—which specify whether the window should have particular **decorations**, such as the menu bar, tool bar, or address (location) bar. These arguments are passed as a comma-delimited string to the *third* argument of `window.open`:

```
var win = window.open('page.html', 'winName',
    'width=640,height=480,'
    + 'scrollbars=yes,resizable=yes,status=yes,'
    + 'toolbar=no,menubar=no,location=no');
```

In our `makePopup` function, the `menubar`, `toolbar`, and `location` arguments are all preset to `no` because these elements are rarely useful for popup windows—they're navigational tools, after all. Popups are mostly used for one-page interfaces, or those in which history navigation is discouraged, such as our survey example, or the logon procedure for a bank's web site.

You can change those arguments if you need to, but the `status` argument should *always* be set to `yes`, because turning it off undermines good usability. (I know—I've mentioned it already, but I'm saying it again because it's important!)

The `resizable` argument may not have any effect—in some browsers, either by design or as a result of user preferences, it's not possible to create non-resizable windows, even if you set this value to `no`. In fact, in Opera 8 for Mac OS X, it's not possible to create custom-sized windows *at all*—a created window will appear as a new tab in the current window. That specific exception might not be significant in itself, but it serves to illustrate the general point that control over the properties of a created window is not absolutely guaranteed.

Once a new window is open, you can bring it into focus using the object's `focus` method. This isn't usually necessary—generally, it happens by default—but the technique may be useful when you're scripting with multiple windows:

```
var cpanel = makePopup('cpanel.html', 480, 240, 'resize');
cpanel.focus();
```

Alternatively, you may want to open a popup but keep the focus in the *primary* window (thereby creating a so-called "popunder"). You can take the focus away from a window using its `blur` method:

```
var cpanel = makePopup('cpanel.html', 480, 240, 'resize');
cpanel.blur();
```

However, in that case you can't predict where the focus will go to next, so it's more reliable to refocus the primary window:

```
var cpanel = makePopup('cpanel.html', 480, 240, 'resize');
self.focus();
```

Opening Off-site Links in a New Window

In the strict versions of HTML 4 and XHTML 1, the `target` attribute for links no longer exists. One interpretation of this is that web pages simply shouldn't open links in new windows; another is that targeting doesn't have universal semantics and therefore shouldn't be defined in HTML.[2]

There are other interpretations, and the arguments are long (and sometimes tedious), but suffice it to say that you may find yourself needing a solution to this problem. Whatever your personal views may be, it's a common request of web development clients.

Solution

This script identifies links by the `rel` attribute value `external`. The `rel` attribute is a way of describing the relationship between a link and its target,[3] so its use for identifying links that point to another site is semantically non-dubious:

File: **offsite-links.html (excerpt)**

```
<a href="http://www.google.com/" rel="external">Google
  (offsite)</a>
```

If each external link is identified like that, a single `document.onclick` event handler can process clicks on all such links:

File: **offsite-links.js**

```
document.onclick = function(e)
{
  var target = e ? e.target : window.event.srcElement;

  while (target && !/^(a|body)$/i.test(target.nodeName))
  {
    target = target.parentNode;
```

---

[2] The CSS 3 working draft includes a set of target properties for link presentation [http://www.w3.org/TR/2004/WD-css3-hyperlinks-20040224/], which could eventually see this mechanism handed to CSS instead. Personally, I hope this never gets past the draft stage, because it's nothing to do with CSS: interface control is no more appropriate in a design language than it is in a semantic markup language!

[3] http://www.w3.org/TR/REC-html40/struct/links.html#h-12.1.2

```
  }

  if (target && target.getAttribute('rel')
      && target.rel == 'external')
  {
    var external = window.open(target.href);

    return external.closed;
  }
}
```

Discussion

Using a single, document-wide event handler is the most efficient approach—it's much better than iterating through all the links and binding a handler to each one individually. We can find out which element was actually clicked by referencing the **event target** property. For more about events and event properties, see Chapter 13, but here's a brief summary of the situation.

Two completely different event models are employed by current browsers. The script establishes which one should be used by looking for e—the event argument that's used by Mozilla browsers, and has been adopted by most other browsers—as opposed to the `window.event` object used by Internet Explorer. It then saves the object property that's appropriate to the model in use: either `target` for Mozilla and like browsers, or `srcElement` for IE.

The target object (if it's not `null`) can be one of three things: a link element node, an element or text node inside a link, or some other node. We want the *first two* cases to be handled by our script, but clicks arising from the last situation may be safely ignored. What we do is follow the trail of parent nodes from the event target until we either find a link, or get to the `body` element.

Once we have a unified target link, we need simply to check for a `rel` attribute with the correct value; if it exists, we can open a window with the link's `href`, and if all of *that* is successful (as judged by the new window object's `closed` property), the handler will return false, preventing the original link from being followed.

Passing a link to `window.open` without defining arguments will create a window with default decorations—as will a link with `target="_blank"`.

The First Test

We use `getAttribute` as the first test for `rel` because attribute-specific properties are only reliable *if* you know for certain that the attribute in question has been assigned a value. We can't go straight to testing `target.rel` against a string, because it might be `null` or `undefined`. This was discussed in more detail in "Reading and Writing the Attributes of an Element" in Chapter 5.

Communicating Between Frames

If you're working in a framed environment, it may be necessary to have scripts communicate between frames, either reading or writing properties, or calling functions in different documents.

If you have a choice about whether or not to use frames, I'd strongly advise *against* doing so, because they have many serious usability and accessibility problems, quite apart from the fact that they're conceptually broken (they create within the browser states that cannot be addressed[4]). But as with your use of popups, in some cases you may not have a choice about your use of frames. So if you really must use them, here's what you'll need to do.

Solution

Let's begin with a simple frameset document:

```
<!DOCTYPE HTML PUBLIC "-//W3C//DTD HTML 4.01 Frameset//EN"
    "http://www.w3.org/TR/html4/frameset.dtd">
<html>
  <head>
    <title>A frameset document</title>
  </head>
  <frameset cols="200, *">
    <frame src="navigation.html" name="navigationFrame">
    <frame src="content.html" name="contentFrame">
    <noframes>
      <p>This frameset document contains:</p>
      <ul>
        <li><a href="navigation.html">Site navigation</a></li>
        <li><a href="contents.html">Main content</a></li>
      </ul>
```

---

[4] http://www.456bereastreet.com/archive/200411/who_framed_the_web_frames_and_usability/

```
    </noframes>
  </frameset>
</html>
```

We can use *four* references for cross-frame scripting:

❑ window or self refers to the current framed page.

❑ parent refers to the page that contains the frame that contains the current page.

❑ top refers to the page at the very top of the hierarchy of frames, which will be the same as parent if there's only one frameset in the hierarchy.

❑ The frames collection is an associative array of all the frames in the current page.

Let's say we have a script in contentFrame that wants to communicate the page in navigationFrame. Both pages are contained in a single frameset—the only one in the hierarchy—so we could successfully make any of the following references from within contentFrame:

❑ parent.frames[0]

❑ top.frames[0]

❑ parent.frames['navigationFrame']

❑ top.frames['navigationFrame']

The frames collection is an associative array (like the forms collection we saw in Chapter 6), so each element can be accessed by either index or name. It's generally best to use the name (unless you have a good reason not to) so that you won't have to edit your code later if the frame order changes. By the same token, parent references in a complex nested frameset can change if the hierarchy changes, so I generally recommend that developers always start referencing from top. Of the above options, the reference I prefer, then, is top.frames['navigationFrame'].

Now that we have a reference to the frame, we can call a function in the other framed page:

File: **frames-navigation.js (excerpt)**

```
var navframe = top.frames['navigationFrame'];
navframe.callMyFunction();
```

Alternatively, we can get a reference to the other framed document, and work with the DOM from there:

File: **frames-navigation.js (excerpt)**

```
var navdoc = navframe.document;
var menu = navdoc.getElementById('menulist');
```

Discussion

Communication between frames is only allowed for documents *in the same domain*—for security reasons, it's not possible to work with a document that was loaded from a different domain than the script. It wouldn't do, for example, for a malicious site owner to load a site that you visit regularly into a frame, and steal the personal data you enter there.

In fact, some browsers let users disallow *all* scripts from communicating between frames, just to eradicate any possibility of a cross-site scripting vulnerability, and there's no way to work around this preference if your script finds itself running in a browser so configured.

If you do have users who are complaining of problems (and they can't or won't change their settings to allow cross-frame scripting), the safest thing to do is simply to avoid cross-frame scripting altogether.

Alternative methods of passing data between pages are discussed in Chapter 6 and Chapter 8.

Getting the Scrolling Position

Page scrolling is one of the least-standardized properties in JavaScript: *three* variations are now in use by different versions of different browsers. But with a few careful object tests, we can reliably get a consistent value.

Solution

There are three ways of getting this information. We'll use object tests on each approach, to determine the level of support available:

File: **get-scrolling-position.js** (excerpt)

```
function getScrollingPosition()
{
  var position = [0, 0];

  if (typeof window.pageYOffset != 'undefined')
  {
    position = [
        window.pageXOffset,
        window.pageYOffset
    ];
  }

  else if (typeof document.documentElement.scrollTop
      != 'undefined' && document.documentElement.scrollTop > 0 ||
    document.documentElement.scrollLeft > 0))
  {
    position = [
        document.documentElement.scrollLeft,
        document.documentElement.scrollTop
    ];
  }

  else if (typeof document.body.scrollTop != 'undefined')
  {
    position = [
        document.body.scrollLeft,
        document.body.scrollTop
    ];
  }

  return position;
}
```

The function can now be called as required. Here's a simple demonstration, using a window.onscroll event handler, that gets the figures and writes them to the title bar:

File: **get-scrolling-position.js** (excerpt)

```
window.onscroll = function()
{
  var scrollpos = getScrollingPosition();
  document.title = 'left=' + scrollpos[0] + ' top=' +
      scrollpos[1];
};
```

note

The Problem with `scroll`

`scroll` is not the most reliable of events: it may not fire at all in Konqueror or Safari 1.0, or when the user navigates with a mouse wheel in Firefox. And if it does fire, it may do so continually and rapidly (as it does in Internet Explorer), which can be slow and inefficient if the scripting you set to respond to the event is very complex.

If you have difficulties of this kind, you may find it better to use the `setInterval` function instead of an `onscroll` event handler. `setInterval` will allow you to call the function at a predictable interval, rather than in response to an event. You can find out more about this kind of scripting in Chapter 14, but here's a comparable example:

```
window.setInterval(function()
{
  var scrollpos = getScrollingPosition();
  document.title = 'left=' + scrollpos[0] + ' top=' +
      scrollpos[1];
}, 250);
```

Discussion

The only real complication here is that IE 5 actually *does* recognize the `documentElement.scrollTop` property, but its value is always zero, so we have to check the value as well as looking for the existence of the property.

Otherwise, it doesn't really matter to us which browser is using which property; all that matters is that our script gets through one of the compatibility tests and returns a useful value. However, the properties used by each browser are shown here for reference:

❏ `window.pageYOffset` is used by Firefox and other Mozilla browsers, Safari, Konqueror, and Opera.

❏ `document.documentElement.scrollTop` is used by IE 6 in standards-compliant mode.

❏ `document.body.scrollTop` is used by IE 5, and IE 6 in "Quirks" mode.

This list doesn't tell the complete story, but it's intended primarily to describe the ordering of the tests. More recent Mozilla browsers (such as Firefox) also support `documentElement.scrollTop` and `body.scrollTop`, by the same rendering mode rules as IE 6. Safari and Konqueror support `body.scrollTop` in either mode. Opera supports all three properties in any mode!

But none of this is important for you to know—browser vendors add these multiple properties to allow for scripts that are unaware of one property or another, not to provide arbitrary choices for the sake of it. From our perspective, the important point is to settle on a set of compatibility tests that ensures our script will work as widely as possible.

Rendering Modes

"Standards" mode and "Quirks" mode are the two main **rendering modes** in use by current browsers. These modes affect various aspects of the output document, including which element is the canvas (`<body>` or `<html>`), and how CSS box sizes are calculated. For more on rendering modes, see Chapter 11.

Making the Page Scroll to a Particular Position

All current browsers implement the same (nonstandard) methods for scrolling a page. At least something here is simple!

Solution

There are two methods that can be used to scroll the page (or rather, the window or frame), either by a particular amount (`window.scrollBy`), or to a particular point (`window.scrollTo`):

File: **scroll-page.js** (excerpt)
```
//scroll down 200 pixels
window.scrollBy(0, 200);
```

File: **scroll-page.js** (excerpt)
```
//scroll across 200 pixels
window.scrollBy(200, 0);
```

File: **scroll-page.js** (excerpt)
```
//scroll to 300 from the edge and 100 from the top
window.scrollTo(300, 100);
```

File: **scroll-page.js** (excerpt)

```
//scroll to the beginning
window.scrollTo(0, 0);
```

These examples say: scroll down by 200 pixels, then across by 200 pixels, then to a point that's 300 pixels from the left and 100 pixels from the top, then back to the top corner.

Getting the Viewport Size (the Available Space inside the Window)

The details of the viewport size are needed for many kinds of scripting, wherever available space is a factor in the script's logic. This solution provides a utility function for getting the viewport size We'll be seeing the function again quite a few times throughout this book!

Solution

The properties we need are implemented in three different ways, like the properties we saw for page scrolling in the previous section ("Making the Page Scroll to a Particular Position"). As was the case in that example, we can use object testing to determine which implementation is relevant, including the test for a zero-value that we need in IE 5 (this test is required for the same reason: because, though the property exists, it isn't what we want):

File: **get-viewport-size.js** (excerpt)

```
function getViewportSize()
{
  var size = [0, 0];

  if (typeof window.innerWidth != 'undefined')
  {
    size = [
        window.innerWidth,
        window.innerHeight
    ];
  }
  else if (typeof document.documentElement != 'undefined'
      && typeof document.documentElement.clientWidth !=
      'undefined' && document.documentElement.clientWidth != 0)
  {
```

```
      size = [
          document.documentElement.clientWidth,
          document.documentElement.clientHeight
      ];
    }
    else
    {
      size = [
          document.getElementsByTagName('body')[0].clientWidth,
          document.getElementsByTagName('body')[0].clientHeight
      ];
    }

    return size;
}
```

The function returns an array of the width and height, so we can call it whenever we need that data:

File: **get-viewport-size.js** (excerpt)

```
window.onresize = function()
{
  var size = getViewportSize();
  alert('Viewport size: [' + size[0] + ', ' + size[1] + ']');
};
```

Summary

We've covered the basics of window and frame manipulation from a pragmatist's point of view in this chapter. We've also talked about principles and techniques that we can use to ensure that scripts like this are as user-friendly and as accessible as we can make them. Doubtless, this kind of work will remain controversial, and clearly we do need *some kind* of targeting mechanism, because even though the use of frames is slowly dying out, the advent of ever more sophisticated interfaces keeps these issues alive.

I rather like the XLink standard's show attribute, which has values like new and replace.[5] These *suggest* a target process (open a new window, and replace the contents of the current window, respectively) but they don't actually *define* specific behaviors. They leave it up to the user agent to control what actually happens, so, for example, new could be used to open tabs instead of windows.

---

[5] http://www.w3.org/TR/xlink/#show-att

8

Working with Cookies

Unless you want to use some unreliable IP detection and database storage techniques, cookies are the only way in which you can share user data between two non-sequential web pages. While CGI parameters require you to pass user data between every page on which the parameters are used, cookies allow you to store data on users' systems and retrieve it minutes, hours, or even days later. This makes cookies perfect for remembering things like users' login names, which pages they visited last, what they dropped into their shopping carts, and when they did so.

Although server-side code is the most robust method of dealing with cookies, sometimes you need to manipulate cookies on the client side. Luckily, JavaScript can read and write the cookies in exactly the same way servers do.

Writing Cookies

Any script—be it server- or client-side—can only read cookies that were set by a web page from the same domain, so cast aside those fantasies of finding out what someone bought on Amazon. If you can read only cookies that you write, you'd better learn how to write them!

Solution

Cookies are stored in the `document` object's `cookie` property. This property is actually a string that's automatically generated by the browser when the page loads. It concatenates all the valid cookie information stored for the current browser address, and makes it available to JavaScript via the DOM.

Within the `cookie` property, cookies are separated by a semicolon (`;`), and traditionally each cookie consists of a name/value pair separated by an equality sign (`=`). An example cookie string looks like this:

```
fur=blue; food=biscuits; name=Cookie_Monster
```

The first step in creating a cookie is to create a string that reflects the name of your cookie, followed by =, followed by the value of the cookie:

File: **write_cookie.js (excerpt)**

```
var cookieName = "login";
var cookieValue = "choc_chip";
var theCookie = cookieName + "=" + cookieValue;
```

Avoid Spaces and Punctuation

When you create your cookie string, make sure that the name or value of the cookie does not include spaces, commas, or semicolons. These characters can cause errors not only with the parsing of the cookie string, but with the sending of cookie data via HTTP headers. The easiest way to avoid entering these characters into `document.cookie` is to pass your cookie value to the `escape` function. This will escape special characters, turning them into their ASCII code equivalents. To read a cookie with escaped characters, you have to reverse the escaping process using the `unescape` function. Don't escape the = that separates the name and value, though: it needs to be present to delimit these two components of the cookie.

Once you've created your cookie string, you have to store it in the browser's cookie jar. Even though `document.cookie` is really just one string, it exhibits special behavior when JavaScript tries to write a cookie to it. Assigning a cookie string to `document.cookie` does not overwrite the entire property, as it would for a normal string. Instead, the cookie string is *added* to `document.cookie`. If the cookie name already exists, the new value automatically replaces the current one:

```
document.cookie = theCookie;
```

Your data is now a cookie! Imagine that `document.cookie` was originally:

```
fur=blue; food=biscuits; name=Cookie_Monster
```

Now, it's:

```
fur=blue; food=biscuits; name=Cookie_Monster; login=choc_chip
```

You can only add one cookie at a time, so even though you can replicate the cookie-semicolon-cookie syntax, you cannot concatenate a number of cookie strings together and add them to `document.cookie` in one go.

Reading a Cookie

It's no good writing a cookie unless you can access it again. The browser automatically fills `document.cookie` with all the valid cookies for the current domain, so there's no chance that you'll read something you're not meant to. However, you can still read the data you set at another time, or from another part of your web site.

Solution

There's nothing glamorous about getting cookies out of `document.cookie`—you have to parse the string yourself and collect your own values. But, once you understand the syntax of the `cookie` property, it's fairly easy to break the process into a couple of `split` method calls:

File: **read_cookie.js** (excerpt)

```
function getCookie(searchName)
{
  var cookies = document.cookie.split(";");

  for (var i = 0; i < cookies.length; i++)
  {
    var cookieCrumbs = cookies[i].split("=");
    var cookieName = cookieCrumbs[0];
    var cookieValue = cookieCrumbs[1];

    if (cookieName == searchName)
    {
```

```
      return cookieValue;
    }
  }
  return false;
}
```

In the `getCookie` function, a split is performed at two levels: the first time, to find each cookie, then, again, to break up the cookie name and its value. It's then a cinch to compare the current cookie name with the one we want.

Let's use the example cookie we created above:

File: **read_cookie.js** (excerpt)

```
var monsterName = getCookie("name");
```

The value of the variable `monsterName` is now `"Cookie_Monster"`.

Setting a Cookie to Expire at a Specific Date and Time

As well as specifying the value of a cookie when you set it, a number of options can be appended to the end of the cookie string that will affect the way the cookie is handled. One of these options allows you to set a date and time at which the cookie will expire.

Solution

By default, cookies are erased once a browser session ends. Alternatively, you can set an expiry date for a cookie, enabling it to exist for a given period of time.

An expiry date is added to the end of the cookie; it must be set apart from the rest of the cookie string by a semicolon, followed by the string `expires=`. The date must be specified in a special GMT string format, which takes the following form:

```
Weekday, DD-Mon-YYYY HH:MM:SS GMT
```

However, there are easier ways to create this awkward string than calculating the exact day of the week on which June 3, 2010 falls.

The `Date` class allows you to specify a more friendly date format, then convert it to a GMT string (for more information on working with dates in JavaScript, see Chapter 9):

File: **set_cookie_expire_date.js** (excerpt)

```
var date = new Date("June 3, 2010");
var cookieDate = date.toGMTString();
```

Once you have the expiry date, attach it to the end of the cookie string, then assign it to `document.cookie`:

File: **set_cookie_expire_date.js** (excerpt)

```
theCookie += ";expires=" + cookieDate;
document.cookie = theCookie;
```

Your cookie data will now be available well into the foreseeable future.

Making a Cookie Accessible Only from a Specific Domain or Path

Although cookies from one domain may not read cookies set by another domain, there are some subtleties of cookie access that you *can* control. These include both the subdomains and directory paths from which a cookie may be read.

Solution

By default, when a cookie is set, it will be readable only by other pages within the full domain. So, if a page at `http://javascript.sitepoint.com/` wrote a cookie, a page at `http://php.sitepoint.com/` would not be able to read it. In order to allow all the subdomains of sitepoint.com to read a cookie, the domain must be set when the cookie is created. To do this, we add `;domain=domainName` to the end of the cookie string:

File: **cookie_specific_domain.js** (excerpt)

```
theCookie += ";domain=sitepoint.com";
document.cookie = theCookie;
```

That cookie is now able to be read by pages from all the subdomains of sitepoint.com, including `http://www.sitepoint.com` and `http://javascript.sitepoint.com`.

As an additional access restriction, by default, cookies are only readable by pages within the current directory, or a subdirectory of the current directory. So, if `http://www.sitepoint.com/scripts/cookie_monster.htm` wrote a cookie, `http://www.sitepoint.com/kermit.htm` would not be able to read it.

To set the highest level path that's allowed to read a cookie, we add `;path=`*pathName* to the end of the cookie string:

File: **cookie_specific_domain.js (excerpt)**
```
theCookie += ";path=/";
document.cookie = theCookie;
```

That cookie is now readable by all pages in or under the root directory; that is, all of the pages on the web site.

Discussion

By default, all cookies are sent to servers over an unsecured channel. If you wish a cookie to be transmitted only to a secure server, i.e., one that uses `https://`, you must attach the **secure** option to the end of your cookie:

```
theCookie += ";secure";
document.cookie = theCookie;
```

The cookie will now be transmitted only if it is requested over a secure channel; otherwise, it will not be sent at all.

Circumventing Browser Restrictions on the Number of Cookies you can Use

Cookies were only designed to store small snippets of data that were relevant to a web site. They were not designed to act as large-scale data repositories. Therefore, some restrictions have been placed upon cookies' storage capacity.

Solution

The string that stores the cookies for a particular host is allowed to store just 4KB of data—4096 characters. In practice, this is not that much of a hindrance, as 4KB represents more than enough data for most of the tasks to which cookies are applied. However, a second restriction on cookies allows a maximum of twenty cookies to be used per domain or server. This *can* affect some web sites, but if you're reaching this limit, there's a method you can use to alleviate its restrictions: use sub-cookies.

The sub-cookie storage method involves storing a number of values inside a single cookie. So, within `document.cookie`, three levels of parsing will be required to get a value. The storage syntax of these sub-cookies is entirely up to you, but it's important that you standardize the syntax, and avoid using your chosen separating characters within names and values. A common scheme is to use colons (`:`) as sub-cookie name/value separators, and slashes (`/`) as sub-cookie separators. This makes the raw `document.cookie` look like this:

```
monsterCookie=fur:blue/food:biscuits/name:Cookie_Monster
```

However, if you're using colons as name/value separators, you'll want to `escape` the cookie value to make sure it doesn't conflict with the cookie syntax:

File: **circumvent_browser_restrictions.js** (excerpt)

```
var cookieName = "monsterCookie";
var cookieValue = "fur:blue/food:biscuits/name:Cookie_Monster";

cookieValue = escape(cookieValue);

var theCookie = cookieName + "=" + cookieValue;

document.cookie = theCookie;
```

After the cookie value is escaped, `document.cookie` will actually look like this:

```
monsterCookie=fur%3Ablue/food%3Abiscuits/name%3ACookie_Monster
```

When you're reading the cookie back in, and looking for a sub-cookie value, you'll have to `unescape` the cookie value, then parse it, to access the sub-cookies. If we put all the parsing layers together, we get a function like this:

File: **circumvent_browser_restrictions.js** (excerpt)

```
function getSubCookie(cookieName, subCookieName)
{
  var cookies = document.cookie.split(";");

  for (var i = 0; i < cookies.length; i++)
  {
    var cookieCrumbs = cookies[i].split("=");

    cookieCrumbs[0] = cookieCrumbs[0].replace(/^\s+/, "");
```

```
if (cookieCrumbs[0] == cookieName)
{
  var cookieValue = cookieCrumbs[1];
  cookieValue = unescape(cookieValue);
  var subCookies = cookieValue.split("/");

  for (var j = 0; j < subCookies.length; j++)
  {
    var subCookieCrumbs = subCookies[j].split(":");

    if (subCookieCrumbs[0] == subCookieName)
    {
      return subCookieCrumbs[1];
    }
  }
}

return false;
}
```

Summary

Now that you know how to read and write cookies using JavaScript, you'll be able to use them to share data across many pages of your web site, and recall important details for users when they return to your site.

In Chapter 12 we'll use cookies to remember the alternate style sheet each user selects, but these principles can just as easily be used to alleviate repetitive form data entry, or to remember users' preferences. Cookies let you fast-track your users' progress toward their goals without having them lift a finger!

9

Working with Dates and Times

Date and time are not the most glamorous of concepts, but these types of data are required frequently for a whole variety of applications. Whether you want to display the date on a page, add a timestamp to a log entry, or calculate how much time will elapse before an event occurs, being able to work effectively with date and time is a necessary and useful skill.

JavaScript provides a Date object from which all other date- and time-related methods derive. We can use these methods to extract various parts of the date—the month, the day, or the number of seconds elapsed in the minute, for example—and then to format that data into the desired output.

Getting the Date and Time

This first solution introduces the Date object, and shows you some very quick and easy ways to create a formatted date and time.

Solution

We begin with a new instance of the Date object:

File: **get-date-and-time.js** (excerpt)

```
var today = new Date();
```

The `today` variable is a `Date` object for the current date, measured in milliseconds since the UTC epoch (midnight on 1 January, 1970), according to local time.

What's "Local" Time?

Local time is the current time wherever your user is located (i.e., based on the internal clock of the host computer, and the time settings of the host operating system). **UTC (Coordinated Universal Time)**[1] is the international standard for time, a more accurately maintained parallel to Greenwich Mean Time.

The actual value you get from this raw `Date` is curious, in that you can compare it against another `Date` numerically (as though it were the number of milliseconds), yet if you output the value, you'll generally get a formatted string! The actual output will vary in different browsers, but will be something like an RFC 2822 formatted date, such as "Mon, 19 Jun 2006 11:33:55 GMT+0100."

If you want to use this output, you *shouldn't* rely on the object-to-string conversion occurring automatically. Rather, call the `Date`'s `toString` method, which produces the formatted date string:

File: **get-date-and-time.js**

```
var today = new Date();
var sentence = today.toString();

alert(sentence);
```

There are two other methods that perform a similar conversion. `toGMTString` formats the date according to Internet GMT conventions (the format used by cookies, as we saw in Chapter 8). `toLocaleString` produces a regional output that varies according to the locale of the user. For example, when you're noting a date in the USA, the convention for doing so requires that the month appears before the day (06/19/2006), while in other countries (such as the UK), the day precedes the month (19/06/2006):

File: **get-date-and-time2.js** (excerpt)

```
var today = new Date();
var gmt = today.toGMTString();
var locale = today.toLocaleString();

alert(gmt);
alert(locale);
```

---

[1]Yes, I *know* the letters don't match.

So gmt would produce a value like "Mon, 19 Jun 2006 10:57:17 GMT," while locale, applied in the UK, would produce a value like "19/06/2005 11:57:17."

Discussion

Basic formatting like this is useful when you need a quick solution, but it doesn't offer any real control over the output. However, the Date class provides a range of methods for extracting *individual parts* of the date and time. We can use these methods together to create whatever custom format we want.

We'll be using many of these methods through this chapter, but before we begin, here's a summary of the most useful:

getFullYear	returns the year as a four-digit number
	There is also a getYear method, but that returns a two-digit number and isn't Y2K safe.
getMonth	returns the month as an integer between 0 and 11
getDate	returns the date as an integer between 1 and 31
getDay	returns the day as an integer between 0 and 6, where 0 is Sunday
getHours	returns the hour as an integer between 0 and 23
getMinutes	returns the minutes as an integer between 0 and 59
getSeconds	returns the seconds as an integer between 0 and 59
getTime	returns the number of milliseconds since the UTC epoch
getTimezoneOffset	returns the difference in minutes between local time and GMT

WARNING

getDate: an Exception to the Rule

Notice that the value returned from getDate is one or higher, while other values start at zero. It's worth keeping an eye out for that difference, because it can easily trip you up if you're associating the numbers with items in an array.

The methods shown here return a value relative to the user's local time, but there are equivalents for returning a UTC time value. These follow a predictable naming convention: `getUTCFullYear`, `getUTCMonth`, `getUTCDate`, and so on.

There are also equivalent setter methods, such as `setFullYear` and `setDate`, which set (rather than get) the corresponding properties of a `Date` object. These may not be useful if the date you're working with is always *now* (a `Date` object created with no arguments, as in the earlier example), but the JavaScript `Date` object is far more powerful. You can modify the date/time of an existing object, or simply create a new object to represent a given time in the past or future, by passing that date as a string argument when you create it.

Formatting a Date into a Sentence

Using some of the methods outlined in the previous discussion, we can create a formatted date that's more precisely tailored to our needs. We can come up with terse or conversational sentences, dates that are incredibly accurate or fairly broad—whatever we need.

In this solution, we'll use **object prototyping** to bind new methods directly to the `Date` class. This makes the functionality more flexible and convenient to use, because we can call our own formatting functions as if they were native methods of the `Date` class. We first saw prototyping in Chapter 4, and it's covered in detail in Chapter 19, but you don't need to understand its finer details to use this solution.

Solution

We'll define two new methods for the `Date` class in this solution. The first does most of the work; the second is there to assist the first:

File: **format-date.js (excerpt)**

```
Date.prototype.getDateString = function(str)
{
  var dnames = ['Sunday', 'Monday', 'Tuesday', 'Wednesday',
      'Thursday', 'Friday', 'Saturday', 'Sunday'];

  var mnames = ['January', 'February', 'March', 'April',
      'May', 'June', 'July', 'August', 'September',
      'October', 'November', 'December'];

  str = str.replace('%day', dnames[this.getDay()]);
```

```
  str = str.replace('%date', this.getDate());
  str = str.replace('%ordinal', this.getDateOrdinal());
  str = str.replace('%month', mnames[this.getMonth()]);
  str = str.replace('%year', this.getFullYear());

  return str;
};

Date.prototype.getDateOrdinal = function()
{
  var n = this.getDate();

  var ord = 'th';

  if (n % 10 == 1 && n % 100 != 11)
  {
    ord = 'st';
  }
  else if (n % 10 == 2 && n % 100 != 12)
  {
    ord = 'nd';
  }
  else if (n % 10 == 3 && n % 100 != 13)
  {
    ord = 'rd';
  }

  return ord;
};
```

To use the `getDateString` method, pass it a string that contains tokens for each of the components of the date sentence: the day (`%day`), date (`%date`), ordinal (`%ordinal`), month (`%month`), and year (`%year`). Any other text passes through unchanged.

For example, a fully-formatted sentence might look like this:

File: **format-date-example.js** (excerpt)

```
var today = new Date();
var sentence = today.getDateString(
    '%day the %date%ordinal of %month %year');

alert(sentence);
```

This script produces an output something like, `"Monday the 19th of June 2006."` Alternatively, you could create a more compact date, in either US or UK format:

```
var today = new Date();
var us = today.getDateString('%month %date%ordinal %year');
var uk = today.getDateString('%date%ordinal %month %year');
```

So the value of us would be `"June 19th 2005"`, while that of uk would be `"19th June 2005"`.

Discussion

The `getDateString` method is pretty straightforward: it's just a series of string replacements that convert tokens (such as `%year`) into values returned from the relevant `Date` method (such as `getFullYear`). The names of days and months are stored in arrays whose indexes correspond with the numbers returned by `getMonth` and `getDay`, so for example, we can return the name of the current month as `mnames[this.getMonth()]`.

The `getDateOrdinal` method in this example is almost identical to the `getOrdinal` function we developed in "Converting Numbers to Ordinals (-st, -nd, -rd, -th)" in Chapter 2.

These two methods are designed to provide dates in a friendly, sentence-style format, but it's also useful in many applications to format dates using international standard notation (ISO 8601),[2] which is the format *YYYYMMDD*. We can drop in another method for this purpose while we're at it.

Creating a date in ISO 8601 format is simply a case of concatenating the date numbers into a string, and adding leading zeros to the month and day as necessary (to get results like `"20270504"` instead of `"202754"`). We also need to add a 1 to the month number, so that, say, January is `"01"` and not `"00"`:

File: **format-date.js** (excerpt)
```
Date.prototype.getISODate = function()
{
  var mth = this.getMonth() + 1;
  mth = (mth < 10 ? '0' : '') + mth;

  var date = this.getDate();
```

---

[2] http://www.cl.cam.ac.uk/~mgk25/iso-time.html

```
  date = (date < 10 ? '0' : '') + date;

  return this.getFullYear() + mth + date;
};
```

Formatting the Time into a 12- or 24-hour Clock

Opinion varies on whether 12- or 24-hour clocks are easier to read, and individual preferences have as much to do with familiarity as anything else. Fortunately, we can provide either format as required.

As with the previous solution, binding a method directly to the Date class makes it more flexible and convenient to use.

Solution

Outputting the time as a 24-hour clock is fairly simple, but we have to do a bit of extra calculation to format the output correctly for 12-hour clocks:

File: **format-time.js**

```
Date.prototype.getTimeString = function(clock)
{
  var str = '';
  var hrs = this.getHours();

  if (clock == 12)
  {
    var meridian = hrs < 12 ? 'am' : 'pm';

    hrs = hrs % 12;
    if (hrs == 0) { hrs = 12; }
    str += hrs;
  }
  else
  {
    str += (hrs < 10 ? '0' : '') + hrs;
  }

  str += ':';
  var mins = this.getMinutes();
  str += (mins < 10 ? '0' : '') + mins;
```

```
  if (clock == 12) { str += meridian; }

  return str;
};
```

To use the `getTimeString` method, simply specify whether to use a 12- or 24-hour clock, and the method will do the rest:

File: **format-time-example.js** (excerpt)

```
var today = new Date();
var now12 = today.getTimeString(12);
var now24 = today.getTimeString(24);

alert('12 hour time: ' + now12);
alert('24 hour time: ' + now24);
```

The returned string has the hours and minutes delimited with colons; if a 12-hour clock is specified, it includes a meridian token (`"am"` or `"pm"`), while for a 24-hour clock the hours include a leading zero (as required).

So `now12` would be something like `"2:27pm"`, while at the same time, `now24` would say `"14:37"`. Midnight is represented by the same convention, as `"12:00am"` or `"00:00"` respectively.

Discussion

The value we get from `getHours` is a number between zero and 23, so if we're using a 24-hour clock, formatting this number is simply a case of adding a leading zero as required, then concatenating that string to the result. Adding the minutes uses exactly the same approach—the figure, plus a leading zero as required.

But if we're using a 12-hour clock, some extra computation is required. We first need to calculate the meridian by testing whether the hours figure is 12 or greater. We then calculate the hour within that meridian by dividing the hours figure by 12 and taking the remainder (resulting in a number between zero and 11). Finally, if the hour is zero, we assign a replacement value of 12, because midnight on a 12-hour clock is 12:00 a.m., and noon is 12:00 p.m.

If you'd like to ascertain the number of seconds as well, add this extra code—it should come after the minutes value is processed, but before the meridian is added at the end:

```
str += ':';
var secs = this.getSeconds();
str += (secs < 10 ? '0' : '') + secs;
```

Now that we have custom formatting methods for both date (from "Formatting a Date into a Sentence") and time, we can use them together, passing the output of getTimeString as part of the input to getDateString:

File: **format-time-example.js** (excerpt)

```
var message = today.getDateString('Created at '
    + today.getTimeString(24)
    + ', on %day, %month the %date%ordinal');
alert(message);
```

This will produce an output like, "Created at 15:04, on Monday, June the 19th." But perhaps you'd prefer something more elaborate:

```
var message = today.getDateString('Inscribed at '
    + today.getTimeString(12)
    + ', on this very %day, the %date%ordinal day of %month'
    + ', in the calendar year %year');
```

This produces the sentence, "Inscribed at 3:04pm, on this very Monday, the 19th day of June, in the calendar year 2005."

Comparing Two Dates

So far we've been working with *today's* date, by creating a Date object with no argument. But if we include a date string as an argument to the Date constructor, it will create a date object for the specified date and time.

This will allow us to input two dates as strings; we'll then be able to work with them as Date objects.

Solution

This function compares two dates and returns the number of years, months, and days between them as an array of three numbers:

File: **get-time-between.js** (excerpt)

```
function getTimeBetween(from, until)
{
  var past = from == '' ? new Date() : new Date(from);
```

```
  var future = until == '' ? new Date() : new Date(until);

  if (past >= future)
  {
    var tmp = past;
    past = future;
    future = tmp;
  }

  var between = [
      future.getFullYear() - past.getFullYear(),
      future.getMonth() - past.getMonth(),
      future.getDate() - past.getDate()
  ];

  if (between[2] < 0)
  {
    between[1]--;
    var ynum = future.getFullYear();

    var mlengths = [
        31,
        (ynum % 4 == 0 && ynum % 100 != 0 || ynum % 400 == 0) ?
        29 : 28,
        31, 30, 31, 30, 31, 31, 30, 31, 30, 31
    ];

    var mnum = future.getMonth() - 1;
    if (mnum < 0) { mnum += 12; }

    between[2] += mlengths[mnum];
  }

  if (between[1] < 0)
  {
    between[0]--;
    between[1] += 12;
  }

  return between;
}
```

To use the function, we specify a date in the past and a date in the future using a compatible format, such as `"19 Jun, 2006"`. If you specify an empty string for either argument, the current date will be used.

Compatible Date Formats

note

The compatible formats are those that are understood by the `Date` object itself: either `"19 Jun, 2006"`, or `"Mon, 19 Jun 2006 15:04:00 GMT+0100"`. The object also understands US time-zone abbreviations (such as PST), and assumes GMT if none is specified (and midnight GMT if no time is specified).

Here's the code we'd use to get the number of years, months, and days between now and a specified event:

File: **get-time-between-example.js** (excerpt)

```
var until = getTimeBetween('', '10 Jun, 2014');
alert(until[0] + 'years ' + until[1] + 'months ' + until[2] +
    'days');
```

We'd use this script to get the number of years, months, and days that had passed since an event:

File: **get-time-between-example.js** (excerpt)

```
var since = getTimeBetween('10 Jun, 2003', '');
alert(since[0] + 'years ' + since[1] + 'months ' + since[2] +
    'days');
```

If you specify a *future date first*, the arguments will just be swapped over—you'll still get the time from the earlier date to the later date.

In the next solution, we'll take these numbers and turn them into a nicely-formatted sentence.

Discussion

The first step in the script is to create a `Date` object for each of the input dates. Although the values are objects, we can still *compare* them as though they were numbers (the number of milliseconds since the UTC epoch), and use that comparison to work out which date occurs in the future (it's the larger amount of time).

Once we know the order of the two dates, we can subtract the years, months, and days in the latter date from their corresponding values in the earlier date, using the relevant `Date` methods.

Yet the final solution is not *quite* as simple as that! We have two specific issues to deal with.

Suppose we have dates of `"22 Jun, 2005"` and `"22 May, 2006"`. We'd get a year difference of one, but a month difference of -1, and obviously that can't be right—we can't have a negative difference. What we actually have is a difference of 11 months (and zero years), so we'll need to adjust our result: if the difference between the number of months is negative, we must add 12 to this number to get the correct positive value, and subtract one from the number of years in order to compensate. This is the same principle as "borrowing from the column to the left" when subtracting large numbers on paper.

The same situation can occur between months and days, but the adjustment is slightly more complex to derive. If we had dates of `"22 Jun, 2006"` and `"19 Jul, 2006"`, we'd get a month difference of one and a day difference of -3, but when we "borrow a month's worth of days" we need to do a bit of extra work, because different months have different numbers of days.

We need to know how many days are in the month *before* our future month, because that's where those remainder days will come from. To calculate this figure, we need to know if the future year is a leap year. That's the purpose of the ternary expression in the second (February) member of the `mlengths` array, which has a condition that expresses the rules for leap years:

File: **get-time-between.js** (excerpt)

```
var ynum = future.getFullYear();

var mlengths = [
    31,
    (ynum % 4 == 0 && ynum % 100 != 0 || ynum % 400 == 0) ?
    29 : 28,
    31,30,31,30,31,31,30,31,30,31
];
```

The final point to note is that we have to do the days/months conversion *before* the months/years conversion, because adjusting the value for months may affect the value for years. And we have our answer!

This handy ability to pass a date string to the `Date` constructor has many other uses. Want to know on which day of the week a particular date falls?

File: **get-time-between.js** (excerpt)

```
function getDayName(thedate)
{
  var dnames = ['Sunday', 'Monday', 'Tuesday', 'Wednesday',
     'Thursday', 'Friday', 'Saturday', 'Sunday'];

  var today = new Date(thedate);

  return dnames[today.getDay()];
}
```

File: **get-time-between-example.js** (excerpt)

```
var dayname = getDayName('1 Jan, 2050');
alert('1 Jan, 2050 is a ' + dayname);
```

Suppose we want to work with the date *in a certain number of days*. We can construct a `Date` object using a number (the number of milliseconds since the UTC epoch) instead of a string, and we can obtain that number for the *current* date using the `getTime` method of `Date`. Once we have the current date in milliseconds, and we've converted the number of additional days to milliseconds, we simply need to pass the result to a new `Date` object:

File: **get-time-between.js** (excerpt)

```
function dateInSomeDays(n)
{
  var today = new Date();

  var seconds = today.getTime();
  seconds += n * 86400000;

  return new Date(seconds);
}
```

File: **get-time-between-example.js** (excerpt)

```
var future = dateInSomeDays(15);
alert('In 15 days, it will be a ' + getDayName(future));
```

`future` is a `Date` object set to 15 days in the future, which we can format or process as normal.

Date Limits

Creating dates at a specific point in time is in fact a limited proposition, though in practice you're unlikely to come up against those limits. The range in which we can create dates stretches +/- 100 million days from the UTC epoch, which is roughly 275,000 years from 1970!

Formatting the Difference Between Dates

Numbers are all very well, but they're not much use to other people if we don't describe what they are!

Solution

In "Comparing Two Dates", earlier in this chapter, we obtained an array that contained the number of years, months, and days between two dates. Now we're going to format those numbers into a coherent string:

File: **format-time-between.js** (excerpt)

```
function formatTimeBetween(difference)
{
  var str = ''

  if (difference[0] > 0)
  {
    str += difference[0] + ' year';
    str += difference[0] == 1 ? '' : 's';
    if (difference[1] > 0)
    {
      str += difference[2] > 0 ? ', ' : ' and ';
    }
    else
    {
      str += difference[2] > 0 ? ' and ' : '';
    }
  }

  if (difference[1] > 0)
  {
    str += difference[1] + ' month';
    str += difference[1] == 1 ? '' : 's';
    str += difference[2] > 0 ? ' and ' : '';
  }

  if (difference[2] > 0)
  {
    str += difference[2] + ' day';
    str += difference[2] == 1 ? '' : 's';
```

```
    }

    return str;
}
```

This function takes a single argument—the array of three numbers returned by getTimeBetween—and returns a string that's formatted according to its content.

Let's look into the past from now:

File: **format-time-between.js (excerpt)**
```
var since = getTimeBetween('10 Jun, 2003', '');
since = formatTimeBetween(since) + ' since Kizzy was born';
alert(since);
```

Or forwards, from now into the future:

File: **format-time-between.js (excerpt)**
```
var until = getTimeBetween('', '8 Sep, 2014');
until = formatTimeBetween(until) + ' until secondary school';
alert(since);
```

Or between any two arbitrary dates:

File: **format-time-between.js (excerpt)**
```
var between = getTimeBetween('10 Jun, 2006', '25 Dec, 2006');
between = formatTimeBetween(between) + ' from birthday to xmas';
alert(between);
```

Discussion

The script needs to work out which delimiter should be used for each part of the string to ensure that, for example, a difference array of [1, 0, 3] would produce "1 year and 3 days", rather than "1 year, 0 months and 3 days".

In this case, the delimiter is the word "and," which comes between years and days. If there were a nonzero number of months, "and" would come instead between the number of months and days. In fact, if any of the figures is zero, the structure of the output sentence will be affected. So, as we consider the delimiter text (if any) to use after each figure, we need to check the values of the other figures.

We also need to add "s" to plural figures, but that's straightforward enough: it's a simple case of ascertaining whether the value is one!

I structured the code in this solution to make it easier to read, but it could be expressed in fewer (though more obscure) lines of code if we made greater use of ternary operators:

```
function formatTimeBetween(difference)
{
  var str = ''
  if (difference[0] > 0)
  {
    str += difference[0]
        + ' year' + (difference[0] == 1 ? '' : 's')
        + (difference[1] > 0
        ? (difference[2] > 0 ? ', ' : ' and ')
        : (difference[2] > 0 ? ' and ' : '')
        );
  }
  if (difference[1] > 0)
  {
    str += difference[1]
        + ' month' + (difference[1] == 1 ? '' : 's')
        + (difference[2] > 0 ? ' and ' : '');
  }
  if (difference[2] > 0)
  {
    str += difference[2]
        + ' day' + (difference[2] == 1 ? '' : 's');
  }
  return str;
}
```

Summary

Personally, I don't believe time really exists at all, but that's not a very useful philosophy when you're late for work!

In this chapter, we've examined some of the more useful `Date` methods, seen how to compare dates to one another, and looked at various ways of formatting dates and times. Though they're not particularly glamorous, these tools will stand you in good stead for your future JavaScript development.

 **Working with Images**

In the early days of the Web, modifying images was almost the only thing you could do with any degree of visual control in a browser. Happily, those days are long gone, but even now images are a staple ingredient of any design that can't be represented with text, boxes, and solid colors alone.

We won't be using the old DOM 0 collection `document.images` in this chapter, because we don't need it. It's generally more future-safe to avoid these old collections, but that's not always possible—we *did* use `document.forms` in Chapter 4, because it provided information that we couldn't easily derive otherwise (see Chapter 4 for a detailed discussion).

Preloading Images

JavaScript has a built-in `Image` class that can be used to preload images. When you create an `Image` object and set its `src`, the browser makes a request for that image, thereby saving it into the cache. Subsequent calls for the same image will draw it from the cache instead of loading it afresh.

Solution

The basic code that preloads an image looks like this:

```
var img = new Image();
img.src = 'chewbacca.gif';
```

If we have several images to preload, we can cache them more efficiently using a
`for` loop. And if all the images have the same file extension, we can make our
code more efficient by adding that extension when we create the image `src`, instead of storing the extension as part of each file's name:

File: **preload-images.js** (excerpt)

```
var imgNames = ['luke', 'obi-wan', 'chewbacca', 'han'];
var imgObjects = [];

for (var i = 0; i < imgNames.length; i++)
{
  imgObjects[i] = new Image();
  imgObjects[i].src = imgNames[i] + '.gif';
}
```

Discussion

Notice that we're storing each `Image` object to an array as we go along, rather
than reusing the same reference for each iteration. We do so because image
loading is **asynchronous** (the load request is made, but the script carries on
without waiting). If we reused a single variable for all iterations, we could end
up storing only the *final* image in the cache, as each request would be overwritten
by the next.

We avoid this possibility by using an array to save the images—we have a unique
reference for each image, so the times and orders in which they're loaded don't
matter. This solution also provides a convenient set of references to our cached
`Image` objects, which could be useful later on.

However, once you've preloaded an image, you don't actually *need* that same
reference to be able to use the image from the cache. Give any `img` element on
your page a `src` that's identical to the `src` of an already-loaded image, and that
image will be found and shared in the cache. The same is true if you need to
preload images for `background-image` swapping, or other CSS effects: once you've
preloaded an image using this method, any further uses of that image will be
drawn from the cache (providing that the browser's cache has not been disabled).

Swapping One Image for Another

Image swapping is a well-known technique, and some of its applications are almost irrelevant today. Mouseover-driven image swapping is a good example: the same effect can be achieved more easily and cleanly using a block-level link and some CSS pseudo-classes. For more information on this technique, see Chapter 4 of *The CSS Anthology: 101 Tips, Tricks & Hacks*,[1] also published by SitePoint.

Nonetheless, there are many uses for programmatic image changing that remain relevant, and we'll look at some of the more interesting applications as we progress through this chapter. This solution introduces the basic technique.

Solution

We can perform an image swap by changing the `src` property of an image. We'll begin with a static `img`, so that we have an image in our page by default:

File: **swap-image.html** (excerpt)

```
<p>
  Luke's father is
  <img id="father" src="darth.gif" alt="Darth Vader">
</p>
```

Now, we need to identify that image in the DOM, and change it to some other image, updating the `alt` text as we go.

As is the case with any DOM script, we can't do this until the DOM is ready (we discussed this in Chapter 5). To trigger it, we'll use the `addLoadListener` construct from Chapter 1 (as a better alternative to `window.onload`):

```
addLoadListener(window.onload = function()
{
  var img = document.getElementById('father');

  img.src = 'chewbacca.gif';
  img.alt = 'Chewbacca';
});
```

---

[1] http://www.sitepoint.com/books/cssant1/

Discussion

When you perform an image swap, the new image is loaded into the **placeholder** of the first. So, if you've defined `width` and `height` attributes on the original `<img>` tag, the new image will be displayed at those same dimensions.

However, we can resize an image after swapping it: we load the new image into an `Image` object, read the `width` and `height` properties from that object, then set the corresponding properties of the `img` element in the document.

Of course, we can't read those values until the new image has loaded, so we can't just slap the image into the page and allow it to load in its own time. Instead, we can *preload* the image using the technique we've just seen, bind an `onload` handler to read the image's `width` and `height` once it has loaded, then perform the image swap with the correct dimensions, as follows:

File: **swap-image.js** (excerpt)

```
addLoadListener(function()
{
  var img = document.getElementById('father');

  var newimg = new Image();

  newimg.onload = function()
  {
    img.src = newimg.src;
    img.width = newimg.width;
    img.height = newimg.height;
  }

  newimg.src = 'chewbacca.gif';
});
```

Note that we set up the `onload` handler before assigning the file name to the `src` property. If we had assigned the `src` first, the `load` event might occur before the `onload` event handler were in place to respond to it.[2]

 ## Beware of this

More experienced coders might think to refer to `newimg` using the special variable `this` within the `onload` event handler. Within event handlers,

---

[2]In particular, this can happen with cached images in Safari.

this generally provides a reference to the object that the handler was assigned to.

Unfortunately, due to an apparent bug in Safari 1.3 and 2.0, this points to window in onload event handlers for Image objects. We must therefore continue to refer to the image as newimg in the above example.

Our final output will change, as Figure 10.1 illustrates.

Figure 10.1. Before and after the image swap

Displaying an Image at Random

Displaying a random image is a trick that comes in handy for promotional as well as decorative purposes—it's often used for tasks like selecting a banner advertisement, or choosing a random product shot to display on an ecommerce site.

Solution

The process of presenting a random image is just like a regular image swap, but instead of having a single, named image, we choose an image at random from a group of images stored in an array. We start with the same static img as before:

File: **random-image.html** (excerpt)

```
<p>
  Luke's father is
  <img id="father" src="darth.gif" alt="Darth Vader">
</p>
```

Next, the script defines a choice of images (with corresponding alt text), and selects one of them using a constrained random number (a technique we saw in "Creating and Constraining Random Numbers" in Chapter 2):

```
                                          File: random-image.js (excerpt)
addLoadListener(function()
{
  var people = [
      ['darth', 'Darth Vader'],
      ['palpatine', 'Emperor Palpatine'],
      ['boba', 'Boba Fett'],
      ['chewbacca', 'Chewbacca']
  ];

  var n = Math.floor(Math.random() * people.length);

  var img = document.getElementById('father');

  img.src = people[n][0] + '.gif';
  img.alt = people[n][1];
});
```

Discussion

We don't preload the selection of images because we'll only need one of them, once, but this solution does assume that the new image is the same size as the original. If that's not the case, we could preload the image and read its properties before doing the switch, as we saw in "Swapping One Image for Another".

We could also add weighting to the choice, so that some options are given preference over others. Weighted random selections are especially useful to those who write games and puzzles, and can be achieved in several ways.

If we simply want to make a choice, using a random number as part of an `if` condition will do the trick:

```
if (Math.floor(Math.random() * 4)) == 0)
{
  : do something here
}
```

Here we've said, "if a random number between zero and three (inclusive) is zero," we'll perform the given action—that's a one-in-four probability.

But in this instance, what we want is to weight the outcome of a random selection, so we select a constrained number, then modify it according to a degree of probability:

```
var n = Math.floor(Math.random() * 4);

if (n > 0 && Math.floor(Math.random() * 2) == 0)
{
  n = 0;
}
```

Here we've said, "if a random number, n, between zero and three (inclusive) is *not* zero, and a different random number between zero and one (inclusive) *is* zero, then set n to zero." So, when n is first generated, there's a one-in-four chance that it will be each of the possible values: 0, 1, 2, or 3. But there's a one-in-two chance that the values 1, 2, and 3 will be reset to zero, so the probability of each of these values occurring is reduced to one-in-eight. We add a probability of three-in-eight to the original one-in-four probability of the value 0 occurring, to get five-in-eight. The resulting probability distribution for this example is shown in Table 10.1.

Table 10.1. Probability distribution

Value of n	Probability
0	62.5%
1	12.5%
2	12.5%
3	12.5%

Making a Slideshow of Several Images

If you have a group of photographs to display, you might decide to offer them as an automated slideshow.

Solution

For this solution, we'll be dealing with high-resolution photographs, and since each image is likely to be quite large, we could be hanging around a long time waiting to preload them all. So instead of caching all the images in advance, we're going to stagger the loading: if we load the next image while the previous one is being displayed, we'll spare our viewers from sitting there watching the photos download line by agonizing line.

The only HTML we need is for the default photograph:

File: **slideshow.html** (excerpt)

```
<img id="photo" src="photos/cliffs.jpg"
    alt="A view of the cliffs from the beach at Colwyn Bay">
```

The slideshow scripting looks like this:

File: **slideshow.js** (excerpt)

```
// length of slideshow timer (seconds)
var timer = 5;

// array of photo names
var photos = [
  ['cliffs', 'A view of the cliffs from the beach at Colwyn Bay'],
  ['moon', 'A full moon shining over the sea'],
  ['landscape', 'A barren desert landscape with very few trees'],
  ['river', 'The river Yangtze snaking off into the distance'],
  ['cave', 'The candle-shaped view from inside Merlin\'s cave'],
  ['beach', 'A small, stony beach at Crackington Haven']
];

var img, count = 1;

function startSlideshow()
{
  img = document.getElementById('photo');
  window.setTimeout('cueNextSlide()', timer * 1000);
}

function cueNextSlide()
{
  var next = new Image();

  next.onerror = function()
  {
    alert('Failed to load next image');
  };

  next.onload = function()
  {
    img.src = next.src;
    img.alt = photos[count][1];

    img.width = next.width;
    img.height = next.height;

    if (++count == photos.length) { count = 0; }
```

```
    window.setTimeout('cueNextSlide()', timer * 1000);
  };

  next.src = 'photos/' + photos[count][0] + '.jpg';
}

addLoadListener(startSlideshow);
```

The first two values define the duration for which each slide remains on screen (in seconds), and the array of photos, respectively. Each member of the `photos` array is itself an array that contains the image name and its corresponding `alt` text. Since all the images are of the same file type (`.jpg`), we can shorten our code by adding that extension at the end of each image request, rather than storing it as part of the filename.

Discussion

The slideshow animation is controlled using a built-in JavaScript function called `setTimeout`, which is used to call a function once, after a set time period. The basic syntax looks like this:

```
window.setTimeout('functionName()', delay);
```

Here, `functionName` is the name of the function to call (you can even supply arguments, if required), and `delay` is the length of the delay in milliseconds. We'll be using this again later in the chapter, but for more details about `setTimeout` and its uses, please see Chapter 14.

Tip

Using Intuitive Values

We define the speed of our slideshow animation as a value in seconds, then convert it to milliseconds within the function, rather than defining it initially as a value in milliseconds. We do this simply because it's easier to deal with the timeframes in seconds than in milliseconds. When you're setting up global variables to configure your script like this, it's a good idea to make them as intuitive as possible.

With each iteration we load the next photo, then cue the start of the *next* iteration from that image's `load` event. Since each iteration is delayed on a timer, the image's loading time can be absorbed into the overall delay. Obviously, we can't predict exactly how long each iteration will take, but we can estimate the time interval based on the average size of the images. An estimate is fine, because no one's likely to notice the small differences in the loading times of the various slides, and you can be absolutely confident that an image will never be displayed before it's fully loaded.

A further consideration when changing each image is that the next one might not (in fact, it probably won't) be the same size as the previous one. But, since we preload each image before it's displayed, that's no problem, either: we read the `width` and `height` properties from the `Image` object, then change the dimensions of our photo accordingly when we swap it.

Making an Image Fade in or out

Fading images is a cool trick (provided it's used judiciously!), and one that's surprisingly easy to implement in most browsers. To create the effect, we'll use a combination of standard and proprietary properties.

Solution

Let's begin with the two images we'd like to fade between:

```
<img id="before" src="anakin.jpg" alt="Anakin Skywalker">
<img id="after" src="darth.jpg" alt="Darth Vader">
```

We also need some static CSS to define the initial opacity of those images (IE's opacity filter takes an integer between zero and 100, while the opacity models used by other browsers use a floating-point number between 0 and 1). Both images are absolutely positioned, so that they're superimposed, and since the `after` image has zero opacity, only `before` will be visible by default:

File: **fade-image.css**

```
#before
{
  opacity:1;
  -moz-opacity:1;
  -khtml-opacity:1;
  filter: alpha(opacity=100);
}

#after
{
  opacity:0;
  -moz-opacity:0;
  -khtml-opacity:0;
  filter: alpha(opacity=0);
```

```
}
#before, #after
{
  position: absolute;
  left: 10px;
  top: 10px;
}
```

If Opacity is not Supported …

In browsers that don't support opacity, like Opera 8.5, both images will be displayed by default. But, as they're superimposed, and the after image will appear on top, only that image will actually be visible to users of these browsers. This is the same visual state we'll reach at the *end* of our scripted transition.

With the CSS locked in, we can add some scripting to create the fade animations. First, we'll use an initialization function that detects which opacity model is in use, defines a reference to the object we want to fade, and determines the number of opacity steps that will be used in the animation, based on the requested duration of the fade, and a global fps (frames per second) variable:

File: **fade-image.js** (excerpt)

```
var fps = 10;

function fade(img, time, dir)
{
  img = document.getElementById(img);
  var steps = time * fps;

  if (typeof img.style.opacity != 'undefined')
  {
    var otype = 'w3c';
  }
  else if (typeof img.style.MozOpacity != 'undefined')
  {
    otype = 'moz';
  }
  else if (typeof img.style.KhtmlOpacity != 'undefined')
  {
    otype = 'khtml';
  }
  else if (typeof img.filters == 'object')
  {
```

```
   otype = (img.filters.length > 0
       && typeof img.filters.alpha == 'object'
       && typeof img.filters.alpha.opacity == 'number')
       ? 'ie' : 'none';
   }
   else { otype = 'none'; }

   if (otype != 'none')
   {
     if (dir == 'out') { dofade(steps, img, 1, false, otype); }
     else { dofade(steps, img, 0, true, otype); }
   }
}
```

The `fade` function then calls `dofade`. Which arguments it passes to this function depend on the value of `dir` (the fade direction argument). It's this function that actually controls the animation:

File: **fade-image.js** (excerpt)

```
function dofade(steps, img, value, targetvisibility, otype)
{
  value += (targetvisibility ? 1 : -1) / steps;
  if (targetvisibility ? value > 1 : value < 0)
      value = targetvisibility ? 1 : 0;

  setfade(img, value, otype);

  if (targetvisibility ? value < 1 : value > 0)
  {
    setTimeout(function()
    {
      dofade(steps, img, value, targetvisibility, otype);
    }, 1000 / fps);
  }
}
```

To avoid undue repetition in our code, the actual application of opacity is abstracted into another function, `setfade`:

File: **fade-image.js** (excerpt)

```
function setfade(img, value, otype)
{
  switch(otype)
  {
    case 'ie':
```

```
      img.filters.alpha.opacity = value * 100;
      break;

    case 'khtml':
      img.style.KhtmlOpacity = value;
      break;

    case 'moz':
      img.style.MozOpacity = (value == 1 ? 0.9999999 : value);
      break;

    default:
      img.style.opacity = (value == 1 ? 0.9999999 : value);
  }
}
```

Finally, we're ready to use the script! To do so, we call the `fade` function with the necessary arguments—the `id` of the image object, the fade duration (in seconds), and the fade direction (`'in'` or `'out'`):

File: **fade-image.js** (excerpt)

```
addLoadListener(function()
{
  fade('before', 5, 'out');
  fade('after', 5, 'in');
});
```

In supporting browsers, our images will cross-fade nicely from one to the other, as shown in Figure 10.2.

Figure 10.2. A cross-fade between two images

Discussion

The `fade` function starts by defining the variables we need for our animation: `img` is a reference to the image we're fading, and `steps` is the number of animation

179

frames that are needed to complete the animation in the specified `time` at the target frame rate (`fps`).

Once we've identified our animation properties, we use feature detection to find out which opacity model is being used by the browser. There are four different models: the standard `opacity` property supported in recent versions of Mozilla and Safari; the `MozOpacity` property of earlier Mozilla builds; the `KhtmlOpacity` of earlier Safari builds; and finally, the `filters.alpha.opacity` used by Internet Explorer 5.5 or later.

Looking into Opacity

The `opacity` property is defined in CSS 3,[3] but only very recent browser builds implement this standard syntax. The earlier opacity models of Mozilla and KHTML browsers were implemented before the standards were stable, and therefore used vendor-specific prefixes[4] (`-moz-` and `-khtml-`) to avoid any conflicts with the standards. Internet Explorer has had opacity much longer than any of its counterparts—since the release of IE 5.5—but its implementation uses a vendor-specific property name (`filter`), which unfortunately means that a standard property with the same name can never be safely implemented by the standards.

We need to do some additional drilling in Internet Explorer to weed out IE 5.0 for Windows and IE 5 for Mac, neither of which supports filters or opacity, though both return values for these properties, nonetheless:

File: **fade-image.js** (excerpt)

```
else if (typeof img.filters == 'object')
{
  otype = (img.filters.length > 0
      && typeof img.filters.alpha == 'object'
      && typeof img.filters.alpha.opacity == 'number')
      ? 'ie' : 'none';
}
```

Finally, once we've calculated all the values we need, we can pass them to the animation function, `dofade`. This function increments or decrements the opacity of the image, then uses `setTimeout` to call `dofade` for the next step of the animation after a delay.

---

[3] http://www.w3.org/TR/2003/CR-css3-color-20030514/#transparency
[4] http://www.w3.org/TR/CSS21/syndata.html#q4

We Have Closure

This example's `setTimeout` syntax uses a **closure** around the call to the fade function. This allows us to pass its arguments directly from the parent scope, instead of having to store them in global variables. For more about scope and inheritance, see Chapter 19.

But, when we actually apply the opacity values (in the `setfade` function), we have one more browser quirk to deal with—surprisingly, with Firefox. It has an unfortunate rendering issue with animated opacity, which can cause a visual "popping" effect when the opacity is set to 1. But if we set the value to just below 1—to `0.9999999`, for example—we can avoid the issue without making any visible difference to the effect.

Cross-fade or Straight Fade?

If you look closely at Figure 10.2, you'll see that our cross-fade effect has an unfortunate side-effect. As one image fades out and the other fades in, the white page background is visible through our semitransparent images. This washes out the colors in both images during the animation.

A more seamless and attractive fade effect can be achieved by performing a straight fade: fade in the "after" image on top of the "before" image, leaving the "before" image fully opaque for the duration of the animation. The colors will transition smoothly to the "after" image without passing through that awkward semitransparent limbo.

Of course, you can only get away with a straight fade if your images have identical dimensions; otherwise, you could end up with the "before" image's edges protruding from the sides of your "after" image as it fades in. When you're dealing with images of different sizes, a cross-fade, as we have created in this solution, is the best choice. To make the transparency during the transition less jarring, try setting your images against a black background.

Making an Image-based Clock that Updates in Real Time

An image-based clock is another one of those things that looks impressive—and comes in handy—yet is surprisingly easy to make. The numbers are simply images, so you can use any fonts or symbols you like to create the clock face, as the example in Figure 10.3 shows.

Figure 10.3. An LCD-style clock with a six-digit display

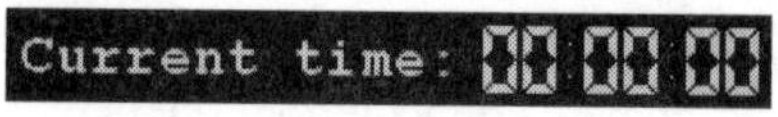

Solution

The basic approach here is to work out the current time (using some of the methods we saw in Chapter 9), then convert it into individual digits. We can then apply those digits to a series of numbered images (`0.gif`, `1.gif`, and so on), to create the visual display.

Once again, we begin with a layout of static images:

File: **image-clock.html** (excerpt)

```
<dl id="clock">
  <dt>Current time:</dt>
  <dd>
    <img id="d0" src="digits/0.gif" alt="0">
    <img id="d1" src="digits/0.gif" alt="0">
    <img src="digits/colon.gif" alt=":">
    <img id="d2" src="digits/0.gif" alt="0">
    <img id="d3" src="digits/0.gif" alt="0">
    <img src="digits/colon.gif" alt=":">
    <img id="d4" src="digits/0.gif" alt="0">
    <img id="d5" src="digits/0.gif" alt="0">
  </dd>
</dl>
```

With a little CSS, this code could produce Figure 10.3.

But, in the interests of improved accessibility, I recommend that we generate the img elements with server-side code, so that it can show the time at page load if JavaScript is not supported.

Each of the digit images is a placeholder for a number between zero and nine. We need to cache those images first, so that there's not a pause before the time is fully displayed:

File: **image-clock.js** (excerpt)

```
var digits = [];
for (var i = 0; i < 10; i++)
{
  digits[i] = new Image();
```

```
  digits[i].src = 'digits/' + i + '.gif';
}
```

Next, we must create a function that works out the time as a six-digit array, and applies those digits to the images:

File: **image-clock.js (excerpt)**

```
function displayTime()
{
  var now = new Date();
  var time = [];

  var hrs = now.getHours();
  hrs = (hrs < 10 ? '0' : '') + hrs;
  time[0] = hrs.charAt(0);
  time[1] = hrs.charAt(1);

  var mins = now.getMinutes();
  mins = (mins < 10 ? '0' : '') + mins;
  time[2] = mins.charAt(0);
  time[3] = mins.charAt(1);

  var secs = now.getSeconds();
  secs = (secs < 10 ? '0' : '') + secs;
  time[4] = secs.charAt(0);
  time[5] = secs.charAt(1);

  for (var i = 0; i < time.length; i++)
  {
    var digit = document.getElementById('d' + i);
    digit.src = digits[time[i]].src;
    digit.alt = time[i];
  }
}
```

Finally we're ready to call the `displayTime` function. We call it immediately, so that the current time is updated straight away, then call it once per second, with `setInterval`, so that it runs perpetually:

File: **image-clock.js (excerpt)**

```
addLoadListener(function()
{
  displayTime();
  setInterval('displayTime()', 1000);
});
```

Discussion

We're calculating each part of the time so that it always results in a two-digit string. Then, we copy those characters into an array using the `charAt` method, which returns the character at a particular index of a string. We always end up with a six-character array, and once we have that, we can convert each value into an image `src`. Using numbers for the image names keeps the script nice and simple: when it all boils down, our clock really is just a bunch of image swaps on a timer.

It's interesting to note how the time is worked out in each iteration: we don't just add one second to the elapsed time; instead, we recalculate the current time afresh. Why do that, you may wonder, when it's easier just to add one second?

We recalculate the time in order to avoid problems with **processor latency**. Applications take turns for a "slice" of CPU time, and the actual time that each application has to wait will vary slightly. A 1000 millisecond timeout may take 1002 milliseconds, for instance, or 1004, and that latency would gradually send the clock out of sync. Querying the system time freshly for each interval avoids this problem. It means that the clock is never *exactly* right (it will always be a few thousandths of a second slow or fast) but, overall, it stays in time with the system clock.

We can use the same principle to make a stopwatch that, similarly, is far more accurate than simply adding to a counter every second. We can make a stopwatch using the same script—almost! The difference is that, instead of displaying the *current time*, it displays the *time elapsed since the first iteration*.

To modify our existing script to do that, we first need a variable for the start time. This must be declared globally (so it's accessible to the `displayTime` function), then defined at initialization:

File: **image-stopwatch.js** (excerpt)

```
var start;
⋮
addLoadListener(function()
{
  start = new Date();

  displayTime();
  setInterval('displayTime()', 1000);
});
```

Within `displayTime`, we need to calculate the time values in a different way. Instead of representing the *current time*, the values must represent the *current time minus the start time*. We can do this by obtaining the start and current time in milliseconds (with the `getTime` method), subtracting one from the other, and then repeatedly dividing that difference to get the various components of the elapsed time:

File: **image-stopwatch.js** (excerpt)

```
var diff = (new Date().getTime() - start.getTime()) % 360000000;
var time = [];

var hrs = Math.floor(diff / 3600000);
hrs = (hrs < 10 ? '0' : '') + hrs;
time[0] = hrs.charAt(0);
time[1] = hrs.charAt(1);
diff -= hrs * 3600000;

var mins = Math.floor(diff / 60000);
mins = (mins < 10 ? '0' : '') + mins;
time[2] = mins.charAt(0);
time[3] = mins.charAt(1);
diff -= mins * 60000;

var secs = Math.floor(diff / 1000);
secs = (secs < 10 ? '0' : '') + secs;
time[4] = secs.charAt(0);
time[5] = secs.charAt(1);
diff -= secs * 1000;
```

You could also include milliseconds by adding the necessary `img` elements:

File: **image-stopwatch.html** (excerpt)

```
<img src="digits/colon.gif" alt=":">
<img id="d6" src="digits/0.gif" alt="0">
<img id="d7" src="digits/0.gif" alt="0">
```

Now, we calculate the extra values in `displayTime`, just after the seconds are calculated:

File: **image-stopwatch.js** (excerpt)

```
var millis = diff;
millis = (millis < 10 ? '0' : '') + millis;
time[6] = millis.charAt(0);
time[7] = millis.charAt(1);
```

You would also need to increase the speed of the `setInterval`, but there's no need to do it every millisecond—quite apart from that activity being incredibly processor-intensive, you'd never be able to see the difference anyway. Once every 50 milliseconds is quite sufficient:

File: **image-stopwatch.js** (excerpt)

```
setInterval('displayTime()', 50);
```

Making a Progress Indicator

When you're preloading lots of images, a progress indicator can be a useful way to show users that something is actually happening. On an application level, it's an essential usability tool (can you imagine a browser with no status bar?). Thus, although this solution is based around image preloading, it can be used more generally for displaying progress within any web application or situation in which progress can be distilled into a number of states over time.

The end result of this solution is depicted in Figure 10.4.

Figure 10.4. A status bar showing 50% progress

Solution

We're going to indicate progress by updating the `width` of a styled `span`, and changing its inner text to give both visual and textual information. The default HTML looks like this:

File: **progress-indicator.html** (excerpt)

```
<p id="indicator">
  <span id="progress">0%</span>
</p>
```

It's styled with this basic CSS:

File: **progress-indicator.css** (excerpt)

```
#indicator
{
  width: 200px;
  border: 1px solid #000;
```

```
  background: #fff;
  color: #000;
}

#progress
{
  display: block;
  width: 0;
  background: #ccc;
}
```

We'll write our script with these styles in mind by changing the `width` of the span, where `0` reflects no progress and `200px` shows that the process is complete. Since the text is also updated to display the progress as a percentage figure, we can use that data to extract the current progress from the indicator.

For a flexible solution let's define two functions to increment the indicator by, or set it to, a particular amount:

File: **progress-indicator.js** (excerpt)

```
function progressBy(n)
{
  var prog = document.getElementById('progress');

  var current = parseInt(prog.firstChild.nodeValue, 10);
  current += n;
  if (current > 100) { current = 100; }

  prog.style.width = (current * 2) + 'px';
  prog.firstChild.nodeValue = current + '%';
}

function progressTo(n)
{
  var prog = document.getElementById('progress');

  prog.style.width = (n * 2) + 'px';
  prog.firstChild.nodeValue = n + '%';
}
```

We can use these functions programmatically to control the progress indicator. For example, we could set it to 50%:

```
progressTo(50);
```

Or increase it by 10%:

```
progressBy(10);
```

Using this control, we can make an image loader that includes progress information. We simply add to each image an `onload` handler that increases the value of the indicator:

File: **progress-indicator.js** (excerpt)

```
addLoadListener(function()
{
  var photoNames = ['mountains', 'cliffs', 'moon'];
  var photoObjects = [];

  for (var i = 0; i < photoNames.length; i++)
  {
    photoObjects[i] = new Image();
    photoObjects[i].src = 'photos/' + photoNames[i] + '.jpg';

    photoObjects[i].onload = function()
    {
      progressBy(Math.ceil(100 / photoNames.length));
    };
  }
});
```

Discussion

The `progressBy` function should be able to accept values that add up to imprecise amounts (e.g., not exactly 100%), but it can't know whether a value that's *less* than that equates to completion. However, we can assert the opposite—that a value *greater* than 100 equates to completion—since our values are a percentage of completion, and by definition that can't be greater than 100.

So what we'll do is cap any figure that's greater than 100; we can see from our image loader exactly why this is necessary.

We're calculating the progress at each `load` event as a percentage of the total number of images, but since we have an *odd* number of images, we're using `Math.ceil` to round that value up to an integer. Rounding it down would produce a total that was less than 100, but of course rounding it up produces a total that's *greater* than 100 (in this case, 102%). We're relying on the figure being capped in `progressBy`—this ensures that the total it displays on completion is correct.

Loading a Single Image

If we were loading a single, very large image, this approach wouldn't work: we don't have a number of states over time that we can pass to the progress indicator, because the browser doesn't give us that information. The best approach to loading a single large image would probably be to use an animated GIF—maybe something like an hourglass animation—which was then removed or replaced when the main image had loaded.

Summary

Using the techniques provided in this chapter, you should now be able to implement any kind of image manipulation you require. Having worked through these solutions, you should also have a sound general approach for calculating and displaying image loading progress.

Detecting Browser Differences

As we saw way back in Chapter 1, the divergent threads from which the current incarnation of JavaScript is derived at least partially explain why different browsers implement JavaScript in different ways. Factors such as backwards compatibility, misinterpretation of the specification, and the natural evolution that occurs in competitive markets cause every browser's implementation of JavaScript to have its own peculiarities.

Yet these differences are nowhere near as damaging as out-of-the-loop observers would have us believe. The core features of the language are remarkably stable among modern browsers (i.e., above version 4 of Netscape and Internet Explorer). However, there are certain areas in which some browsers' continued support for outdated functions makes developing two versions of code unavoidable. Event handling, which we'll examine in Chapter 13, is one such example.

This chapter explains how to cut through the tangle of browsers and ensure that your code runs successfully wherever you intend it to.

Identifying Support for a Particular Feature

To prevent your scripts from falling over in older browsers, it's often necessary to make sure that those browsers don't try to execute your code. However, to try to use browser detection techniques is to fight a losing battle. The list of browsers and browser versions is always growing, so it's almost impossible to keep detection scripts up to date, and user agent strings can be counterfeited, making browser detection much harder than it ought to be.

In most cases, by detecting a certain browser, you're trying to make sure that the client will run your code properly. Instead of dealing with browsers on the basis of what they *appear to be*, it's better to focus on *what they can do*. Detecting whether the user's browser has a particular feature is a simple and foolproof way to ascertain exactly what you want to know, and is far preferable to obtaining the browser's name alone.

Solution

The differences between browsers' varying implementations of JavaScript mean that some features may be implemented using different processes, or not at all. By detecting whether a function or property exists before you use it, you can ensure that all compatible browsers will execute your code, while incompatible browsers will remain unaffected.

The easiest way to detect whether a function or property exists in your current browser is to use the `typeof` operator. By passing any JavaScript value, object, class, method, or property to this operator, you are able to determine its type. If we pass to `typeof` an operand that doesn't exist in the browser, the type `"undefined"` will result.

For instance, we can test whether the current browser supports the `XMLHttpRequest` class like so:

File: **feature-detection.js** (excerpt)

```
var xmlHttpExists = typeof XMLHttpRequest;
```

In Mozilla, Opera 8, or Safari 1.2, the value of the variable `xmlhttpexists` will be `"object"` or `"function"`. However, in Internet Explorer 6 and other older browsers, the value of `xmlhttpexists` will be `"undefined"`.[1]

This method of detection also works for functions, methods, and properties, as well as classes. When you test functions and methods, omit the braces that follow their names; otherwise, the script will try to identify the value that's *returned* by the function or method, which will cause an error if the function or method doesn't exist:

File: **feature-detection.js** (excerpt)

```
var byIdExists = typeof document.getElementById;
```

These tests allow us to provide alternative branches of code for browsers that don't support particular features:

File: **feature-detection.js** (excerpt)

```
if (typeof document.designMode != undefined)
{
  document.designMode = "on";
}
else
{
  return false;
}
```

Don't Test without `typeof`

It's possible to detect the existence of a feature without using `typeof`, as the following code shows:

```
if (feature)
{
    ⋮
}
```

However, this isn't an entirely safe test. We're trying to check whether *feature exists*, not what its value is. If the value of *feature* happens to be `false`, the condition in the code above will evaluate to `false`, even though *feature* actually exists. Furthermore, if the value of *feature* is the number 0, the condition will also evaluate to `false`, because JavaScript treats 0 as `false` when evaluating a condition.

---

[1]For a cross-browser implementation of **XMLHttpRequest** see Chapter 18.

For these reasons, it's safer to use `typeof` whenever you are testing for the existence of a feature.

Identifying a Particular Browser

While the detection of a particular feature is the most robust way to deal with browser differences, sometimes a browser will implement a feature improperly, or with irreparable bugs. In these instances, feature detection won't suffice, so we have to rely upon specific browser detection to weed them out.

Solution

Because of certain browsers' abilities to mimic the user agent strings of other browsers, it's best to use feature differentiation to identify a particular browser where possible. However, in some cases the only recourse is to rely on the `navigator` object, which provides information on a number of aspects of the browser, including the user agent string (`navigator.userAgent`) and the browser vendor (`navigator.vendor`).

The function below uses known profiles of feature support and user agent information to identify browsers correctly, even if they're **spoofing** (using another browser's user agent string):

File: **indentify-browser.js**

```javascript
function identifyBrowser()
{
  var agent = navigator.userAgent.toLowerCase();

  if (typeof navigator.vendor != "undefined" &&
      navigator.vendor == "KDE" &&
      typeof window.sidebar != "undefined")
  {
    return "kde";
  }
  else if (typeof window.opera != "undefined")
  {
    var version = parseFloat(
        agent.replace(/.*opera[\/ ]([^ $]+).*/, "$1"));

    if (version >= 7)
    {
      return "opera7";
    }
```

```
    else if (version >= 5)
    {
      return "opera5";
    }

    return false;
  }
  else if (typeof document.all != "undefined")
  {
    if (typeof document.getElementById != "undefined")
    {
      var browser = agent.replace(/.*ms(ie[\/ ][^ $]+).*/, "$1").
        replace(/ /, "");

      if (typeof document.uniqueID != "undefined")
      {
        if (browser.indexOf("5.5") != -1)
        {
          return browser.replace(/(.*5\.5).*/, "$1");
        }
        else
        {
          return browser.replace(/(.*)\..*/, "$1");
        }
      }
      else
      {
        return "ie5mac";
      }
    }

    return false;
  }
  else if (typeof document.getElementById != "undefined")
  {
    if (navigator.vendor.indexOf("Apple Computer, Inc.") != -1)
    {
      if (typeof window.XMLHttpRequest != "undefined")
      {
        return "safari1.2";
      }

      return "safari1";
    }
    else if (agent.indexOf("gecko") != -1)
    {
```

```
      return "mozilla";
    }
  }
  return false;
}
```

Firstly, Konqueror is detected using the unique `navigator.vendor` property of `"KDE"`. Versions of Konqueror prior to 3.2 offered some incomplete functionality, so we need only worry about returning a value for this version and those that came after it. To do so, we detect the `window.sidebar` object, which is only available in version 3.2 onwards.

We check for Opera next. Although it has the propensity to identify itself as other browsers, Opera is the only browser that has the `window.opera` object, so this is an easy way to identify it. After using this condition, we can safely parse the user agent string, as Opera's version information is included there even if the browser is masquerading as Mozilla or Internet Explorer. The two major milestone releases for which we need to check are Opera 5 and Opera 7, so any version number that's greater than or equal to 7 will return `"opera7"`, and anything between that and Opera 5 will return `"opera5"`.

Once we have detected Opera clients, it's safe to run a test for `document.all`. This is an Internet Explorer property, but it was reproduced by Opera for the sake of compatibility. No other browser makes `document.all` available, so it's a good way to separate Internet Explorer from its competitors. Again, once inside the condition, it's safe to parse the user agent string for `"msie"`. At this stage, we can differentiate between Internet Explorer for Windows and Internet Explorer for Mac OS. The latter doesn't have the `document.uniqueID` property that other versions of Internet Explorer include, so if that property doesn't exist, we know that the client is IE 5 for Mac. The version number is cut down to the integer, except for 5.5, as this has quite a few differences from version 5.

After the Internet Explorer code block, we filter out all ancient browsers by requiring `document.getElementById`. Any browser that doesn't support this method probably won't support much in the way of modern JavaScript, so it's safe to exclude such browsers. If that method *is* supported, we need to distinguish between the remaining significant candidates: Mozilla and Safari.

Although Safari is fairly similar to Mozilla (even going so far as to include the word "gecko" in its user agent string), it always has the `navigator.vendor` value of `"Apple Computer, Inc."`. Version 1.2 of Safari boasted notable improvements over its predecessors, including bug fixes to its rendering capabilities, and support for `XMLHttpRequest`, so it's worthwhile testing for this version in case we need it.

With Safari out of the way, it's safe to look for `"gecko"` in the user agent, and pronounce the browser to be Mozilla if `"gecko"` is present. There are so many different variations of the Mozilla/Gecko engine that it's not really feasible to check for different versions of this, but if you require it, you can always interrogate `navigator.userAgent` within your own code.

Any browser that's not mentioned above can be assumed to have inadequate JavaScript or DOM support, and `false` will be returned.

By calling `identifyBrowser`, you'll receive a string that tells you the browser type and version (if applicable), as listed in Table 11.1.

Table 11.1. Browser identification strings

Browser	`identifyBrowser` string
Unsupported browsers	`false`
Konqueror 3.2 and above	`"kde"`
Opera 5 and Opera 6	`"opera5"`
Opera 7 and above	`"opera7"`
Internet Explorer 5	`"ie5"`
Internet Explorer 5 for Mac	`"ie5mac"`
Internet Explorer 5.5	`"ie5.5"`
Internet Explorer 6 and above	`"ie6"`, `"ie7"`, etc.
Mozilla/Firefox	`"mozilla"`
Safari 1.0 and 1.1	`"safari1"`
Safari 1.2+	`"safari1.2"`

Discussion

In addition to identifying the browser, sometimes it's helpful to know which operating system the browser is running on. This information is included in the user agent string, so it's fairly easy to check that string for any matching operating systems:

File: **indentify-os.js**

```
function identifyOS()
{
  var agent = navigator.userAgent.toLowerCase();

  if (agent.indexOf("win") != -1)
  {
    return "win";
  }
  else if (agent.indexOf("mac") != -1)
  {
    return "mac";
  }
  else
  {
    return "unix";
  }

  return false;
}
```

Detecting Quirks Mode and Standards Mode

If you're familiar with CSS, you'll probably be familiar with Quirks mode and Standards mode. Modern browsers use these two modes to handle the same page differently, employing either the rules that were used by older versions of the browser, or more up-to-date, standards-compliant rules. The mode can affect the way that a page is displayed, so it can be useful to know which mode the browser is using before you change the dimensions or visual properties of elements on the page.

Solution

You can determine whether browsers are handling a document using Standards or Quirks mode by reading the document.compatMode property. If they're running in Quirks mode, most browsers will assign a value of "BackCompat" to this property (although Opera uses the value "QuirksMode"); browsers in Standards mode will return "CSS1Compat" (at present). Based on this, it's safest to test for "CSS1Compat" and, if this is not returned, to assume that the browser is running in Quirks mode:

File: **quirksmode.js** (excerpt)

```
function detectQuirksMode()
{
  if (typeof document.compatMode != "undefined" &&
      /CSS.Compat/.test(document.compatMode))
  {
    return false;
  }

  return true;
}
```

In a document that is rendered in Quirks mode, `detectQuirksMode` will return `true`; otherwise, it will return `false`.

Discussion

The toggle between Quirks and Standards modes is based upon the DOCTYPE declaration at the top of a page. HTML documents without a DOCTYPE will be handled in Quirks mode automatically, but the presence of a DOCTYPE does not exclude the possibility that a document will be rendered in Quirks mode.

For information on the effects of DOCTYPEs, see Holly Bergevin's article on the subject.[2]

Most of the differences between Quirks mode and Standards mode are related to CSS. So if your JavaScript deals with the styling of elements, it will have to deal appropriately with CSS rules. Quirks mode is generally more lenient—it doesn't enforce rules such as the requirement for units on nonzero values—but perhaps the most important discrepancy is the difference in box model calculations, specifically in the way element dimensions are calculated. A more thorough breakdown of the differences between Quirks mode and Standards mode is available in Eric Meyer's article on the topic.[3]

Omitting a DOCTYPE from a page will have little effect on the execution of your JavaScript, though. The only browser that's affected is Internet Explorer 6, which rearranges some of the properties that are used to ascertain window and page dimensions (as noted in Chapter 7).

---

[2] http://www.communitymx.com/content/article.cfm?cid=85FEE
[3] http://www.ericmeyeroncss.com/bonus/render-mode.html

Summary

Although there are differences between the browsers that access your client-side code, this chapter has shown you how to structure your code to handle those differences gracefully.

Whether you need to subtly test for new functionality, or you require the brute force method of individual browser selection, these scripts will let you execute your JavaScript correctly now—and well into the future.

 **Using JavaScript with CSS**

Traditionally, JavaScript and CSS form two separate aspects of web page architecture: behavior and style. However, the inclusion of CSS in the DOM, and JavaScript's ability to manipulate DOM elements, means that the line that divides the two can easily become blurred. The benefits, though, justify such blurring: using CSS and JavaScript, we are able to modify a page's style dynamically and in immediate response to user interaction.

This chapter explains several techniques that we can use to affect the CSS that's applied to documents, to gain selective control over individual elements, or facilitate broad-brush changes across the entire page.

Changing the Style of a Single Element

Although the DOM's style syntax might seem verbose when compared with CSS, JavaScript makes it easy to implement incremental style changes to, for instance, the size, positioning, or color of an element.

Solution

The DOM provides a `style` object as a property of every element. The `style` object represents the `style` attribute in an element's HTML tag, and contains the various CSS properties, providing us very granular control over an element's style. The syntax of the `style` object closely mirrors the syntax used in CSS. Properties that contain hyphens are replaced with **camel casing**, so `font-size` becomes `fontSize` and `margin-top` becomes `marginTop`.

Accessing `float`

Because the word "float" is already reserved in JavaScript, it's not possible to access an object's `floatCSS` property using `style.float`. In fact, browsers use different terms for the `float` property: Internet Explorer uses `style.styleFloat`, while all other browsers use the W3C-specified `style.cssFloat`.

A complete list of the standard DOM CSS 2 properties interface can be found in the W3C's DOM CSS Recommendation.[1]

To set a style via the `style` object, we must assign a valid CSS string value to the property we wish to affect. As an example, consider the CSS-styled heading shown in Figure 12.1.

Figure 12.1. A heading styled with CSS

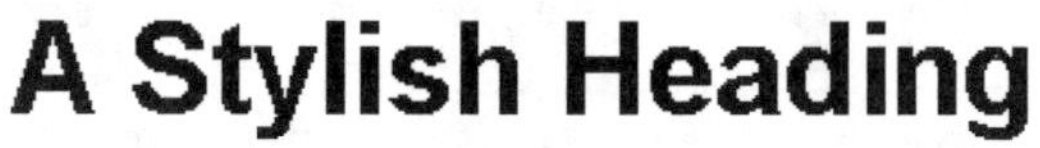

A Stylish Heading

We can change that heading text to white, and the background color to black, using JavaScript:

File: **style_single_element.js** (excerpt)

```
var heading = document.getElementById("heading");

heading.style.color = "#FFFFFF";
heading.style.backgroundColor = "#000000";
```

The heading now looks like Figure 12.2.

---

[1] http://www.w3.org/TR/2000/REC-DOM-Level-2-Style-20001113/css.html#CSS-CSS2Properties

Figure 12.2. The heading after its styles have been modified using JavaScript

Discussion

The `style` object is a direct representation of an element's `style` attribute. Suppose we specified the following inline styles in our HTML:

```
<h1 id="heading"
    style="color: #FFFFFF; background-color: #000000;">
 A Stylish Heading
</h1>
```

We can immediately access those values using the `style` object:

```
var heading = document.getElementById("heading");

var headingColor = heading.style.color;
var headingBGColor = heading.style.backgroundColor;
```

The value of the variable `headingColor` is now `"#FFFFFF"`; the value of the variable `headingBGColor` is now `"#000000"`.

But, if a property has been set in some other manner—such as via a linked style sheet, or a `<style>` tag in the `head` of the document—those values will not be reflected in the corresponding property within the `style` object.

If you wish to obtain the current styles of an element, irrespective of their source, skip one section to "Retrieving the Computed Style of an Element".

Changing the Style of a Group of Elements

CSS is designed to allow groups of elements to be styled easily with a single selector. In Chapter 5, we saw how to add classes to, and remove them from elements; this knowledge will allow you to apply pre-written CSS to elements via JavaScript. However, if you want to create your styles on the fly, things become complicated: the current state of style sheet handling in browsers causes a few problems, as we'll see later in this chapter.

This solution is a more straightforward—but calculation-intensive—solution that we can achieve using some of the basic principles we've already explored.

Solution

We know that we can change the style of an individual element using its `style` object. Extending this, we can modify the style of a group of elements by changing the style of each element individually.

To change the style of every paragraph on a page so that the text is red, we need first to get a collection that contains every paragraph. Then, we can iterate through each of the paragraphs, changing their styles. We can do this easily using the `getElementsByTagName` method:

File: **style_group_elements.js** (excerpt)

```
var paragraphs = document.getElementsByTagName("p");

for (var i = 0; i < paragraphs.length; i++)
{
  paragraphs[i].style.color = "#FF0000";
}
```

As you can see above, to modify a group of elements, all we require is to have those elements in a collection that we can iterate through. Using `getElementsByTagName`, and the custom function `getElementsByAttribute`, which we saw in Chapter 5, it's easy to obtain the group of elements we want to change, and to modify their styles using a `for` loop.

Retrieving the Computed Style of an Element

We can specify the style of an element within an HTML document in three ways: using inline styles, `style` declarations in the `head` of the page, and external CSS files. Although an element's visual appearance is calculated initially by combining all of these sources and determining which style rules will apply, only the inline styles are accessible via an element's `style` object. If you specify CSS styles in any other location, the corresponding `style` object property will be blank.

The **computed style** of an element takes into account all of the sources from which an element can receive its styling, and calculates the values for that element's CSS properties. These computed styles *are* accessible via JavaScript, but not through the `style` object—it takes a bit more code to get to them.

Solution

Current versions of Internet Explorer do not implement the DOM standard method for retrieving the computed styles of an element, so we need to use a code branch to get this information in a cross-browser fashion.

Under the W3C DOM, an element's computed styles can be retrieved from a document's rendering space—`document.defaultView`—using the `getComputedStyle` method. When this method is supplied with an element reference, it returns a `CSSStyleDeclaration` object that behaves similarly to an element's child `style` object. It's a little complex, perhaps, but it boils down to this:

```
var heading = document.getElementById("heading");
var computedStyle = document.defaultView.getComputedStyle(heading,
    null);
var computedFontFamily = computedStyle.fontFamily;
```

The value of the variable `computedFontFamily` is now `"sans-serif"`.

Internet Explorer likes to make things a bit easier. Using the proprietary element property `currentStyle`, we can retrieve the computed style with the syntax we applied to the `style` object:

```
var heading = document.getElementById("heading");
var computedFontFamily = heading.currentStyle.fontFamily;
```

The value of the variable `computedFontFamily` is now `"sans-serif"`.

If we combine these approaches, we can create a cross-browser function for retrieving the computed style:

File: **retrieve_computed_style.js** (excerpt)

```
function retrieveComputedStyle(element, styleProperty)
{
  var computedStyle = null;
```

```
if (typeof element.currentStyle != "undefined")
{
  computedStyle = element.currentStyle;
}
else
{
  computedStyle = document.defaultView.getComputedStyle(element,
      null);
}

return computedStyle[styleProperty];
}
```

Beware of Inconsistent Values

Even though `retrieveComputedStyle` creates a cross-browser method for obtaining the value of a computed style, the *value* that you receive mightn't be consistent across browsers.

Internet Explorer's `currentStyle` object will return the specified style value for the element exactly as it was written in the source. Suppose you have a style selector like this:

```
#heading
{
  width: 10em;
}
```

In this case, the property `heading.currentStyle.width` will return `"10em"`.

The W3C-specified method `getComputedStyle` normalizes all values to predefined units. This means that dimension units such as ems, millimeters, points, and percentages will automatically be converted into pixels, hex color values will be converted into `rgb(x,x,x)`, and so on.

The computed style value returned by `getComputedStyle` for the `width` of the object specified above will always be returned in pixels, but it will vary depending upon the value of an em as calculated for that particular element.

It's arguable which method is best, but you should be aware of this difference if you choose to work with computed styles.

Making a Style Sheet Switcher

Alternative style sheets are one of the most impressive examples of the power of CSS; they give a page the ability to change costumes in the blink of an eye. Although style sheet switching can be implemented on the server side, JavaScript offers a far more fluid and seamless solution.

Solution

We can link to countless alternative style sheets from the `head` of a document. The style sheets are not applied to the page unless they are specifically selected either by the user, or JavaScript.

note

The Importance of `link`

Although there are numerous ways to specify styles, style switching only works with style sheets that are referenced via `link` elements.

Imagine that we've specified some alternate style sheets like this:

File: **style_sheet_switcher.html (excerpt)**

```
<head>
    ⋮
  <link id="styleSerif" rel="alternate stylesheet" type="text/css"
      href="css/text_serif.css" title="Serif Text">
    <link id="styleInverted" rel="alternate stylesheet"
        type="text/css" href="css/inverted.css"
        title="Inverted Color Scheme">
    ⋮
</head>
```

We can make a style switcher by looking through all the `link` elements on the page, finding the ones that are style sheets with titles, and turning on the one we need:

File: **style_sheet_switcher.js (excerpt)**

```
function switchStyleSheet(title)
{
  var links = document.getElementsByTagName("link");

  for (var i = 0; i < links.length; i++)
  {
    var rel = links[i].getAttribute("rel");
```

```
    var linkTitle = links[i].getAttribute("title");

if (/(^| )stylesheet( |$)/.test(rel) && linkTitle != null &&
    linkTitle != "")
{
  links[i].disabled = true;

  if (linkTitle == title)
  {
    links[i].disabled = false;
  }
}
}
}
```

`switchStyleSheet` starts by getting a collection of all the `link` elements on the page. `link` elements are general pointers to resources—not necessarily to style sheets—so, as we cycle through the collection, we check for `rel` attributes that contain the keyword `stylesheet`, along with a `title` attribute. Any linked style sheet without a `title` attribute is actually a persistent style sheet; we don't want to disable these. We want to disable only those style sheets that have `titles`.

The normal style-switching behavior ensures that only one titled style sheet is active at any time. So, as we cycle through each of the titled style sheets, we turn them off by setting their `disabled` property to `true`. The `disabled` property is a Boolean that indicates whether the style sheet in question is being applied to the page. A value of `true` means that the style sheet *isn't* being applied, while `false` means it *is* applied. Right after we set `disabled` to `true`, we check whether the `title` of that style sheet matches the one we want. The `title` of the style sheet we want to make active is passed to `switchStyleSheet` as its only argument. We compare this argument to the `title` of the style sheet in question, and, if the two match, set `disabled` to `false`.

Setting disabled to true

Some browsers will not activate an alternate style sheet unless you first set the `disabled` property to `true`. Once this has been done, the style sheet can be switched on and off.

This is automatically handled in `switchStyleSheet`, because we initially set `disabled` to `true` for every style sheet anyway.

After we've cycled through all the `link` elements, we end up with our selected style sheet activated, and all the other alternate style sheets disabled.

Imagine that our page looks like Figure 12.3 when all alternate styles are turned off.

Figure 12.3. The default page with no alternative styles applied

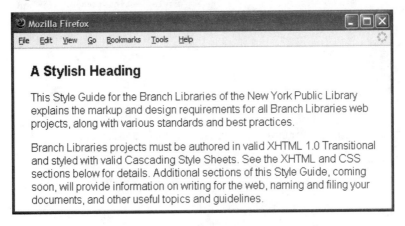

Now, let's switch on the serif text style sheet:

```
switchStyleSheet("Serif Text");
```

Now, the page appears as in Figure 12.4.

Figure 12.4. The page with a serif style sheet applied

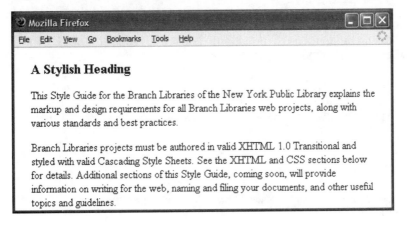

To ensure clean, accessible markup, we can allow users to activate switchStyleSheet via an element such as a hyperlink or a select box that's created dynamically using JavaScript:

File: **style_sheet_switcher.js (excerpt)**

```
addLoadListener(initStyleSwitcher);

function initStyleSwitcher()
{
  if (identifyBrowser() != "ie5mac")
  {
    var links = document.getElementsByTagName("link");
    var newSelect = document.createElement("select");
    var defaultOption = document.createElement("option");

    defaultOption.setAttribute("value", "");
    defaultOption.appendChild(document.createTextNode(
        "Select an alternate style sheet"));
    newSelect.appendChild(defaultOption);

    for (var i = 0; i < links.length; i++)
    {
      var rel = links[i].getAttribute("rel");
      var linkTitle = links[i].getAttribute("title");

      if (/(^| )stylesheet( |$)/.test(rel) && linkTitle != null
          && linkTitle != "")
      {
        var newOption = document.createElement("option");
        newOption.setAttribute("value", linkTitle);
        newOption.appendChild(document.createTextNode(linkTitle));
        newSelect.appendChild(newOption);
      }
    }

    newSelect.onchange = function()
    {
      switchStyleSheet(this.value);
      return true;
    };

    document.getElementsByTagName("body")[0].appendChild(
        newSelect);

    return true;
  }
}
```

```
  return false;
}
```

`initStyleSwitcher` cycles through the `link` elements on the page looking for titled style sheets. When it finds one, it adds that style sheet as one of the options in a `select` element. After all the `link` elements have been parsed, that `select` element is added to the end of the page. Using a simple event handler, any changes to the `select` list are captured, and `switchStyleSheet` is called with the corresponding value, causing the page's style sheets to switch.

We use the `identifyBrowser` function from Chapter 11 to exclude Internet Explorer 5 for Mac because it doesn't handle the dynamic creation of `select` lists very well. As such, it's better to simply disable the switcher on this browser.

Discussion

There are actually three types of style sheet:

persistent
   Persistent styles are applied at all times. A persistent style sheet is set when a `link`'s `rel` attribute is set to `stylesheet` and it has no `title` attribute.

preferred
   Preferred styles are turned on by default, but are turned off when an alternate style sheet is activated. A preferred style sheet is set when a `link`'s `rel` attribute is set to `stylesheet` and it has a `title` attribute.

alternate
   Alternate styles are turned off by default and must be selected in order to be activated. An alternate style sheet is set when a `link`'s `rel` attribute is set to `alternate stylesheet` (or `stylesheet alternate`) and it has a `title` attribute.

Although JavaScript is capable of enabling and disabling any of these types of styles, to keep our style sheet switcher compatible with the behavior offered by the style sheet switchers that are built into some browsers, we modify only the status of preferred and alternate style sheets.

This approach has implications for the way we structure our CSS, because preferred and alternate style sheets will always be applied in combination with any persistent style sheets. This might mean that you need to include in an alternate style sheet some rules that reverse the effects contained in a persistent style sheet, or that you choose not to have any persistent style sheets at all.

It's also possible to apply multiple alternate style sheets simultaneously, though this is not normally desirable.

If we were to set the `disabled` property of both the `Serif Text` style sheet and the `Inverted Color Scheme` style sheet to `false`, our page display would combine the two, as shown in Figure 12.5.

Figure 12.5. The page with both serif text and inverted color style sheets applied

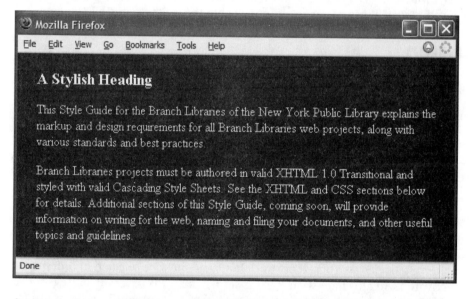

Maintaining Alternate Style Sheet States

Allowing your users to change the style of a page with the flick of a switch is a great idea, but it's fairly useless if every time they go to some other page the styles have reverted to the defaults again.

As we saw in Chapter 8, the easiest way to maintain persistence on the client side is to write cookies that monitor users' preferences no matter where they are in the site. Once this cookie is written, we can check what style the user has selected and apply it automatically to the current page.

Whenever a user switches styles, we have to write a new value for the cookie:

File: **`style_sheet_switcher.js`** (excerpt)

```
function switchStyleSheet(title, media)
{
  ⋮
  document.cookie = "stylesheet=" + title;
}
```

Simple! Now, when a page loads, we have to set the correct style sheet. The best way to do this is on the server side—by writing the correct preferred style sheet—but as an alternative we can include a call to `switchStyleSheet` in a script that occurs *after* the `<link>` tags in the HTML source. Because the script occurs after the `<link>` tags, it will execute only once the `<link>` tags have loaded, so we can be sure that we won't get errors saying that those style sheets don't exist. This method is preferable to using a `load` event listener because the document/window load event only fires after all the page content—including images—has loaded. This often means that most of the page will already be displayed before the load event fires, which would create a flicker in the display as our script updated the page style.

Though this source order execution of the script helps to minimize flickering between styles, it's by no means perfect: it means that our script is no longer independent of the HTML source. However, it's the best solution we have at the moment:

File: **`style_sheet_switcher.js`** (excerpt)

```
stylesheetCookie = getCookie("stylesheet");

if (stylesheetCookie != "")
{
  switchStyleSheet(stylesheetCookie);
}
```

Currently, most browsers that natively handle style switching do not also maintain the style state between different pages. This shortcoming can be rectified by the application of a little background script that regularly checks the alternate style sheets and writes any changes to the style sheet cookie. Then, when a user visits another page, that person's browser-native choice will be maintained.

Time-based functionality is explained in the next chapter, but if you put the script below into action, it will cycle through every two seconds, checking to see which is the currently selected style sheet:

File: **style_sheet_switcher.js** (excerpt)

```
addLoadListener(checkStyleSheet);

function checkStyleSheet()
{
  if (typeof document.styleSheetLinks == "undefined")
  {
    document.styleSheetLinks = [];

    var links = document.getElementsByTagName("link");

    for (var i = 0; i < links.length; i++)
    {
      var rel = links[i].getAttribute("rel");
      var linkTitle = links[i].getAttribute("title");

      if (/(^| )stylesheet( |$)/.test(rel) && linkTitle != null
          && linkTitle != "")
      {
        document.styleSheetLinks[document.styleSheetLinks.length]
            = links[i];
      }
    }
  }

  for (var i = 0; i < document.styleSheetLinks.length; i++)
  {
    if (document.styleSheetLinks[i].disabled == false)
    {
      document.cookie = "stylesheet=" +
          document.styleSheetLinks[i].getAttribute("title");
      break;
    }
  }

  setTimeout("checkStyleSheet()", 2000);
}
```

Because this is a repetitive function, checkStyleSheet creates as a child of the document a special object that is an array of the alternate style sheets on the page. By using this object we avoid having to search for all the style sheets every time checkStyleSheet is called. Instead, on successive executions, checkStyleSheet simply runs through the array of style sheets and checks whether disabled is set to false in any of them. If a user selects a style sheet through the browser, that selection will change the disabled property for that style sheet, and we will detect it. We can then write the style sheet value to a cookie, and store the user's choice for retrieval when they visit another page.

The execution time of two seconds is a reasonable period that balances the performance cost of the calculation against its ability to capture users' actions. Of course, you can change this time to suit your own applications.

Making a Style Sheet Switcher that Handles Multiple Media Types

One of the advantages of style sheets is that they can style a document specifically to suit the display medium that is being used to view them. Both style sheets and alternate style sheets have a `media` attribute that allows us to specify the media to which that style sheet applies, with options including `screen`, `projection`, `print`, `speech`, and `braille`. Using this attribute, we can also provide different style switchers for different media.

Solution

Due to a browser bug in Internet Explorer for Windows, the style switcher we used in the previous solution has to be modified slightly to handle different media types. Internet Explorer does not apply alternate style sheets that have a `media` attribute; however, it does apply them correctly if they are *preferred* style sheets. So, to activate them, we need to change the `rel` attribute as well as the `disabled` property:

File: **style_sheet_switcher_media_types.js** (excerpt)

```
function switchStyleSheet(title, media)
{
  if (typeof media == "undefined" || media == "")
  {
    media = ".*";
  }

  var mediaPattern = new RegExp("(^|,)\s*" + media + "\s*(,|$)");

  var links = document.getElementsByTagName("link");

  for (var i = 0; i < links.length; i++)
  {
    var rel = links[i].getAttribute("rel");
```

```
    var linkTitle = links[i].getAttribute("title");

    if (/(^| )stylesheet( |$)/.test(rel) && linkTitle != null &&
        linkTitle != "")
    {
      var styleMedia = links[i].getAttribute("media");
      if (styleMedia == null || styleMedia == ""
          || styleMedia == "all"
          || mediaPattern.test(styleMedia))
      {
        links[i].disabled = true;
        links[i].rel = "alternate stylesheet";

        if (linkTitle == title)
        {
          links[i].disabled = false;
          links[i].rel = "stylesheet";
        }
      }
    }
  }

  document.cookie = "stylesheet=" + title;
}
```

This extended function first checks to see whether a `media` argument has been passed to it. If not, it matches on all styles with the specified `title` attribute, irrespective of media type. The extra `if` statement makes sure that the media type matches, or is a global type (i.e., it's unspecified or specified as `all`). Our switching code then updates the `disabled` and `rel` properties of each `link` element.

Consider this page:

File: **style_sheet_switcher_media_types.html** (excerpt)
```
<head>
  ⋮
  <link id="styleBig" rel="alternate stylesheet" type="text/css"
    href="css/text_big.css" title="Big Text" media="screen">
  <link id="styleBigP" rel="alternate stylesheet" type="text/css"
      href="css/text_big.css" title="Big Text" media="print">
  ⋮
</head>
```

We execute the extended `switchStyleSheet` function like so:

```
switchStylesheetStyleSheet("Big Text", "print");
```

The resulting changes will not be visible immediately in the browser, but when we print the page, the style switch will be reflected.

Reading and Modifying an Existing Style Sheet

Although the `style` object allows you to modify the styles of an element one by one, the most efficient way to modify the styles of many elements simultaneously is to alter the CSS rules contained in your page's style sheets. CSS has its own special syntax for selecting the elements to which a set of style properties should apply, but JavaScript has full access to these rules, allowing you to change them at will.

Solution

DOM Style Sheet Support in Flux

Dealing with the contents of style sheets is one of the areas of DOM support that is most in flux. Currently, Opera 8.0 and below do not support the reading or manipulation of style sheets at all, and the browsers that do support it have their own individual quirks.

If a browser *does* allow the manipulation of style sheets, the `document.styleSheets` collection will contain references to each of the external style sheets (specified via `<link>` tags or `<style>` tags with `src` attributes), as well as to inline styles included between `<style>` and `</style>` tags. These style sheets are indexed according to their HTML source order.

Safari `document.styleSheets` Collection Quirk

Safari does not include alternate style sheets in the `document.styleSheets` collection, so this will affect the collection's index numbers in this browser.

Each element in `document.styleSheets` offers as a property a collection that allows you to access the rules contained in the corresponding style sheet, indexed according to their source order. The W3C Standard defines this property as `cssRules`, while Internet Explorer for Windows implements it as `rules`. This difference can easily be abstracted using a simple test:

File: **read_modify_existing_style_sheet.js** (excerpt)

```
if (typeof document.styleSheets != "undefined")
{
  var printStyleSheet = document.styleSheets[1];
  var printRules = null;

  if (typeof printStyleSheet.rules != "undefined")
  {
    printRules = printStyleSheet.rules;
  }
  else
  {
    printRules = printStyleSheet.cssRules;
  }
}
```

Once we have a consistent pointer to the `rules` collection, the CSS selector for a particular rule can be accessed using the `selectorText` property, and its style properties can be accessed using its `style` property. This follows the same syntax as the `style` object that we used to access an individual element's style properties earlier in this chapter.

Imagine we have a style sheet that looks like this:

File: **read_modify_existing_style_sheet.css**

```
p {
  font-family: "Comic Sans MS", sans-serif;
  font-weight: bold;
}

a {
  text-decoration: underline;
}
```

Here, we cannot modify the selector text because `selectorText` is read-only; however, we can change any of the style properties. So, for example, we can change all hyperlinks to have an overline:

File: **read_modify_existing_style_sheet.js** (excerpt)

```
if (typeof document.styleSheets != "undefined")
{
  var printStyleSheet = document.styleSheets[1];
  var printRules = null;

  if (typeof printStyleSheet.rules != "undefined")
```

```
  {
    printRules = printStyleSheet.rules;
  }
  else
  {
    printRules = printStyleSheet.cssRules;
  }

  printRules[1].style.textDecoration = "overline";
}
```

Alternatively, instead of hard-coding the index number of the rule we want to change, we could check each rule's selector to find the one we want:

File: **read_modify_existing_style_sheet2.js** (excerpt)

```
for (var i = 0; i < printRules.length; i++)
{
  if (printRules[i].selectorText.toLowerCase() == "a")
  {
    printRules[i].style.textDecoration = "overline";

    break;
  }
}
```

IE Tag Name Quirk

Internet Explorer automatically converts to uppercase all tag names in the CSS selectors, so a becomes A and h2 becomes H2. However, classes and other strings retain their case. This can cause problems with string matching, so be careful to take into account character case differences. This is why the toLowerCase conversion method is used above.

Discussion

Unfortunately, for slightly more complex selectors, the indexing of the rules collection varies wildly between browsers.

Consider grouped selectors, such as:

```
h2, h3, h4
{
  font-weight: bold;
}
```

Internet Explorer for Windows divides each of the components into its own rule, so effectively, it becomes three rules:

```
h2
{
  font-weight: bold;
}

h3
{
  font-weight: bold;
}

h4
{
  font-weight: bold;
}
```

Mozilla 1.6 and below also see three different rules; more recent versions see one rule; Safari sees just the first selector, ignoring the remainder. There are quite a few other differences in the ways different browsers represent selector syntax, including classes and precedent operators. Details of a few of these discrepancies are explained atQuirksMode.org[2].

At this point in time, if you're attempting to modify style sheets in a cross-browser fashion, it's safest to use the simplest rules possible—probably straightforward tag name or ID selection.

Adding New Style Sheet Rules

While the previous tip explained how to modify the *properties* of a style sheet rule, we can't modify the *selector* for a predefined rule using that process. In order to create a new rule, we have to use a dedicated method that's available via the DOM.

---

[2] http://www.quirksmode.org/dom/changess.html

Solution

A Sans-Safari Solution

Although Safari appears to support the DOM functions used here, it doesn't actually implement any of their functionality—calling them does nothing. As such, it's not possible to add new style sheet rules in this browser.

The W3C Standards advocate that, to add a rule to an existing style sheet, we should use the `insertRule` method of the style sheet object. However, the process isn't *quite* that simple. Internet Explorer has chosen to use a completely different method, `addRule`, which takes an entirely different syntax.

`insertRule` takes *two* arguments: a string containing both the selector and style properties, and the index at which you want to insert the rule.

`addRule` takes *three* arguments: a selector string, a style properties string, and an index (although the index is optional).

The easiest way to reconcile these differences is to write an abstracting function:

File: **add_new_style_sheet_rules.js** (excerpt)

```
function addStyleRule(styleSheet, selector, properties, index)
{
  if (typeof styleSheet.addRule != "undefined")
  {
    styleSheet.addRule(selector, properties, index);
  }
  else if (typeof styleSheet.insertRule != "undefined")
  {
    if (typeof index == "undefined")
    {
      index = styleSheet.cssRules.length;
    }

    styleSheet.insertRule(selector + " {" + properties + "}",
        index);
  }

  return true;
}
```

The first `if` statement in this function addresses the Internet Explorer approach to adding style sheet rules, by checking for the existence of `addRule`, then executing the method. If only three arguments were supplied to `addStyleRule` (i.e., no index was supplied), Internet Explorer will automatically append the rule to the end of the style sheet.

The alternative to the Internet Explorer approach is to use the W3C's `insertRule` method, which is handled in the `else` part of the conditional. Because an index is required by this method, we must detect whether one was passed to `addStyleRule`; if not, we calculate the index of the last style rule by getting the `length` of the style sheet's `cssRules` array. Once this is done, we can call `insertRule` with the appropriate arguments.

If we want to add to a style sheet a new rule that overlines hyperlinks when they're moused over, we can use this new function:

File: **add_new_style_sheet_rules.js (excerpt)**

```
if (typeof document.styleSheets != "undefined")
{
  addStyleRule(document.styleSheets[0], "a:hover",
      "text-decoration: overline");
}
```

Safari Workaround

Safari will report `typeof styleSheet.addRule` or `typeof styleSheet.insertRule` as `"function"`, but it hasn't actually implemented either of these functions. Calling them will not produce an error, nor will it achieve anything.

If you're really worried about this, you can add an extra exclusion to the condition around the `addStyleRule` call, using our browser detection function `identifyBrowser` from Chapter 11:

```
if (typeof document.styleSheets != "undefined" &&
    identifyBrowser().indexOf("safari") == -1)
{
  addStyleRule(document.styleSheets[0], "a:hover",
      "text-decoration: overline");
}
```

We can add multiple style properties to the one rule by adding to the list inside the property string (separating properties with semicolons, of course):

File: **add_new_style_sheet_rules2.js** (excerpt)

```
if (typeof document.styleSheets != "undefined")
{
  addStyleRule(document.styleSheets[0], "body",
      "background-color: #000000; color: #FFFFFF;");
}
```

Deleting a Rule from a Style Sheet

Like adding a rule, deleting a rule from a style sheet requires a dedicated DOM method. Again, Internet Explorer uses a different method from the W3C Standard, so a bit of massaging is required to get it to work properly.

Solution

Safari: Style Sheet Rules Stay!

Although Safari appears to support the DOM method `deleteRule` that's used here, it doesn't actually implement any of its functionality—calling it does nothing. It's not possible to delete style sheet rules in this browser.

The W3C Standard method for deleting a style rule is `deleteRule`. Internet Explorer's method is `removeRule`. Both are executed on the style sheet itself and, luckily, they both use the same argument: the index of the rule to delete. If we wanted to remove the first rule in the style sheet, here's how we do it:

File: **delete_rule_style_sheet.js** (excerpt)

```
if (typeof document.styleSheets != "undefined")
{
  var printStyleSheet = document.styleSheets[0];

  if (typeof printStyleSheet.removeRule != "undefined")
  {
    printStyleSheet.removeRule(0);
  }
  else if (typeof printStyleSheet.deleteRule != "undefined")
  {
    printStyleSheet.deleteRule(0);
  }
}
```

Creating a New Style Sheet

Usually, it will suffice to add a new style rule to an existing style sheet. However, in rare cases you may want to create a new style sheet and add rules to this, particularly if you want to use a media type that isn't specified in any of the existing style sheets.

Because we're creating an inline style sheet from scratch, we aren't restricted by the DOM structures required for accessing external files, so this method will work in browsers that don't support the `addStyleRule` function we created earlier, in "Adding New Style Sheet Rules".

Solution

The W3C Standards specify a method for creating a new style sheet, but curiously, the newly created style sheets can't be associated with a document. That's kind of pointless, don't you think?

Thankfully, it's possible to create a new **style** element on a page, then add to it via the `document.styleSheets` collection. As the **style** element is a normal DOM element, we can append text nodes to its contents. This enables us to create style rules for browsers that don't support the standard DOM style functions:

File: **create_new_style_sheet.js** (excerpt)

```
addLoadListener(initNewStyleSheet);

function initNewStyleSheet()
{
  var styleSheet = createNewStyleSheet();

  addHeadStyleRule(styleSheet, "body",
      "background-color: #000000; color: #FFFFFF;");

  return true;
}

function createNewStyleSheet(media)
{
  var isSafari = /safari/.test(identifyBrowser());

  var styleSheet = document.createElement("style");
```

```
  styleSheet.setAttribute("type", "text/css");

  if (typeof media == "undefined")
  {
    styleSheet.setAttribute("media", "all");
  }
  else
  {
    styleSheet.setAttribute("media", media);
  }

  styleSheet = document.getElementsByTagName("head")[0].
      appendChild(styleSheet);

  if (typeof document.styleSheets != "undefined" &&
      document.styleSheets.length > 0 && !isSafari)
  {
    styleSheet = document.styleSheets[
        document.styleSheets.length - 1];
  }

  return styleSheet;
}

function addHeadStyleRule(styleSheet, selector, properties)
{
  var isSafari = /safari/.test(identifyBrowser());

  if (typeof styleSheet.addRule != "undefined" && !isSafari)
  {
    styleSheet.addRule(selector, properties);
  }
  else if (typeof styleSheet.insertRule != "undefined" &&
      !isSafari)
  {
    styleSheet.insertRule(selector + " {" + properties + "}",
        styleSheet.cssRules.length);
  }
  else
  {
    styleSheet.appendChild(document.createTextNode(selector +
        " {" + properties + "}"));
  }

  return true;
}
```

Here, the `addLoadListener` function we saw in Chapter 1 is used to schedule the addition of a new style sheet when the page loads. `initNewStyleSheet` creates a new style sheet by calling `createNewStyleSheet`, then adds a rule to style the page's `body` element by calling `addHeadStyleRule`. Let's look at how both these custom functions work.

`createNewStyleSheet` adds a new `style` element to the `head` of the current document. It adds this element as the last child, so any styles that are specified inside this new style sheet will override other styles specified in the `head`. Although `createNewStyleSheet` sets the `type` attribute statically, it does allow you to specify for the style sheet a media type that's passed in when the function is called. You can supply any valid media type—for example, `all`, `print`, `screen`, `projection`, and so on—but if one is not supplied, it defaults to `all`. The return value from the function is a reference to the style sheet; this allows us to add style rules to it later. A code branch appears here because the different rule addition models require different references. Browsers that support `document.styleSheets` require a reference through this object, whereas less advanced browsers can use only a normal DOM node reference. The one exception is Safari, which has a `document.styleSheets` object, but does not properly implement any of the standard DOM style functions. It's for this reason that we call the function `identifyBrowser` (which we saw in Chapter 11) at the start of `createNewStyleSheet`, and we specifically exclude Safari from returning a `document.styleSheets` reference.

After the style sheet has been created, we end up with a unique reference to it. This is assigned to the variable `styleSheet`, and is passed to the function `addHeadStyleRule` when we want to create a new style rule. Even though they both take the same arguments, and `addHeadStyleRule` builds upon the `addStyleRule` function we created earlier, `addHeadStyleRule` is different from `addStyleRule` because it's designed specifically to add style rules to the head of the document (i.e., not to external files). It's for this reason that we are able to provide backwards compatibility for browsers that don't have special native functions for handling style sheets.

Firstly, `addHeadStyleRule` has to check for Safari, to make sure that browser doesn't try and execute either of the DOM style functions. Then, we try to add the specified style rule using Internet Explorer's `addRule` method, or the standard `insertRule` function. If either of these methods isn't available, we resort to the basic approach: a text node containing an appropriately formatted style rule is appended to the contents of the style element. To simplify matters for this case, no index is provided to either of the other two methods: we just append the rule to the very end of the style sheet.

With this cascade of feature detection, we can now add styles in every modern browser. And you thought it couldn't be done!

Summary

Determining the visual display of elements on a page is one of the most crucial aspects of interface design. As this chapter has shown, not only can JavaScript determine the behavior of an interface, but, via CSS, it can also change the way that an interface appears.

This makes JavaScript doubly useful: it can apply the logic and calculations required to power an application, as well as specifying the form of that application. This makes JavaScript a truly formidable application development environment.

13

Basic Dynamic HTML

Dynamic HTML isn't a single piece of technology that you can point to and say, "This is DHTML." The term is a descriptor that encompasses all of the technologies that combine to make a web page dynamic: the technologies that let you create new elements without refreshing the page, change the color of those elements, and make them expand, contract, and zoom around the screen.

DHTML uses HTML, the DOM, and CSS in combination with a client-side scripting language—JavaScript—to bring life to what was traditionally a static medium. In previous chapters, we learned that we can use JavaScript to manipulate parts of a page to achieve some very handy results. DHTML provides solutions to much more complex problems by assembling these parts into a coherent whole—one that satisfies real-world needs, rather than programming puzzles.

This chapter explores a few of the tools we need in order to create effective user interfaces with DHTML. It then discusses a couple of simple widgets in preparation for the more complex modules we'll consider throughout the rest of this book.

Handling Events

Any interaction that users have with a web page—whether they're moving the mouse or tapping the keyboard—will cause the browser to generate an event.

Sometimes, we want our code to respond to this interaction, so we listen for these events, which let us know when we should execute our code.

Solution

There are two ways to handle events: the short way, and the W3C way. Each has its pros and cons, but both allow you to execute a specified function when an event occurs on a particular element.

The Short Way: Using Event Handlers

The shorter way of handling an event is to use the DOM 0 event handlers that are assigned as shortcut properties of every element. Much as we saw in Chapter 5 when we discussed DOM 0 attribute shortcuts, these event handlers are not future-proof. However, they do offer some advantages over standard W3C event listeners:

❑ Every browser that's currently in operation supports DOM 0 event handlers without the need for code branching.

❑ Each function executed by a DOM 0 event handler has access to the exact element to which the event handler was assigned. (As you'll see later, this is not always available in W3C event listeners.)

The main problem with utilizing DOM 0 event handlers is that they are not designed to work with multiple scripts. Every time you assign a DOM 0 event handler, you overwrite any previously assigned handler for that event. This can interfere with the operation of multiple scripts that require event handling on the same element. With W3C event listeners, you can apply any number of event listeners on the same element, and enjoy the ability to remove any of them at any time.

If you can be certain that your code will not interfere with someone else's event handling (e.g., you're placing events on elements that are created dynamically in your own script), it will be safe to use DOM 0 event handlers. But—all things being equal—it is safer to use the W3C event listeners wherever practical, as we do in this book.

A number of DOM 0 event handlers are available via the browser; Table 13.1 lists the most commonly used handlers.

Table 13.1. DOM 0 event handlers

DOM 0 Event Handler	W3C DOM Event	Indicated Action
onblur	blur	Remove focus from an element by clicking outside or tabbing away from it.
onfocus	focus	Focus the cursor on an element.
onchange	change	Remove focus from an element after changing its content.
onmouseover	mouseover	Move the mouse pointer over an element.
onmouseout	mouseout	Move the mouse pointer out of an element.
onmousemove	mousemove	Move the mouse pointer while it is over an element.
onmousedown	mousedown	Press a mouse button while the pointer is over an element.
onmouseup	mouseup	Release a mouse button while the pointer is over an element.
onclick	click	Press and release the main mouse button or keyboard equivalent (**Enter** key) while the pointer is over an element.
ondblclick	dblclick	Double-click the main mouse button while the pointer is over an element.
onkeydown	keydown	Press a keyboard key while an element has focus.
onkeyup	keyup	Release a keyboard key while an element has focus.
onkeypress	keypress	Press and release a keyboard key while an element has focus.
onsubmit	submit	Request that a form be submitted.
onload	load	Finish loading a page and all associated assets (e.g., images).
onunload	unload	Request a new page to replace the currently-displayed page, or close the window.

In using DOM 0 event handlers, once you have a reference to the element whose events you want to handle, it's a simple matter of assigning a handling function to the appropriate property:

File: **handle_events.js** (excerpt)

```
var mylink = document.getElementById("mylink");

mylink.onclick = engage;
⋮
function engage()
{
  alert("Engage!");

  return false;
}
```

You'll note that, in the function assignment (`mylink.onclick = engage;`), parentheses do not follow the function name. Their inclusion would execute the function immediately, and assign the *return value* as the event handler. By omitting the parentheses, you can assign the function *itself* to the handler. This also means that you cannot supply arguments directly to the handling function: the function must obtain its information through other means.

Tip

Anonymous Functions

Instead of supplying a reference to a named function, you can supply an anonymous function for an event handler:

```
var mylink = document.getElementById("mylink");

mylink.onclick = function()
{
  alert("Engage!");

  return false;
}
```

Depending on whether you need to reuse the handling function (and your own coding preferences), this can be an easier way of writing event handling code.

The return value of the handling function determines whether the default action for that event occurs. So, in the preceding code, if `mybutton` were a hyperlink, its default action when clicked would be to navigate to its `href` location. By returning `false`, the `engage` function does not allow the default action to occur, and the hyperlink navigation will not take place. If the return value were `true`, the default action *would* occur after the event handling function's code had executed.

When an event occurs, detailed information about the how, why, and where of that event is written to an **event object**. In Internet Explorer, this takes the form of a global `window.event` object, but in other browsers the object is passed as an argument to the event-handling function. This difference is fairly easy to address within the handling function:

File: **handle_events2.js (excerpt)**

```
function engage(event)
{
  if (typeof event == "undefined")
  {
    event = window.event;
  }

  alert("The screen co-ordinates of your click were: " +
      event.screenX + ", " + event.screenY);

  return false;
}
```

The event object allows you to find out a range of details, such as which element was clicked, whether any keys were pressed, the coordinates of the event (e.g., where the cursor was located when the mouse button was clicked), and the type of event that triggered the function. Quite a few of the event property names are consistent across browsers, but a few differ. The Mozilla event properties can be viewed at the Gecko DOM Reference,[1] while the Internet Explorer event properties can be seen at MSDN.[2] For properties whose names vary between browsers, the potential for associated problems can normally be rectified with a little object detection; we'll discuss this in detail later in this chapter.

The W3C Way (Event Listeners)

Although the DOM 0 event handlers are quick and easy, they do have limitations (aside from the fact that eventually they will become deprecated). The main advantage of the W3C event listeners is that they natively support the addition and removal of multiple handling functions for the same event on a single element. Event listeners also have the capability to respond to events in several phases (though most browsers don't yet support this capability).

---

[1] http://www.mozilla.org/docs/dom/domref/dom_event_ref.html
[2] http://msdn.microsoft.com/workshop/author/dhtml/reference/objects/obj_event.asp

In the W3C specification, an event can be added to an element using the element's `addEventListener` method, but Internet Explorer for Windows chooses to use a method called `attachEvent`, which has a slightly different syntax.[3]

To add an event listener in every browser except Internet Explorer, you would write code similar to this:

```
var mylink = document.getElementById("mylink");

mylink.addEventListener("click", engage, false);
```

To support Internet Explorer, you'd need this code:

```
var mylink = document.getElementById("mylink");

mylink.attachEvent("onclick", engage);
```

As well as the differing function names, it's important to note that Internet Explorer uses the DOM 0 handler name for the event—`"onclick"`—rather than the true event name: `"click"`. The extra argument that's supplied to `addEventListener` specifies whether the listener is applied during the capture (`true`) or bubble (`false`) event propagation phase. Event propagation is explained in more detail in the discussion below, but bubble is really the most useful choice, and ensures the same behavior in standards-compliant browsers as in Internet Explorer.

The differences between these two approaches are fairly easy to work around using an abstracting function. We can also provide a fallback for browsers that don't support W3C event listeners at the same time:

File: **handle_events3.js (excerpt)**

```
function attachEventListener(target, eventType, functionRef,
    capture)
{
  if (typeof target.addEventListener != "undefined")
  {
    target.addEventListener(eventType, functionRef, capture);
  }
  else if (typeof target.attachEvent != "undefined")
  {
    target.attachEvent("on" + eventType, functionRef);
  }
```

---

[3]Internet Explorer for Mac doesn't support either of these event models, so we have to rely on the DOM 0 handlers to work with events in this browser.

```
else
{
  eventType = "on" + eventType;

  if (typeof target[eventType] == "function")
  {
    var oldListener = target[eventType];

    target[eventType] = function()
    {
      oldListener();

      return functionRef();
    };
  }
  else
  {
    target[eventType] = functionRef;
  }
}
}
```

The first two `if` statements deal with the standards-based and Internet Explorer methods respectively, but the catch-all `else` deals with older browsers that don't support either of these methods, particularly Internet Explorer 5 for Mac. In this last case, a DOM 0 event handler is used, but to ensure that multiple functions can be used to handle a single event for a particular element, a closure is used to execute any existing functions that are attached to the event.

Closures are an advanced feature of JavaScript that relates to scoping (which you can read about in Chapter 19). Closures allow an inner function to reference the variables of the containing function even after the containing function has finished running. Simon Willison has explained their usage in relation to event handlers in some detail.[4] Suffice it to say that closures allow us to stack multiple event handlers in browsers that don't support W3C event listeners.

The cross-browser code for assigning an event listener is as follows:

File: **handle_events3.js** (excerpt)

```
var mylink = document.getElementById("mylink");

attachEventListener(mylink, "click", engage, false);
```

---

[4] http://www.sitepoint.com/blogs/2004/05/26/closures-and-executing-javascript-on-page-load/

Not (quite) the Genuine Article

Although the DOM 0 event handler fallback mimics the ability to add multiple event listeners for one event type on an element, it does not provide exact replication of the W3C event model, because specific handlers cannot be *removed* from an element.

Whereas DOM 0 handlers allowed the cancellation of an element's default action by returning `false`, W3C event listeners achieve this goal slightly differently. To cancel a default action in this model, we need to modify the event object. Internet Explorer requires you to set its `returnValue` property to `false`; standards-based implementations offer the `preventDefault` method to do the same thing. We can create a small function that figures out the difference for us:

File: **handle_events4.js (excerpt)**

```
function stopDefaultAction(event)
{
  event.returnValue = false;

  if (typeof event.preventDefault != "undefined")
  {
    event.preventDefault();
  }
}
```

We can call this function whenever we want to cancel the default action:

File: **handle_events4.js (excerpt)**

```
function engage(event)
{
  if (typeof event == "undefined")
  {
    event = window.event;
  }

  alert("Engage!");

  stopDefaultAction(event);

  return false;
}
```

You still need to return `false` after executing `stopDefaultAction` in order to ensure that browsers that don't support the W3C event model will also prevent the default action.

Safari and W3C Event Listeners

Due to a bug in Safari, it's impossible to cancel the default action of clicking a hyperlink in that browser when using W3C event listeners. To achieve the cancellation, you'll have to use DOM 0 event handlers with a return value of `false`.

Checking for `attachEvent`

Internet Explorer for Windows actually passes an event object to the event-handling function when `attachEvent` is used to attach an event listener. However, we still need to check for the existence of this object for any browsers that use the old event model.

One of the advantages of using W3C event listeners is that you can remove an individual listener from an element without disturbing any other listeners on the same event. This is not possible using the DOM 0 handlers.

Internet Explorer uses the `detachEvent` method, while the standards-compliant browsers instead specify a method called `removeEventListener`. Each of these methods operates fairly similarly to its listener-adding counterpart: an event type must be supplied along with the function that was assigned to handle that event type. The standard method also demands to know whether the event handler was registered to respond during the capture or bubble phase.

Here's a function that supports this approach across browsers:

File: **handle_events5.js (excerpt)**

```
function detachEventListener(target, eventType, functionRef,
    capture)
{
  if (typeof target.removeEventListener != "undefined")
  {
    target.removeEventListener(eventType, functionRef, capture);
  }
  else if (typeof target.detachEvent != "undefined")
  {
    target.detachEvent("on" + eventType, functionRef);
  }
  else
  {
    target["on" + eventType] = null;
  }
}
```

The W3C Event Model and Anonymous Functions

The W3C event model doesn't allow for the removal of anonymous functions, so if you need to remove an event listener, hang onto a reference to the function in question.

In browsers that don't support W3C event listeners, this function removes all event handlers on the given event: it's not possible to remove just one of them and leave the others.

Discussion

Referencing the Target Element

Quite often, you'll want to use the object that was the target of an event inside the event handler itself. With DOM 0 event handlers, the use of the special variable `this` inside a handling function will refer to the event target object. Consider this code:

File: **handle_events6.js** (excerpt)

```
var mylink = document.getElementById("mylink");

mylink.onclick = engage;
:
function engage()
{
  var href = this.getAttribute("href");

  alert("Engage: " + href);

  return false;
}
```

Here, `this` refers to the link with ID `mylink`. We can use it to get the link's `href` attribute.

However, if you use W3C event listeners, the target of the event is stored as part of the event object, under different properties in different browsers. Internet Explorer stores the target as `srcElement`, while the standards model stores it as `target`. But the element to which these properties point isn't necessarily the element to which the event listener was assigned. It is, in fact, the deepest element in the hierarchy affected by the event. Take a look at the following HTML.

File: **handle_events6.html** (excerpt)

```
<p>
  These are the voyages of the <a id="mylink"
      href="enterprise.html">starship Enterprise</a>.
</p>
```

If a `click` event listener were placed on the paragraph and a user clicked on the link, the paragraph's `click` event handler would be executed, but the event target that was accessible through the above-mentioned properties would be the hyperlink. Some browsers (most notably, Safari) even go so far as to count the text node *inside* the link as the target node.

We can write a function that returns the event target irrespective of which property has been implemented, but this does not solve the problem of finding the element to which we originally applied the event listener.[5] Often, the best resolution to this quandary is to iterate upwards from the event target provided by the browser until we find an element that's *likely* to be the element to which we attached an event listener. To do this, we can perform checks against the element's tag name, class, and other attributes.

The abstracting event target function would look like this:

File: **handle_events7.js** (excerpt)

```
function getEventTarget(event)
{
  var targetElement = null;

  if (typeof event.target != "undefined")
  {
    targetElement = event.target;
  }
  else
  {
    targetElement = event.srcElement;
  }

  while (targetElement.nodeType == 3 &&
      targetElement.parentNode != null)
  {
    targetElement = targetElement.parentNode;
```

---

[5]The W3C Standard specifies another property called `currentTarget`, which lets you get the element to which the listener was assigned, but there is no Internet Explorer equivalent. Browsers that support `currentTarget` also set up the event handler-style `this` variable with the same value, but again, without Internet Explorer support, this isn't particularly useful.

```
    }

    return targetElement;
}
```

The `if-else` retrieves the event target across browsers; the `while` loop then finds the first non-text-node parent if the target reported by the browser happens to be a text node.

If we want to retrieve the element that was clicked upon, we then make a call to `getEventTarget`:

File: **handle_events7.js** (excerpt)

```
var mylink = document.getElementById("mylink");

attachEventListener(mylink, "click", engage, false);
:
function engage(event)
{
  if (typeof event == "undefined")
  {
    event = window.event;
  }

  var target = getEventTarget(event);

  while(target.nodeName.toLowerCase() != "a")
  {
    target = target.parentNode;
  }

  var href = target.getAttribute("href");

  alert("Engage: " + href);

  return true;
}
```

Because we know, in this case, that the event-handling function will be attached only to links (<a> tags), we can iterate upwards from the event target, checking for a node name of "a". The first one we find will be the link to which the handler was assigned; this ensures that we aren't working with some element inside the link (such as a `strong` or a `span`).

Obviously, this method of target finding is not ideal, and cannot be 100% accurate unless you have knowledge of the exact HTML you'll be working with. Recently, much effort has gone into resolving this problem, and quite a few of the proposed solutions offer the same `this` variable as is available under DOM 0 event handlers, and in browsers that support the W3C Standard for event listeners (not Internet Explorer).

One such solution is to make the event listening function a method of the target object in Internet Explorer. Then, when the method is called, `this` will naturally point to the object for which the method was called. This requires both the `attachEventListener` and `detachEventListener` to be modified:

File: **handle_events8.js (excerpt)**

```javascript
function attachEventListener(target, eventType, functionRef,
    capture)
{
  if (typeof target.addEventListener != "undefined")
  {
    target.addEventListener(eventType, functionRef, capture);
  }
  else if (typeof target.attachEvent != "undefined")
  {
    var functionString = eventType + functionRef;
    target["e" + functionString] = functionRef;

    target[functionString] = function(event)
    {
      if (typeof event == "undefined")
      {
        event = window.event;
      }
      target["e" + functionString](event);
    };

    target.attachEvent("on" + eventType, target[functionString]);
  }
  else
  {
    eventType = "on" + eventType;

    if (typeof target[eventType] == "function")
    {
      var oldListener = target[eventType];

      target[eventType] = function()
```

```
        {
          oldListener();

          return functionRef();
        }
      }
      else
      {
        target[eventType] = functionRef;
      }
    }
}

function detachEventListener(target, eventType, functionRef,
    capture)
{
  if (typeof target.removeEventListener != "undefined")
  {
    target.removeEventListener(eventType, functionRef, capture);
  }
  else if (typeof target.detachEvent != "undefined")
  {
    var functionString = eventType + functionRef;

    target.detachEvent("on" + eventType, target[functionString]);

    target["e" + functionString] = null;
    target[functionString] = null;
  }
  else
  {
    target["on" + eventType] = null;
  }
}
```

This line of thinking was well represented in entries to Peter Paul Koch's improved addEvent competition.[6]

Another solution by Dean Edwards totally eschews the W3C event model in favor of implementing DOM 0 event handlers with independent add and remove abilities.[7]

---

[6] http://www.quirksmode.org/blog/archives/2005/10/_and_the_winner_1.html
[7] http://dean.edwards.name/weblog/2005/10/add-event/

Although both of these solutions may prove to be well written and robust, they're largely untested as of this writing, so we'll stick with the approach whose flaws we know and can handle: the one presented in the main solution. Besides, in practice, the process of iterating to find an event's target isn't as unreliable as it may appear to be.

What is Event Bubbling, and How do I Control it?

You may have noticed that we needed to supply a third argument to the W3C Standard `addEventListener` method, and that a *capture* argument was included in our `attachEventListener` function to cater for this. This argument determines the phase of the event cycle in which the listener operates.

Suppose you have two elements, one nested inside the other:

```
<p>
  <a href="untimely_death.html">Nameless Ensign</a>
</p>
```

When a user clicks on the link, click events will be registered on both the paragraph and the hyperlink. The question is, which one receives the event first?

The event cycle contains two phases, and each answers this question in a different way. In the **capture** phase, events work from the outside in, so the paragraph would receive the click first, then the hyperlink. In the **bubble** phase, events work from the inside out, so the anchor would receive the click before the paragraph.

Internet Explorer and Opera only support bubbling, which is why `attachEvent` doesn't require a third argument. For browsers that support `addEventListener`, if the third argument is `true`, the event will be caught during the capture phase; if it is `false`, the event will be caught during the bubble phase.

In browsers that support both phases, the capture phase occurs first and is always followed by the bubble phase. It's possible for an event to be handled on the same element in both the capture and bubbling phases, provided you set up listeners for each phase.

These phases also highlight the fact that nested elements are affected by the same event. If you no longer want an event to continue propagating up or down the hierarchy (depending upon the phase) after an event listener has been triggered, you can stop it. In Internet Explorer, this involves setting the `cancelBubble` property of the event object to `true`; in the W3C model, you must instead call its `stopPropagation` method:

File: **handle_events9.js (excerpt)**

```
function stopEvent(event)
{
  if (typeof event.stopPropagation != "undefined")
  {
    event.stopPropagation();
  }
  else
  {
    event.cancelBubble = true;
  }
}
```

If we didn't want an event to propagate further than our event handler, we'd use this code:

File: **handle_events9.js (excerpt)**

```
var mylink = document.getElementById("mylink");

attachEventListener(mylink, "click", engage, false);

var paragraph = document.getElementsByTagName("p")[0];

attachEventListener(paragraph, "click", engage, false);

function engage(event)
{
  if (typeof event == "undefined")
  {
    event = window.event;
  }

  alert("She canna take no more cap'n!");

  stopEvent(event);

  return true;
}
```

Although we have assigned the `engage` function to listen for the `click` event on both the link and the paragraph that contains it, the function will only be called once per click, as the event's propagation is stopped by the listener the first time it is called.

Finding the Size of an Element

There are so many variables that affect the size of an element—content length, CSS rules, font family, font size, line height, text zooming ... the list goes on. Add to this the fact that browsers interpret CSS dimensions and font sizes inconsistently, and you can never predict the dimensions at which an element will be rendered. The only consistent way to determine an element's size is to measure it once it's been rendered by the browser.

Solution

You can tell straight away that it's going to be useful to know exactly how big an element is. Well, the W3C can't help: there's no standardized way to determine the size of an element. Thankfully, the browser-makers have more or less settled on some DOM properties that let us figure it out.

Although box model differences mean that Internet Explorer includes padding and borders inconsistently as part of an element's CSS dimensions, the offsetWidth and offsetHeight properties will consistently return an element's width—including padding and borders—across all browsers.

Let's imagine that an element's dimensions were specified in CSS like this:

File: **find_size_element.css**

```
#enterprise
{
  width: 350px;
  height: 150px;
  margin: 25px;
  border: 25px solid #000000;
  padding: 25px;
}
```

We can determine that element's exact pixel width in JavaScript by checking the corresponding offsetWidth and offsetHeight properties:

File: **find_size_element.js** (excerpt)
```
var starShip = document.getElementById("enterprise");
var pixelWidth = starShip.offsetWidth;
var pixelHeight = starShip.offsetHeight;
```

In Internet Explorer 6, Opera, Mozilla, and Safari, the variable `pixelWidth` will now be set to 450, and the variable `pixelHeight` will be set to 250. In Internet Explorer 5/5.5, `pixelWidth` will be 350 and `pixelHeight` 150, because those are the dimensions at which the broken box model approach used in those browsers will render the element. The values are different across browsers, but only because the actual rendered size differs as well. The offset dimensions consistently calculate the exact pixel dimensions of the element.

If we did not specify the dimensions of the element, and instead left its display up to the default block rendering (thus avoiding the box model bugs), the values would be comparable between browsers (allowing for scrollbar width differences, fonts, etc.).

Attaining the Correct Dimensions

In order to correctly determine the dimensions of an element you must wait until the browser has finished rendering that element, otherwise the dimensions may be different from those the user ends up seeing. There's no guaranteed way to ensure that a browser has finished rendering an element, but it's normally safe to assume that once a window's **load** event has fired, all elements have been rendered.

Discussion

It is possible to retrieve the dimensions of an element minus its borders, but including its padding. These values are accessed using the `clientWidth` and `clientHeight` properties, and for the example element used above their values would be 300 and 100 in Internet Explorer 5/5.5, and 400 and 200 in all other browsers.

There is no property that will allow you to retrieve an element's width without borders *or* padding.

Finding the Position of an Element

Knowing the exact position of an element is very helpful when you wish to position other elements relative to it. However, because of different browser sizes, font sizes, and content lengths, it's often impossible to hard-code the position of an element *before* you load a page. JavaScript offers a method to ascertain any element's position *after* the page has been rendered, so you can know exactly where your elements are located.

Solution

The `offsetTop` and `offsetLeft` properties tell you the distance between the top of an element and the top of its `offsetParent`. But what is `offsetParent`? Well, it varies widely for different elements and different browsers. Sometimes it's the immediate containing element; other times it's the `html` element; at other times it's nonexistent.

Thankfully, the solution is to follow the trail of `offsetParent`s and add up their offset positions—a method that will give you the element's accurate absolute position on the page in every browser.

If the element in question has no `offsetParent`, then the offset position of the element itself is enough; otherwise, we add the offsets of the element to those of its `offsetParent`, then repeat the process for *its* `offsetParent` (if any):

File: **find_position_of_element.js** (excerpt)

```
function getPosition(theElement)
{
  var positionX = 0;
  var positionY = 0;

  while (theElement != null)
  {
    positionX += theElement.offsetLeft;
    positionY += theElement.offsetTop;
    theElement = theElement.offsetParent;
  }

  return [positionX, positionY];
}
```

note

IE 5 for Mac Bug

Internet Explorer 5 for Mac doesn't take the **body**'s margin or padding into account when calculating the offset dimensions, so if you desire accurate measurements in this browser, you should have zero margins and padding on the **body**.

Discussion

The method above works for simple and complex layouts; however, you may run into problems when one or more of an element's ancestors has its CSS `position` property set to something other than `static` (the default).

There are so many possible combinations of nested positioning and browser differences that it's almost impossible to write a script that takes them all into account. If you are working with an interface that uses a lot of relative or absolute positioning, it's probably easiest to experiment with specific cases and write special functions to deal with them. Here are just a few of the differences that you might encounter:

❏ In Internet Explorer for Windows and Mozilla/Firefox, any element whose parent is relatively positioned will not include the parent's border in its own offset; however, the parent's offset will only measure to the edge of its border. Therefore, the sum of these values will not include the border distance.

❏ In Opera and Safari, any absolutely or relatively positioned element whose `offsetParent` is the `body` will include the `body`'s margin in its own offset. The `body`'s offset will include its own margin as well.

❏ In Internet Explorer for Windows, any absolutely positioned element inside a relatively positioned element will include the relatively positioned element's margin in its offset. The relatively positioned element will include its margin as well.

Detecting the Position of the Mouse Cursor

When working with mouse events, such as `mouseover` or `mousemove`, you will often want to use the coordinates of the mouse cursor as part of your operation (e.g., to position an element near the mouse). The solution explained below is actually a more reliable method of location detection than the element position detection method we discussed in "Finding the Position of an Element", so if it's possible to use the following solution instead of the previous one, go for it!

Solution

The event object contains everything you need to know to work with the position of the cursor, although a little bit of object detection is required to ensure you get equivalent values across all browsers.

The standard method of obtaining the cursor's position relative to the entire page is via the pageX and pageY properties of the event object. Internet Explorer doesn't support these properties, but it *does* include some properties that are *almost* the ones we want. clientX and clientY are available in Internet Explorer, though they measure the distance from the mouse cursor to the edges of the browser window. In order to find the position of the cursor relative to the entire page, we need to add the current scroll position to these dimensions. This technique was covered in Chapter 7; let's use the getScrollingPosition function from that solution to retrieve the required dimensions:

File: **detect_mouse_cursor.js** (excerpt)

```
function displayCursorPosition(event)
{
  if (typeof event == "undefined")
  {
    event = window.event;
  }

  var scrollingPosition = getScrollingPosition();
  var cursorPosition = [0, 0];

  if (typeof event.pageX != "undefined" &&
      typeof event.x != "undefined")
  {
    cursorPosition[0] = event.pageX;
    cursorPosition[1] = event.pageY;
  }
  else
  {
    cursorPosition[0] = event.clientX + scrollingPosition[0];
    cursorPosition[1] = event.clientY + scrollingPosition[1];
  }

  var paragraph = document.getElementsByTagName("p")[0];

  paragraph.replaceChild(document.createTextNode(
      "Your mouse is currently located at: " + cursorPosition[0] +
      "," + cursorPosition[1]), paragraph.firstChild);
```

```
    return true;
}
```

`clientX`/`clientY` are valid W3C DOM event properties that exist in most browsers, so we can't rely on their existence as an indication that we need to use them. Instead, within our event handler, we test for the existence of `pageX`. Internet Explorer for Mac does have `pageX`, but it's an incorrect value, so we must also check for `x`. `x` is actually a nonstandard property, but most browsers support it (the exceptions being Opera 8+ and Internet Explorer). It's okay that Opera 8+ doesn't support `x`, because the `else` statement is actually a cross-browser method for calculating the mouse cursor position *except* in Safari, which incorrectly gives `clientX` the same value as `pageX`. That's why we still need to use both methods of calculating the cursor position.

Displaying a Tooltip when you Mouse Over an Element

Tooltips are a helpful feature in most browsers, but they can be a bit restrictive if you plan to use them as parts of your interface. If you'd like to use layers that appear when you want them to, aren't truncated, and can contain more than plain text, why not make your own enhanced tooltips?

Solution

For this example, we'll apply a `class`, `hastooltip`, on all the elements for which we'd like tooltips to appear. We'll get the information that's going to appear in the tooltip from each element's `title` attribute:

File: **tooltips.html (excerpt)**

```
<p>
  These are the voyages of the <a class="hastooltip"
    href="enterprise.html" title="USS Enterprise (NCC-1701) …">
    starship Enterprise</a>.
</p>
```

From our exploration of browser events earlier in this chapter, you'll probably already have realized that we need to set up some event listeners to let us know when the layer should appear and disappear.

Tooltips classically appear in a fixed location when you mouse over an element, and disappear when you mouse out. Some implementations of JavaScript tooltips also move the tooltip as the mouse moves over the element, but I personally find this annoying. In this solution, we'll focus on the mouseover and mouseout events:

File: **tooltips.js** (excerpt)

```
addLoadListener(initTooltips);

function initTooltips()
{
  var tips = getElementsByAttribute("class", "hastooltip");

  for (var i = 0; i < tips.length; i++)
  {
    attachEventListener(tips[i], "mouseover", showTip, false);
    attachEventListener(tips[i], "mouseout", hideTip, false);
  }

  return true;
}
```

We've already coded quite a few of the functions in this script, including addLoadListener from Chapter 1, getElementsByAttribute from Chapter 5, and the attachEventListener function that we created earlier in this chapter, so the bulk of the code is in the event listener functions:

File: **tooltips.js** (excerpt)

```
function showTip(event)
{
  if (typeof event == "undefined")
  {
    event = window.event;
  }

  var target = getEventTarget(event);

  while (target.className == null ||
      !/(^| )hastooltip( |$)/.test(target.className))
  {
    target = target.parentNode;
  }

  var tip = document.createElement("div");
  var content = target.getAttribute("title");
```

```
target.tooltip = tip;
target.setAttribute("title", "");

if (target.getAttribute("id") != "")
{
  tip.setAttribute("id", target.getAttribute("id") + "tooltip");
}

tip.className = "tooltip";
tip.appendChild(document.createTextNode(content));

var scrollingPosition = getScrollingPosition();
var cursorPosition = [0, 0];

if (typeof event.pageX != "undefined" &&
    typeof event.x != "undefined")
{
  cursorPosition[0] = event.pageX;
  cursorPosition[1] = event.pageY;
}
else
{
  cursorPosition[0] = event.clientX + scrollingPosition[0];
  cursorPosition[1] = event.clientY + scrollingPosition[1];
}

tip.style.position = "absolute";
tip.style.left = cursorPosition[0] + 10 + "px";
tip.style.top = cursorPosition[1] + 10 + "px";
document.getElementsByTagName("body")[0].appendChild(tip);

return true;
}
```

After getting a cross-browser event object, and iterating from the base event target element to one with a `class` of `hastooltip`, `showtip` goes about creating the tooltip (a `div`). The content for the tooltip is taken from the `title` attribute of the target element, and placed into a text node inside the tooltip.

To ensure that the browser doesn't display a tooltip of its own on top of our enhanced tooltip, the `title` of the target element is then cleared—now, there's nothing for the browser to display as a tooltip, so it can't interfere with the one we've just created. Don't worry about the potential accessibility issues caused by removing the `title`: we'll put it back later.

Controlling Tooltip Display in Opera

Opera still displays the original `title` even after we set it to an empty string. If you wish to avoid tooltips appearing in this browser, you'll have to stop the default action of the mouseover using the `stopDefaultAction` function from "Handling Events", the first section of this chapter. Be aware that this will also affect other mouseover behavior, such as the status bar address display for hyperlinks.

To provide hooks for the styling of our tooltip, we assign the tooltip element an ID that's based on the target element's ID (*targetID*`tooltip`), and set a `class` of `tooltip`. Although this approach allows for styles to be applied through CSS, we are unable to calculate the tooltip's position ahead of time, so we must use the coordinates of the mouse cursor, as calculated when the event is triggered, to position the tooltip (with a few extra pixels to give it some space).

All that remains is to append the tooltip element to the `body`, so it will magically appear when we mouse over the link! With a little bit of CSS, it could look like Figure 13.1.

Figure 13.1. A dynamically generated layer that appears on mouseover

"Space – the final frontier. These are the voyages of the starship Enterprise, her five-year mission: to explore strange new worlds, to se... boldy go where n...

USS Enterprise (NCC-1701). Starship class: Constitution class. The USS Enterprise was once referred to as the "United Space Ship Enterprise", but ever since has always been "United Star Ship".

When the mouse is moved off the element, we delete the tooltip from the document, and it will disappear:

File: **tooltips.js** (excerpt)

```
function hideTip(event)
{
  if (typeof event == "undefined")
  {
```

```
      event = window.event;
  }

  var target = getEventTarget(event);

  while (target.className == null ||
      !/(^| )hastooltip( |$)/.test(target.className))
  {
    target = target.parentNode;
  }

  if (target.tooltip != null)
  {
    target.setAttribute("title",
        target.tooltip.childNodes[0].nodeValue);
    target.tooltip.parentNode.removeChild(target.tooltip);
  }

  return false;
}
```

Earlier, in showTip, we created a reference to the tooltip element as a property of the target element. Having done that, we can remove it here without needing to search through the entire DOM. Before we remove the tooltip, we retrieve its content and insert it into the title of the target element, so we can use it again later.

Tip

Do those Objects Exist?

You should check that objects created in other event listeners actually exist before attempting to manipulate them, because events can often misfire, and you can't guarantee that they will occur in a set order.

Discussion

One problem with the code above is that if the target element is close to the right or bottom edge of the browser window, the tooltip will be cut off. To avoid this, we need to make sure there's enough space for the tooltip, and position it accordingly.

By checking, in each dimension, whether the mouse position is less than the browser window size minus the tooltip size, we can tell how far to move the layer in order to get it onto the screen:

File: **tooltips2.js (excerpt)**

```javascript
function showTip(event)
{
  if (typeof event == "undefined")
  {
    event = window.event;
  }

  var target = getEventTarget(event);

  while (target.className == null ||
      !/(^| )hastooltip( |$)/.test(target.className))
  {
    target = target.parentNode;
  }

  var tip = document.createElement("div");
  var content = target.getAttribute("title");

  target.tooltip = tip;
  target.setAttribute("title", "");

  if (target.getAttribute("id") != "")
  {
    tip.setAttribute("id", target.getAttribute("id") + "tooltip");
  }

  tip.className = "tooltip";
  tip.appendChild(document.createTextNode(content));

  var scrollingPosition = getScrollingPosition();
  var cursorPosition = [0, 0];

  if (typeof event.pageX != "undefined" &&
      typeof event.x != "undefined")
  {
    cursorPosition[0] = event.pageX;
    cursorPosition[1] = event.pageY;
  }
  else
  {
    cursorPosition[0] = event.clientX + scrollingPosition[0];
    cursorPosition[1] = event.clientY + scrollingPosition[1];
  }

  tip.style.position = "absolute";
```

```
  tip.style.left = cursorPosition[0] + 10 + "px";
  tip.style.top = cursorPosition[1] + 10 + "px";
  tip.style.visibility = "hidden";

  document.getElementsByTagName("body")[0].appendChild(tip);

  var viewportSize = getViewportSize();

  if (cursorPosition[0] - scrollingPosition[0] + 10 +
      tip.offsetWidth > viewportSize[0] - 25)
  {
    tip.style.left = scrollingPosition[0] + viewportSize[0] - 25 -
        tip.offsetWidth + "px";
  }
  else
  {
    tip.style.left = cursorPosition[0] + 10 + "px";
  }

  if (cursorPosition[1] - scrollingPosition[1] + 10 +
      tip.offsetHeight > viewportSize[1] - 25)
  {
    if (event.clientX > (viewportSize[0] - 25 - tip.offsetWidth))
    {
      tip.style.top = cursorPosition[1] - tip.offsetHeight - 10 +
          "px";
    }
    else
    {
      tip.style.top = scrollingPosition[1] + viewportSize[1] -
          25 - tip.offsetHeight + "px";
    }
  }
  else
  {
    tip.style.top = cursorPosition[1] + 10 + "px";
  }

  tip.style.visibility = "visible";

  return true;
}
```

This function is identical to the previous version until we get to the insertion of
the tooltip element. Just prior to inserting the element, we set its visibility to
"hidden". This means that when it's placed on the page, the layer will occupy

the same space it would take up if it were visible, but the user won't see it on the page. This allows us to measure the tooltip's dimensions, then reposition it without the user seeing it flash up in its original position.

In order to detect whether the layer displays outside of the viewport, we use the position of the cursor relative to the viewport. This could theoretically be obtained by using `clientX`/`clientY`, but remember: Safari gives an incorrect value for this property. Instead, we use our cross-browser values inside `cursorPosition` and subtract the scrolling position (which is the equivalent of `clientX`/`clientY`). The size of the viewport is obtained using the `getViewportSize` function we created in Chapter 7, then, for each dimension, we check whether the cursor position plus the size of the layer is greater than the viewport size (minus an allowance for scrollbars).

If part of the layer is going to appear outside the viewport, we position it by subtracting its dimensions from the viewport size; otherwise, it's positioned normally, using the cursor position.

The only other exception to note is that if the layer would normally appear outside the viewport in both dimensions, when we are positioning it vertically, it is automatically positioned above the cursor. This prevents the layer from appearing directly on top of the cursor and triggering a `mouseout` event. It also prevents the target element from being totally obscured by the tooltip, which would prevent the user from clicking on it.

 Tip

Measuring Visible Tooltip Dimensions

In order for the dimensions of the tooltip to be measured it must first be appended to the document. This will automatically make it appear on the page, so to prevent the user seeing it display in the wrong position, we need to hide it. We do so by setting its `visibility` to `"hidden"` until we have finalized the tooltip's position.

We can't use the more familiar `display` property here, because objects with `display` set to `"none"` are not rendered at all, so they have no dimensions to measure.

Sorting Tables by Column

Tables can be a mine of information, but only if you can understand them properly. Having the ability to sort a table by its different columns allows users to view the data in a way that makes sense to them, and ultimately provides the opportunity for greater understanding.

Solution

To start off, we'll use a semantically meaningful HTML `table`. This will provide us with the structure we need to insert event listeners, inject extra elements, and sort our data:

File: **`sort_tables_by_columns.html`** (excerpt)

```
<table class="sortableTable" cellspacing="0"
    summary="Statistics on Star Ships">
  <thead>
    <tr>
      <th class="c1" scope="col">
        Star Ship Class
      </th>
      <th class="c2" scope="col">
        Power Output (Terawatts)
      </th>
      <th class="c3" scope="col">
        Maximum Warp Speed
      </th>
      <th class="c4" scope="col">
        Captain's Seat Comfort Factor
      </th>
    </tr>
  </thead>
  <tbody>
    <tr>
      <td class="c1">
        USS Enterprise NCC-1701-A
      </td>
      <td class="c2">
        5000
      </td>
      <td class="c3">
        6.0
      </td>
      <td class="c4">
        4/10
      </td>
    </tr>
```

First, we need to set up event listeners on each of our table heading cells. These will listen for clicks to our columns, and trigger a sort on the column that was clicked:

File: **sort_tables_by_columns.js** (excerpt)

```
function initSortableTables()
{
  if (identifyBrowser() != "ie5mac")
  {
    var tables = getElementsByAttribute("class", "sortableTable");

    for (var i = 0; i < tables.length; i++)
    {
      var ths = tables[i].getElementsByTagName("th");

      for (var k = 0; k < ths.length; k++)
      {
        var newA = document.createElement("a");
        newA.setAttribute("href", "#");
        newA.setAttribute("title",
            "Sort by this column in descending order");

        for (var m = 0; m < ths[k].childNodes.length; m++)
        {
          newA.appendChild(ths[k].childNodes[m]);
        }

        ths[k].appendChild(newA);

        attachEventListener(newA, "click", sortColumn, false);
      }
    }
  }

  return true;
}
```

Internet Explorer 5 for Mac has trouble dealing with dynamically generated table content, so we have to specifically exclude it from making any of the tables sortable.

Only tables with the `class sortableTable` will be turned into sortable tables, so `initSortableTable` navigates the DOM to find the table heading cells in these tables. Once they're found, the contents of each heading cell are wrapped in a hyperlink—this allows keyboard users to select a column to sort the table by—and an event listener is set on these links to monitor `click` events, and execute `sortColumn` in response. The `title` attribute of each link is also set, providing the user with information on what will happen when the link is clicked.

The `sortColumn` function is fairly lengthy, owing to the fact that it must navigate and rearrange the entire table structure each time a heading cell is clicked:

File: **sort_tables_by_columns.js** (excerpt)

```
function sortColumn(event)
{
  if (typeof event == "undefined")
  {
    event = window.event;
  }

  var targetA = getEventTarget(event);

  while (targetA.nodeName.toLowerCase() != "a")
  {
  targetA = targetA.parentNode;
  }

  var targetTh = targetA.parentNode;
  var targetTr = targetTh.parentNode;
  var targetTrChildren = targetTr.getElementsByTagName("th");
  var targetTable = targetTr.parentNode.parentNode;
  var targetTbody = targetTable.getElementsByTagName("tbody")[0];
  var targetTrs = targetTbody.getElementsByTagName("tr");
  var targetColumn = 0;

  for (var i = 0; i < targetTrChildren.length; i++)
  {
    targetTrChildren[i].className = targetTrChildren[i].className.
      replace(/(^| )sortedDescending( |$)/, "$1");
    targetTrChildren[i].className = targetTrChildren[i].className.
      replace(/(^| )sortedAscending( |$)/, "$1");

    if (targetTrChildren[i] == targetTh)
    {
      targetColumn = i;

      if (targetTrChildren[i].sortOrder == "descending" &&
          targetTrChildren[i].clicked)
      {
        targetTrChildren[i].sortOrder = "ascending";
        targetTrChildren[i].className += " sortedAscending";
```

```
      targetA.setAttribute("title",
          "Sort by this column in descending order");
    }
    else
    {
      if (targetTrChildren[i].sortOrder == "ascending" &&
          !targetTrChildren[i].clicked)
      {
        targetTrChildren[i].className += " sortedAscending";
      }

      else
      {
        targetTrChildren[i].sortOrder = "descending";
        targetTrChildren[i].className += " sortedDescending";
        targetA.setAttribute("title",
            "Sort by this column in ascending order");
      }
    }

    targetTrChildren[i].clicked = true;
  }
  else
  {
    targetTrChildren[i].clicked = false;

    if (targetTrChildren[i].sortOrder == "ascending")
    {
      targetTrChildren[i].firstChild.setAttribute("title",
          "Sort by this column in ascending order");
    }
    else
    {
      targetTrChildren[i].firstChild.setAttribute("title",
          "Sort by this column in descending order");
    }
  }
}

var newTbody = targetTbody.cloneNode(false);

for (var i = 0; i < targetTrs.length; i++)
{
  var newTrs = newTbody.childNodes;
  var targetValue = getInternalText(
      targetTrs[i].getElementsByTagName("td")[targetColumn]);
```

```
for (var j = 0; j < newTrs.length; j++)
{
  var newValue = getInternalText(
      newTrs[j].getElementsByTagName("td")[targetColumn]);

  if (targetValue == parseInt(targetValue, 10) &&
      newValue == parseInt(newValue, 10))
  {
    targetValue = parseInt(targetValue, 10);
    newValue = parseInt(newValue, 10);
  }
  else if (targetValue == parseFloat(targetValue) &&
      newValue == parseFloat(newValue))
  {
    targetValue = parseFloat(targetValue, 10);
    newValue = parseFloat(newValue, 10);
  }

  if (targetTrChildren[targetColumn].sortOrder ==
      "descending")
  {
    if (targetValue >= newValue)
    {
      break;
    }
  }
  else
  {
    if (targetValue <= newValue)
    {
      break;
    }
  }
}

if (j >= newTrs.length)
{
  newTbody.appendChild(targetTrs[i].cloneNode(true));
}
else
{
  newTbody.insertBefore(targetTrs[i].cloneNode(true),
      newTrs[j]);
}
}
```

```
        targetTable.replaceChild(newTbody, targetTbody);

        stopDefaultAction(event);

        return false;
}
```

The first `for` loop that occurs after all the structural variables have been defined sets the respective states for each of the table heading cells when one of them is clicked. Not only are classes maintained to identify the heading cell on which the table is currently sorted, but a special `sortOrder` property is maintained on each cell to determine the order in which that column is sorted. Initially, a column will be sorted in descending order, but if a heading cell is clicked twice consecutively, the sort order will be changed to reflect an ascending sequence. Each heading cell remembers the sort order state it exhibited most recently, and the column is returned to that state when its heading cell is re-selected. The `title` of the hyperlink for a clicked heading cell is also rewritten depending upon the current sort order, and what the sort order would be if the user clicked on it again.

The second `for` loop sorts each of the rows that's contained in the body of the table. A copy of the original `tbody` is created to store the reordered table rows, and initially this copy is empty. As each row in the original `tbody` is scanned, the contents of the table cell in the column on which we're sorting is compared with the rows already in the copy.

In order to find the contents of the table cell, we use the function `getInternalText`:

File: **sort_tables_by_columns.js** (excerpt)

```
function getInternalText(target)
{
  var elementChildren = target.childNodes;
  var internalText = "";

  for (var i = 0; i < elementChildren.length; i++)
  {
    if (elementChildren[i].nodeType == 3)
    {
      if (!/^\s*$/.test(elementChildren[i].nodeValue))
      {
        internalText += elementChildren[i].nodeValue;
      }
    }
```

```
    else
    {
      internalText += getInternalText(elementChildren[i]);
    }
  }

  return internalText;
}
```

getInternalText extracts all of the text inside an element—including all of its descendant elements—by recursively calling itself for each child element and concatenating the resultant values together. This allows us to access the text inside a table cell, irrespective of whether it's wrapped in elements such as spans, strongs, or ems. Any text nodes that are purely whitespace (spaces, tabs, or new lines) are ignored via a regular expression check.

When sortColumn finds a row in the copy whose sorted table cell value is "less" than the one we're scanning, we insert a copy of the scanned row into the copied tbody. For a column in ascending order, we simply reverse this comparison: the value of the row in the copy must be "greater" than that of the scanned row.

However, before a comparison is made, we check whether the contents of the sorted table cell can be interpreted as an integer or a float; if so, the comparison values are converted. This makes sure that columns that contain numbers are sorted properly; string comparisons will produce different results than number comparisons.

Once all of our original rows have been copied into the new tbody, that element is used to replace the old one, and we have our sorted table!

Using the sortableDescending and sortableAscending classes, which are assigned to the currently sorted table heading cells, we can use CSS to inform the user which column the table is sorted on, and how it is sorted, as shown in Figure 13.2 and Figure 13.3.

Figure 13.2. A sortable table sorted in descending order on the fourth column

Star Ship Class	Power Output (Terra Watts)	Maximum Warp Speed	Captain's Seat Comfort Factor ▼
Ferengi Trading Vessel	500	4.0	8/10
USS Enterprise NCC-1701-D	6500	8.5	5/10
USS Enterprise NCC-1701-A	5000	6.0	4/10
Klingon Bird of Prey	3000	6.5	1/10
Class E Geo-stationary Satellite	2	0.1	0/10

Figure 13.3. A sortable table sorted in ascending order on the second column

Star Ship Class	Power Output (Terra Watts) ▲	Maximum Warp Speed	Captain's Seat Comfort Factor
Class E Geo-stationary Satellite	2	0.1	0/10
Ferengi Trading Vessel	500	4.0	8/10
Klingon Bird of Prey	3000	6.5	1/10
USS Enterprise NCC-1701-A	5000	6.0	4/10
USS Enterprise NCC-1701-D	6500	8.5	5/10

Summary

The two main pillars of DHTML are the capturing of events, and the reorganization and creation of page elements via the DOM. Using these principles, it's possible to capture many of the different ways that users interact with a page and make the interface respond accordingly.

As can be seen by the number and quality of JavaScript-enhanced web applications that are now available, the features DHTML can bring to new interfaces represents one of the biggest growth areas for innovative JavaScript. The foundations and basic examples shown in this chapter give you a sense of the power that it can deliver inside a user's browser. We'll expand upon this further in the following chapters as we build some really interesting interfaces.

Time and Motion

The fundamental structure of the Internet is based upon a series of static states, which are generally called pages. In the last chapter, we saw how DHTML could break down this model and create a number of separate states within the same page by reacting to a user's interaction. In this chapter, we take this concept one step further.

Instead of viewing a web page as a discrete set of states, JavaScript allows us to use time and motion to produce truly dynamic pages. Objects can change over time, move fluidly around the page, and be manipulated by users in a manner analogous to real-world interaction. Operations that are now deeply ingrained in desktop applications—such as drag-and-drop objects or slider controls—are good examples of this behavior, and have not yet been made part of the Web.

In the following solutions, you'll learn the basic steps involved in moving objects around a page, then apply these principles as we build real-time interactive systems such as slider controls and drag-and-drop interfaces.

Using `setTimeout` and `setInterval`

Both of these functions are used to execute JavaScript code after a given time period. However, each does so in a way that's more appropriate for some situations than others.

Solution

Both `setTimeout` and `setInterval` have exactly the same syntax. A string of code and a time period in milliseconds is passed to the function, and the code is evaluated after the time period has elapsed.

The difference between these functions is that `setInterval` automatically repeats the execution of the code at ongoing intervals of the time period, whereas `setTimeout` executes the code just once.

Although this makes it seem that `setTimeout` is applicable only to one-off actions, it can still be used to perform repeated operations if we create a **functional loop**—a function that executes again, after a delay, by means of a `setTimeout` call:

File: **settimeout_setinterval.js**

```
showTime();

function showTime()
{
  var today = new Date();
  alert("The time is: " + today.toString());
  setTimeout("showTime()", 5000);
}
```

Once this call is executed, the time will be displayed *approximately* once every five seconds. If `setInterval` were used, the code would look like this:

File: **settimeout_setinterval2.js**

```
setInterval("showTime()", 5000);

function showTime()
{
  var today = new Date();
  alert("The time is: " + today.toString());
}
```

While the two approaches may look extremely similar, and would display very similar results, the most telling difference is this: the `setTimeout` approach does not execute `showTime` every five seconds; it executes `showTime` *five seconds after each call to* `setTimeout`. This means that if the main body of the `showTime` function took two seconds to execute, the function would be executed once every seven seconds. `setInterval`, on the other hand, is not bound by the operation of the function it calls. It simply executes that function regularly at the specified interval.

It is for this reason that `setInterval` is best used for operations in which you require accurate performance at a regular interval. `setTimeout` is more suited to situations in which you don't want to run the risk of having successive calls interfere with each other, particularly where each call involves heavy calculation and long processing times.

Using a Function Pointer

Tip

As well as a string of code, both timing functions can take a function pointer as their first arguments, although Internet Explorer 5 for Mac will silently fail if you do this.

If you use `setTimeout` and `setInterval` in this fashion, they can point to a function that's defined elsewhere:

```
setTimeout(showTime, 500);

function showTime()
{
  var today = new Date();
  alert("The time is: " + today.toString());
}
```

Alternatively, an anonymous function can be declared inline:

```
setTimeout(function(){var today = new Date();
    alert("The time is: " + today.toString());}, 500);
```

Discussion

If left untended, `setInterval` will continue to execute the same code over and over until the browser window is closed, or the user moves to another page. However, there is a way to stop both `setInterval` and `setTimeout` from executing.

When executed, a `setInterval` call returns a **timer ID** that allows you to access the timing function in the future. By passing this ID to `clearInterval`, you are able to halt the execution of that timed process:

File: **settimeout_setinterval3.js (excerpt)**

```
var intervalProcess = setInterval("alert('GOAL!')", 3000);
⋮
var stopGoalLink = document.getElementById("stopGoalLink");
attachEventListener(stopGoalLink, "click", stopGoal, false);
⋮
function stopGoal()
{
  clearInterval(intervalProcess);
}
```

If stopGoalLink is clicked at any time, the interval process will be cancelled and no further iterations of the interval will be executed. The same can be done to a setTimeout call, if it is cancelled before the timeout period has expired:

File: **settimeout_setinterval4.js (excerpt)**

```
var timeoutProcess = setTimeout("alert('GOAL!')", 3000);
⋮
var stopGoalLink = document.getElementById("stopGoalLink");
attachEventListener(stopGoalLink, "click", stopGoal, false);
⋮
function stopGoal()
{
  clearTimeout(timeoutProcess);
}
```

Making an Object Move Along a Set Path

Animations use small visual changes at regular time intervals to trick the brain into seeing fluid movement. This technique has been used for well over 150 years to achieve animated effects across various media, and as we're about to see, computers also use this approach—albeit in a fairly refined fashion.

Solution

If you want to move an absolutely or relatively positioned object, say, 500 pixels from the left edge of the browser window, we can set object.style.left = "500px"; however, the effect that the end user sees will be something akin to teleportation. In order to create a smooth movement from point A to point B, we must divide the intervening space into a series of points, then position the object at each of those points, in turn, for a fraction of a second. This technique creates the illusion that the object is moving towards its destination.

This discussion gives us the perfect opportunity to use one of JavaScript's time delay functions. By moving the object 25 pixels to the right every 50 milliseconds, we can eventually get it to move all the way to our end-point 500 pixels across the screen:

File: **move_object_along_path.js (excerpt)**

```
addLoadListener(initSoccerBall);

function initSoccerBall()
{
  document.getElementById("soccerBall").animationTimer =
      setInterval(
       'moveObject(document.getElementById("soccerBall"),
      500, 0, 25)', 50);
}

function moveObject(target, destinationLeft, destinationTop,
    maxSpeed)
{
  var currentLeft = parseInt(retrieveComputedStyle(target,
      "left"));
  var currentTop = parseInt(retrieveComputedStyle(target, "top"));

  if (isNaN(currentLeft))
  {
    currentLeft = 0;
  }

  if (isNaN(currentTop))
  {
    currentTop = 0;
  }

  if (currentLeft < destinationLeft)
  {
    currentLeft += maxSpeed;

    if (currentLeft > destinationLeft)
    {
      currentLeft = destinationLeft;
    }
  }
  else
  {
    currentLeft -= maxSpeed;
```

```
    if (currentLeft < destinationLeft)
    {
      currentLeft = destinationLeft;
    }
  }

  if (currentTop < destinationTop)
  {
    currentTop += maxSpeed;

    if (currentTop > destinationTop)
    {
      currentTop = destinationTop;
    }
  }
  else
  {
    currentTop -= maxSpeed;

    if (currentTop < destinationTop)
    {
      currentTop = destinationTop;
    }
  }

  target.style.left = currentLeft + "px";
  target.style.top = currentTop + "px";

  if (currentLeft == destinationLeft &&
      currentTop == destinationTop)
  {
    clearInterval(target.animationTimer);
  }
}
```

Our soccer ball animation is set up to execute once the page loads, using the addLoadListener function from Chapter 1. Once it executes, this load event handler calls setInterval, requesting a call to moveObject every 50 milliseconds with the appropriate arguments. This generates the appearance of movement shown in Figure 14.1. The setInterval timer ID is assigned as an extended property of our target object, so we can stop it from executing once the object has reached its destination.

setInterval Inefficiencies and Alternatives

Although getting `setInterval` to execute `document.getElementById` for each iteration may be a little inefficient, the alternative—using an anonymous function to create a closure—would not allow the animation to work in Internet Explorer 5 for Mac. Using a global variable would be downright messy.

`moveObject` takes four arguments: the object to be moved, the final position of the left edge of the object (in pixels) (*destinationLeft*), the final position of the top edge of the object (*destinationTop*), and the number of pixels that the object will be moved each time (*maxSpeed*).

Inside `moveObject`, our first task is to obtain the target object's current position using the `retrieveComputedStyle` function from Chapter 12. This custom function is used so that the initial position of the object can be applied inside a style sheet, and still be retrieved via the function. If no valid value is found for either of the left or top positions, they will be set to zero.

Position Detection Alternatives

This method of position detection relies upon our setting explicit values for the object's position in the CSS, or wanting the animation to start at the origin (0, 0). It is possible to detect the position of an element whose location is not explicitly set—to do so, we use the `getPosition` function from Chapter 13. However, for the reasons explained there, it will not be reliably accurate.

By using the `left` and `top` style properties, `moveObject` assumes that the target object is positioned relatively or absolutely. Statically positioned objects will not be affected by either of these properties, so if you're going to perform animation on static objects, you can replace those property assignments with `marginLeft` or `marginTop`. However, the animation of statically positioned objects results in changes to the surrounding document, which is usually an undesired effect. Hence, this function operates upon relatively or absolutely positioned elements.

Once we've calculated the current position of the object, we must calculate the position of the point to which we want it to move. Depending upon the direction in which the object is moving, we must either add or subtract *maxSpeed*. The direction is determined by comparing the current position to the destination position. If the current position is less than the destination, the element must be moved right and/or down. If the current position is greater than the destination, the element must be moved right and/or up. The destination position is calculated independently for each axis; at the same time, we check whether the planned movement will carry the element beyond its destination point. If it will, the new position is set to equal the destination point.

Once the planned values have been checked, they are assigned to the element's `style.left` and `style.top` properties, which changes its position. If, after this move, the object has reached both its destination ordinates, `clearInterval` is called using the reference to the animation timer that we created earlier. This stops the object's animation. Otherwise, execution continues as normal and `moveObject` will be called again as per the original `setInterval` call.

Figure 14.1. Simulating movement between an object's origin and its destination

Discussion

Movement in the real world is a far more complex process than is moving an object 25 pixels to the right every 1/20th of a second. You could write an entire book on computer animation—and many have—so we won't delve too deeply into it here.

A lot can be gained by experimenting with different types of movement and making subtle changes to the ways that you move objects; however, such experiments can become very specific to the scenario on which you're working, which can make it difficult to produce an all-encompassing solution.

A simple example of more realistic motion is shown below. This modified version of moveObject simulates deceleration in an object's movement as it approaches its destination, as shown in Figure 14.2.

Figure 14.2. Decreasing the distance traveled per frame as the object approaches its destination

File: **move_object_along_path2.js** (excerpt)

```
function moveObjectDecelerate(target, destinationLeft,
    destinationTop, maxSpeed)
{
  var currentLeft = parseInt(retrieveComputedStyle(target,
    "left"));
  var currentTop = parseInt(retrieveComputedStyle(target, "top"));

  if (isNaN(currentLeft))
  {
    currentLeft = 0;
  }

  if (isNaN(currentTop))
  {
    currentTop = 0;
  }

  if (typeof target.floatingPointLeft == "undefined")
  {
    target.floatingPointLeft = currentLeft;
```

```
      target.floatingPointTop = currentTop;
}

var decelerateLeft = 1 + Math.abs(destinationLeft -
    target.floatingPointLeft) / 10;
var decelerateTop = 1 + Math.abs(destinationTop -
    target.floatingPointTop) / 10;

if (decelerateLeft > maxSpeed)
{
  decelerateLeft = maxSpeed;
}

if (decelerateTop > maxSpeed)
{
  decelerateTop = maxSpeed;
}

if (target.floatingPointLeft < destinationLeft)
{
  target.floatingPointLeft += decelerateLeft;

  if (target.floatingPointLeft > destinationLeft)
  {
    target.floatingPointLeft = destinationLeft;
  }
}
else
{
  target.floatingPointLeft -= decelerateLeft;

  if (target.floatingPointLeft < destinationLeft)
  {
    target.floatingPointLeft = destinationLeft;
  }
}

if (target.floatingPointTop < destinationTop)
{
  target.floatingPointTop += decelerateTop;

  if (target.floatingPointTop > destinationTop)
  {
    target.floatingPointTop = destinationTop;
  }
}
```

```
else
{
  target.floatingPointTop -= decelerateTop;

  if (target.floatingPointTop < destinationTop)
  {
    target.floatingPointTop = destinationTop;
  }
}

target.style.left = parseInt(target.floatingPointLeft) + "px";
target.style.top = parseInt(target.floatingPointTop) + "px";

if (target.floatingPointLeft == destinationLeft &&
    target.floatingPointTop == destinationTop)
{
  clearInterval(target.animationTimer);
}
}
```

The major difference between `moveObjectDecelerate` and `moveObject` lies in how far the object is moved in each step. Instead of directly using *maxSpeed* to determine how far the object is moved each time, a relationship is set up between the distance remaining between an object and its destination, and that object's next move. The gist of the algorithm used here is that the distance between the element's current position and its destination is divided by ten. We add one to the resulting figure to make sure that the object moves at least one pixel at each step. Although this approach might seem to suggest that there will be only ten steps between the object's origin and its destination, remember that each time the object moves, the distance between it and its destination is lessened, and so, too, is the calculated increment. As the element moves closer to its destination, it gradually slows down, then comes to a stop on its destination point, as shown in Figure 14.2.

We divide the difference between the element's current position and its destination by ten because this approach creates a nicely paced movement. As with any of the variables in this solution, changing this value will produce a different type of movement; change the variables yourself to create a movement that's just right for *your* animations.

 Tip

Magnitude vs Distance

When we perform the calculations for `decelerateLeft` and `decelerateTop`, we're interested in the magnitude of motion, not the direction, which we determine separately. In order to make sure that we don't get a negative number, the `Math.abs` method is used to obtain the absolute (i.e., positive) distance remaining.

maxSpeed is used to control the speed of the element. The values calculated for the steps of movement can be very large, particularly in the animation's early stages. This would normally cause a large jump in the object's position, creating less-than-ideal animation. By capping its speed with *maxSpeed*, we maintain a nice, smooth flow.

This discussion has presented just one method by which we can calculate an object's deceleration. Depending upon the type of movement you want to achieve, different numbers and different algorithms can be used to calculate an object's velocity. You can make an object accelerate, decelerate, stop gently, stop abruptly, or bounce around on elastic. Robert Penner has created quite a few different models of movement for Flash animation[1] that could easily be transferred from ActionScript to JavaScript. Try some of them yourself.

Making Animation Less Jerky

As it's only an illusion, the best an animation can do is to fool the eye into thinking that an object is moving naturally. A jerky animation breaks this illusion by allowing the user to see the discrete parts that make up the animation. Fortunately, there are a few tricks that you can use to minimize your animation's jerkiness.

Solution

The smoothness of JavaScript animation is governed by quite a few factors:

❑ the length of time between each animation frame

❑ the pixel distance (or amount of change) between frames

❑ the complexity of the animation that's being performed

❑ the speed of the computer on which the animation is running

❑ the speed of the browser in which the animation is viewed

---

[1] http://www.robertpenner.com/easing

You can influence some of these factors; others are beyond your control. Here's a little insight into each area.

Animation Frame Times

In order to move an object across the screen in the previous solution, we used a time interval of 50 milliseconds, which equates to a frame rate of roughly 20 frames per second (20 Hz). As a comparison, movies use a frame rate of 24 Hz or 25 Hz, while television standards vary around the world from 25 Hz to 30 Hz. Although 20 Hz will not produce a perfectly smooth animation, it will produce a reasonably smooth result. The reason why we used this less-than-perfect number was because most average computer systems are not able to handle a higher frame rate. So, to ensure some consistency of speed across systems, it's better to use a lower frame rate than the optimal rate.

Note that increasing the frame rate *will* reduce jerkiness if the computer is capable of rendering the animation at the speed you've chosen. So, if the interval between `moveObject` calls was set to 25 milliseconds, we would achieve a rate of approximately 40 Hz on systems that could handle it:

```
setTimeout(function(){moveObject(target, destinationX,
    destinationY, maxSpeed);}, 25);
```

The frame rates that different computers can handle depend upon the complexity of the animation, how much of the CPU is being used for other applications, and various other factors. So, it's worth your while to experiment with different frame rates for different circumstances.

Doubling the Frame Rate Doubles the Speed

If you double the frame rate of an animation, effectively, you're doubling its speed. So, if you double the frame rate but want an object to cover the same distance in the same amount of time, you must halve the distance the object travels between frames.

Changing Between Frames

Small movements are less noticeable than large movements. On a computer monitor, the smallest possible movement shifts an object by one pixel[2]—the

---

[2]Dynamic antialiasing, supported by Flash and the 3D graphics engines of modern games, makes it possible to display movement in steps that are smaller than a pixel. However, in the world of DHTML, antialiasing is not practical.

minimum unit of display. By composing an animation using the smallest units possible (i.e., one-pixel shifts), you can reduce jerkiness to a minimum; however, you'll also affect the speed at which objects move.

In the example we discussed in the previous solution, we required the object to move 500 pixels at 20 frames per second. If the object moves 25 pixels at a time, it takes one second to reach its destination. If it were to move only one pixel at a time, it would take 25 seconds to travel 500 pixels. Hence, a compromise must be reached between the speed of the animation and its smoothness (the number of discrete points that are used to represent its movement). Smoothness can also be affected by changing the frame rate, as noted above.

Complexity of the Animation

Probably the biggest time-drain in object animation occurs while the browser and computer draw the image on the screen. The browser needs to calculate how the object will appear on the page, as well as how it interacts with other elements; the computer needs to interpret all this information, then get the display onto the monitor.

If you have large animated areas—or a number of objects that are animating simultaneously—this will affect the time it takes for objects to be redrawn, and impact on how jerky their movements look. By reducing the size of an animation, or reducing the number of animations occurring concurrently, you will decrease the complexity of the animation and decrease its jerkiness.

The Speed of the Computer

At its most basic level, JavaScript animation is about calculation. Finding objects, multiplying numbers, drawing colors—all these steps rely on the computer's processing power. Yet your viewers' computing power will vary, and this will affect the way in which your animation performs.

Users' hardware quality is out of your control, but you can ensure that your JavaScript code is as lean as possible and doesn't require redundant processing that could waste CPU power. You may also want to consider the complexity of your animation, as noted above.

The Speed of the Browser

Different browsers obviously use different application code to perform various functions. The time it takes Internet Explorer to perform a regular expression is different from the time it takes Safari to do the same thing; the time it takes Mozilla to calculate the styles for an element is different from the time it takes Opera to perform those calculations.

The differing engines used by browsers affect the way your animations perform, but the choice of browsers your visitors use is out of your hands. The most pragmatic approach you can take is to make sure your JavaScript code and animations are optimized for best performance using the other tips in this solution.

Implementing Drag-and-drop Behavior

Dragging an object and dropping it onto something else is an extremely powerful visual metaphor. It has become a deeply ingrained behavior in many operating systems and applications; Microsoft even went so far as to include proprietary drag-and-drop functionality in Internet Explorer. But, by using some modern JavaScript, you can use this technique on your web pages with full cross-browser support.

Solution

There are two main steps to creating a drag-and-drop interface: defining the visual movement of objects as they are dragged, and defining the "hot zones" to which they can be dragged.

Drag-and-drop behavior can be added to almost any HTML element, but for the purposes of this example we will use as a starting point the basic structure for a shopping cart:

File: **drag_n_drop.html (excerpt)**

```
<ul id="products">
  <li id="shirtArsenal">
    Arsenal Shirt
  </li>
  <li id="shirtLiverpool">
    Liverpool Shirt
  </li>
  <li id="shirtChelsea">
```

```
      Chelsea Shirt
    </li>
    <li id="shirtWestham">
      Westham Shirt
    </li>
  </ul>
  <form id="shoppingCart">
  </form>
```

First, we need to attach event listeners to the draggable objects so that when a user clicks and holds the mouse button on one of them, that object enters a dragging state. We'll use the addLoadListener function from Chapter 1 to install all the listeners when the page loads:

File: **drag_n_drop.js** (excerpt)

```
addLoadListener(initDragNDrop);

function initDragNDrop()
{
  if (identifyBrowser().indexOf("ie") >= 0 &&
      identifyOS() == "mac")
  {
    return false;
  }

  var LIs= document.getElementById("products").
      getElementsByTagName("li");

  for (var i = 0; i < LIs.length; i++)
  {
    attachEventListener(LIs[i], "mousedown", mousedownDragNDrop,
        false);
    LIs[i].style.cursor = "move";
  }
}
```

A browser detection technique from Chapter 11 is used to prevent Internet Explorer 5 for Mac from executing the script. We take this precaution because the values the script returns for object positions and mouse cursor events in this browser are a little buggy; it's safest to serve degraded functionality to IE 5 for Mac.

In all other browsers, the attachEventListener function we saw in Chapter 13 is used to create a cross-browser event listener that fires mousedownDragNDrop when one of the draggable objects receives a mousedown event. As an additional usability helper, when a list item is made draggable, we change its `style.cursor` property to `"move"`. This means that when users mouse over a draggable item, they will be informed that it is draggable by a change in the cursor's appearance.

`mouseDownDragNDrop` makes an object ready to be dragged. It calculates position coordinates, and attaches event handlers that react to mouse movements:

File: **drag_n_drop.js** (excerpt)

```
function mousedownDragNDrop(event)
{
  if (typeof event == "undefined")
  {
    event = window.event;
  }

  if (typeof event.pageX == "undefined")
  {
    event.pageX = event.clientX + getScrollingPosition()[0];
    event.pageY = event.clientY + getScrollingPosition()[1];
  }

  var target = getEventTarget(event);

  while (target.nodeName.toLowerCase() != "li")
  {
    target = target.parentNode;
  }

  document.currentTarget = target;

  var currentLeft = parseInt(target.style.left);
  var currentTop = parseInt(target.style.top);

  if (isNaN(currentLeft))
  {
    currentLeft = "0";
  }

  if (isNaN(currentTop))
  {
    currentTop = "0";
  }

  if (typeof target.originLeft == "undefined")
  {
    target.originLeft = currentLeft;
```

```
    target.originTop = currentTop;
  }

  target.clickOriginX = event.pageX;
  target.clickOriginY = event.pageY;
  target.differenceX = currentLeft - event.pageX;
  target.differenceY = currentTop - event.pageY;

  attachEventListener(document, "mousemove",
      mousemoveCheckThreshold, false);
  attachEventListener(document, "mouseup",
      mouseupCancelThreshold, false);

  stopDefaultAction(event);

  return false;
}
```

You might think that it would be best to put event listeners for `mousemove` and `mouseup` on the draggable object. However, because a browser's display can sometimes get out of sync with the cursor, this approach would make it possible to move the cursor outside of the element while the mouse button was still depressed. Were this to happen, the object would stop moving, and the user would have to go back and click on it again. Also, when the mouse button was released, the `mouseup` event wouldn't register on the draggable object, so the `mousemove` event listener would be active whenever the mouse cursor moved over that object. Confusion would most certainly ensue.

To avoid these problems, we'll install the event listeners onto the `document`. This way, they'll be triggered no matter where the cursor is positioned in relation to the object.

Our listeners need to know which object is currently being dragged, so we've created a property—`document.currentTarget`—to keep track of the currently dragged element. To detect this element, we use the `getEventTarget` function from Chapter 13. However, as we saw in that chapter, this function returns the deepest element in the DOM that is affected by the event, not necessarily the element to which this event listener was attached. To make sure we have the right target element, we check whether the element returned from `getEventTarget` is of the type we need; if it's not, we iterate upwards through its ancestor elements until we find the element we want. As you write the JavaScript code for this process, you'll need to have some knowledge of the structure of your page, but this is the easiest method of consistently finding the target element.

`originLeft` and `originTop` are added as properties of the draggable object the first time it is clicked upon; they store the value of the object's original position so that it can be returned to the origin if an invalid drop is made. `clickOriginX` and `clickOriginY` store the coordinates of the mousedown event itself. These values are used later to determine how far from the mousedown point the user has moved the cursor. `differenceX` and `differenceY` store the difference between the position of the top-left corner of the object and the location of the mousedown event. This information is required because, though we'll use the cursor's coordinates to position the draggable object, the coordinate system used by the cursor differs from that used by the object. The coordinates of the mousedown event (`event.pageX` and `event.pageY`) are calculated using the solution devised in Chapter 13, and require the `getScrollingPosition` function from Chapter 7.

Once a mouse button has been depressed on a draggable object, mouse activity is monitored by two event listeners: `mousemoveCheckThreshold` and `mouseupCancelThreshold`. These are merely interim listeners that allow linked items to be dragged. If the draggable object is a link, or contains any links, those links will still be clickable, but once the user moves the cursor more than three pixels with the mouse button depressed, the list item will enter drag mode.

`mousemoveCheckThreshold` detects whether the cursor has moved those three pixels:

File: **drag_n_drop.js** (excerpt)

```
function mousemoveCheckThreshold(event)
{
  if (typeof event == "undefined")
  {
    event = window.event;
  }

  if (typeof event.pageX == "undefined")
  {
    event.pageX = event.clientX + getScrollingPosition()[0];
    event.pageY = event.clientY + getScrollingPosition()[1];
  }

  var target = document.currentTarget;

  if (Math.abs(target.clickOriginX - event.pageX) > 3 ||
      Math.abs(target.clickOriginY - event.pageY) > 3)
  {
    detachEventListener(document, "mousemove",
      mousemoveCheckThreshold, false);
```

```
    detachEventListener(document, "mouseup",
        mouseupCancelThreshold, false);

  attachEventListener(document, "mousemove", mousemoveDragNDrop,
      false);
  attachEventListener(document, "mouseup", mouseupDragNDrop,
      false);
  attachEventListener(document, "click", clickDragNDrop, false);
  }

  stopDefaultAction(event);

  return false;
}
```

Once `mousemoveCheckThreshold` detects the required movement, it removes the interim event listeners and attaches the real drag-and-drop listeners. We also add a `click` event listener to prevent any links from being followed when the mouse button is released.

The second interim listener, `mouseupCancelThreshold` is triggered when the user releases the mouse button without moving the cursor more than three pixels in any direction. This simply removes our interim listeners, cancelling the drag operation that would otherwise have been initiated:

File: **drag_n_drop.js (excerpt)**

```
function mouseupCancelThreshold()
{
  detachEventListener(document, "mousemove",
      mousemoveCheckThreshold, false);
  detachEventListener(document, "mouseup", mouseupCancelThreshold,
      false);

  return false;
}
```

In `mousemoveDragNDrop`, we use the variables initialized in `mousedownDragNDrop` to display the draggable object in the right place:

File: **drag_n_drop.js (excerpt)**

```
function mousemoveDragNDrop(event)
{
  if (typeof event == "undefined")
  {
    event = window.event;
```

```
}

if (typeof event.pageX == "undefined")
{
  event.pageX = event.clientX + getScrollingPosition()[0];
  event.pageY = event.clientY + getScrollingPosition()[1];
}

var target = document.currentTarget;

target.style.left = event.pageX + target.differenceX + "px";
target.style.top = event.pageY + target.differenceY + "px";

stopDefaultAction(event);

return true;
}
```

The vertical and horizontal positions of the cursor are added to the stored
differenceX and differenceY values for the dragged object, and are then assigned to its top and left style properties. This has the effect of moving the
object around with the cursor.

Applying the Script to Static Elements

The left and top properties only apply to relatively or absolutely positioned
elements. If you must apply this script to static elements, those properties
can be replaced with the marginLeft and marginTop properties.

mousemoveDragNDrop also calls the stopDefaultAction function we saw in
Chapter 13 in order to prevent standard actions—such as text selection—from
occurring while an object is being dragged.

When the mouse button is released, we want the dragging effect to cease. This
is achieved using the mouseupDragNDrop function:

File: **drag_n_drop.js** (excerpt)

```
function mouseupDragNDrop(event)
{
  if (typeof event == "undefined")
  {
    event = window.event;
  }

  if (typeof event.pageX == "undefined")
```

```
{
  event.pageX = event.clientX + getScrollingPosition()[0];
  event.pageY = event.clientY + getScrollingPosition()[1];
}

var hotZone = document.getElementById("shoppingCart");
var hotZonePosition = getPosition(hotZone);
var target = document.currentTarget;

if (!((event.pageX > hotZonePosition[0]) &&
    (event.pageX < hotZonePosition[0] + hotZone.offsetWidth) &&
    (event.pageY > hotZonePosition[1]) &&
    (event.pageY < hotZonePosition[1] + hotZone.offsetHeight)))
{
  target.style.left = target.originLeft + "px";
  target.style.top = target.originTop + "px";
}
else
{
  var cartInput = document.getElementById("cartInput");

  if (cartInput == null)
  {
    var cartInput = document.createElement("input");

    cartInput.setAttribute("id", "cartInput");
    cartInput.setAttribute("name", "cartInput");
    cartInput.setAttribute("type", "hidden");
    cartInput.setAttribute("value", target.getAttribute("id"));
    document.getElementById("shoppingCart").
        appendChild(cartInput);
  }
  else
  {
    cartInput.setAttribute("value",
        cartInput.getAttribute("value") + "," +
        target.getAttribute("id"));
  }

  // In a practical system, you would probably submit the form
  alert("Item dropped on shopping cart!");
  target.style.left = target.originLeft + "px";
  target.style.top = target.originTop + "px";
}

detachEventListener(document, "mousemove", mousemoveDragNDrop,
```

```
      false);
  detachEventListener(document, "mouseup", mouseupDragNDrop,
      false);

  return true;
}
```

Here, the last two calls to the `detachEventListener` function from Chapter 13 remove the event listeners from the `document`, meaning that further interaction won't occur until the user clicks on another draggable object.

Before that, we determine whether the draggable object has been placed on the "hot zone," or whether it should return to its original position. The rather verbose `if` statement in the middle of the function determines whether the current cursor position falls within the boundaries of the hot zone object. If it doesn't, the dragged object is returned to its original position. If an object has been placed in the hot zone, an action is performed. In this example, we create a hidden form field that stores the value of the dragged item, but it could just as easily write to a cookie or send off a remote scripting call.

Lastly, the `clickDragNDrop` function cancels any `click` events that arise during the drag-and-drop process. This stops links from being followed after the mouse button has been released:

File: **drag_n_drop.js** (excerpt)

```
function clickDragNDrop(event)
{
  if (typeof event == "undefined")
  {
    event = window.event;
  }

  detachEventListener(document, "click", clickDragNDrop, false);

  stopDefaultAction(event);

  return true;
}
```

`clickDragNDrop` also removes the event listener that called it; otherwise, links would remain unclickable after you'd finished dragging the item.

The finished script lets you create drag-and-drop interfaces like the one shown in Figure 14.3.

Figure 14.3. Using drag-and-drop behavior to create relationships between two separate objects

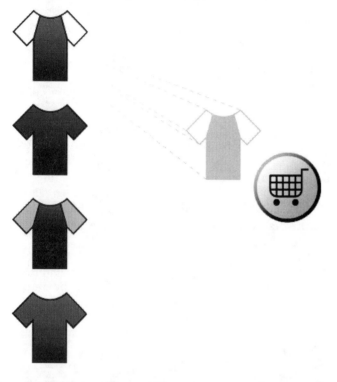

Reordering a List Using Drag-and-drop Functionality

Traditionally, it has been a usability challenge to enable a user to order more than one of a particular item from a store. An obvious solution would be to position arrows next to each the list item, and get the user to click repeatedly on those arrows in order to move an item; however, this solution wouldn't be easy to use. The drag-and-drop capabilities of JavaScript offer a far easier way for users to manipulate lists of items and see their changes reflected in real time.

Solution

A sortable list uses a lot of the code that we created for normal drag-and-drop objects in the previous solution. It differs in that, as the selected item is dragged around, each of the objects in the list must respond to the movement appropriately by reordering the list. Once the dragged object has been dropped and the order finalized, the structure of the list can be recorded in a number of ways.

The HTML for our list looks something like this:

File: **list_order_drag_n_drop.html** (excerpt)

```html
<ol id="footballLadder">
  <li>
    Liverpool
  </li>
  <li>
    Manchester United
  </li>
  <li>
    Arsenal
  </li>
  <li>
    Chelsea
  </li>
  <li>
    West Ham
  </li>
  <li>
    Fulham
  </li>
</ol>
```

The CSS used to position each of our list items is relatively simple, and can be fairly flexible:

File: **list_order_drag_n_drop.css** (excerpt)

```css
ol
{
  list-style: none;
}

li
{
  width: 195px;
```

```
height: 30px;
margin-bottom: 5px;
background-color: #666666;
color: #FFFFFF;
line-height: 30px;
⋮
}
```

The initialization and `mousedown` listeners hardly differ from the drag-and-drop script we developed in "Implementing Drag-and-drop Behavior" earlier in this chapter:

File: **list_order_drag_n_drop.js** (excerpt)

```
addLoadListener(initSortableList);

function initSortableList()
{
  if (identifyBrowser().indexOf("ie") != -1 &&
      identifyOS() == "mac")
  {
    return false;
  }

  var LIs = document.getElementById("footballLadder").
      getElementsByTagName("li");

  for (var i = 0; i < LIs.length; i++)
  {
    attachEventListener(LIs[i], "mousedown",
        mousedownSortableList, false);
    LIs[i].style.cursor = "move";
  }
}

function mousedownSortableList(event)
{
  if (typeof event == "undefined")
  {
    event = window.event;
  }

  if (typeof event.pageY == "undefined")
  {
    event.pageY = event.clientY + getScrollingPosition()[1];
  }
```

```
  var target = getEventTarget(event);

  while (target.nodeName.toLowerCase() != "li")
  {
    target = target.parentNode;
  }

  document.currentTarget = target;

  target.clickOriginY = event.pageY;

  attachEventListener(document, "mousemove",
      mousemoveCheckThreshold, false);
  attachEventListener(document, "mouseup", mouseupCancelThreshold,
      false);

  return true;
}
```

Because the list items will move in only one dimension (vertically), we do not need to worry about handling any horizontal coordinates, but that functionality can easily be incorporated from the previous solution if we need it.

Once a mouse button has been depressed on a draggable object, the mouse movements are initially monitored by `mousemoveCheckThreshold` and `mouseupCancelThreshold`. These functions check for an appropriate amount of cursor movement before initializing the actual drag-and-drop functionality:

File: **list_order_drag_n_drop.js (excerpt)**

```
function mousemoveCheckThreshold(event)
{
  if (typeof event == "undefined")
  {
    event = window.event;
  }

  if (typeof event.pageY == "undefined")
  {
    event.pageY = event.clientY + getScrollingPosition()[1];
  }

  var target = document.currentTarget;

  if (Math.abs(target.clickOriginY - event.pageY) > 3)
  {
```

```
    if (typeof document.selection != "undefined")
    {
      var textRange = document.selection.createRange();
      textRange.collapse();
      textRange.select();
    }

    detachEventListener(document, "mousemove",
        mousemoveCheckThreshold, false);
    detachEventListener(document, "mouseup",
        mouseupCancelThreshold, false);

    attachEventListener(document, "mousemove",
        mousemoveSortableList, false);
    attachEventListener(document, "mouseup", mouseupSortableList,
        false);

    var cloneItem = target.cloneNode(true);
    cloneItem.setAttribute("class", "clone");
    cloneItem.style.position = "absolute";
    cloneItem.style.top = getPosition(target)[1] + "px";
    cloneItem.differenceY = parseInt(cloneItem.style.top) -
        event.pageY;

    cloneItem = target.parentNode.appendChild(cloneItem);

    target.clone = cloneItem;
    target.style.visibility = "hidden";
  }

  stopDefaultAction(event);

  return true;
}

function mouseupCancelThreshold()
{
  detachEventListener(document, "mousemove",
      mousemoveCheckThreshold, false);
  detachEventListener(document, "mouseup", mouseupCancelThreshold,
      false);
  return true;
}
```

Once `mousemoveCheckThreshold` detects the required movement (more than three pixels), the interim event listeners are removed, and the proper drag-and-drop listeners are attached. Just before this, we see a conditional statement that deals with selection. This is a fix for a bug that occurs in lower versions of Internet Explorer for Windows: these browsers don't cancel text selections while an object is being dragged. The fix simply collapses any text selections, nullifying their effects.

Once the new event listeners are added, an exact clone of the target object is created and positioned in the same location as the original. Instead of moving the actual target list item around, we create this absolutely positioned clone and hide the original. We do so because we need to maintain a gap in the list where the dragged item would ordinarily be, and because we need to provide a visual display of the item moving around with the cursor. By creating a clone, and adding it to the end of the list, we get the best of both worlds. The clone's inclusion at the end of the list ensures that it inherits any of the styles associated with the list items, so we don't have to style it manually to match the original list item. And by setting the `visibility` of the target list item to `"hidden"`, we eradicate the need to cancel any click events for any links the item may contain, as hidden elements don't receive events.

Tip

Cloning the Clone

A class of "clone" is added to the clone, just so you can add some extra CSS effects. A good one to use is opacity, which makes the clone seem like a ghost of the original. Note, though, that this simple code doesn't work in all browsers:

```
.clone
{
  opacity: 0.5;
}
```

Once this additional infrastructure has been created, the positions of the clone and the surrounding elements are modified by the listener `mousemoveSortableList`:

File: **list_order_drag_n_drop.js** (excerpt)

```
function mousemoveSortableList(event)
{
  if (typeof event == "undefined")
  {
    event = window.event;
  }
```

```
if (typeof event.pageY == "undefined")
{
  event.pageY = event.clientY + getScrollingPosition()[1];
}

var target = document.currentTarget;
var clone = target.clone;
var plannedCloneTop = event.pageY + clone.differenceY;
var listItems = clone.parentNode.getElementsByTagName("li");
var firstItemPosition = getPosition(listItems[0]);
var lastItemPosition = getPosition(listItems[listItems.length -
    2]);

if (plannedCloneTop < firstItemPosition[1])
{
  plannedCloneTop = firstItemPosition[1];
}
else if (plannedCloneTop > lastItemPosition[1])
{
  plannedCloneTop = lastItemPosition[1];
}

clone.style.top = plannedCloneTop + "px";

var LIs = target.parentNode.getElementsByTagName("li");
var currentItemHigher = true;

for (var i = 0; i < LIs.length; i++)
{
  if (LIs[i] != target && LIs[i] != target.clone)
  {
    if (event.pageY < getPosition(LIs[i])[1] +
        LIs[i].offsetHeight && currentItemHigher)
    {
      target.parentNode.insertBefore(target, LIs[i]);

      break;
    }
    else if (event.pageY > getPosition(LIs[i])[1] &&
        !currentItemHigher)
    {
      target.parentNode.insertBefore(LIs[i], target);
    }
  }
  else
  {
```

```
      currentItemHigher = false;
    }
  }

  stopDefaultAction(event);

  return true;
}
```

The position of the dragged object is managed using the technique explained in the solution in "Implementing Drag-and-drop Behavior"; however, a number of other aspects are peculiar to sortable lists.

Firstly, the position of the clone is constrained at the top and bottom by the first and last items in the list. If users try to drag the clone beyond those boundaries, they will not succeed. Obviously, the clone itself technically is the last item in the list, so we use the second-last item to mark the bottom boundary.

Once the position of the clone has been finalized, we check to see how the other list items should order themselves around its new position. For each list item that isn't either the target or the clone, we check whether its bottom edge is higher than the current cursor position, and assess whether its current location is above the target element. If the list item meets both these requirements, it should be moved below the target element; to do so, we reorder the list using the `insertBefore` DOM function. If it doesn't meet those requirements, we check if instead the top edge of the current list item is lower than the cursor position, and whether the current item is positioned below the target list item. If *these* requirements are met, we rearrange the list so that the current list item is positioned *above* the target list item. In all other cases, we leave the order of the list untouched.

The effect of this script is that, as users move the clone around, their movements automatically change the position of the target list item in the list. This will automatically be reflected in the visual order of the other list items, creating a real-time sorting effect.

When the user releases the mouse button, we tidy up the list by removing the clone and making the target visible again:

File: **list_order_drag_n_drop.js (excerpt)**

```
function mouseupSortableList()
{
  var target = document.currentTarget;
  var clone = target.clone;
```

```
clone.parentNode.removeChild(clone);

target.style.visibility = "visible";

detachEventListener(document, "mousemove",
    mousemoveSortableList, false);
detachEventListener(document, "mouseup", mouseupSortableList,
    false);

return true;
}
```

The drag-and-drop event listeners are removed, and the list is reordered!

The finished script will produce an interface like that shown in Figure 14.4.

Figure 14.4. Putting Manchester United into its rightful position using a drag-sortable list

Making a Scrolling News Ticker

Scrolling news tickers serve two main purposes. Firstly, because they're animated, they attract more attention than static text. Secondly, the ability of scrolling tickers to display a theoretically endless amount of text allows them to squeeze a lot of information into a very small space. Of course, the inappropriate use of tickers can distract users from truly important information and, not surprisingly, users generally find uncontrollable animation to be irritating. It's up to you to use ticker effects wisely.

Solution

The HTML and CSS code for this news ticker is particularly important. The HTML consists of two block elements, one nested inside the other. You can place whatever content you wish inside the innermost block element:

File: **scrolling_news_ticker.html** (excerpt)

```
<div id="newsTicker">
  <div id="newsScroller">
    <strong>Breaking news:</strong> Liverpool defeats AC Milan in
    a penalty shootout after a shock comeback from 3-0 down in the
    second half of the Champions' League final.
  </div>
</div>
```

The following CSS must be applied to the elements:

File: **scrolling_news_ticker.css** (excerpt)

```
#newsTicker
{
  position: relative;
  width: 300px;
  height: 35px;
  overflow: hidden;
}

#newsScroller
{
  position: absolute;
  position/**/: relative;
  height: 35px;
  line-height: 35px;
  white-space: nowrap;
}
```

The relative positioning of newsTicker means that any absolutely positioned elements inside this will be positioned relative to newsTicker itself; the defined height and overflow properties restrict the news ticker display to a single line of text. An explicit width must be defined for newsTicker, but this property can take anything from a pixel value to a percentage. If you want the ticker to span the entire page, just use 100%.

The double declaration of position for newsScroller means that Internet Explorer 5.0 for Windows treats this element as absolutely positioned, while all other browsers treat it as relatively positioned. Ideally, all browsers would be comfortable with the absolutely positioned version, but Opera does not clip absolute elements inside relative elements, so without the second declaration the whole message would be visible in that browser—virtually ruining the news ticker effect. The complexity increases because Internet Explorer 5.0 ignores the `white-space` property and wraps the message. We have to give this browser the absolutely positioned version of the ticker to maintain the horizontal flow of words.

Now, to the JavaScript! Its main function is to determine the width of the inner container, and to animate it the appropriate distance before recycling the content:

```
addLoadListener(initNewsTicker);

function initNewsTicker()
{
  var newsScroller = document.getElementById("newsScroller");

  newsScroller.style.left = 0;

  if (retrieveComputedStyle(newsScroller, "position") ==
      "relative")
  {
    var relativeWidth = newsScroller.offsetWidth;

    newsScroller.style.position = "absolute";
    newsScroller.calculatedWidth = newsScroller.offsetWidth;

    if (relativeWidth > newsScroller.calculatedWidth)
    {
      newsScroller.calculatedWidth = relativeWidth;;
    }

    newsScroller.style.position = "relative";
  }
  else
  {
    newsScroller.calculatedWidth = newsScroller.clientWidth;
  }

  moveNewsScroller();

  return true;
}
```

```
function moveNewsScroller()
{
  var increment = 5;
  var newsScroller = document.getElementById("newsScroller");
  var currLeft = parseInt(newsScroller.style.left);

  if (currLeft < newsScroller.calculatedWidth * -1)
  {
    newsScroller.style.left =
        newsScroller.parentNode.offsetWidth + "px";
  }
  else
  {
    newsScroller.style.left = (parseInt(newsScroller.style.left) -
        increment) + "px";
  }

  setTimeout("moveNewsScroller()", 50);

  return true;
}
```

Unfortunately, when a relatively positioned element occurs inside an element whose overflow is set to "hidden", most browsers will calculate the offsetWidth of the inner element to reflect that of its parent. For this reason, initNewsTicker quickly changes newsScroller's position to "absolute", measures its width, then changes it back to "relative". We then take the largest width between the absolute and relative positions. This process happens almost instantly, but if there were a visible flicker, it would occur only in Opera. For Internet Explorer 5, we simply take newsScroller's clientWidth.

moveNewsScroller then uses a simple linear animation cycle to move news-Scroller to the left. The increment variable can be increased or decreased to affect the speed at which the news ticker scrolls.

The finished result is shown in Figure 14.5.

Figure 14.5. The scrolling news ticker displaying an unlimited amount of information in a limited area

Liverpool defeats AC Milan in a penalty shooto

penalty shootout after a shock comeback from

from 3-0 down in the second half of the Cham

the Champions' League final.

Discussion

For accessibility reasons—and because so many people find movement on web pages annoying—it's a good idea to include a stop/start button for your news ticker. Most users wouldn't bother to start the ticker, which would defeat the purpose of the tool, so we'll make it move by default, and let the user turn the ticker off if they wish.

We'll use JavaScript to add the stop button to our page so that only users who see the scrolling effect will see the button. At the same time, we'll attach a `click` event listener to handle clicks on the button:

File: **scrolling_news_ticker.js (excerpt)**

```
function initNewsTicker()
{
  var newsScroller = document.getElementById("newsScroller");

  newsScroller.style.left = 0;

  if (retrieveComputedStyle(newsScroller, "position") ==
      "relative")
  {
    var relativeWidth = newsScroller.offsetWidth;

    newsScroller.style.position = "absolute";
    newsScroller.calculatedWidth = newsScroller.offsetWidth;

    if (relativeWidth > newsScroller.calculatedWidth)
    {
      newsScroller.calculatedWidth = relativeWidth;
    }

    newsScroller.style.position = "relative";
  }
  else
  {
    newsScroller.calculatedWidth = newsScroller.clientWidth;
  }

  var stopLink = document.createElement("a");
  stopLink.setAttribute("id", "");
  stopLink.id = "stopLink";
  stopLink.setAttribute("href", "");
  stopLink.href = "#";
  stopLink.appendChild(document.createTextNode(
      "Stop/start news ticker"));
  attachEventListener(stopLink, "click", clickStopLink, false);

  var stopButton = document.createElement("div");

  stopButton.appendChild(stopLink);

  var newsTicker = document.getElementById("newsTicker");

  if (newsTicker.nextSibling != null)
  {
    newsTicker.parentNode.insertBefore(stopButton,
        newsTicker.nextSibling);
```

```
  }
  else
  {
    newsTicker.parentNode.appendChild(stopButton);
  }

  moveNewsScroller();

  return true;
}
```

We'll also need a reference to the timer that's used to animate the news ticker. This requires us to edit one line in `moveNewsScroller`:

File: **scrolling_news_ticker.js** (excerpt)

```
function moveNewsScroller()
{
  ⋮
  newsScroller.timeout = setTimeout("moveNewsScroller()", 50);

  return true;
}
```

When the `click` event on `stopLink` is fired, we can start or stop the animation as appropriate:

File: **scrolling_news_ticker.js** (excerpt)

```
function clickStopLink()
{
  var stopLink = document.getElementById("stopLink");

  if (typeof stopLink.stopped != "undefined" && stopLink.stopped)
  {
    moveNewsScroller();
    stopLink.stopped = false;
  }
  else
  {
    clearTimeout(document.getElementById("newsScroller").timeout);
    stopLink.stopped = true;
  }

  return true;
}
```

Figure 14.6 shows the ticker once the button has been added to it.

Figure 14.6. A stop/start button providing user control over the ticker

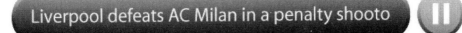

Creating Clip-based Transition Effects

Used appropriately, transitions can help to provide users with visual feedback on their actions, and add a little extra polish to your interfaces. Clip-based transitions manipulate the visible area of an element, so you can use them to produce effects like wipes or collapses. Move over, George Lucas!

Solution

CSS 2 allowed the `clip` CSS property to be applied to any object that *wasn't* absolutely positioned. However, CSS 2.1 reversed this to allow `clip` to be used *only* on absolutely positioned elements. This is the rule that modern browsers apply, so the effects mentioned here will only work for absolutely positioned elements. The principles could be applied to relative or static elements if you modified the dimensions of a containing element with `overflow` set to `hidden`; however, you might find the content of the container reflows as you modify the container's dimensions.

You can start a transition in response to any event—clicking, waiting, moving, typing—but for this example, we'll assume that the user will click on an object.

File: **`clip_transitions.js` (excerpt)**

```
addLoadListener(function(){setTimeout(function(){
    initTransitions();}, 0);});

function initTransitions()
{
  var elements = getElementsByAttribute("class", "transition");

  for (var i = 0; i < elements.length; i++)
  {
    attachEventListener(elements[i], "click", clickTransition,
```

```
             false);
  }

  return true;
}

function clickTransition(event)
{
  if (typeof event == "undefined")
  {
    event = window.event;
  }

  var target = getEventTarget(event);

  while (!/(^| )transition( |$)/.test(target.className))
  {
    target = target.parentNode;
  }

  transitionSquash(target);

  return true;
}
```

That rather confused looking addLoadListener call at the beginning of this script
weeds out any browsers that can't handle functions as arguments to setTimeout
(i.e., Internet Explorer 5 for Mac). As a result of that addLoadListener call,
initTransitions won't be called in that browser, so the page will degrade to
non-JavaScript functionality. We use function references to animate the objects
in this solution because we require a general solution that can be applied to
multiple elements on a page. Earlier in this chapter, we animated a soccer ball
using a method that was compatible with Internet Explorer 5 for Mac, but that
solution required us to hard-code the element that we used. If you'd like to achieve
these transitions in that browser, similar modifications can be made to this code.

initTransitions uses the getElementsByAttribute function from Chapter 5
to attach a click event listener to all elements with a class of transition. That
event listener executes clickTransition, a function whose main purpose is to
get the right event target element from our Chapter 13 custom function
getEventTarget. The listener then makes sure that the selected event target
element is in fact the right element by checking the className for the class
transition. The correct element reference is then passed to transitionSquash
to start the transition animation.

transitionSquash is a transition that appears to squash an object: it reduces the object's height by incrementally clipping its top and bottom edges:

```
function transitionSquash(target)
{
  if (typeof target == "undefined" || typeof target.style ==
      "undefined")
  {
    target = this;
  }

  var increment = 5;
  var width = target.offsetWidth;
  var height = target.offsetHeight;

  if (target.style.clip.indexOf("rect") == -1)
  {
    target.style.clip = "rect(" + increment + "px," + width +
        "px," + (height - increment) + "px,0)";
  }
  else
  {
    var clipDimensions = getClipDimensions(target.style.clip);

    if ((clipDimensions[2] - increment) - (clipDimensions[0] +
        increment) > 0)
    {
      target.style.clip = "rect(" + (clipDimensions[0] +
          increment) + "px," + clipDimensions[1] + "px," +
          (clipDimensions[2] - increment) + "px," +
          clipDimensions[3] + "px)";
    }
    else
    {
      target.style.clip = "rect(" + parseInt(height / 2) + "px," +
          clipDimensions[1] + "px," + parseInt(height / 2) +
          "px," + clipDimensions[3] + "px)";

      return true;
    }
  }

  setTimeout(function(){transitionSquash(target)}, 50);

  return true;
}
```

The first action that `transitionSquash` takes is to check the target object for an existing `clip` property. If a target object doesn't exist, the clipping area of the object is set to five pixels away from the top and bottom, and flush on the left and right sides.

If a clipping area is already defined (i.e., this is a subsequent step of the animation), we go on to reduce the clipping area by the defined `increment`. In order to do this, the current dimensions of the clipping area must be retrieved and modified, progressing the animation. The dimensions of the clipping area are retrieved using the `getClipDimensions` function, which returns an array of integers in the standard CSS dimension order (top, right, bottom, left).

File: **clip_transitions.js** (excerpt)

```javascript
function getClipDimensions(clipString)
{
  var clipValue = clipString.replace(/rect\(((.*)\))/, "$1");

  if (/,/.test(clipValue))
  {
    var clipDimensions = clipValue.split(",");
  }
  else
  {
    var clipDimensions = clipValue.split(" ");
  }

  for (var i = 0; i < clipDimensions.length; i++)
  {
    clipDimensions[i] = parseInt(clipDimensions[i]);
  }

  return clipDimensions;
}
```

This function parses the `clip` property's `rect(top,right,bottom,left)` syntax to retrieve the dimension values as integers. Most browsers separate the values with commas, but Internet Explorer automatically converts the commas to spaces, so we have to be careful when deciding which character to split the string upon.

When defining the new dimensions of the clipping area, `transitionSquash` checks to see whether any part of the object will remain visible. If not, it defines the clipping area to be of zero height (some browsers will display an object with a negative clipping area), and returns from the function without calling `setTimeout` again, thereby ending the transition.

The finished effect should look like Figure 14.7.

Figure 14.7. The squash transition collapsing an object vertically

Discussion

A number of effects are made possible by clip transitions; all you need to do to create a new effect is execute a different function from inside `clickTransition`.

`transitionCurtain` is similar to `transitionSquash`, except that it makes the object collapse horizontally.

File: **clip_transitions2.js** (excerpt)

```
function transitionCurtain(target)
{
  var increment = 5;
  var width = target.offsetWidth;
  var height = target.offsetHeight;

  if (target.style.clip.indexOf("rect") == -1)
  {
    target.style.clip = "rect(0," + (width - increment) + "px," +
        height + "px," + increment + "px)";
  }
  else
  {
    var clipDimensions = getClipDimensions(target.style.clip);

    if ((clipDimensions[1] - increment) - (clipDimensions[3] +
        increment) > 0)
    {
      target.style.clip = "rect(" + clipDimensions[0] + "px," +
          (clipDimensions[1] - increment) + "px," +
          clipDimensions[2] + "px," + (clipDimensions[3] +
          increment) + "px)";
    }
    else
    {
      target.style.clip = "rect(" + clipDimensions[0] + "px," +
```

```
                parseInt(width / 2) + "px," + clipDimensions[2] +
            "px," + parseInt(width / 2) + "px)";

        return true;
      }
    }

    setTimeout(function(){transitionCurtain(target)}, 50);

    return true;
}
```

This transition is illustrated in Figure 14.8.

Figure 14.8. The curtain transition collapsing an object horizontally

transitionShrink collapses the object into the top-left corner. Instead of increment, it uses a variable named steps to determine how many frames should be animated before the object disappears:

File: **clip_transitions3.js** (excerpt)

```
function transitionShrink(target)
{
  var steps = 15;
  var width = target.offsetWidth;
  var height = target.offsetHeight;
  var widthIncrement = parseInt(width / steps);
  var heightIncrement = parseInt(height / steps);

  if (target.style.clip.indexOf("rect") == -1)
  {
    target.style.clip = "rect(0," + (width - widthIncrement) +
        "px," + (height - heightIncrement) + "px,0)";
  }
  else
  {
    var clipDimensions = getClipDimensions(target.style.clip);

    if ((clipDimensions[1] - widthIncrement) > 0)
    {
```

```
    target.style.clip = "rect(0," + (clipDimensions[1] -
        widthIncrement) + "px," + (clipDimensions[2] -
        heightIncrement) + "px," + "0)";
  }
  else
  {
    target.style.clip = "rect(0,0,0,0)";

    return true;
  }
}

setTimeout(function(){transitionShrink(target)}, 50);

return true;
}
```

The finished effect can be seen in Figure 14.9.

Figure 14.9. The shrink transition collapsing an object into the top left corner

These are just some of the ways in which you can use the `clip` property to transition an object. Others you could try include left-to-right wipes, top-to-bottom wipes, and various forms of scaling.

Making a Slider Control

Sliders provide users with a very intuitive way to select data over a fixed, continuous data range. They immediately give users a sense of the position of the current value within a range of values, and also allow users to manipulate that value easily, and see changes in real time.

Solution

A slider is another example of a feature that's available in desktop applications, but is not yet widely used as a native widget inside web browsers. Plain text fields are capable of storing the same data as a slider, so in order to provide graceful degradation for users without JavaScript, we will convert any plain text input that has a class of slider into a slider object:

File: **slider_control.js** (excerpt)

```
addLoadListener(initSliders);

function initSliders()
{
  var sliderReplacements = getElementsByAttribute("class",
      "slider");

  for (var i = 0; i < sliderReplacements.length; i++)
  {
    var container = document.createElement("div");
    var slider = document.createElement("div");
    var newInput = document.createElement("input");
    var sliderReplacementID =
        sliderReplacements[i].getAttribute("id");

    if (sliderReplacementID != null || sliderReplacementID != "")
    {
      container.setAttribute("id", sliderReplacementID +
          "SliderContainer");
    }

    container.className = "sliderContainer";
    slider.className = "sliderWidget";
    slider.style.left =
        sliderReplacements[i].getAttribute("value") + "px";
    slider.valueX =
        parseInt(sliderReplacements[i].getAttribute("value"), 10);

    try
    {
      newInput.setAttribute("id",
          sliderReplacements[i].getAttribute("id"));
      newInput.setAttribute("name",
          sliderReplacements[i].getAttribute("name"));
      newInput.setAttribute("type", "hidden");
      newInput.setAttribute("value",
          sliderReplacements[i].getAttribute("value"));
    }
    catch(error)
    {
      return false;
```

```
    }

    container.appendChild(slider);
    sliderReplacements[i].parentNode.insertBefore(container,
        sliderReplacements[i]);
    sliderReplacements[i].parentNode.replaceChild(newInput,
        sliderReplacements[i]);

    container.input = newInput;

    attachEventListener(slider, "mousedown", mousedownSlider,
        false);
  }

  return true;
}
```

The target element is replaced by two divs that represent the slider control—one nested inside the other—as well as a hidden input that will record the form data that's to be submitted.

Internet Explorer 5 for Mac doesn't allow the type of a newly created input to be changed, so the creation of the hidden input is wrapped inside a try-catch statement. If the creation of the input fails, the function will exit without creating a slider, leaving the plain text input on the page.

If the target element possesses an id, the id of the outer div is modified to allow easy access to the target element's id via either CSS or JavaScript, as are the classes of both divs. If the original form element had a value, the slider's style.left property will be modified appropriately to represent it, and its extended property valueX (which is used later) also will be updated.

Lastly, a reference to the hidden input field is created from the slider container to allow the field's value to be updated dynamically, and a mousedown event listener is placed on the internal div.

This event listener is the gateway to the slider's behavior. When a user presses a mouse button on the slider object, the following familiar drag-and-drop code is initiated:

File: **slider_control.js (excerpt)**

```
function mousedownSlider(event)
{
  if (typeof event == "undefined")
```

```
{
  event = window.event;
}

var target = getEventTarget(event);

while (!/(^| )sliderWidget( |$)/.test(target.className))
{
  target = target.parentNode;
}

document.currentSlider = target;
target.originX = event.clientX;

attachEventListener(document, "mousemove", mousemoveSlider,
    false);
attachEventListener(document, "mouseup", mouseupSlider, false);

stopDefaultAction(event);

return true;
}
```

This function is pretty much identical to the mousedown listener we saw in the drag-and-drop solution that was presented earlier in this chapter. In this case, though, we use a different criterion to verify the target element: we make sure it has a class of sliderWidget. The major differences are incorporated into the mousemove handler:

File: **slider_control.js (excerpt)**

```
function mousemoveSlider(event)
{
  if (typeof event == "undefined")
  {
    event = window.event;
  }

  var slider = document.currentSlider;
  var sliderLeft = slider.valueX;
  var increment = 1;

  if (isNaN(sliderLeft))
  {
    sliderLeft = 0;
  }
```

```
sliderLeft += event.clientX - slider.originX;

if (sliderLeft < 0)
{
  sliderLeft = 0;
}
else if(sliderLeft > (slider.parentNode.offsetWidth -
    slider.offsetWidth))
{
  sliderLeft = slider.parentNode.offsetWidth -
      slider.offsetWidth;
}
else
{
  slider.originX = event.clientX;
}

slider.style.left = Math.round(sliderLeft / increment) *
    increment + "px";
slider.parentNode.input.setAttribute("value",
    Math.round(sliderLeft / increment) * increment);
slider.valueX = sliderLeft;

stopDefaultAction(event);

return true;
}
```

The slider is positioned relative to the mouse cursor using the technique we discussed in "Implementing Drag-and-drop Behavior"; however, we restrict its movement to occur within the boundaries of the slider container. Every slider has to have a finite length, and if the user moves the cursor beyond the boundaries of the slider container, the slider handle shouldn't go with it. Because of this, the slider handle's position is automatically set to zero or to the maximum value, if the cursor goes beyond the left or right boundaries, respectively, of the slider control.

The increment value we're using in this function allows you to specify "notches" on the slider for fixed values. For instance, if your scale went from zero to 100, but you only wanted the user to select multiples of ten, you could set increment to 10. This way, the slider would position itself at the multiple of ten pixels that was closest to the cursor's position. The default value of increment is 1 (i.e., one pixel, in which case the slider moves in a smooth fashion).

Beyond its appearance, any change in the slider's position is reflected in its associated input field. At the moment, this field merely indicates the raw pixel distance from the left boundary of the slider container, but we could easily apply an algorithm to this value in order to calculate some other figure with an offset or a multiplier. In such cases, we'd modify the second-to-last operation with the details of that algorithm. So, if we wanted each pixel on the slider to represent 5°C, the code that assigned the value to the hidden `input` field would look like this:

```
slider.parentNode.input.setAttribute("value",
    Math.round(sliderLeft / increment) * increment * 5);
```

We've simply multiplied the value by five.

The last thing that `mousemoveSlider` does is call the `stopDefaultAction` function we saw in Chapter 13. This function stops the action that would normally occur when the mouse moves; in this case, it stops users from selecting text on the page while they're moving the slider around.

Slider Styling

The values produced by the slider are inseparably tied to the way it is styled. If the slider container is specified to have a width of 200 pixels, and the slider handle has a width of 20 pixels, 180 discrete data points will be available on the slider.

How you relate those points to your own data domain is up to you, but it's generally easiest to assign one pixel to represent one unit. For example, if you have a number scale from zero to 400, set the width of the slider container to 420 and the width of the slider handle to 20.

Once the user has finished selecting the required slider value, the user will release the button and `mouseupSlider` will remove the event listeners that we put in place to handle the slider movement:

File: **slider_control.js** (excerpt)
```
function mouseupSlider()
{
  detachEventListener(document, "mousemove", mousemoveSlider,
      false);
  detachEventListener(document, "mouseup", mouseupSlider, false);

  return true;
}
```

Figure 14.10 shows what the finished slider control should look like.

Figure 14.10. Using a slider control to pick a value within a continuous data range

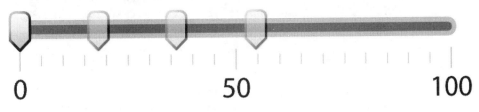

In Chapter 16 we'll revisit this slider widget and look at ways to make it accessible to a variety of different users.

Discussion

To see how we can translate the slider value into a usable number, let's create a widget that allows the user to choose the background color of the page.

In order to build this functionality, we need three inputs that will represent the red, green, and blue color channels:

File: **slider_control_background_color.html** (excerpt)
```
<input id="channelRed" name="channelRed" class="slider"
    type="text" value="0" />
<input id="channelGreen" name=" channelGreen" class="slider"
    type="text" value="0" />
<input id="channelBlue" name=" channelBlue" class="slider"
    type="text" value="0" />
```

Users without JavaScript will see text inputs: they can type in a value for each of the channels, and submit the form. However, we can replace these text boxes with much more intuitive slider controls that update the page in real time.

If we reuse the code from the example above, all we need to do is modify mousemoveSlider to collect the values from each of the sliders, and write them to the background color of the page:

File: **slider_control_background_color.js** (excerpt)
```
function mousemoveSlider()
{
  ⋮
  var redValue =
    document.getElementById("channelRed").getAttribute("value");
```

```
var greenValue =
  document.getElementById("channelGreen").getAttribute("value");
var blueValue =
  document.getElementById("channelBlue").getAttribute("value");
document.getElementsByTagName("body")[0].style.backgroundColor =
  "rgb(" + redValue + "," + greenValue + "," + blueValue + ")";

stopDefaultAction(event);

return true;
}
```

Each of the channels in the RGB color scale has 255 possible values, so if we want to be able represent all the colors in that scale, we must ensure that our sliders have at least 255 discrete data points. If our slider markers were 20 pixels wide, for example, we'd make our slider containers 275 pixels wide.

Figure 14.11 shows our background color sliders in action.

Figure 14.11. Transforming slider values to alter the background color of a page

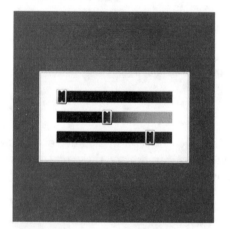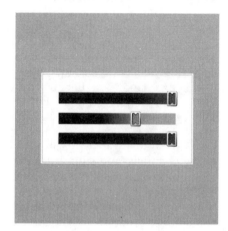

Summary

Because the Internet has traditionally been a static medium, the ability to create movement and respond to user input are some of the most eye-opening and tangible examples of JavaScript's benefits.

These capabilities have been given a bad reputation due to the proliferation of frivolous, nonfunctional eye candy—effects that more often hinder a user's interaction with a web page than help it. Yet real power underlies those tricks. JavaScript gives us the ability to enrich interfaces, create more usable environments, and involve users as they have never been involved before.

This chapter has explained the basic principles by which many valuable effects can be achieved, and has given you a few examples of what JavaScript makes possible within the realm of time-and-motion effects. Yet the greatest applications of this power lie waiting in your imagination.

DHTML Menus and Navigation

DHTML menus are usability and accessibility minefields, and opinion is strongly divided on whether they're useful tools, necessarily evils … or just plain evil!

Personally, I rather like them, but I will concede that it's rare to find a really well-made menu on the Web, though they do exist. In developing an HTML menu, there are quite a few major issues to consider. We'll be looking at these as we move through this chapter, examining the techniques for avoiding or minimizing problems as they arise.

The chapter is divided into two broad solutions—a drop-down or fly-out menu, and a folder tree or expanding menu—each of which is a different beast, functionally speaking. For each solution there are a number of sub-solutions, which build on the original script to add new features, such as timers and menu repositioning capabilities, to the basic fly-out menu.

Throughout this chapter, we'll use the same HTML structure (an unordered list), with CSS styling and JavaScript behaviors. This is a beautiful demonstration of the true separation of content, style, and behavior,[1] and ensures that our menu will degrade gracefully. We'll also set it up so that the underlying content remains

---

[1]Though beautiful, the demonstration is not perfect—our script will still need to know one or two things about the design, and take some of its data from HTML attributes—but in that respect, perfection is almost impossible.

accessible, both for screen readers and other serial browsers, and for legacy browsers and those that lack CSS and scripting support.

List Menu Credits

The technique of using lists for navigation and drop-down menus is credited in part to Mark Newhouse, and his seminal article Taming Lists,[2] and to Eric Meyer's pure CSS menus.[3] The advantage of using lists over tables or divs for navigation is that they have a proper structure and hierarchy, and are semantically close in meaning to a navigation bar. XHTML 2 ratifies this notion with a new nl (navigation list) element.[4]

Before we dive into the scripting, let's look at the HTML:

File: **vertical.html** (excerpt)

```
<ul id="navigation" class="vertical">
  <li><a href="/">Home</a></li>
  <li><a href="/about/">About us</a>
    <ul>
      <li><a href="/services/">Our services</a>
        <ul>
          <li><a href="/manufacture/">Manufacturing</a></li>
          <li><a href="/distribute/">Distribution</a></li>
        </ul>
      </li>
      <li><a href="/products/">Our products</a>
        <ul>
          <li><a href="/widgets/">Widgets</a></li>
          <li><a href="/spoons/">Spoons</a></li>
        </ul>
      </li>
    </ul>
  </li>
  <li><a href="/contact/">Contact us</a>
    <ul>
      <li><a href="/phone/">By phone</a></li>
      <li><a href="/email/">By email</a></li>
    </ul>
  </li>
</ul>
```

---

[2] http://www.alistapart.com/articles/taminglists/
[3] http://www.meyerweb.com/eric/css/edge/menus/demo.html
[4] http://www.w3.org/TR/2005/WD-xhtml2-20050527/mod-list.html

Remember that nested `<ul>` lists go *before* the closing `</li>`, not after it. That's important, because our scripting won't work on a list that's not properly formed.

The `id` attribute will be used to identify the list to our script. The `class` is used partly by the script to determine the orientation of a fly-out menu (because some of the positioning calculations will be different for a horizontal navigation bar), but mostly to apply the CSS. Although this example (and the CSS examples in this chapter) involves a vertical navbar with menus, the script we'll be writing will work equally well for a horizontal navbar, and the necessary CSS for such a menu is included in the archive.

Making a Drop-down or Fly-out Menu

Having established the HTML framework, we need to use some CSS to style our basic navigation bar and menus. The development of that menu is largely outside the scope of this book, and for discussions of the techniques involved I refer you to Rachel Andrew's *The CSS Anthology*.[5] In any case, not much of it is directly relevant to how the script works. Since we have pretty good separation of content from design, we don't need to know a great deal about the CSS to write the JavaScript (and vice versa).

That said, we don't have perfect separation, and some bits are significant, so we'll highlight and discuss those sections as we come across them. Watch also for points at which I've added footnotes to the CSS, to explain a particular rule or choice of syntax.

Here's a complete style sheet that styles the list we've just created as a vertical navigation bar with fly-out menus:

File: **vertical.css (excerpt)**

```css
/* structural styles and offsets */
ul.vertical, ul.vertical li, ul.vertical ul {
  margin: 0;
  padding: 0;
  list-style-type: none;
  font-size: 100%;
}
ul.vertical {
  position: absolute;
  z-index: 1000;
  cursor: default;
```

---

[5] http://www.sitepoint.com/books/cssant1/

```
    width: 8em;
    left: 1em;
    top: 1em;
}
ul.vertical li {
    position: relative;
    text-align: left;
    cursor: pointer;
    cursor: hand;
    width: 8em;
    margin: -1px 0 0 0;
}
ul.vertical ul {
    z-index: 1020;
    cursor: default;
    width: 8.2em;
    margin: -0.5em 0 0 7.5em;
    position: absolute;
    left: -100em;
    top: 0;
    padding: 1px 0 0 0;
}
ul.vertical ul li {
    width: 8.2em;
}
ul.vertical ul ul {
    margin: -0.5em 0 0 7.7em;
}
/* design styles */
ul.vertical ul {
    border-width: 1px;
    border-style: solid;
    border-color: #ffeca7 #a97741 #a97741 #ffeca7;
}

ul.vertical a:link, ul.vertical a:visited {
    display: block;
    cursor: pointer;
    cursor: hand;
    background: #ffc;
    border: 1px solid #edbb85;
    padding: 5px 7px;
    font: normal normal bold 0.7em tahoma, verdana, sans-serif;
    color: #008000;
    text-decoration: none;
    letter-spacing: 1px;
```

```
}

ul.vertical a:hover, ul.vertical a:focus, ul.vertical a:active,⁶
ul.vertical a.rollover:link, ul.vertical a.rollover:visited {
  background: #ffefcf;
  color: #806020;
}

/* browser hacks */
@media screen, projection {
  * html ul.vertical li {⁷
    display: inline;
    f\loat: left;
    background: #fff;
  }
}
* html ul.vertical li { position: static; }
* html ul.vertical a:link, * html ul.vertical a:visited {
    position: relative; }
```

Our list now looks like Figure 15.1.

Figure 15.1. An HTML list styled as a vertical navigation bar

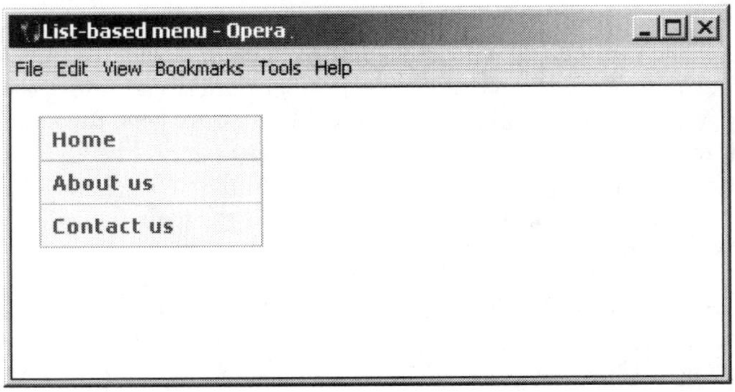

---

⁶The :active pseudo-class can be used to simulate :focus in Internet Explorer 5 and 6. Their implementation of :active is wrong, and they don't support :focus at all, but by a happy coincidence their implementation of :active is almost identical to the correct implementation of :focus! The difference is that when you click a link, and then click Back, or select the previous page from the history, the last link you clicked will still be in its active state and, therefore, will still be highlighted.

⁷These CSS hacks are for Internet Explorer 5 and 6, to stabilize the appearance of the list items. The inline display applies to all versions of IE, but the float applies only to IE 5.5 or later, because the backslash in the rule hides it from IE 5.0.

The menus have a similar layout and appearance to the main navigation bar, but we can't see them yet, because they're hidden by default. To hide them we're not using `display` or `visibility`, because that would make them inaccessible to most browser-based screen readers (which, for the most part, cannot read content that is not visibly displayed[8]).

With that as a given, what we're using instead is a technique known as **offleft positioning**, with which the hidden content is made "invisible" by virtue of being positioned far off the screen:

File: **vertical.css (excerpt)**

```
ul.vertical ul {
    ⋮
    position: absolute;
    left: -100em;
    ⋮
}
```

Since nothing is actually hidden *per se*, the content remains accessible to this group of users, whether they have JavaScript enabled or not.

Accessible ... Almost!

However it won't be *universally* accessible, because there's one group of users who fall through the net: people who use a graphical browser that has CSS enabled but doesn't support the script, or has JavaScript disabled, won't see the submenus at all. Even if we included pure CSS menu triggers, they still wouldn't work for everyone; in fact, inevitably, *whatever* method we use for creating menus, a minority of users are not going to be able to see them. The only part of the structure that *is* universally accessible is the main navigation bar (the top level of links).

What this means in practical use is that *everything that is accessible from the submenus must also be accessible without them*. This can be achieved by ensuring you have additional sub-navigation on the index page of each section, and that you provide options like a site map and search function. Most of this happens quite naturally in the process of putting a site together, but I still recommend you keep it in mind specifically: a dynamic menu is a useful form of site navigation, but it should never be the only one.

Finally, please note that the menus we're making in this solution will only work from mouse events. In Chapter 16, we'll pick them up again and make them accessible from the keyboard.

---

[8] http://www.access-matters.com/2005/04/10/quiz-521-screen-reader-test-1/

Solution

Since we're using offleft positioning to hide the submenus, the work that the script will do in opening and closing them will actually just set their positions, bringing each menu back into view, or moving it off again.

There are two parts to the script. This first is an initialization function called dropdownMenu:

File: **dropdownMenu.js (excerpt)**

```
function dropdownMenu(navid)
{
  var isie = (typeof document.all != 'undefined'
      && typeof window.opera == 'undefined'
      && navigator.vendor != 'KDE');
  if (typeof document.getElementById == 'undefined'
      || (navigator.vendor == 'Apple Computer, Inc.'
      && typeof window.XMLHttpRequest == 'undefined')
      || (isie && typeof document.uniqueID == 'undefined'))
  {
    return;
  }

  var tree = document.getElementById(navid);
  if (tree)
  {
    var items = tree.getElementsByTagName('li');
    for (var i = 0; i < items.length; i++)
    {
      dropdownTrigger(tree, items[i], navid, isie);
    }
  }
}
```

We'll also use a list item initialization function called dropdownTrigger, which binds the necessary event listeners using the generic attachEventListener function we saw in "Handling Events" in Chapter 13:

File: **dropdownMenu.js (excerpt)**

```
function dropdownTrigger(tree, li, navid, isie)
{
  var a = li.getElementsByTagName('a')[0];
  var menu = li.getElementsByTagName('ul').length > 0
      ? li.getElementsByTagName('ul')[0] : null;
```

```
    var horiz = tree.className.indexOf('horizontal') != -1;
    var issub = li.parentNode.id == navid;

    attachEventListener(li, 'mouseover', function(e)
    {
      a.className += (a.className == '' ? '' : ' ') + 'rollover';
      if (menu)
      {
        menu.style.left = horiz
            ? (isie ? li.offsetLeft + 'px' : 'auto')
            : '0';
        menu.style.top = horiz && issub
            ? (isie ? a.offsetHeight + 'px' : 'auto')
            : (isie ? li.offsetTop + 'px' : '0');
      }
    }, false);

    attachEventListener(li, 'mouseout', function(e)
    {
      var related = typeof e.relatedTarget != 'undefined'
          ? e.relatedTarget : e.toElement;
      if (!li.contains(related))
      {
        a.className = a.className.replace(/ ?rollover/g, '');
        if (menu)
        {
          menu.style.left = '-100em';
        }
      }
    }, false);

    if (!isie)
    {
      li.contains = function(node)
      {
        if (node == null) { return false; }
        if (node == this) { return true; }
        else { return this.contains(node.parentNode); }
      };
    }
  }
}
```

Finally, we can initialize the menu onload by calling dropdownMenu with the list id. Here, we're using the encapsulated load solution we built in "Getting Multiple Scripts to Work on the Same Page" in Chapter 1:

File: **dropdownMenu.js (excerpt)**

```
addLoadListener(function() { dropdownMenu('navigation'); });
```

Now, when our menus are in use, they'll look like Figure 15.2.

Figure 15.2. The menus in use

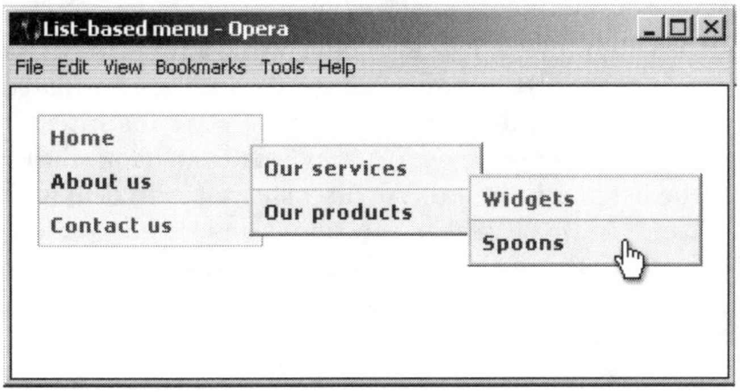

Discussion

Let's begin with the `dropdownMenu` function. The first thing we do is check for Internet Explorer, using the object tests we saw in Chapter 11 to set the `isie` variable. We need that variable straight away in order to test for exclusions. We need DOM support, which filters out older script-supporting browsers such as Netscape 4, but we also need to test for older Safari builds (earlier than 1.2) and IE 5 for Mac. In both cases, the CSS for the submenus isn't stable, so we degrade those builds to unsupported (they can see the navigation bar, but not the submenus). Finally, we can proceed to iterate through the list items, passing each one to the trigger-initialization function, `dropdownTrigger`.

In `dropdownTrigger`, we begin by creating some values for later use: we save references to the link (`a`), and the menu (`menu`), which are used within the open and close functions (this will make the menu toggling faster, since some of its computations have been done in advance). We also save the result of some environment checks: whether this is a horizontal menu (`horiz`), and whether this is a first-level or deeper submenu (`issub`), both of which affect how positioning works.

The Scope of Defined Variables

Since we've defined the variables at this level, they remain global to everything inside `dropdownTrigger`, including the inner functions. The fact that variables defined in a particular scope are available to inner scopes is one of the most powerful features of JavaScript, and is discussed in more depth in Chapter 19.

Now we come to bind our list item event handlers, and we again encounter a problem we saw in Chapter 13. We're using our encapsulated `attachEventListener` function, which delegates to `attachEvent` for Internet Explorer, but within that construct the reference `this` points to `window`, rather than the element to which the listener is bound. We discussed ways to deal with this problem in Chapter 13 and, in this case, the solution is simple because our functions are defined as closures: we already have a reference to the element to which we're binding our listener in the argument `li`, so we can simply use that reference instead of this:

File: **dropdownMenu.js (excerpt)**

```
attachEventListener(li, 'mouseover', function()
{
```

Let's look at what the listeners actually do. In the **list item mouseover** function, the first thing that happens is that a scriptable class name for rollover styles is set. It's set on a link when you mouse over that item, and ensures that, when you move to a link in a submenu, the parent link remains highlighted, which wouldn't happen with pseudo-classes alone. It improves usability by adding context highlighting all the way down the branch you're viewing (and it looks very nice as well). The `rollover` class name ties in with the styles we defined in the original CSS:

File: **vertical.css (excerpt)**

```
ul.vertical a:hover, ul.vertical a:focus, ul.vertical a:active,
ul.vertical a.rollover:link, ul.vertical a.rollover:visited {
  background: #ffefcf;
  color: #806020;
}
```

This effect is also stabilized by the action of **event bubbling**. If you were to roll over a link without having already passed your mouse over its ancestors (which could happen if you came to an already-open menu from outside it), then the rest of the branch wouldn't already be highlighted. By allowing the event to bubble, the rollover is applied to every ancestor. If you're not already familiar with event bubbling, see the section called "Handling Events" in Chapter 13 in Chapter 13.

Regular Expression Trickery

note

When we add the rollover class name, we first check for an existing value before adding a space delimiter, which is necessary to avoid creating a class value such as `rollover` (beginning with a leading space). This is purely to avoid a browser quirk: in some Opera 7 builds, a class is not applied if the attribute value begins with a leading space:

File: **dropdownMenu.js** (excerpt)

```
a.className += (a.className == '' ? '' : ' ') +
    'rollover';
```

When we come to *remove* the class name in the mouse out handler, we might find that it's been applied more than once to the same link, as a result of the event bubbling we've just discussed. To remove the rollovers properly, we need to include a global flag in the replacement expression:

File: **dropdownMenu.js** (excerpt)

```
a.className = a.className.replace(/ ?rollover/g, '');
```

For more about regular expressions, see Chapter 3.

The only other thing that exists in our mouseover function is the show/hide mechanism for the menus, which is simply a set of position toggles that move the menu into place. There's no display or visibility change, because our menus are already displayed and visible, as we saw when we looked at the CSS.

Within that code, we have variations that are specific to Internet Explorer. For example:

File: **dropdownMenu.js** (excerpt)

```
(isie ? li.offsetLeft + 'px' : 'auto')
```

These are needed because IE's menu positioning is different than other browsers'; where most browsers use `position: relative` on the list items, in IE that would expose an obscure and frustrating z-ordering[9] quirk.[10] To accommodate this

---

[9]z-order is the vertical stacking of objects, as defined for normal elements by the CSS `z-index` property.
[10]Where multiple nested elements all have `position: relative`, IE starts erroneous new contexts, resulting in an incorrect stacking order.

quirk, we're using `position: static` on the list items for IE, which means that the coordinate origin for absolutely-positioned menus is different in that browser.

In Internet Explorer, then, the menu's natural position is flush with the left edge of the list item, hence we position it to the right edge using that item's `offsetWidth`; in other browsers, the menu's natural position is *already* flush with the right edge, exactly where we want it, so we position it using the value `auto`. (The offsets that make them overlap the parent are applied from the default CSS, using negative `margin` values.)

In fact, this is true for all the position values: they're either computed for Internet Explorer, or set to zero or `auto` for other browsers, in which they sit in their natural position. I designed the CSS for this example specifically to allow for these nuances, partly so that the later addition of pure CSS menu-triggers is still possible (for browsers other than IE), but largely because it was the most effective way of making the stupid thing behave (but please don't think I'm wantonly IE-bashing here; I have high praise indeed in only a few paragraphs' time!).

In the **list item mouseout** function, we do the opposite job: reset the rollover class name, and reset the positioning styles so that the menus disappear from view.

But there's some interesting event evaluation going on there:

File: **dropdownMenu.js (excerpt)**

```
var related = typeof e.relatedTarget != 'undefined'
    ? e.relatedTarget : e.toElement;
if (!li.contains(related))
{
    :
}
```

`contains` is a method for evaluating the relationship between two nodes in the DOM: it indicates whether one contains the other. We're using it here to evaluate the related-target node (for a `mouseout` event, the related target is the element or other node that the mouse is moving *to*), proceeding only if that node is *not* contained by our current list item (i.e., it's outside that list item). This technique is used to filter out events we're not interested in, for example, the `mouseout` event that fires on an element when the user mouses over an element inside it.

But, fantastically useful as the `contains` method is, it's not defined in any public standard. It's actually proprietary to Internet Explorer (you see—it's not all bad!), so before we can use it, we have to write the function for other browsers. Here, I'm using Jason Davis' solution:[11]

File: **dropdownMenu.js** (excerpt)

```
if (!isie)
{
  li.contains = function(node)
  {
    if (node == null) { return false; }
    if (node == this) { return true; }
    else { return this.contains(node.parentNode); }
  };
}
```

In our evaluation, we ask whether the list item contains the node we're examining:

❑ If that node is `null`, it doesn't exist, and therefore it can't be contained within our list item (`false`).

❑ If that node is the same as the node we're currently examining, the list item *is* that node; therefore it must be contained within it (`true`).

❑ If neither of the above is true, run the function again on the parent node.

And so it travels up the DOM, starting with the node in question, until we either find our list item (`true`) or run out of nodes (`false`). This is an example of a **recursive function**—a function that calls itself.

`contains` is also implemented by Opera, but it doesn't do any harm to re-implement it regardless. However, it needs to be protected from IE, because it throws an error in IE 5 for Mac (that's okay of course: we don't need to recreate the function in that browser, we're simply preventing it from choking on our recreation).

Event Argument not Required

You might have noticed that we create the related-target reference without first having to convert an event argument. Normally, we'd do something like this:

```
if (!e) { e = window.event; }
```

---

[11] http://www.jasonkarldavis.com/

In this case, it isn't necessary because IE is using `attachEvent`, and when that construct is used, an event reference is passed to the function *automatically*. In other words, `e` is *already* a reference to IE's `window.event` object. This is also discussed in Chapter 13.

Adding Arrows to Indicate the Presence of a Submenu

Now that we have a functional menu, it would be nice to open it up beyond the realms of "mystery meat" navigation! When we look at it we have no way of knowing which item contains a sub-branch, unless we actually mouse over that item. We can improve the usability of the menu by adding arrows.

Solution

We're going to add submenu-indicator arrows as CSS background images. Here's the CSS, which uses a list item class name of `hasmenu`, and child selectors from that class (plus equivalent hacks for Windows IE), to redefine the link backgrounds so that they include arrow images:

File: **vertical.css (excerpt)**

```
/* submenu indicator arrows */
ul.vertical li.hasmenu > a:link,
ul.vertical li.hasmenu > a:visited {
  background: url(right-green.gif) #ffc no-repeat 95% 50%;
}

ul.vertical li.hasmenu > a:hover,
ul.vertical li.hasmenu > a:focus,
ul.vertical li.hasmenu > a:active,
ul.vertical li.hasmenu > a.rollover:link,
ul.vertical li.hasmenu > a.rollover:visited {
  background: url(right-red.gif) #ffefcf no-repeat 95% 50%;
}

* html ul.vertical li.hasmenu a:link,
* html ul.vertical li.hasmenu a:visited {
  background: expression(/hasmenu/.test(this.parentNode.className)
      ? "url(right-green.gif) #ffc no-repeat 95% 50%" : "#ffc");
}

* html ul.vertical li.hasmenu a:hover,
```

```
* html ul.vertical li.hasmenu a:active,
* html ul.vertical li.hasmenu a.rollover:link,
* html ul.vertical li.hasmenu a.rollover:visited {
  background: expression(/hasmenu/.test(this.parentNode.className)
    ? "url(right-red.gif) #ffefcf no-repeat 95% 50%" : "#ffefcf");
}
```

We can apply the class name to the relevant list items as they're being initialized. We already have a variable for whether a list item has a submenu, so we can use that as the condition for whether to add the arrow class name (including a test for whether it already has a class, as we did for the link rollovers in the original script).

Below is an excerpt from the dropdownTrigger function; our new code is shown in bold:

File: **dropdownMenu.js (excerpt)**

```
function dropdownTrigger(tree, li, navid, isie)
{
  var a = li.getElementsByTagName('a')[0];
  var menu = li.getElementsByTagName('ul').length > 0
      ? li.getElementsByTagName('ul')[0] : null;
  var horiz = tree.className.indexOf('horizontal') != -1;
  var issub = li.parentNode.id == navid;

  if (menu)
  {
    li.className += (li.className == '' ? '' : ' ') + 'hasmenu';
  }

  attachEventListener(li, 'mouseover', function(e)
  {
    :
```

Figure 15.3. The menus displaying submenu-indicator arrows

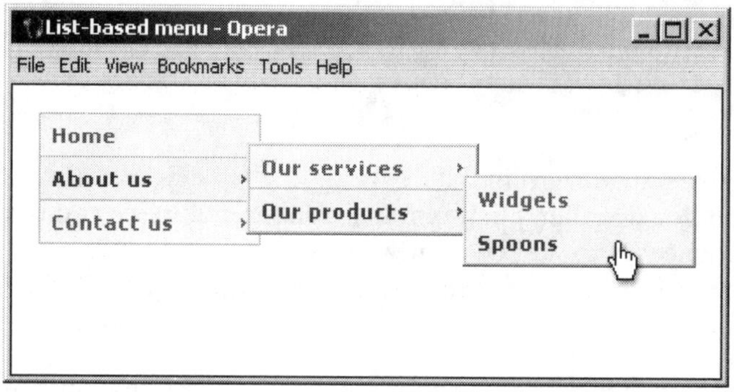

Now our menus will look like Figure 15.3.

Since the rollover is a separate image from the default arrow, we should take the time to cache it. We can do this in the main initialization function as shown below (additions are shown in bold):

File: **dropdownMenu.js** (excerpt)

```
function dropdownMenu(navid)
{
  var isie = (typeof document.all != 'undefined'
     && typeof window.opera == 'undefined'
     && navigator.vendor != 'KDE');
  if (typeof document.getElementById == 'undefined'
     || (navigator.vendor == 'Apple Computer, Inc.'
     && typeof window.XMLHttpRequest == 'undefined')
     || (isie && typeof document.uniqueID == 'undefined'))
  {
    return;
  }

  var rollover = new Image;
  rollover.src = 'right-red.gif';
```

Discussion

The CSS that applies the arrows uses child selectors, but these aren't supported in Windows IE 5 and IE 6, so what we can do instead is apply the rules using an **expression**, for example:

File: **vertical.css** (excerpt)

```
* html ul.vertical li.hasmenu a:link,
* html ul.vertical li.hasmenu a:visited {
  background: expression(/hasmenu/.test(this.parentNode.className)
     ? "url(right-green.gif) #ffc no-repeat 95% 50%" : "#ffc");
}
```

The expression syntax is proprietary to Windows IE, and allows you set a style property value as the result of a JavaScript evaluation. Inside the expression, this is a reference to the element to which the rule applies; here, we're evaluating the class name of its parent to determine whether the background image should be used.

Using a CSS background tied to a single class name makes the arrow images very easy to apply, and easy to deal with in the script: because no new elements have been added, we don't have to consider whether events from those elements will cause any conflicts.

But this choice is not entirely without debate, because it's not exactly clear whether submenu indicator arrows are part of the content or the presentation. They serve a visual purpose, so maybe they're presentational; but they also indicate hierarchy, so maybe they're part of the content.

It's a complicated and rather tedious subject, but on this occasion I'm siding with the arrow being part of the presentation, and I'm going to apply it without a textual equivalent as a CSS background. While I must admit that I think the arrows are actually content, the information they impart is already present in the semantics of the list (the structure itself includes hierarchical information, which a good-quality screen reader like JAWS can interpret), so I don't think it's a tremendous loss to apply them this way.

Navigation Arrows as Content?

If you do decide that the arrows are content, you'll also need to decide how to represent that content textually: even if we used images, they would still need alt text. But what text is appropriate? We certainly can't use a symbol like > or », because those symbols already have other meanings—the former is a greater-than sign, the latter is a French quotation mark—and a screen reader would pronounce those existing meanings.

What we really want is one more character that imparts the same meaning *irrespective of modality*. I don't know if there is a definitive answer here, but the best I can suggest is to use two or three dots (or an ellipsis character, as I've done myself in the past). That should be commonly understood to mean "and there's more" when heard as speech, while doing a similar job when viewed as written text. An alternative could be to use a textual label, such as submenu, written as the alt text of an image.

Adding Timers so the Menus Don't Open and Close so Abruptly

One of the major usability problems with dynamic menus is that they can be very skittish and awkward to use: you have to move your mouse very precisely over a small target area in order to navigate through a structure like the one shown in Figure 15.4.

Figure 15.4. Without timers, mouse movement must be very precise

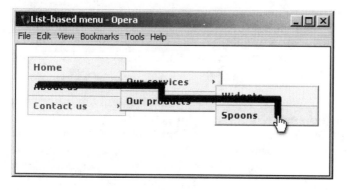

If you move your mouse outside the target area, the menu you're aiming for will close. If you move your mouse outside the structure, the whole thing will close and you'll have to start again. This can be intensely frustrating for users, but we can solve the problem by introducing **open and close timers**.

The addition of timers engenders better usability for anyone who's using a mouse, because timers permit more natural mouse movement. You could move to the link directly, as depicted in Figure 15.5, or with a more erratic path like that in Figure 15.6.

Figure 15.5. With timers, mouse movement can be more direct

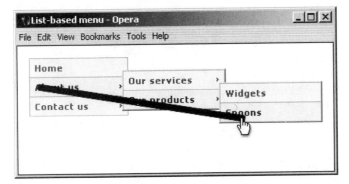

Figure 15.6. With timers, mouse movement can be more erratic

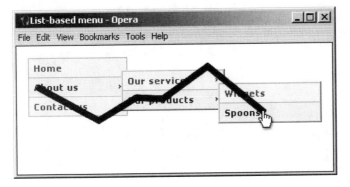

Solution

To add timers to our menu, we need to add some logic to our `mouseover` and `mouseout` event listeners. Rather than opening and closing the menus immediately in response to these events, we must perform these actions after a delay, using `setTimeout`, and cancel these actions when a contradicting event occurs during the delay.

An example of a contradicting event would occur where a `mouseout` event initiates a menu close timer, but a subsequent `mouseover` event on the same element requests that the menu be kept open, thus cancelling the menu close timer.

To modify our script, we first need a new global variable, `branch`, which we'll use to track the currently-open branch. As shown in the code below, this variable is set to a default value in dropdownMenu (additions from the previous script are shown in bold):

File: **dropdownMenu.js (excerpt)**

```
var branch;

function dropdownMenu(navid)
{
  var isie = (typeof document.all != 'undefined'
     && typeof window.opera == 'undefined'
     && !?navigator.vendor != 'KDE');
  if (typeof document.getElementById == 'undefined'
     || (navigator.vendor == 'Apple Computer, Inc.'
     && typeof window.XMLHttpRequest == 'undefined')
     || (isie && typeof document.uniqueID == 'undefined'))
  {
    return;
  }

  var rollover = new Image;
  rollover.src = 'right-red.gif';
  var tree = document.getElementById(navid);
  if (tree)
  {
    branch = tree;
    var items = tree.getElementsByTagName('li');
    for (var i = 0; i < items.length; i++)
    {
      dropdownTrigger(tree, items[i], navid, isie);
    }
  }
};
```

We're also going to need a new function that closes all the menus from a given root node, and a second function to identify unwanted events coming from text nodes in Safari (both of which we'll examine in the discussion):

```
function clearMenus(root)
{
  var menus = root.getElementsByTagName('ul');
  for (var i = 0; i < menus.length; i++)
  {
    menus[i].style.left = '-100em';
  }
}
```

```
function unwantedTextEvent()
{
  return (navigator.vendor == 'Apple Computer, Inc.'
      && (event.target == event.relatedTarget.parentNode
      || (event.eventPhase == 3
      && event.target.parentNode == event.relatedTarget)));
};
```

Now we're ready to implement the timers into our main script, which we'll do by surrounding the show/hide code with calls to setTimeout, passing the existing code as nested closures. Writing them in this format means we can use variables from the function scope directly within the timers; they'll run the code inside after a set amount of time, unless cancelled by a contradicting event (again, additions are shown in bold):

File: **dropdownMenu.js (excerpt)**

```
function dropdownTrigger(tree, li, navid, isie)
{
  var opentime, closetime;
  var a = li.getElementsByTagName('a')[0];
  var menu = (li.getElementsByTagName('ul').length > 0
      ? li.getElementsByTagName('ul')[0] : null);
  var horiz = (tree.className.indexOf('horizontal') != -1);
  var issub = (li.parentNode.id == navid);

  if (menu)
  {
    li.className += (li.className == '' ? '' : ' ') + 'hasmenu';
  }

  attachEventListener(li, 'mouseover', function(e)
  {
    if (unwantedTextEvent()) { return; }
    clearTimeout(closetime);
    if (branch == li) { branch = null; }

    a.className += (a.className == '' ? '' : ' ') + 'rollover';

    if (menu)
    {
      opentime = window.setTimeout(function()
      {
        if (branch)
        {
          clearMenus(branch);
```

```
            branch = null;
        }

        menu.style.left = horiz
            ? (isie ? li.offsetLeft + 'px' : 'auto')
            : '0';

        menu.style.top = horiz && issub
            ? (isie ? a.offsetHeight + 'px' : 'auto')
            : (isie ? li.offsetTop + 'px' : '0');
    }, 250);
    }
}, false);

attachEventListener(li, 'mouseout', function(e)
{
    if (unwantedTextEvent()) { return; }

    var related = typeof e.relatedTarget != 'undefined'
        ? e.relatedTarget : e.toElement;
    if (!li.contains(related))
    {
        clearTimeout(opentime);
        branch = li;

        a.className = a.className.replace(/ ?rollover/g, '');
        if (menu)
        {
            closetime = window.setTimeout(function()
            {
                menu.style.left = '-100em';
            }, 600);
        }
    }
}, false);

if (!isie)
{
    li.contains = function(node)
    {
        if (node == null) { return false; }
        if (node == this) { return true; }
        else { return this.contains(node.parentNode); }
    };
}
}
```

Discussion

The principle here is simple: before opening or closing a menu, wait a specified amount of time; if another event occurs, contradicting the first, cancel the timer and do nothing. Implementing a **close timer** means that mouse movement across a menu can be very imprecise: if your mouse moves briefly off the menu and back again, it doesn't matter.

The **open timer** works on the same principle, but its purpose is slightly different—it's there to ensure that, when moving your mouse from an item to a child menu, you can pass briefly over intervening links without the menu you aim to reach closing, or being replaced by a different one. It also means that when you're navigating elsewhere on the page, such as moving past the menu to get to the browser's Back button, you can move your mouse briefly over the navigation bar without opening any menus at all.

It's because of the open timer that we need the `clearMenus` reset function: this way, when an open timer *does* complete, and a menu is ready to open, any currently-open menus are closed immediately. Without that reset, we'd often see a short pause, equal to the difference between the open time and close time, before the menu closed. We could avoid that pause using fewer lines of code if we restricted the open and close timers to have the same value, but that would be a shame, because their optimum values are different. Based on experimentation and the feedback I get from users of my own sites, I've found that 600ms is the optimum length for a close timer, while a brisk 250ms is about right for an open timer.

We maintain the global `branch` variable so that the reset doesn't conflict with menu opening—if we just performed a tree-wide reset every time, it would be impossible to open menus further than one-level deep, because a `mouseover` on a nested menu would reset all its ancestors. Instead, we do a reset only from the previously-opened branch downwards, which has the effect of closing whichever menu was last opened.

The `branch` variable is maintained from the list item's `mouseout` function, where it's continually set to whichever list item you last moved your mouse off, and is cleared (set back to `null`) either by the `clearMenus` function, or by a contradicting `mouseover` event. The second circumstance is necessary because you might mouse away from the lowest item in a menu, as though to close it, then move back onto that same item, which, without that test, would cause the menus to close. The approach we're taking ensures that the menus are never reset if the `branch` variable is the item you're actually using.

Although the `branch` variable needs to be global (so that it can be referenced from any item), each pair of timers is local to its own menu—each menu has its own pair of timers. You wouldn't want the parent items of a deeply-nested menu to close while you're still using it—you'd want a menu branch to remain open to the point at which you're using it. This means that an event on a menu should cancel not just that menu's timer, but all timers up that branch.

Happily, this occurs naturally through the action of event bubbling, a process that we used for the persistent rollover when we first built the menu, and which is doubly important here. In fact, event bubbling is the *only* reason this works at all!

We could have achieved this effect in other ways, of course. We could have maintained our menu structure from a single pair of timer references in the global scope, for example, but the method we've chosen is entirely self-contained: by writing the timers as closures within the scope of each list item, our script is more effectively encapsulated (and would be easier to convert to object oriented style, which we'll discuss in Chapter 19). It *does* mean that we lose support for Mac IE 5, and Safari 1.0 (neither of which supports the use of `setTimeout` with that syntax); however, we've *already* degraded those builds to unsupported (for other, CSS-related reasons, as we noted earlier), so it's not going to be an issue.

Tip

Less is More!

The fewer variables you have in the global scope, the better. Ideally, we wouldn't have any (apart from functions), because each global variable you use has the potential to conflict with another. This can easily happen when, for example, one person adds a script without knowing the others that will be used on the same page. Even if you completely control the development of a site yourself, once you have more than a couple of scripts, it can be very easy to lose track of the names you've already used.

We could still have a problem with event bubbling in later versions of Safari, because *events can come from text nodes in Safari*,[12] and some of those events are unwanted. For example, moving your mouse from the padding-space of a link onto its text will fire a `mouseover` event on the text node and a `mouseout` event on the link, neither of which we want, because they would bubble up and cause multiple timers to start. But we can't just ignore them entirely, because the links *might not have* any padding, or the mouse might be moving so fast that the text node is the first to receive an event (elements can sometimes fail to fire `mouseover` or `mouseout` events if the movement across them is extremely fast).

---

[12]We first encountered this phenomenon in "Opening Off-site Links in a New Window" in Chapter 7.

This is why we have the `unwantedTextEvent` function: it returns whether an event is unwanted, by those criteria, so that we can use it as a condition in the list item mouse functions.

event Saves the Day

The event references in `unwantedTextEvent` look pretty strange, I know. `event` is Internet Explorer's `window.event` object, but IE doesn't support the property name `relatedTarget`. So, why haven't we passed an event reference?

Well, we haven't had to, because this test for unwanted events needs only to work in Safari (and Konqueror, which uses the same engine), and because Safari and Konqueror implement IE's global `event` object *as well as* the pass-by-reference model used in Firefox and other browsers! It certainly makes life easier here, and could be invaluable in other cases, should you find yourself in a situation where it's impossible or impractical to pass a reference.

Making Sure the Menus Stay Inside the Window

Once we start adding deeper levels to the menu, we may reach a situation where a single branch is too long to fit inside the window. This clearly won't do, because menus that extend outside the window are virtually impossible to use with the mouse. What we need is the ability to detect that kind of situation, then reposition the menus on the fly.

Information Architecture Tip

Even with these measures in place, it's generally considered good usability to keep a menu structure fairly small. A large structure with many deeply-nested branches can be intimidating to use, while a single menu with dozens of items will be too tall to fit inside a window at a resolution of 800x600.

Consider splitting large menus into subgroups, and if the number of subgroups becomes excessive, consider removing the detailed links, limiting yourself to section-index pages. A drop-down menu should not be a sitemap, after all.

Solution

To make the calculations for menu repositioning, every time a menu is opened, we need to know that menu's approximate position with respect to the top-left of the viewport, and the viewport's size. These two functions will give us the data:

File: **dropdownMenu.js** (excerpt)

```javascript
function getRoughPosition(ele, dir)
{
  var pos = dir == 'x' ? ele.offsetLeft : ele.offsetTop;
  var tmp = ele.offsetParent;
  while (tmp != null)
  {
    pos += dir == 'x' ? tmp.offsetLeft : tmp.offsetTop;
    tmp = tmp.offsetParent;
  }
  return pos;
};

function getViewportSize()
{
  var size = [0,0];

  if (typeof window.innerWidth != 'undefined')
  {
    size = [
        window.innerWidth,
        window.innerHeight
    ];
  }
  else if (typeof document.documentElement != 'undefined'
      && typeof document.documentElement.clientWidth != 'undefined'
      && document.documentElement.clientWidth != 0)
  {
    size = [
        document.documentElement.clientWidth,
        document.documentElement.clientHeight
    ];
  }
  else
  {
    size = [
        document.getElementsByTagName('body')[0].clientWidth,
        document.getElementsByTagName('body')[0].clientHeight
    ];
  }

  return size;
}
```

We also need a function to do the actual repositioning work, using data from the previous two:

File: **dropdownMenu.js (excerpt)**

```
function repositionMenu(menu)
{
  var extent = [
      getRoughPosition(menu, 'x') + menu.offsetWidth + 25,
      getRoughPosition(menu, 'y') + menu.offsetHeight + 25
  ];
  var viewsize = getViewportSize();

  if (extent[0] > viewsize[0])
  {
    var offset = menu.offsetWidth
        + menu.parentNode.parentNode.offsetWidth;
    var inset = menu.parentNode.offsetWidth
        - menu.offsetLeft;

    menu.style.left = (0 - offset + (inset * 2)) + 'px';
  }
  if (extent[1] > viewsize[1])
  {
    var current = parseInt(menu.style.top, 10);
    var difference = (extent[1] - viewsize[1]);

    menu.style.top = (current - difference) + 'px';
  }
}
```

Finally, we can call the repositioning function from our list item mouseover function (additions from the previous script are shown in bold):

File: **dropdownMenu.js (excerpt)**

```
attachEventListener(li, 'mouseover', function(e)
{
  if (unwantedTextEvent()) { return; }
  clearTimeout(closetime);
  if (branch == li) { branch = null; }

  a.className += (a.className == '' ? '' : ' ') + 'rollover';

  var target = typeof e.target != 'undefined'
      ? e.target : e.srcElement;
  while (target.nodeName.toUpperCase() != 'LI')
```

```
{
  target = target.parentNode;
}
if (target != li) { return; }

if (menu)
{
  opentime = window.setTimeout(function()
  {
    if (branch)
    {
      clearMenus(branch);
      branch = null;
    }

    menu.style.left = horiz
        ? (isie ? li.offsetLeft + 'px' : 'auto')
        : '0';

    menu.style.top = horiz && issub
        ? (isie ? a.offsetHeight + 'px' : 'auto')
        : (isie ? li.offsetTop + 'px' : '0');

    repositionMenu(menu);
  }, 250);
}
}, false);
```

Discussion

Before we examine how the repositioning works, let's look briefly at the two utility functions, `getRoughPosition` and `getViewportSize`.

The first function, `getRoughPosition`, finds the position of an object on the page, but as we saw in the earlier section called "Finding the Position of an Element" in Chapter 13, such a simple routine is rarely very accurate: it doesn't include the borders on intermediate elements, nor does it cater for the various browser quirks and variations. In this case, however, we don't really need very accurate figures; we simply need to know if a menu is near, or past, the edge of the viewport, so a simple function like this is good enough. We will, of course, have to allow for broad inaccuracies, so when we actually come to use the function, we'll include a generous buffer zone of 25 pixels to that end.

The second function, `getViewportSize`, simply works out the current viewport size using a variety of browser-dependent properties, and is identical to the solution we saw in "Getting the Viewport Size (the Available Space inside the Window)" in Chapter 7.

Now, let's turn to the function that actually does the repositioning. Within the list item mouseover listener you can see that `repositionMenu` is called immediately after the default positioning. That's simple enough. However, what we have here is a structure of many nested items, inside which events are allowed to bubble freely. Suddenly, that's a problem for us—the bubbling means that the menu we examine when we come to repositioning is always the lowest menu in that branch (the first submenu from the navbar). We can't stop that bubbling, as we rely on it for other purposes in the script, but we do have to do *something* if we want this repositioning to work.

What we have to do is *allow* it to bubble, but ensure that the menu positioning code only acts on the true target, not any subsequent bubble phases. That's the purpose of this code:

File: **dropdownMenu.js** (excerpt)

```
var target = typeof e.target != 'undefined'
    ? e.target : e.srcElement;
while (target.nodeName.toUpperCase() != 'LI')
{
  target = target.parentNode;
}
if (target != li) { return; }
```

The `li` reference is the list item to which the handler is bound, but the `target` variable will refer to whichever node the event has bubbled to at that point in time, "rounded-up," so to speak, to the nearest list item (because the bubbling events can also come from intermediate elements—from links and, in Safari, from the text node inside a link).

The end result is that the code responsible for timer management and rollover styling (both of which come before the above fragment in the mouseover listener) bubbles freely, as it needs to, but the menu positioning code is ignored unless the listener is dealing with the primary target. We could have done the same job more simply if we had been able to use the `eventPhase` property (to determine at what stage of event propagation the function is being called), but that property isn't supported in Internet Explorer 5 or 6.

Now that we are able to reference the right menu, and we have window-size and position-finding functions that can establish that a menu needs to be moved, what kind of repositioning do we want? We have two options:

❏ Move the menu back just enough that it doesn't go over the edge of the window (let's call this **position rounding**).

❏ Invert the menu's position so that it opens to the other side of its parent (**position inversion**).

In fact both approaches are useful for different directions of overflow. Let's begin with the horizontal overflow, and a menu structure that looks like Figure 15.7 when fully expanded.

Figure 15.7. A large menu structure fully expanded

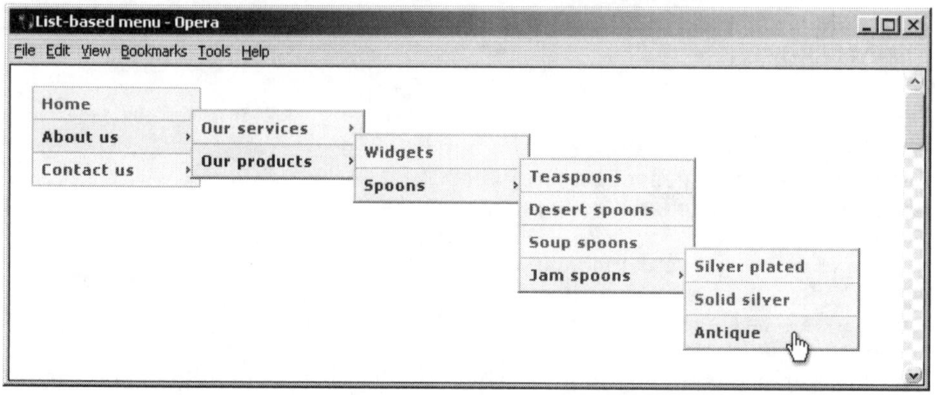

If our window was only half that width and we used position rounding on the Widgets/Spoons menu, what would happen to the levels beyond that menu? Those menu levels would *also* go over the edge. They'd be repositioned in the same way, ending up almost directly on top of their parent. We would see something like Figure 15.8.

Figure 15.8. Menus stacking on top of each other: not good

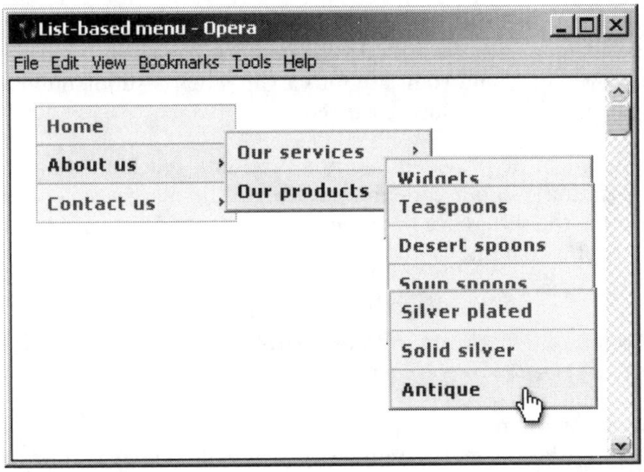

That won't do at all! Let's try position inversion, which will give us a much neater layout, as shown in Figure 15.9. A further child menu might have room to open normally, or it might be repositioned back to the left, as necessary. The menus will still stack up after a certain number of levels, but in two columns instead of one, ensuring that they remain usable.

Figure 15.9. Menus stacking in two neat columns: much better

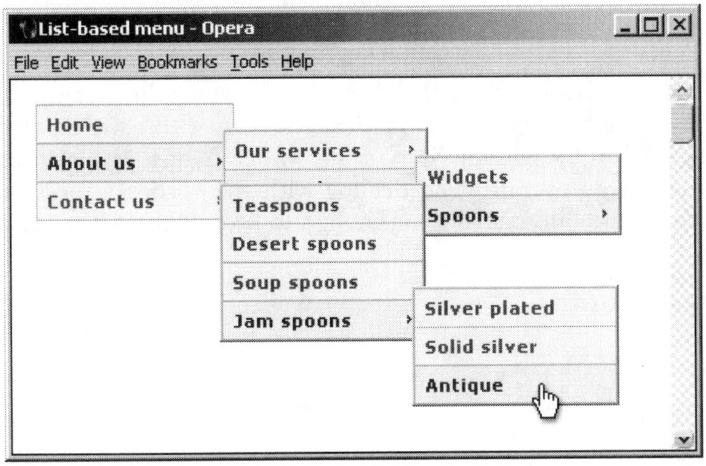

Margins and Menu Overlap

note

You'll notice that the submenus overlap their parents' right edges slightly, which is achieved using a negative `margin` in our CSS. However, if not accounted for, that overlap would translate into a gap when a submenu was repositioned to the left, as we've just discussed.

The `margin` value might be provided in a non-pixel unit (such as `em`, as it is in this demonstration), so our code must calculate the margin as a pixel value by ascertaining the difference between the menu's `offsetLeft`, and the `offsetWidth` of its parent:

File: **dropdownMenu.js** (excerpt)

```
var inset = menu.parentNode.offsetWidth
    - menu.offsetLeft;
```

To re-implement the margin on the repositioned menu, we add *twice* the margin to its `left` position (once to remove the gap, and a second time to create an equivalent overlap of the parent menu's left edge):

File: **dropdownMenu.js** (excerpt)

```
menu.style.left = (0 - offset + (inset * 2)) + 'px';
```

Now, let's look at the possibility of a vertical overflow. Here, position rounding is the solution we want, because the horizontal shift was really all that was needed to avoid obscuring parent menus. Menus are never going to stack directly on top of each other now: we can be sure that a child menu will always be to the left or right of its parent.

Indeed, if we used position inversion for the vertical axis, we could be moving the menu quite a way up, possibly out of practical reach. A menu with many items could be quite tall, and a window is typically wider than it is high, so, typically, we have less leeway overall when dealing with the vertical aspect of menu positioning. We should only move it far enough to keep it above the fold, as shown in Figure 15.10.

Figure 15.10. Menus repositioned to stay above the fold

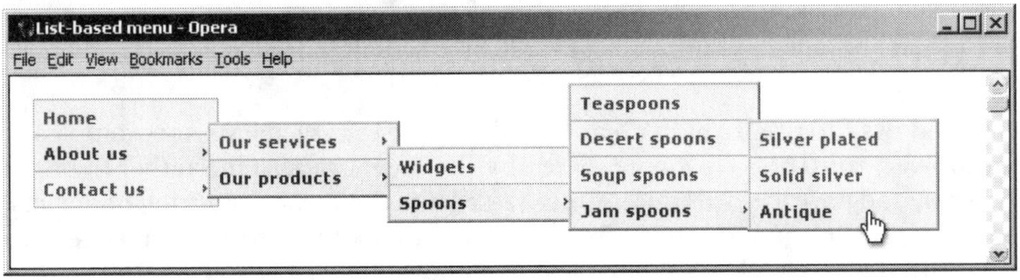

Now, with both kinds of repositioning in force, even a large structure constrained in a small space remains usable, displaying similarly to Figure 15.11.

note

Need Scrolling?

These repositioning functions don't allow for page scrolling. In practice, scrolling is seldom necessary, because most sites have their main navigation bar at or near the top of the page. But if you do need that capability, you can simply add the scrolling amounts to the viewport size figures, using data from the `getScrollingPosition` function we built in "Getting the Scrolling Position" in Chapter 7.

Figure 15.11. A large menu structure in a very small space

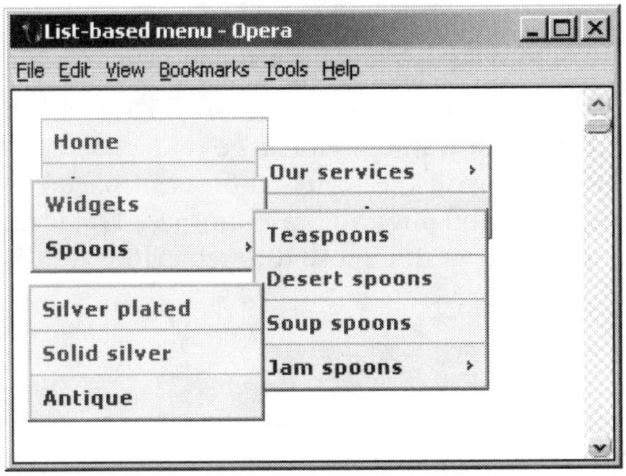

Making the Menus Display Over `select` Elements

In Windows Internet Explorer 5 and 6, HTML `select` elements are examples of **windowed controls**. They're rendered by the operating system, rather than the browser, and have a **z-order** of infinity (z-order is the vertical stacking of objects, as defined for normal elements by the CSS `z-index` property). In practice, this means that when a DHTML layer and a windowed control coincide, the control will show through, as illustrated in Figure 15.12.

Figure 15.12. A menu coinciding with a `select` element in Windows IE

However, in IE 5.5 and IE 6 the `iframe` element has unique properties—it's a window-level object like any other window or frame, so it can go on top of other window-level objects, but it can *also* fall in with the regular z-order of page elements. The practical upshot of this is that if you put an `iframe` *between* a DHTML layer and a windowed-control, the control doesn't show through! How cool is that?

Solution

To apply this technique to our menu, we simply need to create `iframe` layers on the fly. Each time a menu is opened, we'll create a new `iframe` and position it directly underneath that menu, removing it when the menu is closed. Here are the functions we'll need:

File: **dropdownMenu.js (excerpt)**

```
function createIframeLayer(menu)
{
  var layer = document.createElement('iframe');
  layer.tabIndex = '-1';
  layer.src = 'javascript:false;';
  menu.parentNode.appendChild(layer);

  layer.style.left = menu.offsetLeft + 'px';
  layer.style.top = menu.offsetTop + 'px';
  layer.style.width = menu.offsetWidth + 'px';
  layer.style.height = menu.offsetHeight + 'px';
}

function removeIframeLayer(menu)
{
  var layers = menu.parentNode.getElementsByTagName('iframe');
  while (layers.length > 0)
  {
    layers[0].parentNode.removeChild(layers[0]);
  }
}
```

These `iframe`s are styled with the following CSS, which places them *between* the list item and the menu in the stacking order:

File: **vertical.css (excerpt)**

```
/* iframe layer */
ul iframe {
  position: absolute;
  z-index: 1010;
  border: none;
}
```

Finally, we need to add this behavior to the list item functions. First, we call `createIframeLayer` in the mouseover listener, immediately *after* the other positioning code (this way, we create the `iframe` layer at the menu's final position, which saves having to reposition them both). It's wrapped in an object test that applies to Windows IE only (additions from the previous script are shown in bold):

File: **dropdownMenu.js (excerpt)**

```
attachEventListener(li, 'mouseover', function(e)
{
  if (unwantedTextEvent()) { return; }
```

```
clearTimeout(closetime);
if (branch == li) { branch = null; }

a.className += (a.className == '' ? '' : ' ') + 'rollover';

var target = typeof e.target != 'undefined'
    ? e.target : e.srcElement;
while (target.nodeName.toUpperCase() != 'LI')
{
  target = target.parentNode;
}
if (target != li) { return; }

if (menu)
{
  opentime = window.setTimeout(function()
  {
    if (branch)
    {
      clearMenus(branch);
      branch = null;
    }

    menu.style.left = horiz
        ? (isie ? li.offsetLeft + 'px' : 'auto')
        : '0';

    menu.style.top = horiz && issub
        ? (isie ? a.offsetHeight + 'px' : 'auto')
        : (isie ? li.offsetTop + 'px' : '0');

    repositionMenu(menu);

    if (typeof document.uniqueID != 'undefined')
    {
      createIframeLayer(menu);
    }
  }, 250);
}
}, false);
```

Then, we call `removeIframeLayer` at both the points at which menus are closed. The first is the list item mouseout:

File: **dropdownMenu.js (excerpt)**

```
attachEventListener(li, 'mouseout', function(e)
{
  if (unwantedTextEvent()) { return; }

  var related = typeof e.relatedTarget != 'undefined'
      ? e.relatedTarget : e.toElement;
  if (!li.contains(related))
  {
    clearTimeout(opentime);
    branch = li;

    a.className = a.className.replace(/ ?rollover/g, '');
    if (menu)
    {
      closetime = window.setTimeout(function()
      {
        menu.style.left = '-100em';

        removeIframeLayer(menu);
      }, 600);
    }
  }
}, false);
```

We call removeIframeLayer a second time at the reset function, clearMenus:

File: **dropdownMenu.js (excerpt)**

```
function clearMenus(root)
{
  var menus = root.getElementsByTagName('ul');
  for (var i = 0; i < menus.length; i++)
  {
    menus[i].style.left = '-100em';
    removeIframeLayer(menus[i]);
  }
}
```

We don't need to perform any browser checks to call removeIframeLayer, because the code inside it will apply only if an iframe layer has already been created.

Discussion

The iframe has absolute positioning within the same context as the menu (i.e., the menu and the iframe are siblings within a positioned parent element). This makes it easy for us to place the `iframe` underneath the menu, and set its dimensions to match those of the menu using the offset properties of the menu itself (`offsetLeft`, `offsetWidth`, and so on).

Nobody will see the `iframe` layer, since it has no borders, and its size and position perfectly match the size and position of the menu, but it will sit there doing its job, obscuring `select` elements and other windowed controls. In fact, this trick is so robust that it also works for Flash, Java applets—even embedded media players!

Let's set a couple of extra properties, just for safety's sake. The negative `tabIndex` value takes the `iframe` out of the page's tab order (otherwise, users would be able to navigate to it with the keyboard, which would cause confusion). We set `src` so that we don't experience any problems with SSL pages. In IE, `iframes` with no set `src` automatically load about:blank. IE considers this an insecure page, and would generate a warning dialog that reads: "This page contains both secure and non-secure items."

We can avoid this problem by setting the `src` to `'javascript:false;'`, because the document is then deemed to be within the same security zone as the host page. Note that we must set the `src` *before* appending the `iframe` to the page; if we do it afterwards we'll get that "click" sound of a link being followed every time a new `iframe` is created.

Note that this trick only works in IE 5.5 or later, because of the unique properties of an `iframe` in those versions; the solution doesn't work in IE 5.0, even though this browser is equally affected by the original problem. IE 5.0 is a little-used version, and usage rates are in steep decline, so you'd be forgiven for overlooking the browser on this occasion. If you do want to cater for its followers, you can fall back on the older, more brutal technique of hiding all `select` elements whenever the menus open, and showing them as the menus are closed. This method is less subtle because it hides *all* `select` elements *completely*, even if a menu only partially overlaps, or indeed, is nowhere near those elements!

To implement this alternative solution, we'll need to define a show/hide function:

File: **dropdownMenu.js** (excerpt)

```
function toggleSelects(vis)
{
  if (typeof document.uniqueID != 'undefined'
      && typeof document.body.style.scrollbarTrackColor ==
      'undefined')
  {
```

```
      var selects = document.getElementsByTagName('select');
      for (var i = 0; i < selects.length; i++)
      {
        selects[i].style.visibility = vis;
      }

      return true;
  }

  return false;
}
```

The function uses a combination of object tests to identify Windows IE 5.0, then returns true or false on the basis of whether or not it ran (and therefore, whether or not the browser is Windows IE 5.0). This means we can use it as both a function call *and* a condition directly from our iframe functions, so that they either hide all select elements, or create the iframe layer. Here's the code (additions are shown in bold):

File: **dropdownMenu.js (excerpt)**

```
function createIframeLayer(menu)
{
  if (!toggleSelects('hidden'))
  {
    var layer = document.createElement('iframe');
    layer.tabIndex = '-1';
    layer.src = 'javascript:false;';
    menu.parentNode.appendChild(layer);

    layer.style.left = menu.offsetLeft + 'px';
    layer.style.top = menu.offsetTop + 'px';
    layer.style.width = menu.offsetWidth + 'px';
    layer.style.height = menu.offsetHeight + 'px';
  }
}

function removeIframeLayer(menu)
{
  if (!toggleSelects('visible'))
  {
    var layers = menu.parentNode.getElementsByTagName('iframe');
    while (layers.length > 0)
    {
      layers[0].parentNode.removeChild(layers[0]);
    }
```

```
    }
}
```

However, the behaviors we get are not quite what we need. We don't want to display the select elements whenever *any* menu is closed: we only want to display them when *all* of the menus are closed, and to do so, we'll need to change the way those elements are reset. Apply the following modification to the list item mouseout function (additions are shown in bold):

```
attachEventListener(li, 'mouseout', function(e)
{
  if (unwantedTextEvent()) { return; }

  var related = typeof e.relatedTarget != 'undefined'
      ? e.relatedTarget : e.toElement;
  if (!li.contains(related))
  {
    clearTimeout(opentime);
    branch = li;

    a.className = a.className.replace(/ ?rollover/g, '');
    if (menu)
    {
      closetime = window.setTimeout(function()
      {
        menu.style.left = '-100em';

        if (toggleSelects('visible') && tree.contains(related))
        {
          toggleSelects('hidden');
        }
        else
        {
          removeIframeLayer(menu);
        }

      }, 600);
    }
  }
}, false);
```

Here, we're calling toggleSelects directly, rather than having it called indirectly from removeIframeLayer. Only Windows IE 5.0 will return true; therefore, only that browser will go on to the second condition—another contains evaluation that assesses whether the event's related target is still inside the tree (so one or more menus are still open), or is outside the tree completely (so all menus are closed). That gives us the information we need: we have to show the elements again, but we can hide them immediately if the mouse is still inside the tree. The overall effect is that the `select` elements appear to remain constantly hidden.

Remember that `contains` is proprietary to IE. However, we needn't worry about this call tripping up other browsers, since they won't look past the call to `toggleSelects`, which will return `false`.

Making a Folder Tree or Expanding Menu

An **expanding menu** (sometimes also known as a "switch menu" or "contracting menu") begins with almost exactly the same HTML framework as our drop-down/fly-out menu. The only difference is a change in the main `ul` class name, from `vertical` to `expanding`. The styling, as shown in Figure 15.13, is quite similar to that of a vertical navbar with fly-out menus, except that the menus have static, rather than absolute positioning (and the arrows point downwards).

The behaviors are quite different, though, because the menus are triggered using `click` events, rather than `mouseover` events, which means that the usability issues we'll need to tackle will be different from those we saw in the previous solution. In some cases, they'll be simplified—we don't really need timers any more, and we certainly don't need menu repositioning—but we will encounter other usability issues, and a serious accessibility trap that we haven't seen before.

A **folder tree menu** is a variation on the expanding menu theme, with slightly different styling. Generally, a folder tree menu's sublevels are indented, and icons—such as folder/file icons or the plus/minus symbols seen in a Windows-style folder tree—appear beside each menu item, as shown in Figure 15.14.

Figure 15.13. An HTML list styled as an expanding menu

Figure 15.14. A folder tree menu with plus/minus icons

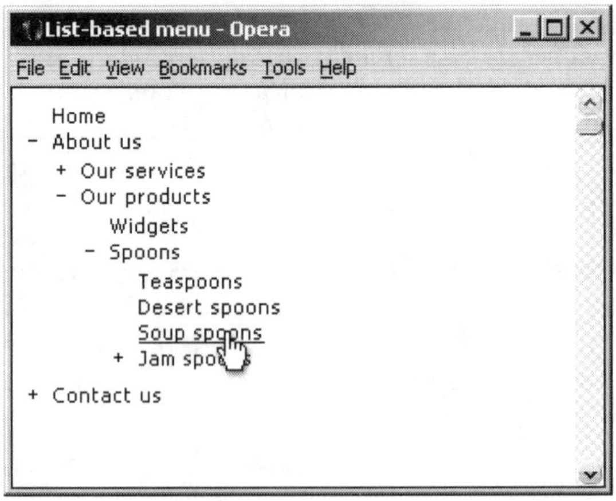

We'll account for both those icon variations in due course, but let's begin by building the basic framework. We've already seen the HTML; here's the CSS for an **expanding menu**:

File: **expanding.css**

```
/* structural styles and offsets */
ul.expanding, ul.expanding li, ul.expanding ul {
  margin: 0;
  padding: 0;
```

```
    list-style-type: none;
    font-size: 100%;
}
ul.expanding {
  position: relative;
  cursor: default;
  width: 8.2em;
}
ul.expanding li {
  position: relative;
  text-align: left;
  cursor: pointer;
  cursor: hand;
  width: 8.2em;
  margin: -1px 0 0 0;
}
ul.expanding ul {
  cursor: default;
  width: 8.2em;
  padding: 2px 0;
  position: absolute;
  left: -100em;
}
ul.expanding ul li {
  width: 8.2em;
}

/* design styles */
ul.expanding a:link, ul.expanding a:visited {
  display: block;
  cursor: pointer;
  cursor: hand;
  background: #ffc;
  border: 1px solid #edbb85;
  padding: 5px 7px;
  font: bold 0.7em tahoma, verdana, sans-serif;
  color: #008000;
  text-decoration: none;
  letter-spacing: 1px;
}
ul.expanding a:hover, ul.expanding a:focus, ul.expanding a:active,
ul.expanding a.rollover:link, ul.expanding a.rollover:visited {
  background: #ffefcf;
  color: #806020;
}
```

```
/* submenu indicator arrows */
ul.expanding li.hasmenu > a:link,
ul.expanding li.hasmenu > a:visited {
  background: url(down-green.gif) #ffc no-repeat 95% 50%;
}
ul.expanding li.hasmenu > a:hover,
ul.expanding li.hasmenu > a:focus,
ul.expanding li.hasmenu > a:active,
ul.expanding li.hasmenu > a.rollover:link,
ul.expanding li.hasmenu > a.rollover:visited {
  background: url(down-red.gif) #ffefcf no-repeat 95% 50%;
}
* html ul.expanding li.hasmenu a:link,
* html ul.expanding li.hasmenu a:visited
  background: expression(/hasmenu/.test(this.parentNode.className)
      ? "url(down-green.gif) #ffc no-repeat 95% 50%" : "#ffc");
}
* html ul.expanding li.hasmenu a:hover,
* html ul.expanding li.hasmenu a:active,
* html ul.expanding li.hasmenu a.rollover:link,
* html ul.expanding li.hasmenu a.rollover:visited {
  background: expression(/hasmenu/.test(this.parentNode.className)
    ? "url(down-red.gif) #ffefcf no-repeat 95% 50%" : "#ffefcf");
}

/* browser hacks */
@media screen, projection {
  * html ul.expanding li {
    display: inline;
    f\loat: left;
    background: #fff;
  }
}
```

This creates a menu which will eventually look like the one shown in Figure 15.13. That image shows where we're going, but at this point, using straight CSS, our menu has no submenu indicator arrows, nor are any of its menus visible by default. Let's implement the basic expanding menu functionality now.

Solution

To begin, we need a primary initialization function; this is called treeMenu. It's similar to the dropdownMenu initialization function we wrote in the section called "Making a Drop-down or Fly-out Menu" at the start of this chapter, but simpler, since we have only one special case to deal with. (It affects Safari and Opera, and is catered for by the call to `displayReset`, which we'll examine in the discussion below.)

File: **treeMenu.js** (excerpt)

```
function treeMenu(navid)
{
  if (typeof document.getElementById == 'undefined') { return; }

  var rollover = new Image;
  rollover.src = 'down-red.gif';

  var tree = document.getElementById(navid);
  if (tree)
  {
    var items = tree.getElementsByTagName('li');
    for (var i = 0; i < items.length; i++)
    {
      treeTrigger(tree, items[i], navid);
    }

    if (navigator.vendor == 'Apple Computer, Inc.'
        || typeof window.opera != 'undefined')
    {
      displayReset(tree);
    }
  }
}

var isreset = false;

function displayReset(tree)
{
  var menus = tree.getElementsByTagName('ul');
  for (var i = 0; i < menus.length; i++)
  {
    menus[i].style.display = 'none';
    menus[i].style.position = 'static';
  }
  isreset = true;
}
```

Next, we have a list item initialization function that works rather differently from the equivalent in our drop-down menu script:

File: **treeMenu.js** (excerpt)

```
function treeTrigger(tree, li, navid)
{
  var a = li.getElementsByTagName('a')[0];
  var menu = li.getElementsByTagName('ul').length > 0
      ? li.getElementsByTagName('ul')[0] : null;

  if (menu)
  {
    li.className += (li.className == '' ? '' : ' ') + 'hasmenu';
  }

  li.onclick = function(e)
  {
    var target = e ? e.target : window.event.srcElement;
    while (target.nodeName.toUpperCase() != 'LI')
    {
      target = target.parentNode;
    }
    if (target == this && isreset)
    {
      if (menu)
      {
        if (menu.style.display == 'none')
        {
          menu.style.display = 'block';
        }
        else
        {
          menu.style.display = 'none';
        }
        return false;
      }
      else
      {
        return true;
      }
    }
  };

  attachEventListener(a, 'keyup', function(e)
  {
    if (!isreset && e.keyCode == 9)
    {
      displayReset(tree);
    }
```

```
  }, false);

  var moves = 0;
  attachEventListener(a, 'mousemove', function()
  {
    if (!isreset)
    {
      moves++;
      if (moves > 2) { displayReset(tree); }
    }
  }, false);
}
```

Finally, as before, we call our main initialization function from the load event, passing the list id:

File: **treeMenu.js (excerpt)**

```
addLoadListener(function() { treeMenu('navigation'); });
```

Discussion

The treeTrigger function starts by performing many of the same tasks the dropdownTrigger function did in our drop-down menu example: it stores a reference to the link and the submenu (if one exists), adds a class name to identify which items should have indicator arrows, and binds an event listener to each list item to facilitate opening and closing the submenus. Two additional event listeners, keyup and mousemove, are used for links. These listeners are related to solving the accessibility trap I mentioned earlier; we'll discuss this in depth shortly.

But let's begin with the simplest aspect: the list item click event handler. Here, we have to do the same kind of target filtering that we performed on our drop-down menu, and for the same reason: to establish whether this event comes directly from the element to which this handler was assigned (this), or has bubbled from another. Without this filter, we wouldn't know if we were responding to a click on the list item that contains the menu, or a list item contained *within* that menu.

Avoiding a Safari Bug

You'll notice that the script uses a DOM 0 event handler to respond to click events, rather than the less intrusive attachEventListener method we've used elsewhere. This tactic helps us avoid a bug in Safari.[13] Although we're responding to `click` events on behalf of list items, it's the links inside those list items that people will actually click. To use these links as menu open and close toggles, we'll need to *prevent those links from being followed*.

In Chapter 13 we saw a method that we can use to prevent the default action of an event. That method was `stopDefaultAction`, and it works all the time for almost every browser. Almost. In Safari, the method simply fails to work, and the browser follows the link as normal. As far as I know, there isn't an effective workaround for this bug, other than to fall back on a DOM 0 handler with which we can simply return `false`. This approach works fine in all browsers, which is why we've used it here.

With the workaround in place, our function simply displays or hides the menu. But hang on … didn't we say that using `display` or `visibility` properties to show and hide elements makes our menus inaccessible to browser-based screen readers?

Indeed, *by default*, the menus are hidden using the offleft positioning technique we saw previously. It solved a usability problem in that example, but in this case it's actually *detrimental* to users of graphical browsers. Links that are positioned in this way are still accessible via the keyboard, even though they're not visible on the screen, so, if we used this solution, users who tabbed through the list (or otherwise navigated by keyboard) would navigate to menu items they couldn't see!

The problem is complicated further by the fact that we have to return `false` on menu-triggering links, and the `click` events which trigger the function can be fired by the keyboard as well as the mouse (for instance, by pressing **Enter** on a link that has focus). So if we returned `false` in every case we'd be preventing keyboard navigation of our menus for anyone using a browser-based screen reader, because activating the link would do nothing at all!

One way to deal with the first problem is to add `focus` event listeners to every link, so that the menus open automatically. This would ensure that all menu levels are always accessible to sighted keyboard users; however, this solution doesn't allow users to *control* the opening and closing of menu branches from the keyboard (which would be far more usable). Nor does it address the second problem in any way: we still need to know what to do—whether or not to follow the link—when a link receives a `click` event.

---

[13]At the time of writing, the bug occurs in versions of Safari up to and including version 2.0.1.

In order to address the second problem, we must think more carefully about how the menu will be navigated by keyboard. Ultimately, both our accessibility problems and our usability preferences are part-and-parcel of the same issue; we have to address them together.

What we really need is a means of *identifying* browser-based screen readers that would allow us to use display toggles and provide a means for evaluating click events. We can't directly identify such devices, because they don't identify themselves differently from the browser they're used with. But we can *infer* their use indirectly, because they *don't generate the same set of events* that the browser generates on its own. We can use these disparities to "detect" the browsing devices in question, and respond accordingly.

This technique is covered in a lot more depth in Chapter 16, but in summary, browser-based screen readers rarely generate keydown or keyup events as a result of the user pressing **Tab** to navigate between links; however, some screen readers do generate these events when modifier keys like **Shift** are used, or when other actions occur, such as the user pressing **Enter** to activate a link.

It's a Hack!

This technique is a hack—there's no other word for it—because it makes inferences about devices based on behaviors that could change in future versions. But, at present, it allows us to cater for the original accessibility problem in a way that would otherwise be impossible, as far as I know. Without it, our tree menu would be useless for all browser-based screen readers.

So, to solve the problem, we attach a key handler to each of the links and test for keyCode 9 (the **Tab** key). If we receive an event with that keyCode we'll know it came from a graphical browser, not a browser-based screen reader.[14] In such cases, we can call displayReset:

File: **treeMenu.js (excerpt)**

```
attachEventListener(a, 'keyup', function(e)
{
  if (!isreset && e.keyCode == 9)
  {
    displayReset(tree);
  }
}, false);
```

---

[14]This solution was tested in JAWS 5.0 and 6.2, Connect Outloud 2.0, Windows Eyes 5.0, Hal 6.5 and Home Page Reader 3.0. Please see Chapter 16 for more details.

The `displayReset` function iterates through and hides all the menus (which gives us the keyboard behaviors we want for graphical browsers, solving the first problem). To say that we've removed those menus from the display, we set the `isreset` flag, which we can use later to process `click` events. If the flag has not been set, we know that we're not dealing with a graphical browser. Therefore, we don't have to toggle the menu display: we can follow the link as normal (solving the second problem).

We'll have to do the same thing for mouse events, so that mouse navigation still works properly. However, in doing so we have to overcome another behavioral quirk of various browser-based screen readers: some generate a complement of *mouse events* when a link is actuated with the keyboard. For example, Dolphin Hal 6.5 generates `mouseover`, `mousemove`, and `mousedown` events at the same time as it generates a `click` event. But it only generates *one of each*, so we can use a `mousemove` handler that counts for *multiple* events to filter the events that are generated. A graphical browser used in conjunction with a mouse will generate several `mousemove` events on a link before it generates a `click` event, while a screen reader generates only one `mousemove`, just before the link is followed. Therefore, if we receive several events within the lifetime of the script, we can assume that the visitor is using a graphical browser:

File: **treeMenu.js** (excerpt)

```
var moves = 0;
attachEventListener(a, 'mousemove', function()
{
  if (!isreset)
  {
    moves ++;
    if (moves > 2) { displayReset(tree); }
  }
}, false);
```

Regardless of which event actually triggers the reset, we need only go through the script once. Therefore, in both instances, `displayReset` is called only if the `isreset` flag has not already been set.

Before we can consider our solution complete, we need to consider one more category of browsers: voicing or speaking browsers such as Opera 8 with Voice, Firefox with the FoxyVoice extension, and Safari 2 using VoiceOver (the speech capability introduced in Mac OS 10.4). Each of these tools is designed to supplement visual browser use, rather than to act as the sole browsing tool for a person who's completely blind, so they need to be treated in the same way as a graphical browser. But Safari with VoiceOver and Opera with Voice fall through the net, because they don't quite generate the same set of events as those browsers generate on their own.

Safari with VoiceOver does generate `keyup` events when the user navigates with the **Tab** key, but not when custom navigation keystrokes (such as **Ctrl-Option-→** for "move to next link") are used.

Opera with Voice may not generate key events at all, because it allows users to navigate using voice commands alone. Actually, Opera has a range of navigation keys (users can press **A** and **Q** to move between links, while the arrow keys allow spatial navigation), so the original test for `keyCode` 9 wouldn't cater for Opera anyway. We could add extra key-codes to the test condition, but the solution we're about to step through will cover it from another direction.

All we need to do to fix this problem is to apply `displayReset` at menu initialization when we detect Opera:

File: **treeMenu.js** (excerpt)

```
if (navigator.vendor == 'Apple Computer, Inc.'
    || typeof window.opera != 'undefined')
{
  displayReset(tree);
}
```

Since no other browser-based screen readers integrate with Safari or Opera,[15] actual users will not be affected.

Indicating Expanded Branches in a Menu

In a Windows-style folder tree menu, each submenu usually is supplemented by an icon; + (plus) denotes a closed sub-branch (meaning "click to expand") and – (minus) denotes an open sub-branch ("click to collapse"). On different systems, the icons may vary—your system may show a folder or other icon—but the principle is the same. For the most part, adding these icons is simply a case of changing the CSS, that is, removing the indicator arrows that change with the link state, and replacing them with icons that change with the menu state.

A little scripting is involved, but it's identical regardless of whether you're adding icons to a folder tree, or highlighting expanded elements in an expanding menu. So far, we've been building an expanding menu, but at the end of this solution,

---

[15]The vast majority of readers only work with Internet Explorer, but GW Micro's Windows Eyes 5.5 (beta, at the time of writing) also claims to work with Firefox.

we'll see how to turn it into a folder tree. You can then continue development using the menu type you need.

Solution

The scripting aspect of this solution is based on the approach we used in our fly-out menu: we'll set a particular class name when a branch is in use (in this case, "in use" means the submenu is open), and remove the class when the menu is not in use. Here's the list item `click` event handler again, with the necessary additions in bold:

File: **treeMenu.js (excerpt)**

```
li.onclick = function(e)
{
  var target = e ? e.target : window.event.srcElement;
  while (target.nodeName.toUpperCase() != 'LI')
  {
    target = target.parentNode;
  }
  if (target == this && isreset)
  {
    if (menu)
    {
      if (menu.style.display == 'none')
      {
        menu.style.display = 'block';
        a.className += (a.className=='' ? '' : ' ') + 'rollover';
      }
      else
      {
        menu.style.display = 'none';
        a.className = a.className.replace(/ ?rollover/g, '');
      }
      return false;
    }
    else
    {
      return true;
    }
  }
};
```

Simple, isn't it? If we add that script to our expanding menu, the revised menu code will highlight not only menu items that we roll over, but submenu items that have been opened, finally achieving the look we saw back in Figure 15.13.

Discussion

But what about folder tree icons? First, let's rework the link and arrow styles so that our background-color and arrow change applies *only* once a submenu has been expanded (not when it is moused over):

```
/* design styles */
ul.expanding a:link, ul.expanding a:visited {
  display: block;
  cursor: pointer;
  cursor: hand;
  background: #ffc;
  border: 1px solid #edbb85;
  padding: 5px 7px;
  font: bold 0.7em tahoma, verdana, sans-serif;
  color: #008000;
  text-decoration: none;
  letter-spacing: 1px;
}

ul.expanding a:hover, ul.expanding a:focus, ul.expanding a:active,
ul.expanding a.rollover:link, ul.expanding a.rollover:visited {
  color: #806020;
}

/* submenu indicator arrows */
ul.expanding li.hasmenu > a:link,
ul.expanding li.hasmenu > a:visited {
  background: url(down-green.gif) #ffc no-repeat 95% 50%;
}
ul.expanding li.hasmenu > a.rollover:link,
ul.expanding li.hasmenu > a.rollover:visited {
  background: url(down-red.gif) #ffefcf no-repeat 95% 50%;
}
* html ul.expanding li.hasmenu a:link,
* html ul.expanding li.hasmenu a:visited {
  background: expression(/hasmenu/.test(this.parentNode.className)
      ? "url(down-green.gif) #ffc no-repeat 95% 50%" : "#ffc");
}
* html ul.expanding li.hasmenu a.rollover:link,
* html ul.expanding li.hasmenu a.rollover:visited {
```

```
    background: expression(/hasmenu/.test(this.parentNode.className)
        ? "url(down-red.gif) #ffefcf no-repeat 95% 50%" : "#ffefcf");
}
```

Figure 15.15 illustrates the difference between a submenu that has been moused over and one that has actually been expanded. Previously, these different states had the same styles.

Figure 15.15. Two states of link appearance

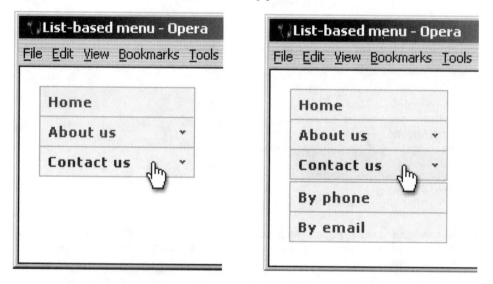

By changing the rules in this way, we've created the states we need for plus/minus icons—they can change and persist from menu opening, but are unaffected by link mouseovers! Now that we've worked out our selector structure, we can adjust the style sheet to give us the look we want for our folder tree menu:

File: **foldertree.css**

```
/* structural styles and offsets */
ul.foldertree, ul.foldertree li, ul.foldertree ul {
  margin: 0;
  padding: 0;
  list-style-type: none;
  font-size: 100%;
}
ul.foldertree {
  position: relative;
  cursor: default;
```

```
  width: 8.2em;
}
ul.foldertree li {
  position: relative;
  text-align: left;
  cursor: pointer;
  cursor: hand;
  width: 8.2em;
  margin: -1px 0 0 0;
}
ul.foldertree ul {
  cursor: default;
  width: 8.2em;
  padding: 2px 0;
  position: absolute;
  left: -100em;
  margin: 0 0 0 1em;
}
ul.foldertree ul li {
  width: 8.2em;
}

/* design styles */
ul.foldertree a:link, ul.foldertree a:visited {
  display: block;
  cursor: pointer;
  cursor: hand;
  padding: 1px 0 1px 15px;
  font: 0.7em tahoma, verdana, sans-serif;
  color: #000;
  text-decoration: none;
  letter-spacing: 1px;
}
ul.foldertree a:hover, ul.foldertree a:focus,
ul.foldertree a:active {
  text-decoration: underline;
  color: #007;
}

/* plus/minus icons */
ul.foldertree li.hasmenu > a:link,
ul.foldertree li.hasmenu > a:visited {
  background: url(plus.gif) no-repeat 1% 50%;
}
ul.foldertree li.hasmenu > a.rollover:link,
ul.foldertree li.hasmenu > a.rollover:visited {
```

```
    background: url(minus.gif) no-repeat 1% 50%;
}
* html ul.foldertree li.hasmenu a:link,
* html ul.foldertree li.hasmenu a:visited {
    background: expression(/hasmenu/.test(this.parentNode.className)
        ? "url(plus.gif) no-repeat 1% 50%" : "transparent");
}
* html ul.foldertree li.hasmenu a.rollover:link,
* html ul.foldertree li.hasmenu a.rollover:visited {
    background: expression(/hasmenu/.test(this.parentNode.className)
        ? "url(minus.gif) no-repeat 1% 50%" : "transparent");
}


/* browser hacks */
@media screen, projection {
    * html ul.foldertree li {
        display: inline;
        f\loat: left;
        background: #fff;
    }
}
```

This style sheet will style our list to look like the one in Figure 15.14. But don't forget to change the icon caching![16]

File: **treeMenu.js** (excerpt)

```
function treeMenu(navid, indexpage)
{
    if (typeof document.getElementById == 'undefined') { return; }

    var rollover = new Image;
    rollover.src = 'minus.gif';
```

If you're working through these examples step by step, you'll now either have an expanding menu with arrows, or a folder tree menu with icons. Both these menus are behaviorally identical; the only difference is their styling, and this will remain the case as we move through the final two solutions in this chapter: the JavaScript is the same, whichever design you're using.

---

[16] The version of treeMenu.js distributed in the code archive caches both down-red.gif and minus.gif, so the script can be used with both menu styles.

Allowing Only One Menu Branch to Be Open at Any Time

Whether or not you want this behavior will depend on what you're doing with your menu. For example, a folder tree menu that's to be used as a directory browser might be better off without it, so that you can have as many branches open as you need. On the other hand, an expanding menu that's used for site navigation could probably benefit from this behavior, as the menu would likely be easier to understand if only one navigable branch can be open at any time.

Solution

To make this solution work, we need to run a reset function in response to every menu-opening event. This function will reset all menus that descend from *siblings* of the newly-opened menu. Here's the reset function:

File: **treeMenu.js** (excerpt)

```
function clearSiblingBranches(trigger)
{
  var menus = trigger.parentNode.getElementsByTagName('ul');
  for (var i = 0; i < menus.length; i++)
  {
    menus[i].style.display = 'none';
    var a = menus[i].parentNode.getElementsByTagName('a')[0];
    if (a)
    {
      a.className = a.className.replace(/[ ]?rollover/g, '');
    }
  }
}
```

To add it to our main function, we'll call it *directly before* a menu-opening event. Here's the list item click function again (additions are shown in bold):

File: **treeMenu.js** (excerpt)

```
li.onclick = function(e)
{
  var target = e ? e.target : window.event.srcElement;
  while (target.nodeName.toUpperCase() != 'LI')
  {
    target = target.parentNode;
```

```
    }
    if (target == this && isreset)
    {
      if (menu)
      {
        if (menu.style.display == 'none')
        {
          clearSiblingBranches(this);
          menu.style.display = 'block';
          a.className += (a.className=='' ? '' : ' ') + 'rollover';
        }
        else
        {
          menu.style.display = 'none';
          a.className = a.className.replace(/ ?rollover/g, '');
        }
        return false;
      }
      else
      {
        return true;
      }
    }
};
```

Discussion

The simplicity of this solution belies its usefulness! As you can see from the code, the reset simply iterates through all menus descending from the parent menu of our trigger (i.e., all sibling menus of that trigger and their descendants). If we call the reset just before a menu opens, it will effectively close all branches except the newly-opened one. Nice!

Opening the Current Sub-branch Automatically

For the final solution in this chapter, we'll look at a neat usability enhancement for navigational tree menus. This enhancement compares the current page against the links in the list, then opens the relevant branch to show users where they are.

Solution

We need three new functions for this solution. First and foremost is a slightly complicated function called findHere, which will work out which link in the navigation bar corresponds to the current page address:

```
function findHere(tree, navid, indexpage)
{
  var page = document.location.href;
  page = page.replace(indexpage, '').replace(/,/g,'%2C');
  var links = tree.getElementsByTagName('a');
  var matches = [];
  for (var i = 0; i < links.length; i++)
  {
    var href = links[i].href;
    if (href && !/[a-z]+\:\/\//.test(href))
    {
      matches = [];
      break;
    }

    href = href.replace(indexpage, '').replace(/,/g,'%2C');
    if (href != '' && page.indexOf(href) != -1)
    {
      matches[matches.length] = links[i];
    }
  }
  if (matches.length < 1) { return; }

  var probabilities = [];
  for (i = 0; i < matches.length; i++)
  {
    href = matches[i].href;
    probabilities[i] = [0, href];

    for (var j = 0; j < href.length; j++)
    {
      if (href.charAt(j) == page.charAt(j))
      {
        probabilities[i][0] ++;
      }
    }
  }

  probabilities.sort(compare);
```

```
    href = probabilities[0][1];
    for (i = 0; i < links.length; i++)
    {
      if (links[i].href == href)
      {
        youAreHere(links[i], href, navid);
        break;
      }
    }
}
```

We also need a `compare` function, for sorting a matrix inverse-numerically (using the method we saw in Chapter 4):

File: **treeMenu.js** (excerpt)

```
function compare(a, b)
{
  return b[0] - a[0];
}
```

Then, once we've found the applicable link, we have a function that applies the necessary attributes:

File: **treeMenu.js** (excerpt)

```
function youAreHere(link, href, navid)
{
  link.className += (link.className == '' ? '' : ' ') +
      'rollover';
  var li = link.parentNode;
  var menu = (li.getElementsByTagName('ul').length > 0
      ? li.getElementsByTagName('ul')[0] : null);
  if (menu)
  {
    menu.style.display = 'block';
    menu.style.position = 'static';
  }

  var text = ((link.getAttribute('title') && link.title != '')
      ? link.title : link.firstChild.nodeValue);

  link.title = text + (link.href == href
      ? ' [you are here]' : ' [you\'re in this section]');
  if (li.parentNode.id != navid)
  {
    link = li.parentNode.parentNode.getElementsByTagName('a')[0];
    youAreHere(link, href, navid);
```

```
    }
}
```

To make all this run, we have to make three modifications to our existing code. First, we edit the `displayReset` function (the function that overrides the positioning of submenus); otherwise, it would cause an unwanted reset when a pre-opened structure was first used. We'll need to arrange the code so that it still applies universal static positioning to override the positioning, but only sets `display` to `none` on a menu that *isn't already shown*. We can detect such menus from looking at their current `position` values (additions are shown in bold):

File: **treeMenu.js** (excerpt)

```
function displayReset(tree)
{
  var menus = tree.getElementsByTagName('ul');
  for (var i = 0; i < menus.length; i++)
  {
    if (menus[i].style.position != 'static')
    {
      menus[i].style.display = 'none';
    }
    menus[i].style.position = 'static';
  }
  isreset = true;
}
```

Next, we add the call to `findHere` from our main initialization function, `treeMenu` (additions are shown in bold):

File: **treeMenu.js** (excerpt)

```
function treeMenu(navid, indexpage)
{
  if (typeof document.getElementById == 'undefined') { return; }
  var rollover = new Image;
  rollover.src = 'minus.gif';

  var tree = document.getElementById(navid);
  if (tree)
  {
    var items = tree.getElementsByTagName('li');
    for (var i = 0; i < items.length; i++)
    {
      treeTrigger(tree, items[i], navid)
    }
```

```
    if (navigator.vendor == 'Apple Computer, Inc.'
        || typeof window.opera != 'undefined')
    {
      displayReset(tree);
    }

    findHere(tree, navid, indexpage);
  }
}
```

Finally, the `treeMenu` function itself takes a second argument, `indexpage`, which is passed on to the `findHere` function and used to specify the name of default index pages (such as `index.html`, or `default.php`). This is so that, for example, `/about/index.html` is recognized as being the same page as `/about/`.

Specify this value as an argument to the original initialization call (additions are shown in bold):

File: **treeMenu.js (excerpt)**

```
addLoadListener(function(){treeMenu('navigation','index.html');});
```

Discussion

The first thing we do in the `findHere` function is establish the current page address, which includes a replacement for the default page name (`indexpage`), and replaces commas for the benefit of Internet Explorer 6, which doesn't correctly equate a comma with its escaped equivalent.

Then, we can iterate through the links in the navbar and compare each `href` with the address. But we have to check that the `href` we get is actually a **qualified value** (a value that includes the domain and protocol) because in older Safari builds it comes back as the literal attribute value, which is of no use for this comparison. In that situation, we reset the "possible matches" array and stop, effectively abandoning the whole function.

Here, we're actually comparing whether or not the page address contains this `href` as a substring: if it does, we're part of the way to establishing that they're the same; if it doesn't, well, obviously they're not the same, so there's no point comparing them further.

We have to determine a "best match" from the array of possible matches. This is done by comparing each character of the `href` against the same character of the page URI, and building up an array of likelihoods to discover which `href` has the highest overall score. The highest score is deemed to be the current page. If a perfect match is not found, the script will end up with the closest match; this will most likely be a section index or parent of the current page, if one exists, or the main index page, if no better match is found.

Now that we know where we are, we can apply the necessary attributes both to our link (adding the rollover style, and appropriate `title` text), and to the menu that contains it (making it visible). Although this code will still apply to browser-based screen readers, and will make a visible difference in the host browser, there won't be a difference to the screen reader itself—the entire tree is still accessible as through scripting and CSS were not enabled.

In order to show a nested menu, we also have to open its parents. Thankfully, since our menu structure is hierarchical, we have no problem asserting that the parent items of the link we have identified are the parent sections of that page, so we can simply walk back up the tree! The `youAreHere` function is recursive (just like the `contains` method we saw at the beginning of this chapter); it calls itself up the branch, applying the necessary attributes, until it reaches the root list.

Summary

In this chapter, we've built two kinds of dynamic menu: a drop-down or fly-out menu, and a folder tree or expanding menu. We've examined accessibility and usability issues as they arise, and looked at some innovative techniques for improving the situation. Using and expanding on these ideas, you can build sophisticated and eminently usable dynamic navigation systems, while remaining confident that you're not falling into the conventional traps.

We've also touched on a few aspects of accessible scripting. We'll explore these ideas further in Chapter 16, where we'll also come back to our drop-down menu, upgrading it for three (yes, *three*) forms of keyboard navigation!

16 JavaScript and Accessibility

At this point in the Web's evolution, it's still impossible to give definitive advice on how best to marry JavaScript and accessibility, particularly when it comes to screen readers and other assistive devices, because implementations vary so much, and technologies change so rapidly. Yet despite—and because of—that fact, accessibility is an incredibly exciting area to work in, so at the very least I hope to impart some of my enthusiasm for the subject in this chapter.

This focus of this book in on practical implementations, and in that respect this chapter is no different than the others, focused as it is on the current needs of users. Certainly, we may allow ourselves room for speculation, and experiment with ideas for the future, but the bottom line is that people are using the Web *now*, in imperfect circumstances, and there are numerous things that we can and should do to improve the situation.

Some of the issues surrounding this topic have become slightly confused in recent times, not just in regard to the definition of accessibility, but over the differing needs of users: keyboard and screen-reader users are often seen as a single group, when in fact the needs and interactions of a screen reader user often diverge sharply from those of a *sighted* keyboard user. We'll see many examples of this as we go through the chapter.

But first, we need to cover some theoretical ground, so let's begin by discussing what accessibility actually is.

Is JavaScript Inaccessible?

Is concrete inaccessible?

Certainly it has the potential to be, if it's created as a structure that's physically impossible for some people to use, as stairs would be to a person using a wheel-chair. Yet that same concrete could have created a ramp, which is accessible both to people using wheelchairs and those on foot. So the concrete itself is neither accessible nor inaccessible—it's just a medium. And so is JavaScript.

However, that doesn't mean we can forget the whole point of accessibility and just carry on regardless! Oh, no. Although JavaScript is no more inaccessible than any other aspect of web development, it's loaded with the potential to restrict user access through circumstances that range from simple to extremely complex! There are so many ways in which a script could cause problems, or fail to accommodate one or more groups of users, that if we are to begin to address the possibilities and create accessible scripts, we must start by looking at the whole spectrum of potential access barriers.

Solution

What exactly do we mean when we say, "accessible?" To whom are we making our scripts accessible? And why do we need to do this, anyway?

What is Accessibility?

The answer to this question is not quite as straightforward as I wish it were. In recent months, there's been a lot of debate among developers about whether "accessibility" means "catering to the needs of people with disabilities" or "catering to the needs of all users."[1] The premise under which we'll work in this chapter is a compromise between the two: *accessibility is about catering to everyone, but with priority and emphasis on the needs of people with disabilities*.

---

[1] A lively debate on the topic is documented at http://www.accessifyforum.com/viewtopic.php?t=3159, but it's not for the faint-hearted—it throws up more questions than it answers, and gets slightly confrontational in places. I refer to it because it illustrates the strength of passion and reason on both sides (and because I'm in it, making my views pretty clear!). For discussions that focus more on the reason and less on the passion, you might try http://www.alistapart.com/articles/pdf_accessibility#multiple and http://www.autisticcuckoo.net/archive.php?id=2005/08/24/joe-clark-on-accessibility.

When we talk about "accessibility problems" we're talking about issues that affect people because of attributes they can't readily change—a person who's blind can't just decide to see. By contrast, someone who surfs the Web with JavaScript turned off simply because they want to has made a choice, and one they could easily change if they felt inclined.

I think it's absolutely right to be significantly more concerned with limitations over which people have no choices, than those over which they do. But that doesn't mean that people who fall into the latter category aren't important. And, even more crucially, at what point can we assume to *know* which category users and their particular access limitations fall into? How can we ever know (short of asking them) whether users without JavaScript have made that choice consciously? Has the choice been made for them as a result of circumstances beyond their control?

We can predict the amount of choice involved in some issues, though. For example, when an issue affects users on the basis of their ability to see, then the question is definitely one of disability. When an issue affects people who don't have JavaScript support, the question might not be one of disability, but there's no way we can know whether it is or not. Even if we could know (for example, by asking them), the answer wouldn't matter unless that circumstance were true for *all* non-JavaScript users.

We couldn't restrict our accessibility efforts exclusively to disabled users, even if we wanted to. However, this chapter does show how we can put a priority on the needs of those users, while improving accessibility for all.

Who are the Affected Users?

Many groups of users face specific accessibility barriers, but not all of them are directly affected by scripting practice. Color-blindness is one example where the considerations are visual and design-based, and are more to do with CSS than anything else.

There are other issues which, while being significant to a script, are not really programming considerations as much as they are application design considerations. For example, flashing colors and animation (which could be dangerous to someone who has photosensitive epilepsy), may simply be unnecessary. If these effects are necessary, then we face certain planning considerations: do we choose to have a feature that's static by default and animated by preference (so a user chooses the animation, rather than having it happen automatically), or do we decide to warn users in advance that it will occur? (Some applications, such as DHTML games, may be innately fast-paced and visual, and it may be impossible to make them accessible without fundamentally changing their nature.)

The issue of support for JavaScript itself should already be quite familiar to you, as we covered it back in "Providing for Users who Don't Have JavaScript (Progressive Enhancement)" in Chapter 1. Suffice it to say that if client-side scripting is not available, redundant functionality should be provided. But we will encounter situations in which the question of scripting support is not a black and white issue—browser-based screen readers are among the devices that *do* support JavaScript, but only in a very piecemeal way, so we'll have to turn our attention to them specifically.

To summarize, through the course of this chapter we'll look at two groups of users whose particular needs and interactions impact directly on the way an application is programmed:

❑ people who navigate using the keyboard

❑ people who use a screen reader

I'm not saying that these are the *only* groups of users who are affected, because there are definitely others. For example, the needs and interactions of visually impaired users who use screen magnification software may also be different from those of other users, but the developer community at large is only beginning to come to terms with the impacts of such users' needs. There may also be implications in some kinds of scripting for people who have cognitive disabilities; for example, the speed of a news ticker or other animation may need to be made adjustable to accommodate different reading speeds.

However, I must admit that I have very little experience in those areas. So, while I will point out relevant issues and considerations as they arise, the bulk of this chapter is concerned with the two core user groups mentioned above.

The needs of these two groups are often very different, and we'll examine and discuss these variations through this chapter. Nevertheless, a person who uses a screen reader is almost certain to be navigating with the keyboard, so in that sense catering to the keyboard user is the primary concern of accessible scripting. (Obviously, the mouse user is equally important, but I'm assuming you don't need me to tell you that!)

In Another User's Shoes

Tip If you're not in the habit of navigating web sites with the keyboard, try it now. Spend some time getting a feel for what it's like, seeing where difficulties arise, and thinking about how those issues could be avoided.

Making Scripts Accessible to the Keyboard

Now that we've established the need for support, what are the basic practicalities of scripting for the keyboard?

Solution

The biggest implication of scripting for the keyboard is that interactions are limited to elements that can accept the focus universally, primarily links (`<a href>`) and form controls (`<input>`, `<select>`, `<textarea>`, and `<button>`). It's also possible to give focus to the `area` elements in an image map, a `frame` or `iframe`, in some cases an `object`, and in most browsers, the `document` or `documentElement` itself.

This further implies that the events that we can handle using keyboard interactions are limited to those events that the keyboard actually can generate, primarily `focus`, `blur`, `click` (activating a link or button with the keyboard is programmatically the same as clicking it with a mouse), and the three key-action events, `keydown`, `keyup`, and `keypress`.

Of course, we still have to cater to programmatic events like `readystatechange` and the infamous `load` event, proprietary events such as `activate` in IE, and mode-independent events like a form's `submit` event. Even so, we're left with a pretty small collection, not a million miles away from the toolset we had in the days of Netscape 3!

However, this doesn't mean we'll be consigning mouse-specific events to the trash completely; nor does it relegate elements that can't take focus to the sidelines altogether. It just means we'll have to rethink our approach to some things. Improving access is about providing **equivalence**, which is not the same as equality—it doesn't necessarily matter if we provide different paths for different users, as long as everyone has a path to an equivalent end result.

Discussion

In purely practical terms, it's not a major limitation that only certain elements can accept the focus. Styled links can do the job a lot of the time, although a link still needs an `href` if it is to take focus; if the link's only function is scripting-related, that often results in the need for links to have # or `javascript:void(null)`, or a similar, essentially junk `href`. The cure for this problem could be the `button` element, which is incredibly flexible in that it can contain *other* HTML, as well as being able to accept focus regardless of whether or not it has a value.

However, there is a real limitation of semantics here, because the range of meaning we can express using these elements is limited. Furthermore, the native behaviors of the elements are fixed. Let's look at the kinds of problems these issues can cause.

For the issue of semantics, the problem is one of confusion for non-graphical user agents: devices that rely on element semantics to convey meaning cannot accurately convey the fact that an element has been enhanced with dynamic behaviors. How would you know, for example, that a button labeled Add item to cart would run a process on the current page, rather than loading a new page?

To the visual user, it might not matter, but to users of screen reader it matters a great deal, because screen readers have unique difficulties interpreting content that updates without reload (which we'll examine in detail later in this chapter). There's also a problem with using "junk" `href` values in that, to the reader, they appear like a bunch of links that all go to the same page. Once any of them is activated, they're *all* announced as visited links from that point forward. Obviously, this can be very confusing.

As for the second issue—limitations arising from the fixed nature of the elements' native behaviors—the problem is one of repetition and irritation for keyboard users, because they'll have to do more work to navigate around a page.

The best way to illustrate this is with a DHTML menu, and here I'm using the example from a 2005 conference paper, *DHTML Accessibility—Fixing the JavaScript Accessibility Problem*,[2] by Rich Schwerdtfeger and Becky Gibson of IBM:

> Most DHTML menus don't act like regular menus with respect to keyboard access. If you can use the keyboard to get to the menu at all, a common mistake is to put each menu item in the

---

[2] http://www.csun.edu/cod/conf/2005/proceedings/2524.htm

tab order (often accomplished by making each menu item an
`<a>`). In fact, the correct behavior for menus is that the entire
menu should be in the tab order once, and arrow key navigation
should be supported.

Now, personally, I don't completely agree with the claim that this is the "correct"
behavior for menus. I would caution developers against thinking that web-based
GUI widgets should behave exactly like those of an operating system GUI (even
within web applications), because the behavioral norms exhibited on the Web
are not identical to those exhibited within an operating system. To stay with this
example, DHTML menus typically have a capability that OS menus do not,
whereby a single item is both a menu-opening trigger and a link (in OS menus,
they're only ever one or the other).

The paper continues:

Despite this limitation, Internet Explorer filled a hole in the
HTML specification which allows elements with a `tabindex` <
0 to receive focus without being entered in the tab order. We
now treat this as a best practice and it has also been implemented
in Firefox and Mozilla. So, it's now possible for HTML authors
to do the right thing with respect to keyboard navigation.

In IE and recent versions of Firefox and Mozilla, we can indeed give *any* element
the ability to take focus simply by giving it a `tabindex` value. The traditional use
of `tabindex` is actually counterproductive from an accessibility standpoint, because
every browser implements it slightly differently, and no one browser gets it quite
right. The upshot of this is that it's better not to use `tabindex` at all—it's better
simply to allow elements to fall into their natural, source-code order.

But if we're careful, we *can* use this attribute in an accessible manner, because
we can use the special `tabindex` value `0`, which means an element is tab-navigable
in its natural place in the tab order (essentially, `0` is an "auto" setting). Indeed,
we can use the two values, `0` and `-1`, to create a keyboard-navigable menu like
the one shown in Figure 16.1.

A user who navigates with the **Tab** key will have only the menu itself in the
native order, which reduces the amount of manual tabbing they have to do to
move past it. To let users drill into the contents of a single menu, we have to
script for the up and down arrow keys, and programmatically focus each link.

Figure 16.1. Using custom `tabindex` attributes with a DHTML menu

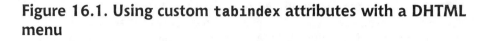

Now we've got a navigational paradigm that *requires* scripting. If we're going to use it, we'll have to design our menu without these custom tab indexes (so that the links are natively navigable), then apply the indexes dynamically. In fact, we'd have to take this approach anyway—for the sake of backwards compatibility—so okay, that's no more of an issue than script support itself.

But what have most users gained from this solution that we couldn't have achieved using cross-browser scripting and without these additional tab indices? Well, on a purely superficial level, it achieves very little. We don't have a native behavioral paradigm, because it takes scripting to make this solution work, and if we're going to add scripting, why wouldn't we just use all four arrow keys to provide two-dimensional navigation throughout? Why should we mess about with **Tab** and arrow combinations? (Later in this chapter we'll be looking at accessible menus in more depth, at which point we'll review both methods of applying keyboard navigation: from the **Tab** key, and from the four arrow keys.)

However, there is another, deeper level at which the benefits of this solution become far more significant. For a screen reader, the richer element semantics are very important, because they can convey more specific information about an element—for example, in navigation developed using this approach, the focus will be announced as a "list," rather than a "link" or "button." The behavior of our menu is also more consistent with what happens now with other widgets; for example, you **Tab** to a `select` element, then use the up and down arrow keys to move between the options. Fundamentally, a screen reader is a linear (one-dimensional) access device, so tab navigation plus up/down drilling makes much more sense conceptually, and is easier to visualize, than two-dimensional navigation.

IBMis currently working with GW Micro (the makers of Windows Eyes) and the Mozilla Foundation, under the project title of DHTML Accessibility,[3] not just to implement compatibility with generically focusable elements, but to introduce

---

[3] http://www.mozilla.org/access/dhtml/

"roles" and "states" (defined by element attributes) that can convey information about the nature and state of elements. This solves the semantics problem, and means that any appropriate element can convey all the necessary information: its own meaning, its behavioral role, and its current state.

These are very exciting developments and I, for one, will be watching them with great interest, but I want to remain firmly practical—this is not something we can really use *now*, because it's not backwards-compatible: it provides no functionality at all to browsers other than IE or Firefox, and offers only very limited functionality to device combinations other than Firefox 1.5 plus Windows Eyes 5.5.

Even if we put aside the additional role and state information, and looked only at custom tab indexes as a means of providing keyboard navigation, we can't implement even *that* solution at the moment, because the vast majority of current screen readers don't generate the key events we'd need as a basis for the additional scripting (something we'll also get into in depth a little later in this chapter). If we used this technique to create a DHTML menu, we'd actually be making the links *inaccessible* to some, though they were accessible before!

So my working conclusion for now is that, while this may become a best practice technique in the future, it's not a widely useful or recommendable technique at the moment.

Using Device-independent Event Handlers

What are device-independent event handlers? A figment of the W3C's imagination!

A more useful answer is that device-independent event handlers are those that have equal semantics irrespective of the device or method that's used to fire them. The ideal example is `actuate`, a theoretical event that would fire from any action that actuated (e.g., clicked) a link or other element. But as the HTML Techniques for WCAG 1.0 concede,[4] no device actually implements such an event.

---

[4] http://www.w3.org/TR/WCAG10-HTML-TECHS/#directly-accessible-scripts

The Client-side Scripting Techniques for WCAG 2.0[5] (Working Draft[6] recommend the use of an event called `activate` instead of `click`—a strange thing to suggest, given that this event doesn't really exist, either! At least, it doesn't exist in any standard implementation. Ironically, it *does* exist as a proprietary event in Windows IE, although it means something else entirely (it's equivalent to the `focus` event, except that it bubbles; we'll examine this difference shortly).

Perhaps the guidelines are referring to the DOM 2 User Interface event `DOMActivate`,[7] or maybe they intend it purely as a theoretical example like `actuate`; undoubtedly this will be clarified in a later draft.

Solution

The nearest thing we have to a universal, device-independent event is `click`. This event is generated in all major desktop browsers—as well as the vast majority of popular screen readers and assistive devices—when the user clicks an element with the mouse, or sets focus on it and presses **Enter** (or **Space**, or whatever key the device is using). In some PDAs, a `click` event can be fired by tapping an element with the stylus,[8] and there are other, equivalent actions in other devices.

There are other events that, similarly, are not truly device-independent, though they're close enough for most practical purposes; these are events that, in theory, could be device-independent, but are actually implemented by current browsers as events from the mouse or the keyboard. To give some other examples, `mouseover` events might come from a track-ball, `mousemove` events might be generated by the analog stick on a Sony PSP, and `focus` events can be generated by spoken navigation commands in Opera 8 with Voice.

In theory, we want to be able to support *any* mode of interaction, from whatever device it is sent, so that all potential users have the same capacity to input or receive information. In practice, our scripts will be dealing with *two* kinds of interaction for any given task. We refer to these as "mouse" and "keyboard" interaction, but they could include a variety of different, equivalent actions.

---

[5] http://www.w3.org/TR/WCAG20-SCRIPT-TECHS/

[6] At the time of writing, this document was a working draft dated June 2005.

[7] http://www.w3.org/TR/DOM-Level-2-Events/events.html#Events-eventgroupings-uievents

[8] This assumes that the device supports JavaScript and `click` events to some extent. In Pocket IE for Windows Mobile 2003, for example, inline event handlers are supported with the `onclick` attribute, but DOM event handlers (the `onclick` property) are not.

Making Scripts Accessible to the Keyboard as well as the Mouse

With two discrete forms of interaction for any given script, we may (or may not) require two separate approaches ... so how do we actually implement solutions that incorporate both? Let's begin by discussing how *not* to do it.

The WCAG (Web Content Accessibility Guidelines) 1.0 techniques documentation suggests that the best approach is to provide redundant input mechanisms—to provide *two* handlers that "pair" together for the same element—and the examples it gives are things like `keydown` to be paired with `mousedown`, or `keyup` to go with `mouseup`. However, this is the wrong way of looking at the situation, because keyboard and mouse events are conceptually different things, and in many cases they behave *completely differently*, as we'll see in the following discussion.

Solution

I think it's more helpful to think in terms of **behavioral pairing**, than event pairing. If, for example, you have a piece of functionality that's driven by a `mousedown` event, don't think, "How can I use a `keydown` event to make this work?" Instead, ask yourself, "How can I make this work from the keyboard?"

Perhaps I'm just splitting hairs, but I don't think so. Phrased the second way, the question leads to different answers. The first question asks about a specific approach, which may or may work; the second question simply asks if there *is* an approach, so it's open to any compatible solution.

Perhaps, in our hypothetical case, the solution is to extend the same functionality using a completely different mechanism: a different button or interface trigger, for example, which may end up being activated by a `keydown` event after all; but instead it might just as easily be a `focus` event or a `click`. The event itself is not the point; the point is to provide *something* that ultimately achieves the same (or an equivalent) end result.

I hesitate to use the tired expression "think outside the box" because, as we know, there is no box. Still, that phrase comes to mind: scripting for the keyboard is a different discipline than scripting for the mouse, with different issues and considerations. I find it much more productive to approach keyboard behaviors from scratch, as a unique set of interactions, rather than trying to adapt existing mouse behaviors to suit the keyboard. Scripting for the keyboard isn't difficult, but it is conceptually different from the way most of us are used to thinking about interactive scripting, and *that's* the point.

Let's get more practical now. We'll look at a few different kinds of scripts that originally were triggered by mouse events, to see if we can find an approach that makes them accessible to the keyboard as well.

We won't go into great detail about any particular script in this solution. Instead, we'll be looking more closely at general ideas, with code snippets for examples. In the solutions that follow, we'll pick up some of these ideas and take them further to create specific and usable scripts.

Rollovers and Revealing Content

A simple rollover effect might just be a change to a `color` or `background-image` on a link. You're probably more than experienced in using links whose `display` property is set to `block`, giving them the predictable dimensions to house a background image that can be swapped without the need for scripting, thanks to the `hover`, `focus`, and `active` pseudo-classes.

Scripted rollovers are generally just as easy to extend to the keyboard, provided that they're based on links or other elements that can take focus. Here's a simple effect that's powered by toggling a class name (this simplified example uses the `attachEventListener` function from Chapter 13):

```
attachEventListener(link, 'mouseover', function()
{
  link.className = 'rollover';
}, false);

attachEventListener(link, 'mouseout', function()
{
  link.className = '';
}, false);
```

We can apply a pair of `focus` and `blur` listeners to do the same job:

```
attachEventListener(link, 'focus', function()
{
  link.className = 'rollover';
}, false);

attachEventListener(link, 'blur', function()
{
```

```
  link.className = '';
}, false);
```

But when it comes to handling events on groups of elements, the situation is more complicated, because *focus events don't bubble*. We could handle a mouse event on any element by using a single document-level listener:

```
attachEventListener(document, 'mouseover', function(e)
{
  var target = typeof e.target != 'undefined'
      ? e.target : e.srcElement;

  : target is whatever node the event bubbles up from

}, false);
```

This works because the mouse events bubble up from the points at which they occur, but as the `focus` and `blur` events don't bubble, such a function would handle only the events that occurred on the element to which the listener was assigned—leaving out any of its descendants.

Actually, focus events *do* bubble in Mozilla browsers, but they're not supposed to; they don't bubble in Opera, Safari, or Internet Explorer. IE 5.5 onwards has the proprietary event `activate`, which is functionally similar to `focus`, except that it does bubble; Safari implements the DOM2 UI Event `DOMFocusIn`,[9] which also does (and is supposed to) bubble; and, since Mozilla's focus events bubble anyway, we could have a partial solution as follows:

```
var focusevent = isie ? 'activate' :
    issafari ? 'DOMFocusIn' : 'focus';
attachEventListener(document, focusevent, function(e)
{
  : and so on...

}, false);
```

However, this doesn't include Opera, or IE 5.0, or indeed *any future browser* that follows the norm of not bubbling focus events, because the default case here is Mozilla's atypical behavior. Ultimately, this solution is of little real use.

If we want something that amounts to a document-wide focus handler, we'll just have to bind `focus` and `blur` handlers to every element individually (and that's

---

[9] http://www.w3.org/TR/DOM-Level-2-Events/events.html#Events-eventgroupings-uievents

exactly what we're going to do later in this chapter, when we make `title`-attribute tooltips accessible to the keyboard).

Form Validation

Making client-side form validation accessible to the keyboard is pretty easy, because the relevant events are mode-independent. The `change` event fires after the value of a form control changes; `select` fires when text within it is selected; `submit` and `reset` fire from form submission and resetting, respectively. But in none of these cases does it matter *how* the event was fired—whether the user was navigating or selecting with the keyboard, clicking or highlighting with the mouse, the events were fired just the same.

Of course, this implies that accessible form scripting must use the right events for the task—don't link a form validation function to the `click` event of the submit button itself, because there are other, entirely independent actions that can submit a form (such as pressing **Enter** when the focus is in a text field). The `submit` event itself bubbles, so you could use a single document-level event listener for all the forms on a page.

If you are performing client-side validation, it's worth thinking about where to send keyboard focus when notifying the user of errors or omissions. For example, a validation function that was bound to the `submit` event of a form might generate an `alert` dialog with details of the error, or it might highlight the erroneous field by changing its border and label text. In both cases, you can make it easier for a keyboard user to get to the problem field if you send focus to it automatically, using the programmatic `focus` method of the field element:

```
function checkUsernameForm(frm)
{
  if (frm['username'].value == '')
  {
    alert('Please enter your username');

    frm['username'].focus();

    return false;
  }

  return true;
}
```

This is a fair use of the method, I think, but be aware that the `focus` method can be dangerous: moving the focus around can be very disorientating for a user, particularly if he or she can't see, or fails to notice the cursor move. However, I think this solution is okay in this case, because if the user submits a form and receives that message, the element that's referred to is the logical place to go.

Other uses of this method spring to mind, and though at first they appear to improve usability, they may actually do just the opposite. The example I'm thinking of is a form that asks for credit card details by presenting four text boxes, each of which takes four numbers. As the user enters the last digit into each box, the focus is shifted automatically to the next box. I've encountered forms like this on a few occasions, but I wasn't expecting that focus-shifting behavior. I was looking down at the keyboard and pressing **Tab** myself after each group of four digits; the result was that only the first and third boxes had numbers in them, while the rest of my typing filled the subsequent form fields. It was inconvenient for me, but it could have been worse—and probably has been for other users of the same sites.

The size of the problem depends on context, of course—behavior like this might be a massive time-saver for someone entering credit card data into a company's internal web-based application on a regular basis; but for the casual user entering his or her details to buy something online, this unexpected behavior could be anything from surprising to intensely frustrating. Think very carefully before you use the `focus` method.

Beware of the `blur`

There's also a programmatic `blur` method (which does what it says on the tin) but you shouldn't use it, because it's ambiguous about *where* it sends the focus. Thus, the focus is ultimately "lost," and the browser is forced to replace it. The actual results of its implementation will vary, but usually the focus will be replaced in the address bar or other window control—whatever's immediately after or before the page in the window's overall tab order. Effectively, the user loses his or her place in the document, and is forced to start again from the top. The worst use of `blur` is so appalling that I fear I would insult your intelligence by suggesting you would even consider it:

```
<a href="/" onfocus="this.blur()">
```

Suffice it to say never, *ever* use this approach: it makes the element (and, potentially, the rest of the page) completely inaccessible to the keyboard.

Another example of dubious use of the `focus` method involves forcing a form element to retain the focus until its value is properly completed. A script might employ a `blur` event listener to validate the field, and then send focus back to it immediately, but this is a bad practice because it forces a change in the natural browsing behavior of keyboard and mouse users alike. It could also be incredibly confusing for someone who has a cognitive disability; for most users it's likely be very annoying. Overall, I would go so far as to discourage *any* kind of element-specific validation mechanism—save validation for the `submit` event.

I also recommend that you avoid disabling buttons based on the states of other fields. Arriving at the Submit button of a form to find it disabled can unsettle users ("Why is this button disabled? How am I supposed to submit the form?"), assuming that the user can get to it at all—some screen readers don't include disabled elements in the reading order, so they wouldn't even know the button was there (so the question would become simply, "How do I submit this form?"). Users who do see the button won't know it has a dependency to other field values (unless you tell them of course, but why go through that learning curve?). I think it's much better—because it's common and well understood—to allow the form to be submitted as the user chooses, and only then to warn of missing or invalid data.

Drag-and-drop Functionality

Drag-and-drop functionality is complicated to script at the best of times, never mind trying to make it more accessible! At first glance it looks impossible, because the dynamos of drag-and-drop behaviors are `mousemove` events, for which there are no keyboard equivalents. But with a bit of lateral thinking it *can* be done.

Imagine a vertical list or a column of boxes, much like the one we built in "Re-ordering a List Using Drag-and-drop Functionality" in Chapter 14, that can be reordered using drag-and-drop functionality. The mouse picks up an object, moves it, then snaps it to a new position, but the end result of those actions is simply a *change in the order* of the objects: the one you dragged has moved up or down by a given number of positions. Couldn't we get to that same end result using commands from the up and down arrow keys?

Indeed we could, but we'll need an element to act as an "anchor" for the keyboard: an element that can take focus (either the draggable object itself, or something inside it), and handle events from the arrow keys.

Figure 16.2 depicts a box that indicates mouse behaviors; the darker strip at the top is the "grab" element for the mouse. You can click on it and, holding the house button down, drag the box around.

Figure 16.2. A draggable box with a "grab" element for the mouse

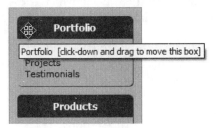

Now, if we add a link inside the grab element, and style it to look like a graphical icon, as shown in Figure 16.3, that icon can be the anchor for keyboard navigation.

Figure 16.3. The same box again with an anchor for keyboard navigation

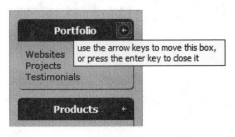

The icon serves a double purpose here. As well as being the keyboard anchor for drag-and-drop actions, it acts as a toggle to show and hide the box's content area (when the user either presses **Enter**, or clicks on it with the mouse). These screenshots were generated by a script that's too large to reproduce here, but if you'd like to download and play with it, you can find it on my web site.[10]

A DHTML slider control is another example in which drag-and-drop functionality can be retrofitted for the keyboard, as arrow-key events can be translated to left and right dragging actions. Later in this chapter, we'll build that exact capability into the slider control we made in "Making a Slider Control" in Chapter 14.

AJAX and other Remote Scripting Techniques

The core of AJAX scripting deals with programmatic events—things like the `readystatechange` event of `XMLHttpRequest`, or the `load` event of an `iframe`

---

[10] http://www.brothercake.com/site/resources/scripts/dbx/

used for data retrieval (we'll delve into both techniques fully in Chapter 18). The users' modes of interaction don't make any difference to the ways in which these events behave, so we don't need to consider them especially.

But we do have two important things to consider. First, how are those processes triggered? If a request or process is to be triggered by a user action, we must ensure that the same process can be triggered by a keyboard user. Second, we must think about how we'll format the response.

In addressing the second issue, we must carefully construct the response HTML, to make sure we maintain a *usable tab order*. For example, if we use the response data to create a new `select` element from which the user can select a further option, we must ensure that the selector is inserted near the trigger element, rather than being appended to the `body`, so that keyboard users can get straight to it.

Making `title` Attribute Tooltips Display on Focus

The `title` attribute is designed to provide supplementary information about a link, form control, or other element, and is usually rendered in graphical browsers as a tooltip like the one shown in Figure 16.4.

Figure 16.4. A link's `title` attribute rendered as a mouseover-driven tooltip

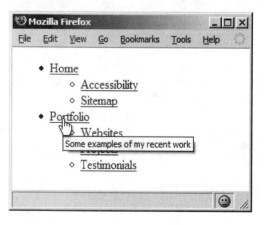

In screen readers and other aural user-agents, the `title` text may be spoken in a different tone, or with other contextual information (or it may not be spoken at all—it's generally an optional setting).

The disadvantaged in this paradigm are sighted keyboard users, for whom `title` text is generally not available at all. The majority of browsers don't display this information when the user is navigating to an element using the keyboard; indeed, some elements that rely on their `title` attributes to be of any use, such as `abbr` (abbreviation) elements, simply are not accessible to the keyboard.

But there is one significant exception that I'm aware of, which is that Opera facilitates spatial navigation (hold down the **Shift** key, then move around using the arrow keys). With this mechanism, it's possible to navigate to `abbr` (among other selected elements), in which case the title text *is* shown as a tooltip!

But in browsers other than Opera (can you tell I'm a fan?) this information generally is not available. We can't do anything about elements that don't receive the focus, but with some nifty DOM scripting, we *can* improve the situation for links, form controls, and other elements that take focus.

Solution

This solution is somewhat similar to the nicely-styled tooltips we saw in "Displaying a Tooltip when you Mouse Over an Element" in Chapter 13. However, what we're doing here is *supplementing*, rather than replacing, the existing tooltips, so we're going to try to style them to match those previously-created tooltips using CSS 2 System Colors.[11]

These will apply the same font and colors used in the native OS tooltip, ensuring that it remains accessible to people who use a specific color scheme (e.g., high contrast). However, system colors don't work in Safari, so in that browser we'll just have to use the tooltips' default styles, and use a less-than-ideal CSS hack to apply the difference:

File: **tooltips.css**

```
div.tooltip {
  background: InfoBackground;
  font: small-caption;
```

---

[11] See http://www.w3.org/TR/CSS21/ui.html#system-colors for more information. Note that System Colors are deprecated in the CSS 3 Color Module in favor of System Appearance properties, as part of the Basic User Interface Module (Working Draft) [http://www.w3.org/TR/2003/WD-css3-ui-20030703/#system].

```
      border: 1px solid InfoText;
      color: InfoText;
      padding: 2px 4px;
      text-align: left;
      position: absolute;
      width: auto;
      height: auto;
}

div[class~="tooltip"] {
      background: #feffc8;
      font: normal normal normal 11px verdana,sans-serif;
      border: 1px solid #c3c3c3;
      color: #000;
}

div[class~="tooltip"]:lang(en) {
      background: InfoBackground;
      font: small-caption;
      border: 1px solid InfoText;
      color: InfoText;
}
```

The first set of rules defines the default styling, which applies to all browsers; the second set applies the alternative, non-system font and colors to CSS 2-capable browsers; the third reapplies the system colors to any CSS 2 browser that also understands the lang pseudo-class (which excludes Safari). This risk here is that if a future version of Safari (or any other browser) adds support for lang without also providing support for system colors, the hack will break.

In our script, we're going to iterate through all elements, attempting to bind a focus event listener to each. When a given element receives the focus, a new element will be created, styled using those system colors, and populated with the title text from the focused element.

We begin with an initialization function that binds the necessary event listeners with our ever-useful attachEventListener function:

File: **tooltips.js (excerpt)**

```
addLoadListener(initTooltips);

function initTooltips()
{
  var keyflag = false;
  attachEventListener(document, 'keydown', function()
```

```
{
  keyflag = true;
}, false);
attachEventListener(document, 'keyup', function()
{
  keyflag = false;
}, false);

var eles = typeof document.all != 'undefined'
  ? document.all : document.getElementsByTagName('*');
for (var i = 0; i < eles.length; i++)
{
  if (eles[i].getAttribute('title'))
  {
    attachEventListener(eles[i], 'focus', createTooltip, false);
    attachEventListener(eles[i], 'blur', removeTooltip, false);
    attachEventListener(eles[i], 'mouseover', function()
    {
      if (!keyflag) { removeTooltip(); }
    }, false);
  }
}
}
```

This initialization function is called from the `load` event, using the generic `addLoadListener` function from Chapter 1.

The `document.all` Collection

Here, we're using the proprietary `document.all` collection—a relic of the browser wars that shouldn't normally be employed. However, in this case, `document.all` is necessary to support Windows IE 5, which doesn't implement the `'*'` notation for fetching all elements.

The real work of the script is done by two functions that create and remove the custom tooltips:

File: **tooltips.js (excerpt)**

```
var timer, tooltip = null;

function createTooltip(e)
{
  var target = typeof e.target != 'undefined'
      ? e.target : e.srcElement;
  timer = window.setTimeout(function()
  {
```

```
    removeTooltip();

  if (!tooltip)
  {
    tooltip = document.createElement('div');
    tooltip.appendChild(document.createTextNode(target.title));
    tooltip.className = 'tooltip';
    document.getElementsByTagName('body')[0].
        appendChild(tooltip);

    if (tooltip.offsetWidth > 300)
    {
      tooltip.style.width = '300px';
    }

    var position = [
        getRoughPosition(target, 'x'),
        getRoughPosition(target, 'y') + target.offsetHeight + 5
    ];

    tooltip.style.left = position[0] + 'px';
    tooltip.style.top = position[1] + 'px';

    var size = [
        tooltip.offsetWidth,
        tooltip.offsetHeight
    ];
    var viewport = getViewportSize();
    var scrolling = getScrollingPosition();

    if ((position[0] + size[0]) >= (viewport[0] + scrolling[0]))
    {
      position[0] -= (size[0] - target.offsetWidth);
      if (position[0] < 0) { position[0] = 0; }
      tooltip.style.left = position[0] + 'px';
    }
    if ((position[1] + size[1]) >= (viewport[1] + scrolling[1]))
    {
      position[1] -= (size[1] + target.offsetHeight + 10);
      if (position[1] < 0) { position[1] = 0; }
      tooltip.style.top = position[1] + 'px';
    }
  }
}, 400);
}
```

```
function removeTooltip()
{
  if (tooltip)
  {
    tooltip.parentNode.removeChild(tooltip);
    tooltip = null;
  }
  clearTimeout(timer);
}
```

This tooltip creation script relies heavily on three other utility functions we've used before:

❑ getRoughPosition, from Chapter 15, for finding the position of the original element

❑ getScrollingPosition and getViewportSize, from Chapter 7, to ascertain the page scroll position and the space that's available inside the window

Discussion

The two keyboard event listeners at the start of the initialization function maintain a keyflag variable that indicates whether or not a key is pressed:

File: **tooltips.js (excerpt)**

```
var keyflag = false;

attachEventListener(document, 'keydown', function()
{
  keyflag = true;
}, false);

attachEventListener(document, 'keyup', function()
{
  keyflag = false;
}, false);
```

We need this extra scripting for Opera, because the use of spatial navigation generates mouseover events as well as focus events. The mouse events are used in the script to clear the tooltip, so that our custom tooltips don't conflict with the native tooltips for people who use both the mouse and keyboard at different times. But if we allowed that to happen while spatial navigation was taking place, the tooltips wouldn't work at all: every action would create and then instantly remove the tooltip.

Since spatial navigation involves holding down the **Shift** key, we create and use the `keyflag` variable to determine whether a `mouseover` event really comes from a mouse (because the flag is `false` when the event fires), and only clear the tooltip if it does:

File: **tooltips.js (excerpt)**
```
attachEventListener(eles[i], 'mouseover', function()
{
  if (!keyflag) { removeTooltip(); }

}, false);
```

The main `createTooltip` function is bound to each element using a `focus` event. This function stores a reference to the target element, then starts a 400ms timer to enclose the rest of the code. The timer helps improve usability, as it lets the script avoid quickly creating and destroying lots of tooltips as users **Tab** through a list.

Once the timer has finished, its inner function begins with a call to `removeTooltip`, which removes any existing tooltip and clears the `timer` variable set by `createTooltip`. This means that if another `focus` event occurs *before* the timer has completed, that iteration will be abandoned and a new one will start, ultimately ensuring that only one tooltip can ever be visible at any time.

Creating the tooltips is a pretty straightforward process. We create a new `div` element with the appropriate class name and the target element's `title` text, then append it to the `body`. The width is restricted to 300 pixels so that the text of large tooltips wraps, and is easier to read.

Then comes the most intensive work: positioning and repositioning the tooltip. We begin by finding the position of the target element, and positioning the tooltip in the same place, though the tooltip is offset by the target element's height (so it's underneath, not directly on top) and a small margin (which improves its appearance):

File: **tooltips.js (excerpt)**
```
var position = [
    (getRoughPosition(target, 'x')),
    (getRoughPosition(target, 'y') + target.offsetHeight + 5)
];
tooltip.style.left = position[0] + 'px';
tooltip.style.top = position[1] + 'px';
```

We must also make sure that the tooltip remains inside the viewport, so we use its position and size, along with the viewport size and scrolling position, to determine whether the tooltip has run off the edge of the viewport. If it has, we recalculate its position to orient it from the other side of the original target, finally limiting its position to zero (so that it won't be repositioned off the viewport's other side):

File: **tooltips.js** (excerpt)

```
var size = [
    tooltip.offsetWidth,
    tooltip.offsetHeight
];
var viewport = getViewportSize();
var scrolling = getScrollingPosition();

if ((position[0] + size[0]) >= (viewport[0] + scrolling[0]))
{
  position[0] -= (size[0] - target.offsetWidth);
  if (position[0] < 0) { position[0] = 0; }]
  tooltip.style.left = position[0] + 'px';
}
if ((position[1] + size[1]) >= (viewport[1] + scrolling[1]))
{
  position[1] -= (size[1] + target.offsetHeight + 10);
  if (position[1] < 0) { position[1] = 0; }
  tooltip.style.top = position[1] + 'px';
}
```

The default position of a custom tooltip will be just beneath its trigger, as show in Figure 16.5.

Figure 16.5. The **title** attribute as a focus-driven tooltip

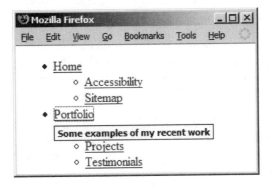

But the tooltip's size and position are flexible, so it works even when space is at a premium, as in Figure 16.6.

Figure 16.6. The same tooltip in a very confined space

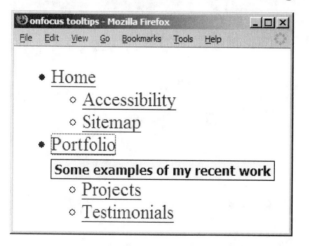

This solution also overcomes a common limitation of built-in tooltips, in that it scales with font size, as shown in Figure 16.7.

Figure 16.7. The same tooltip with larger text

Figure 16.7 illustrates the appearance of the tooltip in Firefox, using CSS 2 System Colors. I don't know why the `font` value displays bold text, given that the native tooltip isn't bold by default, but I'm reluctant to override that manually—tweaking the appearance of system fonts somewhat defeats the point of using them.

You'll remember that we couldn't apply CSS 2 System Colors in Safari, because it doesn't support them (and would render the tooltips as completely black boxes), so the fallback colors are based on the default appearance of Safari's native tooltips, and end up looking like those in Figure 16.8.

Figure 16.8. The same tooltip in Safari

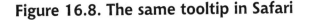

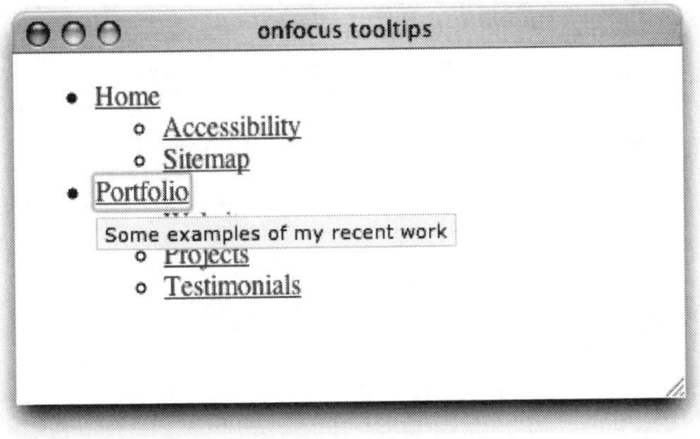

Making a DHTML Menu Accessible to the Keyboard

Our second major solution in Chapter 15 created a folder tree or expanding menu, and that solution is already accessible to keyboard users (including those using screen readers), because we had to consider these people in order to make the menus work properly for *any* user. In that solution, we employed an inference technique for identifying screen readers; we'll be looking at this technique in more depth in "Making Scripts Accessible to Screen Readers" later in this chapter.

However, you may recall that the *first* main solution, a drop-down or fly-out menu, wasn't completed within the scope of that chapter—the solution we produced was only fully accessible to people using a mouse.

At the time, I promised we'd come back to that issue, and here we are! In this solution and the next, we're going to improve our original script to provide *multiple* modes of keyboard navigation. In all browsers, we'll add support for users to navigate using **Tab** and **Shift-Tab** (or equivalent keystrokes—for example, in Opera, the link navigation keys are **A** and **Q**). We're also going to add support for spatial navigation in Opera, while for Firefox, Safari, and Internet Explorer for Windows, we'll implement a similar kind of two-dimensional navigation facility that employs the arrow keys.

The baseline script we're starting with is the finished DHTML menu solution from the section called "Making a Drop-down or Fly-out Menu" in Chapter 15, including all the usability enhancements we designed for it; if you haven't already read that solution, I recommend you do so first, otherwise much of what we talk about here will be completely abstract. For these examples, we'll continue to use a vertical navigation bar with fly-out menus, but the solution will cater equally to a horizontal version, and indeed we'll have some special considerations to talk about in that case.

Solution

Let's begin by adding basic keyboard navigation using **Tab** and **Shift-Tab** (or their equivalents). We can already **Tab** through the links, of course, and press **Enter** to activate any of them, but we need some scripting to make the menus appear and disappear.

On each link we need a `focus` event listener, which will use essentially the same code as the `mouseover` listener. To save repetition, we'll abstract that event listener into a function:

File: **dropdownMenuKeyboard.js** (excerpt)

```
function showMenu(menu, horiz, issub, li, a, isie)
{
  menu.style.left = horiz
      ? (isie ? li.offsetLeft + 'px' : 'auto')
      : '0';

  menu.style.top = horiz && issub
      ? (isie ? a.offsetHeight + 'px' : 'auto')
      : (isie ? li.offsetTop + 'px' : '0');

  repositionMenu(menu);

  if (typeof document.uniqueID != 'undefined')
  {
    createIframeLayer(menu);
  }
}
```

We also need two new iterative functions—the first to show all the menus necessary to reveal a particular submenu, the second to hide all the nested submenus of a given menu:

File: **dropdownMenuKeyboard.js (excerpt)**

```
function showAncestors(tree, menu, horiz, issub, isie)
{
  clearMenus(tree);

  while (menu.id != tree.id)
  {
    var li = menu.parentNode;
    var a = li.getElementsByTagName('a')[0];

    showMenu(menu, horiz, issub, li, a, isie);

    menu = li.parentNode;
  }
}

function resetSiblingBranches(trigger, tree)
{
  clearMenus(trigger.parentNode);

  var links = trigger.parentNode.getElementsByTagName('a');
  for (var i = 0; i < links.length; i++)
  {
    links[i].className =
        links[i].className.replace(/ ?rollover/g, '')
  }
}
```

Next, we need to make a few alterations to the original dropdownTrigger function, to modify the existing mouseover event listener and add the new focus listener (additions and changes to the original script are shown in bold below):

File: **dropdownMenuKeyboard.js (excerpt)**

```
function dropdownTrigger(tree, li, navid, isie, horiz)
{
  var opentime, closetime;
  var a = li.getElementsByTagName('a')[0];
  var menu = li.getElementsByTagName('ul').length > 0
      ? li.getElementsByTagName('ul')[0] : null;
  var issub = li.parentNode.id == navid;

  if (menu)
  {
    li.className += (li.className == '' ? '' : ' ') + 'hasmenu';
  }
```

```
attachEventListener(a, 'focus', function(e)
{
  clearTimeout(closetime);

  a.className += (a.className == '' ? '' : ' ') + 'rollover';

  resetSiblingBranches(li);
  if (menu)
  {
    showMenu(menu, horiz, issub, li, a, isie);
  }

  var parent = li.parentNode;
  if (parent != tree)
  {
    if (parent.style.left == '' ||
        parent.style.left == '-100em')
    {
      showAncestors(tree, parent, horiz, issub, isie);
    }
    if (toggleSelects('visible') && tree.contains(e.srcElement))
    {
      toggleSelects('hidden');
    }
  }
}, false);

attachEventListener(li, 'mouseover', function(e)
{
  if (unwantedTextEvent()) { return; }
  clearTimeout(closetime);
  if (branch == li) { branch = null; }

  a.className += (a.className == '' ? '' : ' ') + 'rollover';

  var target = typeof e.target != 'undefined'
      ? e.target : window.event.srcElement;
  while (target.nodeName.toUpperCase() != 'LI')
  {
    target = target.parentNode;
  }
  if (target != li) { return; }

  if (menu)
  {
```

```
      opentime = window.setTimeout(function()
      {
        if (branch)
        {
          clearMenus(branch);
          branch = null;
        }

        resetSiblingBranches(li);
        showMenu(menu, horiz, issub, li, a, isie);
      }, 250);
    }
  }, false);

  attachEventListener(li, 'mouseout', function(e)
  {
    if (unwantedTextEvent()) { return; }

    var related = typeof e.relatedTarget != 'undefined'
        ? e.relatedTarget : e.toElement;
    if (!li.contains(related))
    {
      clearTimeout(opentime);
      branch = li;

      a.className = a.className.replace(/ ?rollover/g, '');
      if (menu)]
      {
        closetime = window.setTimeout(function(
        {
          menu.style.left = '-100em';

          if (toggleSelects('visible') && tree.contains(related))
          {
            toggleSelects('hidden');
          }
          else
          {
            removeIframeLayer(menu);
          }

        }, 600);
      }

    }, false);
```

```
if (!isie)
{
  li.contains = function(node)
  {
    if (node == null) { return false; }
    if (node == this) { return true; }
    else { return this.contains(node.parentNode); }
  };
}
```

Finally, we'll perform some surgery on the dropdownMenu initialization function, to create new values and bind additional methods (again, additions and alterations are shown in bold):

File: **dropdownMenuKeyboard.js** (excerpt)

```
var branch;

function dropdownMenu(navid)
{
  var isopera = typeof window.opera != 'undefined';
  var isie = typeof document.all != 'undefined'
      && !isopera && navigator.vendor != 'KDE';
  var issafari = navigator.vendor == 'Apple Computer, Inc.';

  if (typeof document.getElementById == 'undefined'
      || (issafari && typeof window.XMLHttpRequest == 'undefined')
      || (isie && typeof document.uniqueID == 'undefined'))
  {
    return;
  }

  var rollover = new Image;
  rollover.src = 'right-red.gif';
  rollover = new Image;
  rollover.src = 'down-red.gif';

  var tree = document.getElementById(navid);
  if (tree)
  {
    var horiz = tree.className.indexOf('horizontal') != -1;
    branch = tree;
    var items = tree.getElementsByTagName('li');
    for (var i = 0; i < items.length; i++)
    {
      dropdownTrigger(tree, items[i], navid, isie, horiz);
    }
```

```
    var eles = typeof document.all != 'undefined'
        ? document.all : document.getElementsByTagName('*');
    for (i = 0; i < eles.length; i++)
    {
      attachEventListener(eles[i], 'focus', function(e)
      {
        var target = typeof e.target != 'undefined'
            ? e.target : e.srcElement;
        if (!tree.contains(target))
        {
          resetSiblingBranches(items[0]);
        }
      }, false);
    }

    if (!isie)
    {
      tree.contains = function(node)
      {
        if (node == null) { return false; }
        if (node == this) { return true; }
        else { return this.contains(node.parentNode); }
      };
    }
  }
}
```

We don't need any blur event listeners because, as it turns out, all the necessary menu closing and resetting will be triggered from other focus events. I'll explain why below.

Discussion

We need to make sure that all the menus are closed when the user navigates away from the tree entirely, so that they're not left with residual menus covering other elements on the page. It sounds simple enough, but detecting that situation is surprisingly awkward.

If we were responding to a mouseout event, we could simply check the event's relatedTarget property (or toElement in IE—the element that the mouse is moving *to*), and check if it was outside the menu tree. But we can't do that from a blur event, because *blur events don't have a related target property*. I have no idea why this is the case, it's just a fact.

A document-level `focus` listener seems like a logical alternative. If we receive a focus event that bubbles up from *any* element, we can check if it's outside the menu tree. But that won't work either, because as we've seen already in this chapter, `focus` *events don't bubble*.

What we're left with is a reliable, if somewhat inefficient, solution: we must bind a `focus` event listener to every element in the document. The listener will perform that same check to see whether or not the event target is outside the menu tree, and will reset the menu state if it is:

File: **dropdownMenuKeyboard.js (excerpt)**

```
var eles = typeof document.all != 'undefined'
    ? document.all : document.getElementsByTagName('*');
for (i = 0; i < eles.length; i++)
{
  attachEventListener(eles[i], 'focus', function(e)
  {
    var target = typeof e.target != 'undefined'
        ? e.target : e.srcElement;
    if (!tree.contains(target))
    {
      resetSiblingBranches(items[0]);
    }
  }, false);
}
```

note

The Custom contains Method

Again, to check if an event is inside or outside the tree, we have created a custom `contains` method. This method evaluates the relationship between nodes, as we discussed in the section called "Making a Drop-down or Fly-out Menu" in Chapter 15.

File: **dropdownMenuKeyboard.js (excerpt)**

```
if (!isie)
{
  tree.contains = function(node)
  {
    if (node == null) { return false; }
    if (node == this) { return true; }
    else { return this.contains(node.parentNode); }
  };
}
```

The new `resetSiblingBranches` function simply closes all menus and clears all highlighted links beginning from a specified root node. Passing the first list item in the tree (member 0 in the `items` collection we defined at the start of the script) has the effect of resetting the entire menu structure.

Our shiny, new `focus` event listener essentially recreates the mouse behaviors, but this time, it does so *without* any open or close timers (because they're not necessary for keyboard navigation, and would just amount to pointless pauses). However, we'll still have to reset any currently running close timer, in case a menu is closed with the mouse but then keyboard navigation supersedes that action. A small addition to the `mouseover` listener—a call to `resetSiblingBranches`—is necessary for the same reason: the mouse navigation needs to reset any changes to the menu structure that were made via keyboard navigation.

The `focus` listener is bound to each link, not each list item (as is the case for the mouse listeners), because we won't get `focus` events from list items, and as we know, they don't bubble up from the links:

File: **dropdownMenuKeyboard.js (excerpt)**

```
attachEventListener(a, 'focus', function(e)
{
  clearTimeout(closetime);

  a.className += (a.className == '' ? '' : ' ') + 'rollover';

  resetSiblingBranches(li);
  if (menu)
  {
    showMenu(menu, horiz, issub, li, a, isie);
  }

  var parent = li.parentNode;
  if (parent != tree)
  {
    if (parent.style.left == '' || parent.style.left == '-100em')
    {
      showAncestors(tree, parent, horiz, issub, isie);
    }

    if (toggleSelects('visible') && tree.contains(e.srcElement))
    {
      toggleSelects('hidden');
    }
```

```
    }
}, false);
```

The only other significant difference between this code and the equivalent mouse behaviors is the call to `showAncestors`, which comes into play when a user tabs backwards through the menu structure:

File: **dropdownMenyKeyboard.js** (excerpt)

```
if (parent.style.left == '' || parent.style.left == '-100em')
{
  showAncestors(tree, parent, horiz, issub, isie);
}
```

When navigating backwards, it's possible to go straight from a navigation bar link to a deeply-nested menu link, but of course that menu *won't be visible*, because you didn't navigate through its ancestors on your way there. We can test for this situation by checking whether the parent menu has a `style.left` value that's consistent with it being hidden, then iterating backwards[12] up the tree, showing each ancestor menu:

File: **dropdownMenyKeyboard.js** (excerpt)

```
function showAncestors(tree, menu, horiz, issub, isie)
{
  clearMenus(tree);

  while (menu.id != tree.id)
  {
    var li = menu.parentNode;
    var a = li.getElementsByTagName('a')[0];

    showMenu(menu, horiz, issub, li, a, isie);

    menu = li.parentNode;
  }
}
```

---

[12]I wonder if iterating backwards should be called "reiteration."

Making a DHTML Menu Usable via the Keyboard

The preceding solution is certainly accessible—every menu and link is now available to the keyboard—but the behaviors are not as smooth as they are for mouse users. Navigating to a deeply nested link still involves of lot of key presses, because tabbing is a one-dimensional operation (forwards or backwards), yet our menu is really a two-dimensional structure (we can move up and down through nested menus, and left and right between sibling menu items). Wouldn't it be cool if we could reconcile that with two-dimensional navigation keys?

The arrow keys are the obvious and intuitive choice. In fact, Opera already has the functionality we want, and almost no effort is required to make it work for our menus! If we use the spatial navigation paradigm we first looked at in "Making `title` Attribute Tooltips Display on Focus", Opera users can navigate around the entire menu structure by holding down **Shift** and moving the mouse cursor around with the arrow keys. This action also fires `focus` events, when relevant, so the menus will open and close as they do for mouse users.[13]

But we still have Firefox and other Mozilla browsers, Safari, and Internet Explorer to think about. For these browsers, we'll create similar functionality with custom scripting, using the arrow keys alone.

Solution

To begin with, we need a simple but highly effective utility function called `cleanUselessWhitespace`. This function, which is based on a method by Alex Vincent,[14] removes all the unwanted whitespace text nodes from inside the tree (including tabs, spaces, and line breaks between list items). It makes our job a whole lot easier, because node references will then be predictable (e.g., an `li` element's `nextSibling` property is another `li` tag, not the whitespace in between):

File: **dropdownMenuKeyboard.js (excerpt)**

```
function cleanUselessWhitespace(node)
{
```

---

[13]The only change that was required to make this work was the addition of `display: table` to the navigation bar list items' CSS! Don't ask me why that makes a difference, but it literally does make *all* the difference; without it, Opera can't latch onto the menu links reliably, so it's basically unusable.

[14] http://weblogs.mozillazine.org/weirdal/

```
for (var x = 0; x < node.childNodes.length; x++)
{
  var child = node.childNodes[x];
  if (child.nodeType == 3 && !/\S/.test(child.nodeValue))
  {
    node.removeChild(node.childNodes[x]);
    x--;
  }
  if (child.nodeType == 1)
  {
    cleanUselessWhitespace(child);
  }
}
}
```

Next, we add the function that does the real work here; called arrowKeyNavigation, it processes each key command, then sends focus to the appropriate element:

File: **dropdownMenuKeyboard.js (excerpt)**

```
function arrowKeyNavigation(tree, link, keycode, horiz)
{
  var li = link.parentNode;
  var menu = li.getElementsByTagName('ul').length > 0
      ? li.getElementsByTagName('ul')[0] : null;
  var parent = li.parentNode;

  switch (keycode)
  {
    case 37:
      parent = parent.parentNode;
      if (tree.parentNode == parent) { parent = null; }
      if (parent)
      {
        parent.firstChild.focus();
      }
      break;
    case 38:
      var previous = li.previousSibling;
      if (!previous)
      {
        previous = li.parentNode.childNodes
            [li.parentNode.childNodes.length - 1]
      }
      previous.firstChild.focus();
      break;
```

```
      case 39:
        if (menu)
        {
          menu.firstChild.firstChild.focus();
        }
        break;
      case 40:
        var next = li.nextSibling;
        if (!next)
        {
          next = li.parentNode.childNodes[0];
        }
        next.firstChild.focus();
        break;
    }
}
```

Finally, we can add a document-level key listener to kick all that into action. Here's an excerpt from the dropdownMenu function to the extent necessary to show you the new code (additions are shown in bold):

File: **dropdownMenuKeyboard.js (excerpt)**

```
function dropdownMenu(navid)
{
  var isopera = typeof window.opera != 'undefined';
  var isie = typeof document.all != 'undefined'
      && !isopera && navigator.vendor != 'KDE';
  var issafari = navigator.vendor == 'Apple Computer, Inc.';

  if (typeof document.getElementById == 'undefined'
      || (issafari && typeof window.XMLHttpRequest == 'undefined')
      || (isie && typeof document.uniqueID == 'undefined'))
  {
    return;
  }

  var rollover = new Image;
  rollover.src = 'right-red.gif';
  rollover = new Image;
  rollover.src = 'down-red.gif';

  var tree = document.getElementById(navid);
  if (tree)
  {
    var horiz = tree.className.indexOf('horizontal') != -1;
    branch = tree;
```

```
var items = tree.getElementsByTagName('li');
for (var i = 0; i < items.length; i++)
{
  dropdownTrigger(tree, items[i], navid, isie, horiz);
}

if (!isopera)
{
  cleanUselessWhitespace(tree);

  var keyevent = issafari || isie ? 'keydown' : 'keypress';
  attachEventListener(document, keyevent, function(e)
  {
    var target = typeof e.target != 'undefined'
        ? e.target : e.srcElement;
    if (tree.contains(target) && target.getAttribute('href'))
    {
      if (/^(37|38|39|40)$/.test(e.keyCode.toString()))
      {
        arrowKeyNavigation(tree, target, e.keyCode, horiz);

        if (typeof e.preventDefault != 'undefined')
        {
          e.preventDefault();
        }
        return false;
      }
    }
    return true;

  }, false);
}
```

Discussion

Here, we're responding to arrow key events (which are key codes 37 to 40, inclusive), then translating those directions into element references.

Figure 16.9 shows a point on the menu from which all possible movements would lead us to other menu items. From this diagram, we can see what the relationships are:

left (key code 37)   means the parent item of the current menu

up (key code 38)   means the previous sibling of the current item

right (key code 39)   means the first item in the current item's child menu

down (key code 40)   means the next sibling of the current item

Figure 16.9. Four directions of possible movement from a submenu link

Of course, an element won't always be available in any given direction, so we'll have to check each menu item for possible exceptions: if an item has no submenu, there isn't going to be anything to the right; from the main navigation bar, there won't be anything to the left; for movements up and down, we can cycle continually through the items, jumping back to the top when we reach the bottom of a menu, and jumping to the bottom when we reach the menu's top.

The core code for translating these four possible directions of movement into a new focus target takes place in `arrowKeyNavigation`, the code for which was given above.

However, there are certain circumstances in which this simple keyboard navigation model breaks down. The main one is associated with menu repositioning, which we implemented in "Making Sure the Menus Stay Inside the Window" in Chapter 15. Pressing the right arrow to go to a submenu that has been shifted to the left no longer makes sense, as Figure 16.10 shows.

Figure 16.10. The repositioned Spoons submenu changes the meaning of "left" and "right"

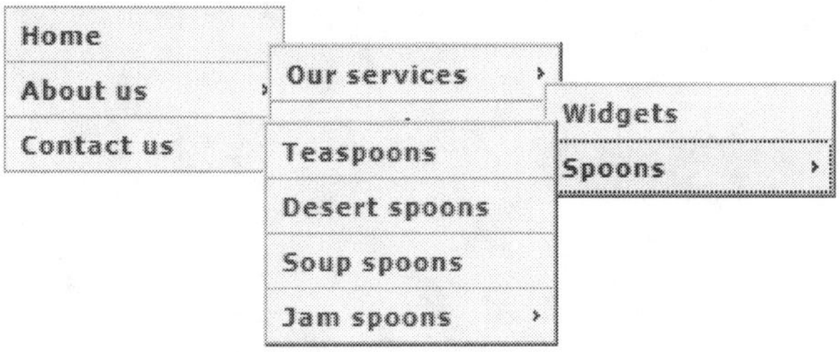

The Spoons submenu has been moved to the left side of its parent menu, so intuition clearly demands that the *left* arrow should go to the submenu, not the right arrow. We're going to have to check for this possibility, and remap the keystrokes accordingly.

We'll also have to do some remapping for a horizontal navigation bar, because the top-level list of links is a row, not a column (but this does not apply to the submenus, which continue to behave as described above!). So within that navigation bar, we'll need to swap the meanings of up and left movements, as well as the down and right movements. Finally—and also for a horizontal navigation bar—when the user presses the up arrow from the first item in a first-level submenu, we'll want to move focus back up to the navigation bar, instead of cycling round to the bottom of the submenu. This means we'll have to convert that particular keystroke from up to left.

Let's create a new function to perform the relevant key conversions that will allow us to handle all these exceptions. `mapKeyCode` will convert the code of the actual key that was pressed to the correct code for the existing navigation logic. As we have three exceptions, this function will perform one of three types of mapping (in the order in which we've just discussed them):

File: **dropdownMenuKeyboard.js** (excerpt)

```
function mapKeyCode(keycode, type)
{
  switch (type)
  {
    case 0:
      if (keycode == 37) keycode = 39;
      else if (keycode == 39) keycode = 37;
      break;

    case 1:
      if (keycode % 2) keycode++;
      else keycode--;
      break;

    case 2:
      if (keycode == 38) { keycode = 37; }
      break;
  }

  return keycode;
}
```

We need to call this code from the main arrowKeyNavigation function, *just before* we check the key code for the action to be performed:

File: **dropdownMenuKeyboard.js** (excerpt)

```
function arrowKeyNavigation(tree, link, keycode, horiz)
{
  var li = link.parentNode;
  var menu = li.getElementsByTagName('ul').length > 0
    ? li.getElementsByTagName('ul')[0] : null;
  var parent = li.parentNode;

  if (menu)
  {
    if (getRoughPosition(menu, 'x')
      < getRoughPosition(li.parentNode, 'x'))
    {
      keycode = mapKeyCode(keycode, 0);
    }
  }
  else if (parent != tree)
  {
    if (getRoughPosition(parent.parentNode.parentNode, 'x')
      > getRoughPosition(parent, 'x'))
    {
      keycode = mapKeyCode(keycode, 0);
    }
  }

  if (horiz)
  {
    if (parent == tree)
    {
      keycode = mapKeyCode(keycode, 1);
    }
    else if (parent.parentNode.parentNode == tree
      && li == li.parentNode.firstChild)
    {
      keycode = mapKeyCode(keycode, 2);
    }
  }

  switch (keycode)
  {
    :
```

The last tricky thing we've done here has to do with the default actions associated with all these arrow key presses. These events would normally cause window scrolling to occur—something which, obviously, we want to prevent. However, we can't prevent scrolling for *all* arrow key presses, or we'd be breaking part of the user interface. We should only prevent scrolling under the right circumstances. So, within our event listener setup code in dropdownMenu, we use the contains method to check if the event target is a hyperlink inside the menu tree; we also check the keyCode to confirm that the event is an arrow key press. If everything checks out, we trigger our arrowKeyNavigation function and cancel the default action. Here's the relevant code:

File: **dropdownMenuKeyboard.js (excerpt)**

```
if (tree.contains(target) && target.getAttribute('href'))
{
  if (/^(37|38|39|40)$/.test(e.keyCode.toString()))
  {
    arrowKeyNavigation(tree, target, e.keyCode, horiz);
    if (typeof e.preventDefault != 'undefined')
    {
      e.preventDefault();
    }
    return false;
  }
}
```

To trigger all this we use one of two different key events, depending on the browser, as different browsers have different ideas about which event equates to (and hence, can be used to suppress) the action of window scrolling. In Safari and Internet Explorer it's keydown, while in Mozilla browsers it's keypress, hence the code branching:

File: **dropdownMenuKeyboard.js (excerpt)**

```
var keyevent = issafari || isie ? 'keydown' : 'keypress';
attachEventListener(document, keyevent, function(e)
{
  ⋮
```

Making a DHTML Slider Control Accessible to the Keyboard

In "Making a Slider Control" in Chapter 14, we built a slider widget that translates mouse movement into values sent to a hidden form field. This was carefully designed to deal with real data that's submitted with the form as normal, so that it degrades gracefully to a regular text field if scripting is not supported.

But the slider only works for mouse users, and even once it's retrofitted for the keyboard, the slider remains inaccessible to some screen reader users, who won't be able to use the widget and can't navigate to the hidden field that represents its data.

This solution sorts that problem out, so if you haven't already read the original solution I strongly recommend you do so.

Solution

We begin by changing a key aspect of what the scripting actually achieves. We no longer want to *remove* the original text fields and replace them with hidden fields; instead, we want to apply offleft positioning to move the text fields off the screen (just as we did for our DHTML menus), then add the custom widgets. This will ensure that the field remains accessible to screen reader users, even if the custom widget doesn't work. Changes from the original code are shown in bold below:

File: **slider.js** (excerpt)

```
function initSliders()
{
  var sliderReplacements = getElementsByAttribute("class",
      "slider");

  for (var i = 0; i < sliderReplacements.length; i++)
  {
    var container = document.createElement("div");
    var slider = document.createElement("button");
    slider.setAttribute("type", "button");

    container.className = "sliderContainer";
    slider.className = "sliderWidget";
    slider.style.left =
        sliderReplacements[i].getAttribute("value") + "px";
    slider.valueX = parseInt(
        sliderReplacements[i].getAttribute("value"), 10);
    sliderReplacements[i].className += " offleft";

    container.appendChild(slider);
    sliderReplacements[i].parentNode.insertBefore(container,
        sliderReplacements[i]);
```

```
container.input = sliderReplacements[i];

attachEventListener(slider, "mousedown", mousedownSlider,
    false);
attachEventListener(slider, "focus", focusSlider, false);
attachEventListener(slider, "blur", blurSlider, false);

document.ismouse = false;
attachEventListener(slider, "mouseover", mouseoverSlider,
    false);
attachEventListener(slider, "mouseout", mouseoutSlider,
    false);
}

return true;
}
```

The slider button itself needs to be an element that's able to take focus, and button is the obvious choice. In fact, this element specifically had to be a button element, rather than an input of type button, because the latter doesn't work in Safari—for some (unknown) reason it doesn't fire any mousedown events, which makes it stop functioning as a slider for mouse users. A button element works, and is semantically just as good; plus it also gives us richer design potential since further elements can be contained inside it.

Styled Link vs Form Element

note

If we'd used a styled link instead of a form element, we'd have created a usability problem in Opera (as well as making our script less accurate semantically). Opera uses different navigation keystrokes for links than it does for form controls. If the slider could not be reached using the same keystrokes that are used to access other form elements, this would clearly undermine its usability as a form control.

The next consideration is that some of the code we'll need for keyboard-initiated movement is the same as for mouse-initiated movement. Let's abstract the original slider positioning logic into a separate function:

File: **slider.js** (excerpt)

```
function incrementSlider(slider, sliderLeft, increment, event)
{
  if (sliderLeft < 0)
  {
    sliderLeft = 0;
```

```
  }
  else if (sliderLeft >
      (slider.parentNode.offsetWidth - slider.offsetWidth))
  {
    sliderLeft = slider.parentNode.offsetWidth -
        slider.offsetWidth;
  }
  else
  {
    slider.originX =
        typeof event != "undefined" ? event.clientX : 0;
  }

  slider.style.left =
      Math.round(sliderLeft / increment) * increment + "px";
  slider.parentNode.input.value =
      Math.round(sliderLeft / increment) * increment;
  slider.valueX = sliderLeft;
}
```

Once we make the necessary adjustment to the mousemoveSlider function (shown in bold), we'll have made all the necessary changes to the original script:

File: **slider.js (excerpt)**

```
function mousemoveSlider(event)
{
  if (typeof event == "undefined")
  {
    event = window.event;
  }

  var slider = document.currentSlider;
  var sliderLeft = slider.valueX;
  var increment = 1;

  if (isNaN(sliderLeft))
  {
    sliderLeft = 0;
  }

  sliderLeft += event.clientX - slider.originX;

  incrementSlider(slider, sliderLeft, increment, event);

  stopDefaultAction(event);
```

```
    return true;
}
```

Now let's define the new functions we need—focus and blur listeners that identify when the user navigates to or away from the slider control:

File: **slider.js** (excerpt)

```
function focusSlider(event)
{
  if (typeof event == "undefined")
  {
    event = window.event;
  }
  var target = getEventTarget(event);

  target.className += " sliderFocus";

  if (document.ismouse) { return false; }

  document.currentSlider = target;
  target.originX = 0;

  target.pressed = false;
  target.repeatRate = 400;
  target.currentRate = target.repeatRate;

  attachEventListener(document, "keydown", keydownSlider, false);
  attachEventListener(document, "keyup", keyupSlider, false);

  return true;
}

function blurSlider(event)
{
  if (typeof event == "undefined")
  {
    event = window.event;
  }
  var target = getEventTarget(event);

  target.className = target.className.replace(" sliderFocus", "");

  detachEventListener(document, "keydown", keydownSlider, false);

  return true;
}
```

We also need `keydown` and `keyup` listeners to handle arrow-key events, and translate them into the appropriate actions:

File: **slider.js (excerpt)**

```
function keydownSlider(event, repeatKey)
{
  if (typeof event == "undefined")
  {
    event = window.event;
  }

  var slider = document.currentSlider;
  var sliderLeft = slider.valueX;
  var increment = 1;

  if (isNaN(sliderLeft))
  {
    sliderLeft = 0;
  }

  if (slider.pressed && event != null) { return false; }
  else { slider.pressed = true; }

  if (event != null)
  {
    repeatKey = event.keyCode;
  }
  else if (slider.currentRate == slider.repeatRate)
  {
    slider.currentRate = slider.repeatRate / 20;
  }
  else
  {
    increment = 3;
  }

  sliderLeft += repeatKey == 39 ? increment
      : repeatKey == 37 ? 0 - increment
      : 0;

  incrementSlider(slider, sliderLeft, increment);

  slider.repeater = setTimeout(function()
  {
    keydownSlider(null, repeatKey);
```

```
  }, slider.currentRate);

  return true;
}

function keyupSlider(event)
{
  var slider = document.currentSlider;

  clearTimeout(slider.repeater);
  slider.currentRate = slider.repeatRate;
  slider.pressed = false;
}
```

We also need new `mouseover` and `mouseout` listeners, which simply set and clear a `document.ismouse` flag. This flag is used within the `focusSlider` function to determine whether a `focus` event came from the keyboard, or from a click of the mouse button (this can generate a focus event if the clicked element doesn't already have focus). In the latter case, we want to ignore most of the code in `focusSlider` so as not to conflict with the mouse behaviors (for example, setting the `target.originX` value to zero would override the value set by `mousedownSlider` in all browsers except Opera, because of the order in which the events fire):

File: **slider.js** (excerpt)

```
function mouseoverSlider()
{
  document.ismouse = true;
}
function mouseoutSlider()
{
  document.ismouse = false;
}
```

That's it! Our slider control can now be used with the keyboard as well as the mouse, and remains accessible to both screen readers and non-script browsers in its original, semantic form.

Discussion

Obviously, there are some pretty tricky details being managed in the code above. Let's dive in!

When a user holds down a key, the repeat rate of the associated `keydown` event is not predictable, if indeed it repeats at all (in this case, it doesn't repeat for Opera or Safari). As such, we'll have to take control of the repeat rate ourselves: only the first, discrete `keydown` event will be handled (until another `keyup` event has occurred); the repeat will be implemented manually using `setTimeout`.

This also allows us to enhance the usability of the slider by implementing a delay before it repeats. You can see in the `focusSlider` function that the initial `repeatRate` is set to 400ms: it takes 400ms after the first `keydown` for the second slider value change to occur; but when it *does* occur, the `keydownSlider` function divides the repeat rate by 20, so that it shoots up to 20ms and stays there. This means users can easily select from a large range of numbers by holding down the arrow key, but they can still micro-adjust the figure by pressing and releasing it more quickly.

For the repeating calls to `keydownSlider`, we store and pass the `keyCode` value back through the timer as a second argument, and replace the first argument—the event object—with `null`. By checking for that `null` value (and confirming that the button is held down with the help of a `pressed` property), the function is able to identify and filter out any repeating `keydown` events that are produced natively by the browser:

File: **slider.js (excerpt)**

```
if (slider.pressed && event != null) { return false; }
else { slider.pressed = true; }
```

The `keyupSlider` function resets all of that, stopping the timer, resetting the repeat rate, and clearing the `pressed` property. The `focus` and `blur` event listeners initialize and reset this property, and handle the rollover effect; but their primary task is to add and remove the key listeners in the same way that the original `mousedown` and `mouseup` listeners functioned for the other mouse listeners.

Before we leave this solution, I'd like to point out that it isn't perfect! First, it has an issue with excessive redundancy, in that the buttons are empty elements for screen reader users, while the original text fields are unnecessary elements for visual users. In neither case is this a problem—it doesn't prevent the widget from working as intended—but it does mean that all users will be left with some redundant elements in their flow. The only way I've found to avoid this problem is to use the *original text field* as the slider control itself, but under this approach the styling possibilities are severely restricted.

The slider has what potentially is a more serious problem for any users who need their keyboards to operate with a specific repeat rate or repeat delay, for example, people who have restricted movement in their hands and require a longer repeat delay to compensate. The script overrides the native speeds and implements custom values, because this was the only way I found to create stable, cross-browser behaviors, but this may make some of the interactions involved impossible; for example, a user might not be able to press and release an arrow key quickly enough to micro-adjust the slider value.

Making Scripts Accessible to Screen Readers

How do screen readers handle JavaScript? Badly!

Almost all of the screen readers in current use are browser-based readers, which means they either work in tandem with, or directly embed, a regular graphical browser (usually Internet Explorer, although Windows Eyes 5.5 also works with Firefox).

An assumption under which many people begin coding is that a screen reader is just like a text-only browser. This is not correct. A reader is nothing like a text browser, because text browsers don't support CSS or JavaScript; browser-based screen readers do.

 Tip

Hear the Web for Yourself!

To get a rough idea of what it's like to use the Web with a screen reader, imagine that a friend or colleague looks at a web page (or actually ask them to do so!) and then reads it to you *over the phone*. They can tell you the `alt` text of images, the `label`s for form controls, and maybe even the `title`s of links. But for the most part, all you can hear is what they can see by default.

The most popular readers in current use are JAWS, Windows Eyes, Hal, Connect Outloud, and Home Page Reader. If you're in a position to try any of these applications, I'd strongly encourage you to do so—you'll be amazed at the empathy and insights you can gain from even very limited experience with these tools.

Better yet, you could go to a local university or college and visit their center for students with disabilities, where you may be able to arrange to be present when someone is using a screen reader to use the Web.

We've already seen the need for scripting to be accessible to the keyboard (or equivalent pointing/actuating device), and how the same baseline should be used for people using screen readers, who are almost certain to be navigating with the keyboard.

But beyond these basics, what we find is that browser-based screen readers *don't behave the same as the browser behaves alone*, yet they *don't behave like non-script browsers, either*. You could say that for these devices, JavaScript is "sort of" supported.[15]

Sounds confusing, right? But this could also be useful: it may allow us actually to *identify* a browser-based screen reader, as distinct from a browser being used on its own, if we could reference the differences in event behavior! In fact, we know this can work, because we've used the technique already in "Making a Folder Tree or Expanding Menu" in Chapter 15. But, as we noted at the time, this approach is clearly a hack that's defensible only because it's better than nothing at all—assuming that we have no other alternative.

But in some cases we do have an alternative. Every situation is different, and just because the hack-based approach worked well in "Making a Folder Tree or Expanding Menu" in Chapter 15 doesn't mean that it's the right solution for all situations; it's just one possible approach to consider. What we would like to be able to develop is a *range* of techniques and ideas to add to our scripting arsenal, so that we can approach *any* given application with a variety of ideas for making it work, or at least to make it safe (i.e., implemented in a way that allows a screen reader to fall back on non-script functionality).

We won't get a complete answer here—in fact, in truth, we'll barely scratch the surface! But what I hope to convey more than anything else is a number of ways to *think* about scripting that you may not have considered before.

To that end, this solution is split into three parts. The first part examines how JavaScript actually behaves in a range of current screen readers, so you can gauge the impact and get a sense of what already works, what can be adapted, and what can't. The second part will outline a general hack for inferring the identity of a screen reader, so that we have at least one technique for "making safe" a script that would otherwise be unusable. In the third and final part, having been through the nitty-gritty, we'll step back to take a broader, more academic look at the subject, at which point we'll reach a surprising best-practice recommendation for building accessible web applications!

---

[15]I don't like to use the phrase "partially supported" in this case, because it feels like that implies a neat, discrete subset of functionality. In fact, what we have here is far more nebulous and imprecise, and "sort of" sums that up much better!

JavaScript Behaviors

Over the last few months, I've been involved in researching how the leading screen readers and other assistive devices respond to JavaScript: what kind of events they generate or respond to, under what circumstances. The research is based at Access Matters,[16] and is coordinated by Bob Easton, Derek Featherstone, Mike Stenhouse and myself, using test data that was provided initially by us (through controlled testing), but more importantly, by readers of the Access Matters blog (who are "real users" in the sense that they're running the test without being concerned by the way it works). I'm grateful to all who took part in that testing—without them, we'd know a great deal less than we do now. The test produced a lot of data—more than I can possibly reproduce here—so if you're interested in the nitty-gritty, see the resources at Access Matters.[17]

Briefly, what we're finding through this research is that script support in screen readers is incredibly erratic and fragmentary. Yet that isn't the biggest problem. There are ways and means by which we can create usable hooks (for example, all the screen readers we tested generate `click` events on links and form controls), but the real sticking point is what to do next. When the script modifies what is displayed by the browser, *how does a screen reader user know that the content has changed?*

A sighted user has random access to a page, by virtue of looking at different bits of it; if something changes, that user's visual attention is drawn to it. But people who are blind have no such access. Their approach to a page is linear, so if part of the page changes before or after the users' current focus, they won't notice it happen, and may not subsequently realize it has happened even when they reach the portion of the page that has changed.

A screen reader *doesn't* announce dynamic changes to the DOM. Those changes just happen in the background, so any given change will more than likely go unnoticed, unless *we* notify the user in some way.

And—this is the $64,000 question—just how do we do that? There are many possibilities, with many variables to consider, so let's explore the jungle and see if we can find the temple!

---

[16] http://www.access-matters.com/

[17] http://www.access-matters.com/index/index-of-javascript-tests/

Rollovers and Revealing Content

We have a nice easy start to this one. Essentially, most rollover effects are aesthetic (they look nice, but convey no actual information), so generally we don't need to be concerned about whether they work for assistive devices, only whether there's likely to be any conflict.

There isn't. Take the focus-driven rollovers we developed in "Making Scripts Accessible to the Keyboard as well as the Mouse", for example. *Most screen readers don't generate* `focus` *events on links*, so they won't trigger the script. But even if they do, all the script does is change the `class` of a link to apply a color change, and that's not a problem to any device—it won't be seen, but it won't do any harm either.

But isn't a rollover informational, in that it confirms the nature of the link (as being a link, not just styled text)? Well yes, it is, but it's information that's only relevant to a sighted user—a screen reader has semantics to fall back on, and will pronounce or announce links differently from regular text (for example, JAWS says "link" or "visited link" after the text, while Home Page Reader in its default configuration uses a different voice).

That example notwithstanding, some effects really are informational and relevant to this group of users, for example, if the rollover exposes another element with new information, or it's something more complex like a DHTML menu.

We looked at accessible fly-out menus earlier in this chapter, and we determined that there were no additional usability considerations over and above how we built the menu in the first place. The structure is an HTML list and uses positioning on the menus to show and hide them; that visual difference is irrelevant to the spoken output of a screen reader, so it doesn't matter whether the scripting works or not, the user will always be able to access the complete menu.

This kind of progressive enhancement generally is the best approach for any kind of content that is "revealed," or otherwise not apparently visible by default: don't generate the content on the fly; have it sitting there in the source code, and just reveal it on the fly. It doesn't matter if the reader doesn't support the script, because the content is there anyway and nothing has changed; if the reader *does* support the script, it *still* doesn't matter, because the content is only changed visually.

But (and this is a very crucial "but"), when hiding content visually we *mustn't actually hide it* (using `visibility`, `display`, `overflow`, or `clip`), because that will also hide it from most screen readers.[18] We discussed this already in the section called "Making a Drop-down or Fly-out Menu" in Chapter 15, but I'll reiterate it here because it's so important. What we must do instead is use the offleft positioning technique, so that the content is rendered but not apparently visible. The CSS for "hidden" and "visible" states might look like this:

```
.hidden
{
  position: absolute;
  left: -100em;
}

.visible
{
  position: static;
}
```

This approach ensures accessibility in the pure sense because all the available content is accessible, but it doesn't provide *ideal usability* as it adds to the number of items in the overall tab order. A user may have to navigate through a lot more elements to find what they want, as they don't have the same random-access capabilities enjoyed by a sighted mouse user. While that might not be a major issue for ad-hoc items or a small navigational tree, it could become a real pain for a large and complex example.

This really is a judgment call—do you provide this kind of implementation, or leave it out entirely, deferring instead to linked information on another page (for example, link to items in a separate glossary instead of having popup definitions)? Sometimes, less is more.

Form Validation

The most important thing when it comes to forms is *don't unduly mess with the focus*. Just as we discussed in "Making Scripts Accessible to the Keyboard as well as the Mouse" (in relation to form validation and general keyboard navigation), *most* uses of the `focus` method and *all* uses of the `blur` method are dubious, and could be very confusing to a screen reader user.

---

[18]This is true for most elements, most of the time—but there are exceptions. For example, JAWS may speak the text in a `label` element even if it's not displayed. But as a general rule of thumb, it's safest to assume that any element that is completely hidden with any of the noted properties is not accessible to screen readers.

Even so, client-side validation is very difficult to implement in a way that screen readers can comprehend. The main consideration (which in fact applies to server-side validation as well) is that error messages must be inserted in a logical place, that is, inside the `labels` for the fields to which they relate. The best recommendation I've seen[19] is to use an additional `em` element to add emphasis to the message, which can then also be used as a styling hook:

```
<label for="uname">Username
  <em>must not contain spaces</em>
</label>
```

But if we want a screen reader to hear that, how do we inform it that the message is there? We could send focus to the relevant `input` element, but that would usually come *after* the `label`, so the user might not hear it. (With implicit association the `input` might be inside the `label`, but it would still generally come after the `label` text.)

Actually, this depends upon the screen reader in question—JAWS, for example, does read the text of an associated `label` when you focus a form field, but Home Page Reader does not. So, for properly accessible client-side validation, the best thing might be to send the focus to the start of the form, either by dynamically resetting the `action` of the `form` to an ID reference in the page when a validation error occurs (e.g., `form.action = "#form"`), or by using `document.location` to do the same thing (e.g., `document.location.replace('#form')`). Or perhaps the answer is simply to use an `alert` dialog for the error message.

But would any of those approaches work? We don't yet have enough information to know, as we're now beginning to question the ways in which screen readers behave in response to dynamically updated content. We need to continue our investigation into more complex forms of scripting.

Non-user-initiated Scripts

The impacts of automatically initiated scripts depend entirely on what they do. The bottom line here is whether they do something at load time, and the result is static from that point on, or whether they do something periodically or asynchronously, such that the content will change *after* the page has finished loading.

---

[19] http://simplyaccessible.org/article/form-error-messages

Don't Change the Page Address Automatically

Don't do anything that changes the page address *automatically*. For example, don't use client-side redirects (either in JavaScript or with a `meta` tag), because these are often disorienting or just plain annoying to users, who cannot control the redirects with most browsers.

If you're implementing a navigational `select` element, for example, make it work from an explicit Go button rather than in response to the `change` event, because most keyboard users select from options with the up and down arrows alone,[20] or by pressing letter keys to jump to specific items (for example, typing **C** three times in a country selector to choose Canada). If the selector activates `onchange`, the highlighted option would immediately be followed, preventing the user from choosing any of the further options.

If the output of a script is static after load time—for instance, part of the page itself is generated with JavaScript, or a random image `src` is selected for an ad banner using JavaScript—this poses no problem for screen reader users. The output will appear to the screen reader no differently than it does to the native browser (where scripting is enabled, of course).

But if it's dynamic output that updates periodically or asynchronously, the situation can become a great deal trickier, and in some cases, the application can break or become useless. Consider a list of news items that updates itself periodically: in one sense, the change doesn't need to be notified, because it's relevant not when it happens, but when you want to read the text; it can update silently in the background until then, and that's fine. But what happens if it updates *while you're reading it*? How confusing would that be?

Let's find out! Here's a simple script that tests the premise. I wouldn't consider this a finished or usable news ticker script; it's simply the bare bones we need to test this question:

File: **news.js**

```
var items = [
    'First news item',
    'Second news item',
    'Third news item',
    'Fourth news item',
    'Fifth news item',
    'Sixth news item',
    'Seventh news item',
```

---

[20] As opposed to **Alt-arrow**, which can open a `select` menu as it appears for the mouse.

```
    'Eighth news item',
    'Ninth news item',
    'Tenth news item'
];

var count = 0;
function updateNews()
{
  var list = document.getElementById('news');
  while (list.childNodes.length > 0)
  {
    list.removeChild(list.firstChild);
  }

  for (var i = count; i < count + 5; i++)
  {
    var n = i >= items.length ? i - items.length : i;
    var li = document.createElement('li');
    var a = li.appendChild(document.createElement('a'));
    a.href = '#';
    a.appendChild(document.createTextNode(items[n]));
    list.appendChild(li);
  }
}

window.onload = function()
{
  updateNews();
  window.setInterval(function()
  {
    count++;
    if (count == items.length) { count = 0; }
    updateNews();

  }, 510000);
};
```

The HTML for this is an ordered list, and is empty by default (which, again, is not suitable for a public web site, as the end user may not support scripting, but it's fine for our test):

File: **news.html (excerpt)**

```
<ol id="news">
</ol>
```

The results from this test are diverse, and actually provide behavioral insights over and above what we're looking for here: as well as telling us how this particular script behaves in each device, the results begin to answer the wider question of how screen readers behave when the DOM is updated after load time (more on this shortly).

To avoid getting too bogged down in detail here, I won't reproduce the test results in full.[21] For our purposes, I'll summarize each screen reader, with an overall assessment of its ability to handle dynamic content, and the potential for confusion that such dynamism could cause the user:

Home Page Reader: moderate dynamic capability, high confusion potential
The content doesn't update dynamically when reading the page automatically, but it does update when navigating manually, so in theory you can hear any five of the news items, though it won't be readily apparent how the user can control *which* five they hear. The content will continue to update as the user navigates manually through the list, but when it does change, Home Page Reader forces the user to update. By "forces the user to update" I mean that the program presents a *modal* choice to the user, forcing them either to reload, or redraw the page! Either of these actions ultimately resets the cursor back to the top of the page, which means that unless a user can get through *all* the items before *any* dynamic change occurs, the scripted list will effectively become an impenetrable wall to keyboard navigation!

JAWS: low dynamic capability, low confusion potential
A JAWS user will hear only the first five items, no matter how they interact with the page, as though the content were generated once and remained static from then on; that being the case, there are no further behavioral issues.

Windows Eyes: low dynamic capability, moderate confusion potential
Windows Eyes displays almost the same behavior as JAWS, except that the content does update when the page is redrawn (for example, if you move the application focus to a different window, then back to Internet Explorer). So while a user might be able to hear all ten news items eventually, this behavior is not coherently controllable.

Dolphin Hal: high dynamic capability, high confusion potential
Dolphin Hal exhibits similar behavior to Home Page Reader, with a similar behavioral quirk: the content is dynamic while the users navigate manually, but any content update that occurs while they're navigating through the list

---

[21] If you'd like to look through them in detail, I refer you to my forthcoming article on SitePoint, a link to which will be published at http://www.sitepoint.com/books/jsant1/.

itself will send the page focus back to the top of that list! Just as with Home Page Reader's modal response, this behavior could create an impenetrable barrier to keyboard navigation.

Connect Outloud: high dynamic capability, moderate confusion potential
The list is fully dynamic via any mode of interaction, so a user can hear all ten news items if they navigate manually through the list, or if they come back to it from time to time. This could be adequately usable providing that the ticker is properly explained with preceding text, and it's certainly the most dynamic behavior we've seen from any screen reader so far. But simply as a result of the ticker's dynamic characteristics (and remember, the user can't actually see it), some quite strange and potentially confusing eventualities are possible. For example, if the user were to **Tab** backwards from one link to the previous one, at exactly the same time as the ticker updated, the user would hear exactly the same link text spoken again!

Thankfully, none of the devices did the very worst thing I feared they might—update the spoken output mid-sentence, resulting in fragmentary, meaningless speech. Sure, I would have been very surprised to find a device that actually did this, but I'm still very relieved to have my expectations confirmed!

To summarize the ability of screen readers to handle dynamic content, they offer *moderate dynamic capability, high confusion potential.* (And there's high confusion potential for us developers as well!) Support can go either way, but neither way is ideal—low dynamic capability gives us little to work with, but high dynamic capability implies higher confusion potential. How can we possibly hope to provide real-time dynamic functionality to any of these users without obfuscating the heck out of their web experience at the same time?

Maybe we've just been unlucky, and have chosen a bad example!

Indeed, in the case of a *scrolling* news ticker such as the one we built in "Making a Scrolling News Ticker" in Chapter 14, the outlook is a whole lot better. In this instance, the content is there by default; all that changes is the visual position of one element inside another, the inner element being partially obscured using `overflow: hidden`. We know from other people's research that some screen readers can't see content that's obscured *completely* using `overflow`,[22] but in this case the content is only *partially* obscured. Does that affect how it's perceived by any of the screen readers?

---

[22] http://www.access-matters.com/2005/04/24/quiz-527-screen-reader-test-7/

Happily, the answer is a resounding *no*! In all tested screen readers, when reading automatically and navigating manually, the CSS and scripting makes no difference whatsoever: the content remains accessible at all times.

At last—something that *just works*!

AJAX and other Remote Scripting Techniques

Given everything we've found out so far, the biggest problem we're going to face should be pretty obvious: the problem isn't how we trigger the script, it's what we do with the response.

We need to do some more testing, and try several possible means of notifying the user that an update has taken place. Again, I won't bog you down with too much detail about the behavior of each device, and I refer you again to my article on SitePoint if you want the nitty-gritty.

All the tests begin with a triggering link. The test is performed by navigating to the link with the keyboard, and pressing **Enter** to actuate it:

File: **ajax1.html (excerpt)**

```
<p>
  <a href="./" id="trigger">This link is the trigger.</a>
</p>
```

That script triggers some JavaScript that makes an XMLHttpRequest request, then performs a variety of tasks with the response text, using an element with ID re-sponse in the document:

```
window.onload = function()
{
  var trigger = document.getElementById('trigger');
  var response = document.getElementById('response');

  trigger.onclick = function()
  {
    var request = null;
    if (typeof window.ActiveXObject != 'undefined')
    {
      try { request = new ActiveXObject('Microsoft.XMLHTTP'); }
      catch (err) { request = null; }
    }
    else if (typeof window.XMLHttpRequest != 'undefined')
    {
```

```
        request = new XMLHttpRequest();
    }

    if (request != null)
    {
        request.onreadystatechange = function()
        {
            if (request.readyState == 4
                && /^(200|304)$/.test(request.status.toString())))
            {
                : do something with the response
            }
        }

        request.open('GET', 'test.php?msg=Hello+World', true);
        request.send(null);
    }

    return false;
    };
};
```

The `test.php` script simply outputs a message to be sent to the browser by way of a response—it could have been anything:

File: test.php

```php
<?php
echo "And here's the response - " . $_GET['msg'];
?>
```

For the first group of tests, the `response` element in the HTML was a link. The text in the link was updated, then a couple of different tricks were used to try to get the screen reader to say it—using the `focus` method to set focus on it, or using the `document.location` property to jump to the element's ID:

File: ajax2.js (excerpt)

```javascript
request.onreadystatechange = function()
{
    if (request.readyState == 4
        && /^(200|304)$/.test(request.status.toString()))same
    {
        response.innerHTML = request.responseText;
        document.location = '#response';
    }
}
```

In the former case (setting focus), only JAWS 5.0 and Connect Outloud responded as hoped—they read the updated text in the link and said nothing further. Other devices either did nothing at all (such as Hal), or read a different part of the page instead (JAWS 6.2 and later versions did this, re-reading the top-level heading again, instead of the updated link text).

The latter example (using `document.location`) produced slightly better, but more varied results: in Hal and all versions of JAWS, the response works as intended; in Connect Outloud and Home Page Reader, the updated link text is spoken as we'd hoped, but the reader doesn't stop—it carries on reading to the end of the page; in Windows Eyes, the reader skips the updated link and starts reading from the element after it!

For the second group of tests, I switched the `response` link for a form element—either a text field or a button—to see if that would produce more consistent results. There were three variants: writing to a button and then focusing it; writing to a text field and then focusing it; and finally, writing to a text field and then selecting the text (using some proprietary methods we'll meet properly in "Creating an Auto-complete Text Field" in Chapter 18):

File: **ajax6.js** (excerpt)

```
request.onreadystatechange = function()
{
  if (request.readyState == 4
      && /^(200|304)$/.test(request.status.toString()))
  {
    response.value = request.responseText;
    if (typeof response.createTextRange != 'undefined')
    {
      var range = response.createTextRange();
      range.select();
    }
    else if (typeof response.setSelectionRange != 'undefined')
    {
      response.setSelectionRange(0, response.value.length);
    }
  }
}
```

For all three variations, the pattern of success and failure was exactly the same: it worked perfectly in JAWS 5.0 and Connect Outloud (although they also announced the element by saying, for example, "button" after the text), but failed to work in later versions of JAWS, or in Windows Eyes. The failures paralleled the browsers' behavior with links—Windows Eyes would start reading from the element after the response, while later JAWS versions would read some other, unrelated element instead. In Hal and Home Page Reader, these tests produced no response at all.

Finally, for the sake of completeness, I turned to a simple `alert` dialog, to check that it worked as expected:

File: **ajax4.js** (excerpt)

```
request.onreadystatechange = function()
{
  if (request.readyState == 4
      && /^(200|304)$/.test(request.status.toString()))same
  {
    alert(request.responseText);
  }
}
```

This should be safe for everyone, but astonishingly, it isn't. Windows Eyes 5.0 *doesn't always speak the dialog text*—sometimes it just announces the dialog, and doesn't tell you what it says!

Overall, the results from these tests suggest that there's *no reliable way to notify screen readers of an update in the DOM*—there are piecemeal approaches that work for one or more devices, but no overall approach or combination of approaches that would cover them all, given that even the humble `alert` may not work correctly in Windows Eyes.

Tricks and Hacks

Now that we've looked at numerous different kinds of scripting, we have some idea of what's okay, and what's far from okay. We may be faced with a situation in which a particular script simply cannot be used in good conscience, unless we can find a way to make it *not apply* to screen readers.

That's where this part of the solution comes into play. We can't identify screen readers directly, because the vast majority don't identify themselves any differently than the browser would on its own. But we can use the data we *do* have to infer their identity indirectly, so that we can filter out dangerous scripting and let them fall back on static content.

We've already seen this technique work in the folder tree menu we made in "Making a Folder Tree or Expanding Menu" in Chapter 15. In that example, we needed to differentiate `click` events on certain links: in a graphical browser we wanted those links to open a submenu and then return `false`, but in a screen reader we wanted to follow the link as normal and ignore the menu script, because otherwise the links would appear to do nothing at all (the change being a purely visual one).

To make this work, there needed to be some interaction—we cannot infer the use of a screen reader automatically, so this is *not* something we can do at load time to determine whether a script should initialize. It's something we can only do *after* a minimum amount of interaction has taken place, and that minimum is *having navigated between two links*.

None of the screen readers we've tested generate `keydown` or `keyup` events from the **Tab** key when navigating between links; but some do generate them from modifier keys like **Shift**, or from other actions like pressing **Enter** to actuate a link. If we attach a `keyup` listener to one or more links, and test for `keyCode 9` (the **Tab** key), we'll know that, if we receive that event, it came from a vanilla browser (i.e., a browser used on its own), not a browser-based screen reader. For our folder tree menu, the links in the list itself provide that interactive input, so as long as neither the very first, nor the very last navigation bar link has a submenu, we'll always have enough data to assess accurately whether the browser is being used alone before any menu-opening `click` event can occur.

We also have to identify mouse navigation, but here we run into another behavioral quirk of some browser-based screen readers, which is that some of these tools also generate a complement of mouse events when a link is actuated with the keyboard. Dolphin Hal 6.5, for example, generates `mouseover`, `mousemove`, and `mousedown` events at the same time as a `click` event. But it only generates one instance of each event, so if we use a `mousemove` handler that counts for multiple events, it will provide the filter we need. A graphical browser used in tandem with the mouse will have generated several `mousemove` events on a link before a `click` event is generated, but the reader will generate only one, just before actuating the link. So, if we receive several of these events before a `click` event, we can be sure that a graphical browser is being used.

The code below has been abstracted into a generic utility and test function (which would be initialized by a `load` event listener, and uses the `attachEventListener` and `detachEventListener` functions from Chapter 13):

File: **reader-detector.js**

```
function readerDetector()
{
  var isreader = (typeof window.opera == 'undefined'
       && navigator.vendor != 'Apple Computer, Inc.');
```

```
var test = document.getElementById('testlink');

function keyupTest(e)
{
  if (!e) { e = window.event; }
  if (e.keyCode == 9)
  {
    isreader = false;
  }
}

var moves = 0;
function mousemoveTest()
{
  if (isreader)
  {
    moves ++;
    if (moves > 2) { isreader = false; }
  }
}

attachEventListener(test, 'keyup', keyupTest, false);
attachEventListener(test, 'mousemove', mousemoveTest, false);

test.onclick = function()
{
  alert(isreader
      ? 'Screen reader' + '     [isreader=' + isreader + ']'
      : 'Vanilla browser' + '     [isreader=' + isreader + ']');
  detachEventListener(test, 'keyup', keyupTest);
  detachEventListener(test, 'mousemove', mousemoveTest);
  return false;
};
}
```

The test-case HTML looks like this:

```
<ul>
  <li><a href="#">Priming link</a></li>
  <li><a href="#" id="testlink">Test link</a></li>
</ul>
```

This script correctly identifies the following devices, used with the keyboard: JAWS 5.0–6.2, Connect Outloud 2.0, Home Page Reader 3.02 and 3.04, Hal 6.5, and Windows Eyes 5.0 and 5.5 (with Internet Explorer or Firefox). It also identifies correctly all the major desktop browsers in their vanilla state, used with either the keyboard or the mouse.

Currently, there are no browser-based readers based in Opera or Safari, hence either of these browsers will immediately set the `isreader` variable to `false` in the script above. Otherwise, the variable defaults to `true`, and is set to `false` by the combinations of events we have just discussed.

This approach works for links, but it won't work for form elements, because navigating between form elements in these devices generates a lot more events than do links, and there isn't enough of a consistent discrepancy between the various browsers and screen readers to be able to make the distinction.

Also, this solution is unable to allow for mouse navigation in a screen reader, as it's similarly not possible to differentiate between the standalone browser and the screen reader. Somebody who does navigate with a mouse can be reasonably assumed not to be blind, though they may be partially sighted and may use a reader to assist navigation. Opera and Safari themselves do have voice capabilities, and these are also designed for users who are not (or are not completely) blind. So we're talking in both cases about groups of users whose typical interactions are no different than those of a sighted user; from a programming perspective, we shouldn't need to identify them separately.

Is this a completely safe hack that we can use from now on with free abandon? Not entirely. Like any hack, it's an imperfect solution, in this case because it makes inferences based on *known* behavioral profiles of the *most popular, current* screen readers. Inferences can break over time as new versions are released; they may fail in programs other than those that have been tested; and of course, they may simply be an incomplete picture, potentially affected by circumstances that the testing didn't reveal.

But the hack is better than nothing, especially if the alternative is a script that creates unsolvable accessibility barriers. The obvious retort would be, "Well, don't use those scripts at all, then!" That's a fair comment, but is it realistic? Could you stay, and are you now, on the right side of that opinion? Consider: any script that uses a `click` handler on a link, and degrades to a regular `href`, might not work at all for a screen reader user, which would create an accessibility barrier. Yet implementing scripts on links like this is a best-practice technique that's used all over the place for a wide range of tasks.

I'm not trying to scare you here, nor am I being intentionally perverse. I simply want to drill home what I believe is a pretty fundamental point: *sometimes, imperfect solutions will have to do, if the alternative is to do nothing.*

In some cases, there is a viable alternative. As we've seen in examples through this chapter, some kinds of scripts can be made safe for screen readers without resorting to hacks—it just takes some thought and careful adjustment to the details of their implementation, and some awareness of the different ways in which people will actually use them. Some kinds of scripts are just fine anyway, without any special consideration. Hooray for small mercies!

But we're still left with big chunks of unsolved puzzle—scripting that simply doesn't work, or cannot be made safe for screen reader users. Most notable among these problem areas is the task of making asynchronous updates to the DOM, for which there's apparently no single, reliable means of informing the screen reader user that a change has occurred—not even the traditional `alert` dialog can provide us with a rock-solid prop.

Towards Best Practice

At the London @media conference in 2005, Derek Featherstone suggested (somewhat controversially at the time) that the best way to provide a consistent experience for people using older screen readers might be to *ask them to turn JavaScript off*.[23] I strongly disagreed at the time, because I couldn't see how that was any different to asking *another* group of users to *turn JavaScript on* (something we go out of our way to avoid doing).

The Mission

I really wanted to create a coherent solution for this book—to find a way of making dynamic client interfaces work in screen readers and other assistive devices. I wanted it for my own sake as much as theirs and yours. I wanted it for the sake of professional pride!

But I haven't found one, and I must tentatively conclude that there isn't one *at present*. I stress the "at present" because we simply don't know enough to draw a firm conclusion; we don't even know what all the issues are! As I said at the start of this section, what we've done here has barely scratched the surface of this issue, and what will transpire over the next few months and years is anybody's guess.

---

[23] http://www.boxofchocolates.ca/archives/2005/06/12/javascript-and-accessibility

Yet in reevaluating the original premise to try to understand all this, I came to a startling conclusion: making dynamic client interfaces work in screen readers was *never the point* of this exercise; the point is to make the *applications themselves* work effectively in screen readers!

Interactions are just details, and perhaps what we've really been doing here is projecting our own desires and preferences onto users for whom they're not really relevant. Maybe dynamic client interfaces don't benefit screen reader users at all, and it would work best for screen readers and their users if we played to the kinds of interaction for which these devices were originally designed.

The Joy of Mode

The failure of `alert` dialogs to provide a reliable solution, and subsequent thoughts and discussions on the general subject of modal dialogs, made me realize that modal interaction is a fantastic thing, because modal interaction is always task-focused. It begins from the premise that a user wants to *do* something (which invariably they do; usually it's only we programmers who have a holistic view of an application), and limits his or her choices within a particular dialog to options that progress that task. Think of the number of "wizards" used in Windows, how easy they are to use, and consequently, how popular they've become.

Now, built-in dialogs themselves are not the answer, partly because we know they're not completely reliable, and partly because they're so restrictive in terms of the ways in which we can format them and the kinds of responses they can provide (not to mention the way they look!). But they do suggest a feasible approach: modality.

Do we have a paradigm on the Web that can create that kind of modality, while still providing a rich canvas for visual and interface design? What mechanism can do that while *also* providing continual, live, and accurate progress information to a screen reader, or any device, about what the host environment is doing?

Reaching toward a Best Practice Approach

The answer to the above questions? *Individual page requests*, and the states and interactions of HTTP!

What I'm basically suggesting here, from these (albeit limited) test results, is that conventional submit and response functionality is infinitely better, from a screen reader's perspective, than remote scripting applications that update pages without reload. If the end goal is building accessible web applications, then for this group of users, the best approach may be to forget about JavaScript altogether!

What is this heresy? Am I trying to talk down one of the most exciting developments in the Web in recent years? Not at all! I'm certainly not drawing a line under AJAX and calling it "inaccessible." I'm merely stressing the point that *applications should work using either mode of interaction*—through traditional post and response, or through remote scripting—and that perhaps the way to differentiate the options for different users is to offer them a choice of interaction, rather than trying to infer their environment and make that decision for them.

Either way, what I'm taking about is progressive enhancement, which makes it possible to serve all users from a single application, without having to compromise anyone's experience, or divide users on the notion that one approach is "better" than another. Just as XHTML 1 is designed to allow it to be handled by any device—even those that were made before it existed—so modern scripting should be designed with the same ideals, by progressive enhancement from a mode- and device-independent core.

It could be that the lynch-pin of any solution is the user's *choice* of mode, regardless of whether that choice should be offered to users up-front, or made for them programmatically. If a user approaches the page with JavaScript turned off, they've already made their choice, otherwise it's still viable; yet in some cases we have a good idea of which mode suits which users better, and that leaves us either wanting to make the choice programmatically (a ticklish business, as we've seen), or offering it to users in advance (in which case it may be difficult to explain).

In most cases, I think the latter option is better. It's better to explain a difficult choice and risk users making the wrong one for themselves, than to take the choice away and risk imposing the wrong one upon them, but circumstances may allow you to avoid the choice altogether (as they did for our folder tree menu).

Into the Future

Maybe (and very ironically) Flash represents the best hope for dynamic client interfaces! Recent versions of Flash have specific capabilities for providing metadata to certain screen readers (JAWS and Windows Eyes), and offer a directly detectable programming environment, with far more in the way of status and object information than is currently available through JavaScript.

But screen reader vendors themselves may reasonably be hoped to respond to the increasing popularity of remote scripting by providing the necessary hooks and feedback to help make it accessible to users. Maybe IBM, in its work with screen reader and browser vendors, will pave the way for the DOM to provide this kind of interface in a clean and accessible way.

Or maybe Derek was right all along, and we should just ask people using a screen reader to turn JavaScript off!

Summary

In this chapter, we've outlined what we mean by accessible scripting, and discovered that making scripts accessible to *sighted* keyboard users is possible for basically anything—we didn't see a single case in which a script was fundamentally unadaptable, even if some circumstances required some careful, creative thinking to make the scripts so.

But the situation is more difficult for screen reader users, because some kinds of scripts are simply impossible to implement in some or all devices, as our testing has revealed. The key remaining question seems to focus on how and whether we try to filter out scripting ourselves, or whether we ask those who are affected to change their browser configurations until such time as the technology is up to the task.

The bulk of this chapter has talked about issues relating to keyboard navigation and screen readers, but there's much more to accessibility than that. For instance, there are numerous groups of users for which we still haven't catered properly, because I honestly don't know what to tell you about them! We may find out through research that, for example, AJAX applications can be used to benefit people with cognitive disabilities. Or we may find out that a general recommendation to turn off JavaScript benefits other groups of users besides those we've considered.

I never expected us to solve it all, but we do know a great deal more than we did at the start of this chapter. Not bad!

Using JavaScript with Flash

Flash occupies an unusual position in the structure of the Internet. It has become almost as ubiquitous as HTML itself, yet it isn't built into any of the browsers natively. Instead, Flash relies on a separate plugin to function properly.

It's because of this unsteady existence that developers are sometimes required to act as intermediaries between the world of Flash and the world of HTML. This chapter introduces a few pieces of JavaScript that can help you successfully integrate Flash into your pages, and make informed decisions about whether or not to do so.

Detecting whether Flash is Installed in a Browser

Although *most* web users can view Flash, there's still a substantial number who can't, and there are always going to be versions of Flash that can't handle your new-fangled technology. So before you decide to use Flash objects on your web page, you should be certain that the user's browser supports them.

Solution

Almost all Flash detection scripts prior to 2005 required a clunky VBScript workaround in order to determine which version of the Flash plugin Internet Explorer was using; however, Bobby van der Sluis managed to find a pure JavaScript method for doing this, and coded it into Unobtrusive Flash Objects.[1] This gives us a nice clean way to detect the version of Flash that's being used by any browser.

Although standard objects are available to detect the plugins available in a user's browser, Internet Explorer for Windows always leaves those objects empty, so we need to access its ActiveX objects in order to get the right information. Fortunately, Internet Explorer for Mac is able to handle standard plugin detection, so it's not left out in the cold:

File: **detect_flash.js**

```
var flashInfo = getFlashVersion();

alert("This browser has Flash version: " + flashInfo["major"] +
    "." + flashInfo["build"]);

function getFlashVersion()
{
  var flashVersion = new Array();

  flashVersion["major"] = 0;
  flashVersion["build"] = 0;

  if (navigator.plugins &&
      typeof navigator.plugins["Shockwave Flash"] == "object")
  {
    var description =
        navigator.plugins["Shockwave Flash"].description;

    if (description != null)
    {
      var versionString =
          description.replace(/^.*\s+(\S+\s+\S+$)/, "$1");

      flashVersion["major"] =
          parseInt(versionString.replace(/^(.*)\..*$/, "$1"));
      flashVersion["build"] =
```

[1] http://www.bobbyvandersluis.com/ufo/

```
            parseInt(versionString.replace(/^.*r(.*)$/, "$1"));
      }
   }
   else if (typeof window.ActiveXObject != "undefined")
   {
      try
      {
         var flashObject =
            new ActiveXObject("ShockwaveFlash.ShockwaveFlash");
         var description =
            flashObject.GetVariable("$version");

         if (description != null)
         {
            var versionNumbers =
               description.replace(/^\S+\s+(.*)$/, "$1").split(",");

            flashVersion["major"] = parseInt(versionNumbers[0]);
            flashVersion["build"] = parseInt(versionNumbers[2]);
         }
      }
      catch(error)
      {
      }
   }

   return flashVersion;
}
```

getFlashVersion can be run at any stage of a page's loading procedure because it queries only global browser properties. This allows you to execute it immediately in the head of your document and use its value later.

Standards-compliant browsers fill the navigator.plugins property, which we check for the existence of the "Shockwave Flash" plugin; we then parse that plugin's description to obtain its version numbers. The description follows the form "Shockwave Flash 7.0 r19", and we're particularly interested in those last two numbers. The integer before the decimal point is the major version number of the plugin, while the number that follows the r is the plugin's build version. Although most significant changes occur between major versions of the software, differences do exist between build versions, so this information is available if you require it.

Internet Explorer on a Windows platform will not store any plugins in the navigator.plugins object, so the second branch of the above code is designed for this browser. We try to create a new ActiveX object of type `"Shockwave-Flash.ShockwaveFlash"`, and if it's successful, we are able to query it for its version information. Internet Explorer's version description takes the form `"WIN 7,0,19,0"`, where the major version is the first number and the build version is the third number. This requires us to use a slightly different set of regular expressions to divide the string up into the parts we need, but once the versions have been ascertained, they are assigned to `flashVersion`, which is used as `getFlashVersion`'s return value.

Once `flashInfo` has been assigned, we can use its associative array values to perform tests on the current Flash version, and act accordingly:

```
var flashInfo = getFlashVersion();

if (flashInfo["major"] > 6 ||
    (flashInfo["major"] == 6 && flashInfo["build"] >= 65))
{
    ⋮
}
```

Tip

Don't Test for a Single Version

If you're testing for a particular version of Flash, you should never check for that version alone, like this:

```
if (flashInfo["major"] == 6)
{
    ⋮
}
```

This kind of test does not make your script future-proof, because future versions of Flash will fail that test even though they will most likely meet the requirements for which you're trying to test.

The script in the solution above tests for a Flash version greater than 6, or a build version greater than or equal to 65. This allows higher versions to pass the test, and means it won't be broken whenever a new version of the plugin is released.

Communicating Between JavaScript and Flash

Flash has its own scripting language called ActionScript, which is actually similar to JavaScript as it was based on the same standard (ECMA-262). However, that doesn't mean the two languages are interchangeable. If you want a Flash file to interact with the JavaScript on the HTML page that contains it, you need a way for the two to communicate, and depending upon what you want to achieve, you might have quite a challenge ahead.

Solution

A very simple way to have a Flash file execute a JavaScript command is to use the ActionScript function `getURL`. Using `getURL`, you can make a "command line" JavaScript call using the `javascript:` "faux URL" syntax that you can also type into your browser's location bar.

If we had a JavaScript function called `uniteFlashJS` on our web page, we could call it from within a Flash movie by executing this piece of ActionScript:

File: **communicate_javascript_flash.fla (excerpt)**

```
getURL("javascript:uniteFlashJS()");
```

`uniteFlashJS` would then execute and do whatever it has to do. Simple!

Discussion

There are two other methods by which JavaScript and Flash can communicate, but both have drawbacks and limitations. Of the two, probably the second method is the most viable, given its broader browser compatibility.

FSCommand

The formalized method of interaction between JavaScript and Flash movies involves the use of Flash's **FSCommand** feature. However, this functionality is currently only available in browsers that support ActiveX or LiveConnect (a Java module), which at the moment includes Internet Explorer for Windows and older versions of Netscape (versions 4.x and 6.2). The newest version of Netscape—version 8—also supports FSCommand, but only if it's in Internet Explorer emulation mode.

The code requirements for FSCommand are very light. In order to execute a Flash action from JavaScript you simply need to execute the method on a reference to the Flash object—just like a DOM method. Take a look at the Flash object in the following HTML:

File: **communicate_javascript_flash2.html** (excerpt)

```
<object id="movie"
    classid="clsid:d27cdb6e-ae6d-11cf-96b8-444553540000">
  <param name="movie" value="intro.swf" />
  <embed name="movie" src="intro.swf"
      type="application/x-shockwave-flash" swLiveConnect="true" />
</object>
```

We could stop the movie by executing the ActionScript method `stop` on it:

File: **communicate_javascript_flash2.js** (excerpt)

```
document.getElementById("movie").stop();
```

note

Enabling LiveConnect

In order to enable LiveConnect, Netscape requires you to include the attribute `swLiveConnect="true"` in the `<embed>` tag. Because it is a Java module, LiveConnect will take a few seconds to load, so be sure to take this into account if you wish to use FSCommand.

There is a limited set of methods that can be accessed using this interface, but they're more than powerful enough to perform almost any task you need to execute in your Flash movie. The full list is available in the Flash online documentation.[2]

If we're approaching the situation from the opposite direction—that is, we need to communicate from Flash to JavaScript—it's almost as simple.

Since version 3 of Flash, ActionScript has had a function called `fscommand` that allows a Flash movie to interact with the browser's client-side scripting. It doesn't, however, directly execute a client-side function. Instead, when `fscommand` is executed, it's mapped to a particular function on the client side. The name of that function is the ID of the movie, followed by `_DoFSCommand`. The arguments that are passed to `fscommand`—two strings called *command* and *args*—are forwarded

---

[2] http://www.macromedia.com/support/flash/publishexport/scriptingwithflash/scriptingwithflash_03.html

to this mapped function, and it is from there that you must perform your own JavaScript calculations.

For the example Flash object above, the mapped function would have to be called `movie_DoFSCommand`; once inside it, we can do whatever we wish with the arguments it is passed. Generally, the *command* argument will specify the action to be taken, and the *args* argument supplies any data that's needed for its execution:

File: **communicate_javascript_flash3.js** (excerpt)

```
function movie_DoFSCommand(command, args)
{
  switch (command)
  {
    case "changeColor":
      changeColor(args);
      break;

    case "changeBackgroundColor":
      changeBackgroundColor(args);
      break;
  }

  return true;
}
```

VBScript Required

Internet Explorer integrates FSCommand using an ActiveX object, so when `fscommand` is executed in ActionScript, it tries to communicate with a VBScript function. Therefore, a VBScript handler must be set up to forward the FSCommand arguments on to the corresponding JavaScript function. To do this, include this short piece of code in the `head` of your page:

File: **communicate_javascript_flash3.html** (excerpt)

```
<script type="text/VBScript">
sub movie_FSCommand(ByVal command, ByVal args)
    call movie_DoFSCommand(command, args)
end sub
</script>
```

If your Flash object has a different ID than `movie`, simply substitute that at the beginning of the function name.

Flash/JavaScript Integration Kit

Although FSCommand *is* the mandated method of communication between JavaScript and Flash, its lack of support across most browsers makes its viability questionable on an open system. To counteract this, two programmers from Macromedia—Christian Cantrell and Mike Chambers—have created an API that uses a feature that was introduced in Flash 6.

The Flash/JavaScript Integration Kit[3] uses ActionScript's `LocalConnection` function to set up between Flash and JavaScript a gateway that handles communication between the two languages. This solution does require you to include a JavaScript file on affected pages, upload an SWF file to your server, and incorporate two Flash library files into your Flash authoring process, so its inner workings are outside the scope of this book; however, it has been proven to work in Internet Explorer 6 for Windows, Opera 8 for Windows and Mac, Safari 1.2, and Firefox for Windows, Mac and Linux.

The kit is easily installed. You simply need to copy a couple of files to your local server and reference one of them—`javaScriptFlashGateway.js`—from the HTML pages that require it. Once this is done, it takes just two lines of code to make a JavaScript to Flash call:

```
var flashProxy = new FlashProxy(uid,
    '/path/to/JavaScriptFlashGateway.swf');

flashProxy.call('myActionScriptFunction', 'my string', 123, true,
    new Date(), null);
```

The first line creates an instance of the Flash proxy, which acts as the gateway between the JavaScript and the Flash movie. You need to pass it the ID of the Flash movie with which you'll be communicating, as well as the path of the Flash gateway file you copied to your server.

Once this object has been instantiated, you're free to execute functions inside the Flash movie using the `call` method. `call`'s first argument is the name of the ActionScript function you want to execute; its remaining arguments comprise any data that you wish to pass to that function. The kit includes a data serializer, so you can pass objects, arrays, strings, dates, numbers, booleans, and nulls, to be converted automatically into a format that can be sent and read by Action-Script.

---

[3] http://weblogs.macromedia.com/flashjavascript/

In order to receive calls from a Flash movie to JavaScript, nothing extra needs to be done to the HTML other than including the `javaScriptFlashGateway.js` file. Some bindings *do* need to be set up in the target Flash movie, but these are all well-documented in the kit's own documentation. If you're keen, the best approach is to download it and try it for yourself.

Summary

While previously, developers have taken an all or nothing approach—all Flash, or all HTML—the growing demand to include rich media alongside accessible content has highlighted the need to merge traditional HTML web pages with individual Flash components. Recent JavaScript/Flash modules such as Scalable Inman Flash Replacement,[4] Unobtrusive Flash Objects,[5] and the Flash/JavaScript Integration Kit have shown that JavaScript and Flash can combine to produce some fantastic results, while still providing for non-Flash, non-JavaScript users.

The solutions contained in this chapter should have helped ease the burden of simultaneously providing Flash and non-Flash content, while showing you some ways in which the two media can strengthen one another through combined interaction. Although communication between the two areas isn't as robust as it could be, the ability to achieve such communication in a majority of modern browsers bodes well for the future integration of Flash, HTML, and JavaScript into one big experience.

[4] http://www.mikeindustries.com/sifr/
[5] http://www.bobbyvandersluis.com/ufo/

18 Building Web Applications with JavaScript

As technology improves and people spend larger proportions of their day online, the Internet is increasingly being used to deliver applications that were once the domain of the desktop. The success of sites such as GMail,[1] Basecamp,[2] and Flickr[3] have shown that static web pages are seriously hampered in their ability to cater to the ever-expanding needs and desires of online users.

The type of interaction that is required for an application like this is vastly different from the traditional browsing experience that has made up most of the Internet's history. Quick response times, fluid interfaces, and granular data transmission are all factors that can help or hinder an application's usability. JavaScript is perfectly positioned to step into this arena and create some truly innovative offerings.

This chapter delves into some of the foundations of online application design, including data transmission using remote procedure calls (RPC) via AJAX/XMLHttpRequest, the replication of traditional application interface elements, and some features that can make your own projects shine.

---

[1] http://www.gmail.com/
[2] http://www.basecamphq.com/
[3] http://www.flickr.com/

Retrieving Data Using XMLHttpRequest

Although XMLHttpRequest has been around since 1999, since the coining of the term **AJAX** (Asynchronous JavaScript and XML), a much stronger focus has been placed on its capabilities as a data transmission module for JavaScript-driven web pages.

Although it's not mentioned in any standard defined by the W3C, Internet Explorer 5+ for Windows, Mozilla 1.0, Safari 1.2, and Opera 8.0 offer XMLHttpRequest as a client-side data transmission object, making it a de facto standard that may oust the W3C's proposed DOM Level 3 Load and Save specification.[4] It's probably a good idea that we learn how to use XMLHttpRequest!

Solution

For any modern browser except Internet Explorer 5 and 6, we can create an XMLHttpRequest object like this:

```
var requester = new XMLHttpRequest();
```

However, in Internet Explorer, XMLHttpRequest is implemented as an ActiveX object, so an object is created like this:

```
var requester = new ActiveXObject("Microsoft.XMLHTTP");
```

IE and XMLHttpRequest

The way that XMLHttpRequest is implemented in Internet Explorer means that if a user has *trusted* ActiveX controls disabled they will be unable to use XMLHttpRequest, even if JavaScript is enabled. A lot of people disable *untrusted* ActiveX controls, but the disabling of trusted ActiveX controls is less frequent.

Apparently, Internet Explorer 7 will implement XMLHttpRequest as a native JavaScript object that does not require ActiveX, but we'll have to wait and see.

To cope with the different object creation syntax used by different browsers, it's best to use a try/catch structure that provides you with the correct object automatically, and returns an error if the XMLHttpRequest object is not available:

---

[4] http://www.w3.org/TR/DOM-Level-3-LS/

File: **retrieve_data_xmlhttprequest.js** (excerpt)

```
var requester;
try
{
  requester = new XMLHttpRequest();
}
catch (error)
{
  try
  {
    requester = new ActiveXObject("Microsoft.XMLHTTP");
  }
  catch (error)
  {
    requester = null;
  }
}
```

The try/catch structure is necessary for instantiating ActiveX objects because, if a user has disabled ActiveX controls, an object test will indicate that they are still available, though it will throw an error when you actually try to create one.

If you weren't able to create an XMLHttpRequest object at all, the requester variable will be null. It's easy to test for this, and branch to some non-AJAX fallback code (such as submitting a form).

Thankfully, the major differences between browser implementations of XMLHttpRequest end there; all the basic data communication methods can be called using the same syntax, irrespective of which browser they're running in.

Accessing the API Documentation

The Internet ExplorerXMLHttpRequest API documentation is available from MSDN.[5]

The Mozilla documentation is available at MDC.[6]

Meet MSXML

Microsoft's XMLHttpRequest functionality is actually built upon an XML parsing library that's independent of the browser, and is known as MSXML. Quite a few versions of MSXML may be available from a user's browser, but

---

[5] http://msdn.microsoft.com/library/en-us/xmlsdk/html/xmobjpmexmlhttprequest.asp
[6] http://developer.mozilla.org/en/docs/XMLHttpRequest

the syntax above uses the default version (possibly a lower version than the highest available).

Newer versions have more functionality, such as support for XPath expressions and XML namespace management, so if you have a particular need for this advanced functionality, you should check for the exact version you need:

```
var requester;
try
{
  requester = new XMLHttpRequest();
}
catch (error)
{
  try
  {
    requester = new ActiveXObject("Msxml2.XMLHTTP.5.0");
  }
  catch (error)
  {
    try
    {
      requester = new ActiveXObject("Msxml2.XMLHTTP.4.0")
    }
    catch (error)
    {
      requester = null;
    }
  }
}
```

However, this is only advisable if you are working in a known browser environment (e.g., an intranet). Otherwise, the default XMLHTTP object will be more than adequate for passing data back and forth with a server.

More information about MSXML[7] is available on MSDN.

Requesting Data from a Server

Once an XMLHttpRequest object has been created, you must call two separate methods in order to get it to retrieve data from a server.

open initializes the connection that you wish to make; it takes two required arguments and several optionals. The first argument is the type of request you want

---

[7] http://msdn.microsoft.com/library/en-us/xmlsdk/html/7e831db8-9d0a-43ff-87e9-11382721eb99.asp

to send, and the second is the location from which you wish to request data. For instance, if you wished to use a GET request to access feed.xml at the root of your server, you would initialize the XMLHttpRequest object like this:

```
requester.open("GET", "/feed.xml");
```

The URL can be either relative or absolute, but due to cross-domain security concerns, the target must reside on the same domain as the page that requests it.

XMLHttpRequest Calls via HTTP Only

Quite a few browsers will only allow XMLHttpRequest calls via HTTP, so if you're running files locally via file:// URLs, these browsers will not allow you to make an XMLHttpRequest call.

The open method also takes an optional third boolean argument that specifies whether the request is made asynchronously (true, the default) or synchronously (false). With a synchronous request, the browser will freeze until the object has completed, and will not allow any user interaction until it does so. An asynchronous request occurs in the background, allowing other scripts to run, and permitting the user to continue to access the browser. It is recommended that you use asynchronous requests, otherwise you run the risk of a user's browser locking up while it waits for a request that went awry. open's optional fourth and fifth arguments are a username and password for authentication purposes when accessing a password-protected URL.

Once open has been used to initialize a connection, the send method activates the connection and makes the request. send takes one argument that allows you to send CGI data along with the call. Internet Explorer dictates that it is optional, but Mozilla will return an error if no value is passed, so it is safest to call it with null if you have no parameters to pass:

File: **retrieve_data_xmlhttprequest.js** (excerpt)

```
requester.send(null);
```

When sending CGI variables using the GET request method, you have to hard-code the variables into the open URL:

File: **retrieve_data_xmlhttprequest.js** (excerpt)

```
requester.open("GET",
    "/query.php?name=Clark&email=superman@justiceleague.xmp");
requester.send(null);
```

When you're sending CGI variables using the POST request method, you can pass the CGI variables to the send method:

```
requester.setRequestHeader("Content-Type",
    "application/x-www-form-urlencoded");
requester.open("POST", "/query.cgi");
requester.send(
    "name=Clark&email=superman@justiceleague.xmp");
```

An Opera Requirement

Opera requires you to set the Content-Type header of a POST request correctly. Other browsers don't require it, but it's the safest thing to do.

Once you have called send, XMLHttpRequest will contact the server and retrieve the data that you requested; however, in the case of asynchronous requests, your code will keep running while the request is processed. In order to find out when the object has finished retrieving data, you must use an event handler. In the case of an XMLHttpRequest object, you need to handle changes to its readyState property. This property indicates the status of the object's connection, and can be any of:

0   uninitialized

1   loading

2   loaded

3   interactive

4   complete

Changes in the readyState property can be monitored using a onreadystatechange handler:

```
requester.onreadystatechange = readystatechangeHandler;
```

readyState increments from 0 to 4, and the onreadystatechange event handler is called for each increment; however, we only really want to know when the connection has completed (4), so our handler needs to check for this. Upon the script's completion, we also have to check whether the XMLHttpRequest object successfully retrieved the data, or was given an HTTP error code such as 404 (page not found). This can be determined from the request object's status property, which contains an integer code. 200 (OK) and 304 (Not Modified) are codes that indicate that data has been retrieved successfully (from the server and from the browser cache, respectively), but the value can be any of the other valid HTTP codes that servers return. If the request was not successful, you must specify a course of action for your program to take:

File: **retrieve_data_xmlhttprequest.js** (excerpt)

```
requester.onreadystatechange = function()
{
  if (requester.readyState == 4)
  {
    if (requester.status == 200 || requester.status == 304)
    {
      success(requester);
    }
    else
    {
      failure(requester);
    }
  }

  return true;
};
```

Even though the XMLHttpRequest object allows you to call the open method multiple times, each object can be used effectively only for one call, as the readystatechange event does not occur again once readyState changes to 4 (in Mozilla). Therefore, you will have to create a new XMLHttpRequest object every time you want to retrieve new data from a server.

Parsing the Data

Following a successful request, two properties of the XMLHttpRequest object can contain data:

responseXML   responseXML stores a DOM-structured object of any XML data that was retrieved by the object. This object is navigable using the standard JavaScript DOM properties and methods we explored in Chapter 5, such as getElementsByTagName, childNodes and parentNode.

responseText   responseText stores the data as a text string. If the content type of the data reported by the server was text/plain or text/html, this is the only property that will contain data. A copy of any XML data will also be placed here as a string of XML code, as an alternative to responseXML.

Depending upon the complexity of your data, it may be easier to return data as a plain text string, thereby making the "XML" in XMLHttpRequest redundant. However, for more complex data structures, you'll probably want to transmit the data as XML, as shown here:

File: **retrieve_data_xmlhttprequest_data.xml**

```
<?xml version="1.0" ?>
<user>
  <name>Barry Allen</name>
  <email>the_flash@justiceleague.com</email>
</user>
<user>
  <name>Hal Jordan</name>
  <email>green_lantern@justiceleague.com</email>
</user>
```

We are able to access different parts of the data using standard DOM access methods:

File: **retrieve_data_xmlhttprequest.js (excerpt)**

```
var users = requester.responseXML.getElementsByTagName("user");

for (var i = 0; i < users.length; i++)
{
  alert("User " + (i + 1) + " name: " +
      users[i].getElementsByTagName("name")[0].firstChild.
      nodeValue + "\nUser " + (i + 1) + " e-mail: " +
      users[i].getElementsByTagName("email")[0].firstChild.
      nodeValue);
}
```

Beware Whitespace

note

You must also be careful about whitespace—any indenting of values in the XML data may produce unwanted whitespace in the value, or add additional text nodes to the DOM structure, both of which your code will need to handle.

Once you've parsed the data from the XMLHttpRequest object, you're free to change, delete and write it onto your web page any way you like.

Discussion

Caching

The caching principles that apply to other requests also apply to `XMLHttpRequest` calls. This means that if you repeatedly contact the same server-side script for data, you mightn't get the most recent version: you may instead receive a cached version supplied by the browser (or a proxy).

There are a couple of solutions to this problem. Firstly, you could append a unique number to the URL of every request that you make via `XMLHttpRequest`. This is just a dummy CGI variable that differentiates each URL: you don't actually use it in the server-side script. The unique number can be produced by appending the current date in milliseconds to your second `open` argument:

```
requester.open("GET", "query.php?timestamp=" +
    new Date().getTime());
requester.send(null);
```

The other (cleaner) client-side solution is to set the `If-Modified-Since` header of your `XMLHttpRequest` request to a date in the past, so that it always gets the latest version from the server:

```
requester.setRequestHeader("If-Modified-Since",
    "Sat, 1 Jan 2000 00:00:00 GMT");
requester.open("GET", "query.php";
requester.send(null);
```

An even cleaner server-side approach is to set the `Expires` header for the documents returned from the server-side script so that they expire immediately. In PHP, this would be:

```
header('Expires: -1');
```

From a client-side perspective, the easiest solution is probably the first one, but the latter will have the fewest undesirable side-effects (such as cluttering your browser's cache with many responses to timestamped URLs).

AJAX Frameworks

Because the communication of data is such a common need—and is easily abstracted—many people have already taken the task of implementing `XMLHttpRequest` off your hands by providing JavaScript frameworks for web application development. These not only include the JavaScript modules with which your pages need to interact in order to send and receive data, but also supply the server-side code that handles JavaScript remote procedure calls.

A few of the more popular frameworks include:

❑ Prototype

http://prototype.conio.net/

❑ Dojo

http://dojotoolkit.org/

❑ Sajax

http://www.modernmethod.com/sajax/

In addition to data handling, Prototype and Dojo are fully-featured application development frameworks that can also help you to create degradable functionality, include interactive components, and modify your web pages dynamically.

Retrieving Data *without* Using XMLHttpRequest

Although `XMLHttpRequest` provides a standard communication interface for most modern browsers, it's not supported in some of the older but still-current versions such as Opera 7 and Internet Explorer 5 for Mac. One way to get around the lack of `XMLHttpRequest` in these browsers is to make the remote procedure call using an `iframe`.

`iframes`—the modern brothers of `frames`—allow you to embed one web page inside another. We can control an `iframe` with script in the containing page, making it request pages from the server, then parse the results for data. This approach is not as clean as `XMLHttpRequest`, nor is it as well-suited to dealing with XML data, but it's a technique that has been used for many years.

Solution

The two main stages of using an `iframe` for a remote procedure call are the creation of the `iframe`, and the execution of code once the data has loaded. The `iframe` can be created using the methods we discussed in Chapter 5. However, Internet Explorer 5 for Windows doesn't allow you to access the properties of a dynamically created `iframe`, so in this browser we must resort to the nonstandard (but widely supported) `innerHTML` property to create an `iframe`:

File: **retrieve_data_iframe.js** (excerpt)

```javascript
function createIframeRPC()
{
  var body = document.getElementsByTagName("body")[0];
  var iframe = document.createElement("iframe");

  iframe.setAttribute("id", "iframeRPC");

  body.appendChild(iframe);

  if (typeof iframe.document != "undefined" &&
      typeof iframe.contentDocument == "undefined" &&
      typeof iframe.contentWindow == "undefined")
  {
    body.removeChild(iframe);

    var iframeHTML = '<iframe id="iframeRPC"></iframe>';

    body.innerHTML += iframeHTML;

    iframe = document.getElementById("iframeRPC");
    iframe.contentWindow = new Object();
    iframe.contentWindow.document = new Object();
    iframe.contentWindow.document.location = new Object();
    iframe.contentWindow.document.location.iframeRef = iframe;
    iframe.contentWindow.document.location.replace =
        locationReplaceIE5;
  }

  iframe.style.position = "absolute";
  iframe.style.left = "-1500em";
  iframe.style.top = "0";
  iframe.style.width = "0";
  iframe.style.height = "0";
  iframe.setAttribute("tabIndex", "-1");
```

```
    return true;
}
```

First, we create the `iframe` using standard DOM methods and append it to the end of the `body` element; then, we check to see if we can access the document that's nested inside it. Internet Explorer 5 will allow us to see `iframe.document`, but we won't be able to manipulate its properties, so we have to substitute the DOM-created `iframe` for a more primitive one.

Inside the check for IE 5, we remove the already created `iframe`, then append some raw HTML to the `body` element using `innerHTML`. To allow us to access that `iframe` using the same properties we'd use with Internet Explorer 5.5 and 6, we have to create a few new object properties that replicate the standard `iframe` window structure. Basically, we have to make it seem like the `location.replace` method may be called as follows (which it can in other browsers):

```
iframe.contentWindow.document.location.replace()
```

Because IE 5 doesn't support this, we install our own custom function, `locationReplaceIE5`, to do the same job:

File: **retrieve_data_iframe.js (excerpt)**

```
function locationReplaceIE5(URL)
{
  this.iframeRef.setAttribute("src", URL);

  return true;
}
```

Now that our `iframe` is in place and operational, we hide it by making it as small as possible and moving it far off the left-hand side of the screen. It's inadvisable to set the `iframe`'s `display` property to `none` because Netscape 6 will then completely ignore it. We also have to set the `iframe`'s `tabIndex` attribute to −1 so that it won't interfere with the actions of keyboard users tabbing around the page.

Once the `iframe` has been created, we're ready to begin transmitting data. Calling `executeIframeRPC` with a URL will load that URL into the `iframe`, effectively sending off a remote procedure call:

File: **retrieve_data_iframe.js (excerpt)**

```
function executeIframeRPC(URL)
{
```

```
  var iframe = document.getElementById("iframeRPC");

  if (typeof iframe.contentDocument != "undefined")
  {
    iframeDocument = iframe.contentDocument;
  }
  else if (typeof iframe.contentWindow != "undefined")
  {
    iframeDocument = iframe.contentWindow.document;
  }
  else
  {
    return false;
  }

  iframeDocument.location.replace(URL);

  return true;
}
```

Internet Explorer uses a different method for accessing the document inside the
`iframe` than other browsers, so we have to check for the appropriate object before
proceeding. Once we've found it, we can then `replace` the current location with
the new one we're trying to communicate with. It's possible to simply change
the `src` attribute of the `iframe`; however, in some browsers, this will place an
entry into the browser's history and adversely affect the behavior of the Back
button. `location.replace` seamlessly updates the `iframe`'s location and allows
the Back button to go to the previous user-navigated page, instead of just invisibly
returning the `iframe` to its original blank location.

Prepare for a Slight Browser Delay

If you wish to call `executeIframeRPC` immediately after you create the
`iframe`, you should place the call inside a `setTimeout` function call with
a 10 millisecond delay, because some browsers will take a moment or two
to realize that the `iframe` exists.

`executeIframeRPC` will accept any well-formed URL, including CGI GET variables.
This enables us to send parameters to a script on our server:

```
executeIframeRPC("/scripts/getSecretIdentity.php?hero=Hawkgirl");
```

iframe Security Limitation

`iframe` scripting is limited by the same cross-domain security measures as `XMLHttpRequest`, so you will only be able to make remote procedure calls to scripts that reside on the same domain as the page that is calling them.

Once the call is made, the server-side script will begin to execute ... but how can we get data out of it? No handy events like `readystatchange` exist for `iframes`, so we have to cheat a little: we get the server to output the very JavaScript code that we want to execute when the response arrives.

When the URL of the `iframe` changes, it waits for the server's response and loads what is sent back by the script—a web page. Inside this web page, it's possible to write out some JavaScript that will be executed once that page has finished loading in the `iframe`. As luck would have it, an `iframe` can execute any JavaScript functions that are available in its parent, so we can call a special RPC "response handler" function from inside the `iframe`.

The HTML that is returned from the server to the `iframe` should look something like this:

File: **retrieve_data_iframe_query.html**

```
<html>
<head>
<script type="text/javascript">
  window.parent.handleRPCData("Shayera Hol");
</script>
</head>
</html>
```

The code inside the `script` element will be executed as soon as it is received. The `iframe` references its parent window using `window.parent`, and any JavaScript function available in the parent can be executed using that reference. In this case, we send some data to our handling function, `handleRPCData`:

File: **retrieve_data_iframe.js** (excerpt)

```
function handleRPCData(data)
{
  alert("The remote data was: " + data);

  return true;
}
```

You can do anything you want with the data inside this function, but here we're just creating a simple `alert` box that contains the returned information.

Because the data is passed as a JavaScript variable, you aren't limited to receiving strings of text. You can pass any valid JavaScript data structure—floats, integers, arrays, objects ... anything:[8]

```html
<html>
<head>
<script type="text/javascript">
  var secretIdentities = [["Black Canary", "Dinah Lance"],
      ["The Atom", "Ray Palmer"], ["The Flash", "Barry Allen"]];

  window.parent.handleRPCData(secretIdentities);
</script>
</head>
</html>
```

Creating Custom Dialogs (Such as Popup Forms)

Dialogs—such as `alert` or `confirm` popups—are a really quick and easy way of garnering information from a user without having to create a new page. They're also good in situations where you don't want to break the flow of user interaction, like the middle of a form. But the native browser dialogs are extremely limited in terms of the information they can display, the ways in which the user can interact with them, and how they look. If you really want to have useful dialogs, the best way to ensure that might be to make your own.

Solution

The recent resentment towards popup windows means that you've probably got less than a 50% chance of successfully opening one in response to user interaction. By writing your dialogs into the current page, you'll permit them to function perfectly, and you'll gain a whole lot more control over them.

---

[8]This capability is behind the recent development of the JavaScript Object Notation (JSON) data format [http://www.json.org/].

Creating an in-page dialog is simple—it draws directly on the element creation techniques that I introduced in Chapter 5. Let's take an ordinary hyperlink and cause it to display a custom dialog:

File: **custom_dialogs.js (excerpt)**

```
addLoadListener(initDialog);

function initDialog()
{
  var permissions = document.getElementById("permissions");

  permissions.onclick = createDialog;

  return true;
}

function createDialog()
{
  try
  {
    var body = document.getElementsByTagName("body")[0];

    var dialog = document.createElement("div");
    dialog.className = "customDialog";
    dialog.style.visibility = "hidden";
    dialog.style.position = "absolute";

    var dialogTitle = document.createElement("h1");
    dialogTitle.appendChild(document.createTextNode(
        "Change Security Permissions"));
    dialog.appendChild(dialogTitle);

    var dialogMessage = document.createElement("p");
    dialogMessage.appendChild(document.createTextNode(
        "Do you wish to give Clayface access to the self " +
        "destruct codes?"));
    dialog.appendChild(dialogMessage);

    var dialogButton1 = document.createElement("input");
    dialogButton1.setAttribute("type", "button");
    dialogButton1.setAttribute("value", "Yes");
    attachEventListener(dialogButton1, "click", dialogClick,
        false);
    dialog.appendChild(dialogButton1);

    var dialogButton2 = document.createElement("input");
```

```
    dialogButton2.setAttribute("type", "button");
    dialogButton2.setAttribute("value", "No");
    attachEventListener(dialogButton2, "click", dialogClick,
        false);
    dialog.appendChild(dialogButton2);

    var dialogButton3 = document.createElement("input");
    dialogButton3.setAttribute("type", "button");
    dialogButton3.setAttribute("value", "Cancel");
    attachEventListener(dialogButton3, "click", dialogClick,
        false);
    dialog.appendChild(dialogButton3);

    body.appendChild(dialog);

    var scrollingPosition = getScrollingPosition();
    var viewportSize = getViewportSize();

    dialog.style.left = scrollingPosition[0] +
        parseInt(viewportSize[0] / 2) -
        parseInt(dialog.offsetWidth / 2) + "px";
    dialog.style.top = scrollingPosition[1] +
        parseInt(viewportSize[1] / 2) -
        parseInt(dialog.offsetHeight / 2) + "px";
    dialog.style.visibility = "visible";

    dialogButton1.focus();
  }
  catch(error)
  {
    return true;
  }

  return false;
}
```

addLoadListener (from Chapter 1) is used to execute initDialog once the page has loaded. Inside initDialog, we divert the normal action of our link to createDialog; however, we don't do so using our usual attachEventListener function, because, as we saw in Chapter 13, Safari is unable to stop a link's default action via W3C event listeners. Therefore, we use the reliable DOM 0 onclick event handler. If users' browsers don't have JavaScript enabled, they'll go to the link's normal href location, so your server-side scripts should handle this case appropriately, serving up a page that's equivalent to the dialog.

createDialog goes about creating the HTML elements for the dialog. Obviously, this will be highly tailored to the particular purpose you want to achieve, but generally you will have a title, message, and action buttons. This code block is wrapped in a try/catch structure because Internet Explorer 5 for Mac doesn't allow you to change the type of a newly created input. This means we can't create buttons, so if an error is thrown while we're doing this, we continue with the normal link action, taking the user to the server-side contingency page.

We place event listeners on the buttons so that we can react when the user clicks on one. The handling functions can do whatever you require of the dialog, but in this example, dialogClick will pass the button value on to a new page, or close the dialog and unlock the page if "Cancel" is clicked:

File: **custom_dialogs.js (excerpt)**

```javascript
function dialogClick(event)
{
  if (typeof event == "undefined")
  {
    event = window.event;
  }

  var target = getEventTarget(event);

  while (target.nodeName.toLowerCase() != "input")
  {
    target = target.parentNode;
  }

  var value = target.getAttribute("value");

  if (value == "Cancel")
  {
    var dialog = target;

    while (dialog.className != "customDialog")
    {
      dialog = dialog.parentNode;
    }

    closeDialog(dialog);
  }
  else
  {
    window.location.href = "permissions.php?action=" + value;
  }
```

```
  return true;
}
```

Closing the dialog removes the dialog container from the DOM:

```
function closeDialog(dialog)
{
  dialog.parentNode.removeChild(dialog);

  return true;
}
```

The last part of `createDialog` positions the dialog squarely in the middle of the browser window—no matter where the page is currently scrolled to—using a combination of `getScrollingPosition` and `getViewportSize` (from Chapter 7). Previously, the `visibility` style property of the dialog container was set to `"hidden"`, so we can add it to the page, get its dimensions, and reposition it without the user seeing it jump around.

After the code has finished adding the dialog to the page, the focus is set to the first dialog button. This not only helps keyboard users to access the dialog immediately, but also lets you set the default action, which can speed up interaction.

Once we add our own CSS to the elements inside the dialog, we end up with a rather attractive, customized dialog that matches our own application interface, as shown in Figure 18.1.

Figure 18.1. A customized dialog

Discussion

An even better way to focus the user's attention onto the dialog is to mask the page behind it with a dark, translucent color. By decreasing the brightness of the background elements, the foreground elements (i.e., the dialog) will demand more attention.

In order to achieve this effect, we must create an empty element and set its dimensions to equal the dimensions of the entire page. Here's the function we'll use to calculate these dimensions:

File: **custom_dialogs2.js** (excerpt)

```
function getPageDimensions()
{
  var body = document.getElementsByTagName("body")[0];
  var bodyOffsetWidth = 0;
  var bodyOffsetHeight = 0;
  var bodyScrollWidth = 0;
  var bodyScrollHeight = 0;
  var pageDimensions = [0, 0];

  if (typeof document.documentElement != "undefined" &&
      typeof document.documentElement.scrollWidth != "undefined")
  {
    pageDimensions[0] = document.documentElement.scrollWidth;
    pageDimensions[1] = document.documentElement.scrollHeight;
  }

  bodyOffsetWidth = body.offsetWidth;
  bodyOffsetHeight = body.offsetHeight;
  bodyScrollWidth = body.scrollWidth;
  bodyScrollHeight = body.scrollHeight;

  if (bodyOffsetWidth > pageDimensions[0])
  {
    pageDimensions[0] = bodyOffsetWidth;
  }

  if (bodyOffsetHeight > pageDimensions[1])
  {
    pageDimensions[1] = bodyOffsetHeight;
  }

  if (bodyScrollWidth > pageDimensions[0])
```

```
  {
    pageDimensions[0] = bodyScrollWidth;
  }

  if (bodyScrollHeight > pageDimensions[1])
  {
    pageDimensions[1] = bodyScrollHeight;
  }

  return pageDimensions;
}
```

`getPageDimensions` consolidates the properties supported by various browsers to determine the actual size of the page.

We can now create an empty element of the correct dimensions just before we create the dialog itself:

File: **custom_dialogs2.js (excerpt)**

```
function createDialog()
{
  var body = document.getElementsByTagName("body")[0];
  var pageDimensions = getPageDimensions();
  var viewportSize = getViewportSize();

  if (viewportSize[1] > pageDimensions[1])
  {
    pageDimensions[1] = viewportSize[1];
  }

  var dropSheet = document.createElement("div");

  dropSheet.setAttribute("id", "dropSheet");
  dropSheet.style.position = "absolute";
  dropSheet.style.left = "0";
  dropSheet.style.top = "0";
  dropSheet.style.width = pageDimensions[0] + "px";
  dropSheet.style.height = pageDimensions[1] + "px";
  body.appendChild(dropSheet);

  try
  {
    var dialog = document.createElement("div");
    :
```

The vertical page dimension has to be checked against the height of the viewport, because the height of the page content may be less than that of the window, and this can cause a strange appearance in the "drop sheet."

When the dialog is closed, we will also have to remove the colored drop sheet:

File: **custom_dialogs2.js** (excerpt)

```
function closeDialog(dialog)
{
  var dropSheet = document.getElementById("dropSheet");

  dropSheet.parentNode.removeChild(dropSheet);
  dialog.parentNode.removeChild(dialog);

  return true;
}
```

With some tricked-out CSS styling, you can give the new element a translucent background color, or provide it with a tiling background image for those browsers that don't support opacity:

File: **custom_dialogs2.css** (excerpt)

```
#dropSheet
{
  background-color/**/: #000000;
  background-image: url(../images/dots.gif);
  background-image/**/: none;
  opacity: 0.35;
  filter: alpha(opacity=35);
}
```

Internet Explorer 5 (which doesn't support opacity) will not read the background-color, but it will understand background-image, which simulates a shaded background. All other browsers will cancel the background-image, then apply an appropriate opacity property to give us a black drop sheet with 35% opacity, producing the effect shown in Figure 18.2.

Figure 18.2. A transparent drop sheet covering the page behind the customized modal dialog

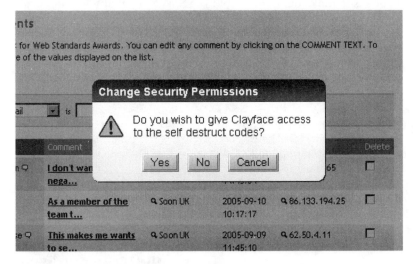

Creating Editable Elements

Form elements do not offer a great number of possibilities when it comes to the visual formatting of their contents. They don't support any child HTML elements, so it's impossible to let users change colors, styles, or preview elements on-the-fly.

However, one feature that's supported by a number of browsers allows users to edit and create content much more freely than usual, though you'll need JavaScript to get it going.

Solution

The property `designMode` is a nonstandard addition to the DOM, but it is currently supported by Internet Explorer for Windows 5.5+, Mozilla/Firefox, and Safari 1.3+. Once `designMode` has been set to `true` on an element, it allows that element to receive text input and facilitates other editing capabilities. The Internet Explorer and Safari implementations allow *any* element to be editable, but only Mozilla allows for an entire document to be editable.

The most obvious use for content editing capabilities like these is in an inline editor for a content management system (CMS) or forum, so the easiest way to explain designMode is to make our own simple WYSIWYG (what you see is what you get) editor.

The HTML element that's closest to a WYSIWYG editor is textarea, so we'll use that as a baseline element to which browsers without designMode will degrade:

File: **editable_elements.html (excerpt)**

```
<form action="submit.php">
  <textarea id="content" name="content" class="wysiwyg">
    ⋮
  </textarea>
</form>
```

Because Mozilla supports designMode only on entire documents, and because our editor is inline, the textarea has to be replaced by an iframe—the only element that will allow us to insert a new document inside the existing one:

File: **editable_elements.js (excerpt)**

```
addLoadListener(initWYSIWYG);

function initWYSIWYG()
{
  if (typeof(document.designMode) == "string" &&
      (document.all || document.designMode == "off"))
  {
    var textareas = getElementsByAttribute("class", "wysiwyg");

    for (var i = 0; i < textareas.length; i++)
    {
      convertWYSIWYG(textareas[i]);
    }
  }

  return true;
}

function convertWYSIWYG(textarea)
{
  var textareaID = textarea.getAttribute("id");
  var textareaName = textarea.getAttribute("name");
  var textareaValue = textarea.value;

  var input = document.createElement("input");
```

```javascript
input.setAttribute("type", "hidden");
input.setAttribute("id", textareaID);
input.setAttribute("name", textareaName);
input.value = textareaValue;

var iframe = document.createElement("iframe");
iframe.className = "wysiwygIframe";
textarea.parentNode.replaceChild(iframe, textarea);

if (typeof iframe.document != "undefined" &&
    typeof iframe.contentDocument == "undefined" &&
    typeof iframe.contentWindow == "undefined")
{
  iframe.parentNode.replaceChild(textarea, iframe);

  return false;
}

iframe.parentNode.insertBefore(input, iframe);

iframe.contentWindow.document.open();
iframe.contentWindow.document.write(
    '<html><head><style type="text/css">' +
    '@import "css/editable_elements_iframe.css";</style>' +
    '</head><body>' + input.value + '</body></html>');
iframe.contentWindow.document.close();
iframe.contentWindow.document.designMode = "on";

var form  = iframe.parentNode;

while (form != null && form.nodeName.toLowerCase() != "form")
{
  form = form.parentNode;
}

if (form != null)
{
  attachEventListener(form, "submit", function() {
      input.value = iframe.contentWindow.document.
      getElementsByTagName("body")[0].innerHTML;}, false);
}

return true;
}
```

Our `addLoadListener` function from Chapter 1 executes `initWYSIWYG` on page load. This function detects whether the current browser supports editable content by checking for the existence of the `designMode` property. The remaining checks within `initWYSIWYG`'s first `if` statement are necessary because the `designMode` property existed in earlier versions of Safari, but the functionality was not yet implemented.

If editable content is supported, we use the `getElementsByAttribute` function from Chapter 5 to retrieve all the elements with a `class` of `wysiwyg`, and send them off to `convertWYSIWYG` to be changed into editable `iframe`s.

`convertWYSIWYG` firstly creates a hidden `input` field that mirrors the `textarea`. Because the `textarea` is a form element but an `iframe` is not, we need to create an equivalent form element that will be submitted when the form is submitted. The hidden `input` gets the same ID and `name` attribute as the `textarea`, as well as the `textarea`'s initial `value`. Once this has been done, we are able to perform a direct replacement between a newly created `iframe` and the `textarea`.

After we insert the `iframe`, we need to check whether we can access its properties. As we saw in "Retrieving Data *without* Using `XMLHttpRequest`" earlier in this chapter, Internet Explorer 5 for Windows has problems with DOM-created `iframe`s. However, in this situation the problem isn't resolvable, so we need to revert to the `textarea` if we can't access the `iframe` properly.

Once the `iframe` has been inserted into the page, we can write its contents. However, because a newly created `iframe` is a bit of a weird creature, we can't insert nodes directly into its DOM: we have to rely on the rather ancient `open` and `write` methods to place content in there as a string. Once that's been done, we flick the switch by setting `designMode` to `"on"`. We now have an editable `iframe` on the page.

designMode Woes

Sometimes you may experience random errors when trying to edit content inside the `iframe`. These could arise because some browsers can't handle an immediate change of `designMode` on new `iframe`s. Try putting the `designMode` change inside a `setTimeout` of 100ms or so:

```
setTimeout(function(){
    iframe.contentWindow.document.designMode = "on";},
    100);
```

That solution looks okay, but it's no good if we can't get the data out of the `iframe` when the form is submitted. To this end, `convertWYSIWYG` also sets up an event listener to copy the contents of the `iframe`'s `body` element to our hidden `input` when the form is submitted. Because the form data can only be submitted as a string, the easiest way to get the `body`'s contents is via the `innerHTML` property.

We've now got an editable HTML element that can be submitted to a server, but it still does little more than the `textarea`. Some browsers have a few editing shortcuts, like **Ctrl-B** to bold text, or **Ctrl-I** to italicize text, but they're not consistent, visible, or comprehensive enough to use on their own. Luckily, a programmatic interface for editing the contents of the `iframe` is available. Once `designMode` is switched on, an in-built method—execCommand—is able to perform a variety of operations on the document's content, from bolding text to creating links and inserting images. Each browser implements a different engine for editable regions, so you'll have to check out the documentation to see what's available:

❏ *Creating Editable Web Pages in Internet Explorer 5.5*

   http://msdn.microsoft.com/library/en-us/dnmshtml/html/createwp.asp

❏ *The Mozilla Midas specification*

   http://www.mozilla.org/editor/midas-spec.html

There are quite a few common features. Two of these—and perhaps the most common editing operations—are the creation of bold and italic text.

In order to bold selected text, we call `execCommand` like this:

```
iframe.contentWindow.document.execCommand("bold", false, null);
```

In order to italicize selected text, we call `execCommand` like this:

```
iframe.contentWindow.document.execCommand("italic", false, null);
```

The first parameter is a string that corresponds to the command that you wish `execCommand` to perform. The second parameter is a Boolean flag for user interface interaction; however, its value always has to be `false`, as a value of `true` throws an error in Mozilla. The last parameter is a string value, which some commands will need in order to execute. If there is no value, it must be set to `null`, otherwise Mozilla will throw another error.

Using these commands, we can modify `convertWYSIWYG` to include an interface for the editable area that provides buttons for our formatting functions:

```
function convertWYSIWYG(textarea)
{
  ⋮
  var toolbar = document.createElement("div");
  toolbar.className = "wysiwygToolbar";
  iframe.parentNode.insertBefore(toolbar, iframe);

  var buttonBold = document.createElement("a");
  buttonBold.className = "wysiwygButtonBold";
  buttonBold.setAttribute("href", "#");
  buttonBold.appendChild(document.createTextNode("Bold"));
  buttonBold.command = "bold";
  buttonBold.iframe = iframe;
  buttonBold.onmousedown = mousedownToolbar;
  buttonBold.onclick = executeWYSIWYG;
  toolbar.appendChild(buttonBold);

  var buttonItalic = document.createElement("a");
  buttonItalic.className = "wysiwygButtonItalic";
  buttonItalic.setAttribute("href", "#");
  buttonItalic.appendChild(document.createTextNode("Italic"));
  buttonItalic.command = "italic";
  buttonItalic.iframe = iframe;
  buttonItalic.onmousedown = mousedownToolbar;
  buttonItalic.onclick = executeWYSIWYG;
  toolbar.appendChild(buttonItalic);

  return true;
}

function executeWYSIWYG(event)
{
  this.iframe.contentWindow.document.execCommand(this.command,
      false, null);
  this.iframe.contentWindow.focus();

  return false;
}

function mousedownToolbar()
{
  return false;
}
```

Each new button is a link that stores a command string for `execCommand` and a reference to its associated `iframe`. These properties are used when the link is clicked and `executeWYSIWYG` is called. The `click` event is handled through a DOM 0 `onclick` event handler because Safari can't cancel the default action of links through W3C event listeners. Another concession to Safari is the need for an `onmousedown` event handler; without this, Safari loses the selection in the `iframe`, so it would be impossible to apply any commands to selections in the editable area. This handler calls what is perhaps the shortest function you'll ever see: it simply returns `false` to cancel the default action.

After a toolbar button is clicked, `executeWYSIWYG` translates the button's value into a valid action and passes it to `execCommand`, which modifies the `iframe`'s document appropriately. Because the buttons are outside the `iframe`, the focus of the cursor will change when we click on them, so the last thing that `executeWYSIWYG` does is refocus the cursor on the `iframe`.

We now have our own little editor! With a little bit of judicious styling, as in Figure 18.3, it can begin to look like the real thing.

Figure 18.3. An editable `iframe` with styled buttons for formatting

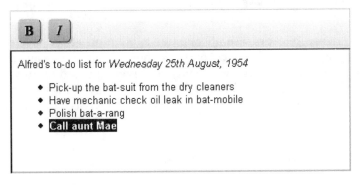

Discussion

As mentioned in the main solution, each browser has its own editing engine for use with editable content, and each engine produces different markup to a different degree of validity.

Internet Explorer will insert tags with uppercase attributes, Mozilla inserts line breaks instead of paragraphs, and they both insert non-semantic markup when all you want is a `<strong>` tag. It's a slippery slope of feature bloat once you decide to implement your own fully-functional editor, especially if you decide to eschew `execCommand` in favor of your own transformation routines.

There already exist a few editors, of differing levels of complexity. You might want to try these before delving into `designMode` yourself:

❑ widgEditor

http://www.themaninblue.com/experiment/widgEditor/

❑ TinyMCE

http://tinymce.moxiecode.com/

❑ FCKEditor

http://www.fckeditor.net/

Controlling Text Selections

Text selections are, in essence, a way of visually marking content on a page. Users can utilize text selections to indicate which parts of the content they want a program to act on (e.g., to copy, replace, or format), and programs can use text selections to highlight text selections to the user. This tip explores text selection from both perspectives, and shows how you can use it in your JavaScript applications.

Solution

Perhaps the simplest form of text selection control is the ability for JavaScript to retrieve the text that a user has selected on a page:

File: **text_selections.js** (excerpt)

```javascript
function retrieveSelection()
{
  var selectedText = "";

  if (typeof window.getSelection != "undefined")
  {
    selectedText = window.getSelection();
```

```
}
else if (typeof document.getSelection != "undefined")
{
  selectedText = document.getSelection();
}
else if (typeof document.selection != "undefined")
{
  selectedText = document.selection.createRange().text;
}

return selectedText;
}
```

The `getSelection` methods in use here are DOM 0 functions, and they both function identically; it's just that different browsers have attached them to different objects (older versions of Opera and Internet Explorer for Mac use `document.getSelection`, while Mozilla and Safari use `window.getSelection`). However, Internet Explorer does not provide a `getSelection` method; instead, it opts to use a feature called **Ranges** as a way of identifying the selected text.

An understanding of Ranges is essential to a deeper understanding of text selection control in browsers. While we are used to selecting text with a mouse or keyboard, this merely creates a visual selection of the content; a Range defines an actual section of the DOM. The two are independent of one another—you can have a Range without a selection and a selection without a Range—but browsers generally have functions that can convert between the two.

In the code above, Internet Explorer for Windows uses the `document.selection` object to access the current selection, and the `createRange` method on that object makes a Range that corresponds to that selection. Once we have that Range, the text that it contains is available via its `text` property.

A Range consists of two boundary points—the start and the end—and its `text` property consists of any text *between* tags that falls within those boundaries. Consider this HTML:

File: **text_selections.html** (excerpt)

```
<h2 id="originHeading">
  Origin of the JLA
</h2>
<p class="bodyText">
  The Justice League's first origin, according to 1962's …
</p>
```

Imagine that a user selected text as shown in Figure 18.4.

Figure 18.4. Simple text selection

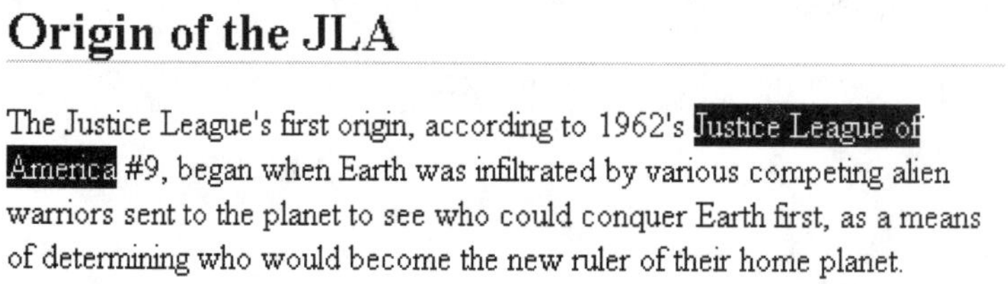

Origin of the JLA

The Justice League's first origin, according to 1962's Justice League of America #9, began when Earth was infiltrated by various competing alien warriors sent to the planet to see who could conquer Earth first, as a means of determining who would become the new ruler of their home planet.

In this case, the value returned by `retrieveSelection` would obviously be `"Justice League of America"`. But what happens if the selection spans HTML elements, as in Figure 18.5?

Figure 18.5. A more complex text selection

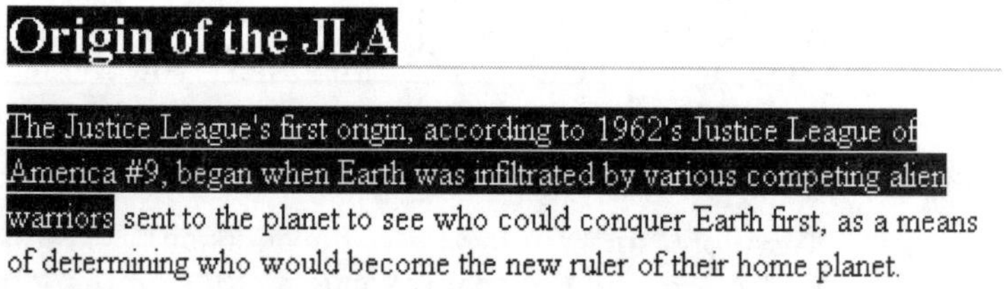

Origin of the JLA

The Justice League's first origin, according to 1962's Justice League of America #9, began when Earth was infiltrated by various competing alien warriors sent to the planet to see who could conquer Earth first, as a means of determining who would become the new ruler of their home planet.

We still retrieve only the textual components, so the returned value would be `"Origin of the JLAThe Justice League's first origin, according to 1962's Justice League of America #9, began when Earth was infiltrated by various competing alien warriors."`

Browser support for Ranges is still a little sketchy. Internet Explorer for Windows and Mozilla/Firefox have well-formed Range interfaces, but they are implemented using different syntax. Safari follows the Mozilla implementation of Ranges, but lacks a few of its features; Internet Explorer for Mac doesn't support Ranges at all, while Opera supports Ranges only on specific elements—namely text `inputs` and `textareas` (strangely enough, Mozilla *doesn't* support Ranges on text `inputs` and `textareas`, but that functionality can be faked using some of its selection functions).

Because of this limited Range support, Internet Explorer for Windows, Mozilla, and Safari are the only browsers that support the generic creation of text ranges in a document. But as luck would have it, those are the browsers that support our editable content area.

To extend our editor to allow the insertion of custom code—like emoticons—we insert a new button when the editor is initialized. Then, when it is clicked, we use the current selection point to determine where to place the code:

File: **text_selection2.js** (excerpt)

```
function convertWYSIWYG(textarea)
{
  ⋮
  var buttonSmile = document.createElement("a");
  buttonSmile.className = "wysiwygButtonSmile";
  buttonSmile.setAttribute("href", "#");
  buttonSmile.appendChild(document.createTextNode("Smile"));
  buttonSmile.emoticon = ":)";
  buttonSmile.iframe = iframe;
  buttonSmile.onmousedown = mousedownToolbar;
  buttonSmile.onclick = insertEmoticon;
  toolbar.appendChild(buttonSmile);

  return true;
}

function insertEmoticon()
{
  var iframeWindow = this.iframe.contentWindow;
  var iframeDocument = iframeWindow.document;
  var selection = null;
  var range = null;

  if (typeof iframeWindow.getSelection != "undefined")
  {
    selection = iframeWindow.getSelection();

    if (typeof selection.getRangeAt != "undefined")
    {
      range = selection.getRangeAt(0);
    }
    else if (typeof selection.baseNode != "undefined")
    {
      range = iframeDocument.createRange();
      range.setStart(selection.baseNode, selection.baseOffset);
```

```
    range.setEnd(selection.extentNode, selection.extentOffset);

    if (range.collapsed)
    {
      range.setStart(selection.extentNode,
          selection.extentOffset);
      range.setEnd(selection.baseNode, selection.baseOffset);
    }
  }

  var rangeCopy = range.cloneRange();
  var insertText = iframeDocument.createTextNode(this.emoticon);

  rangeCopy.collapse(true);
  range.deleteContents();
  rangeCopy.insertNode(insertText);

  selection.collapse(insertText, this.emoticon.length);
}
else if (typeof iframeDocument.selection != "undefined")
{
  selection = iframeDocument.selection;
  range = selection.createRange();
  range.pasteHTML(this.emoticon);
}
else
{
  return false;
}

iframeWindow.focus();

return true;
}
```

Once the extra button has been created in convertWYSIWYG, insertEmoticon is ready to handle any clicks on it. The code is horribly branched due to the current piecemeal implementation of Ranges, but the results are the same in every browser.

The first branch after the event detection determines how the selection object is obtained. Mozilla and Safari both support window.getSelection, so they meet the first condition, but the creation of a Range from that selection differs in each browser. Mozilla employs a shortcut method—getRangeAt—that does all the hard work for us, returning the Range at the specified index (technically a selection can consist of more than one Range, but a user-defined selection will consist of only one).

With Safari, we have to go the long way around, creating an empty Range, and setting its start and end points to the start and end points of the selection. The `baseNode` and `extentNode` properties specify the parent DOM element of the selection's start and end points respectively, while `baseOffset` and `extentOffset` specify the character offsets within those nodes. These pairs of values can be passed to the Range methods `setStart` and `setEnd` to set the boundary points of the Range. Mozilla doesn't include the properties `baseNode` or `extentNode`, so we aren't able simply to use this method for both browsers.

Range Start and End Points

When specifying the start and end points of a Range object, the end point must always be *equal to or after* the start point. Assuming left-to-right text flow, if a user makes a selection from right to left, the `baseNode/baseOffset` values will mark the right edge of the selection, and the `extentNode/extentOffset` values will mark the left. If we use these values to create a Range it will be empty; however, there's no easy way to determine whether the `baseNode` is before or after the `extentNode`. So, once the normal method has been tried, you must check to see whether the Range is collapsed (`range.collapsed`) and, if it is, reverse the order of the boundary points used to initialize the Range.

Once we have a consistent Range object, we delete the selected text using `deleteContents`, then insert the emoticon by creating a text node out of the emoticon characters, and passing that node to `insertNode`, which inserts the supplied node at the beginning of the Range.

A copy of the original Range has to be made and used as the target of `insertNode` because, if `deleteContents` is called on a Range that spans HTML elements, the Range will end up between the elements, and the inserted content will appear out of place. The copy retains its starting position inside the first element, so inserted content will be placed correctly.

The last thing to do is position the caret after the newly inserted content. The selection's `collapse` method does this by taking a node reference and a node offset, and collapsing the selection to that location. By giving it the new text node and its string length, we position the caret after the new emoticon.

The code branch for Internet Explorer's Range handling is a good deal shorter. A Range corresponding to the selection is created by executing `createRange` on the `document.selection` object, and then the contents of the Range are overwritten by `pasteHTML`. Unlike the `insertNode` method used in the opposite branch, `pasteHTML` does not really insert the content into the DOM; it treats the document as a string of text and overwrites the contents of the Range with the supplied string. However, both methods produce the same result, and your new editor, shown in Figure 18.6, will be all smiles!

Figure 18.6. The WYSIWYG editor with a new emoticon insertion feature

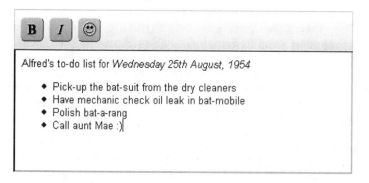

Creating an Auto-complete Text Field

Typing in repetitive data, or having to remember long strings, can quickly wear a user out. If your application is able to preempt the content a user is typing into a text field, and offer a number of possible suggestions, this will save the user time, prevent frustration, and improve accuracy—the less a user types, the fewer errors they can make.

Auto-complete text fields offer a great balance between ease of use and unobtrusiveness. A user can type away unhindered if the system's guess is wrong, but if the guess is right, they can use that suggestion without pressing another key!

Solution

There are really two parts to this solution. The first is an auto-complete feature on the text field itself, and the second is a dynamically generated drop-down of suggestions from which the user can select an option to enter into the text field. Auto-completion of the text field relies upon Range control that is not available in some browsers—Opera only introduced Range functions in version 8, so previous versions will be excluded at this stage. Similarly, Internet Explorer for Mac doesn't implement Ranges, and although Safari does have Range capabilities, they don't work on form elements. Mozilla's Range interface doesn't support form elements; however, it does have some special selection functions that we can use instead.

The suggestion drop-down can be implemented in all modern browsers. The two features are independent of each other, so if a browser doesn't support auto-completion, it will at least get the drop-down suggestions, which are equally useful.

Before a program can guess what the user is typing, it has to have a list of possible values, so you'll need to create an array to hold these. In this example, it's assumed that the values are written into the page by the server, though the way in which the server gets the values is up to you. They could be based on a predefined list, the past history of the current user, or today's horoscope, but the more helpful they are, the more effective your auto-complete field will be.

For this example, let's assume the user has typed in some email addresses on previous occasions:

File: **auto-complete_text_field.js** (excerpt)

```
var emailAddresses = [
    "greenarrow@justiceleague.xmp",
    "greenflame@justiceleague.xmp",
    "greenhornet@dccomics.xmp",
    "greenlantern@justiceleague.xmp",
    "magneto@example.net",
    "mistermiracle@justiceleague.xmp",
    "redronin@sitepoint.com",
    "redtornado@justiceleague.xmp"
];
```

The auto-complete will run on a text input field, so we'll need to get the input field and handle any keystrokes that are made on it:

File: **auto-complete_text_field.js** (excerpt)

```
addLoadListener(initAutoComplete);

function initAutoComplete()
{
  var email = document.getElementById("email");

  email.setAttribute("autocomplete", "off");
```

```
  attachEventListener(email, "keydown", keydownAutoComplete,
      false);
  attachEventListener(email, "blur", blurAutoComplete, false);

  return true;
}

function keydownAutoComplete(event)
{
  if (typeof event == "undefined")
  {
    event = window.event;
  }

  switch(event.keyCode)
  {
    case 9:      // tab
    case 13:     // enter
    case 16:     // shift
    case 17:     // ctrl
    case 18:     // alt
    case 20:     // caps lock
    case 27:     // esc
    case 33:     // page up
    case 34:     // page down
    case 35:     // end
    case 36:     // home
    case 37:     // left arrow
    case 39:     // right arrow
      break;

    case 38:     // up arrow

      var target = getEventTarget(event);
      var autoCompleteDropdown =
          document.getElementById("autoCompleteDropdown");

      if (autoCompleteDropdown != null)
      {
        var childLis = autoCompleteDropdown.childNodes;
        var selected = false;

        for (var i = 0; i < childLis.length; i++)
        {
          if (childLis[i].className == "hover")
          {
```

```
          selected = true;

          if (i > 0)
          {
            childLis[i].className = "";
            childLis[i - 1].className = "hover";

            target.value = childLis[i - 1].firstChild.nodeValue;
          }

          break;
      }
    }

    if (!selected)
    {
      childLis[0].className = "hover";

      target.value = childLis[0].firstChild.nodeValue;
    }
  }

  stopDefaultAction(event);

  break;

case 40:    // down arrow
  var target = getEventTarget(event);
  var autoCompleteDropdown =
      document.getElementById("autoCompleteDropdown");

  if (autoCompleteDropdown != null)
  {
    var childLis = autoCompleteDropdown.childNodes;
    var selected = false;

    for (var i = 0; i < childLis.length; i++)
    {
      if (childLis[i].className == "hover")
      {
        selected = true;

        if (i < childLis.length - 1)
        {
          childLis[i].className = "";
          childLis[i + 1].className = "hover";
```

```
                    target.value = childLis[i + 1].firstChild.nodeValue;
                }

                break;
            }
        }

        if (!selected)
        {
            childLis[0].className = "hover";

            target.value = childLis[0].firstChild.nodeValue;
        }
    }

    stopDefaultAction(event);

    break;
case 8:      // backspace
case 46:     // delete

    if (typeof autoCompleteTimer != "undefined")
    {
        clearTimeout(autoCompleteTimer);
    }

    autoCompleteTimer = setTimeout("generateDropdown(false)",
        500);

    break;

default:

    if (typeof autoCompleteTimer != "undefined")
    {
        clearTimeout(autoCompleteTimer);
    }

    var target = getEventTarget(event);
    var inputRanges = "false";

    if (typeof target.createTextRange != "undefined" ||
        typeof target.setSelectionRange != "undefined")
    {
```

```
        inputRanges = "true";
    }

    autoCompleteTimer = setTimeout("generateDropdown(" +
        inputRanges + ")", 500);
  }

  return true;
}
```

`initAutoComplete` is executed on page load using the `addLoadListener` function from Chapter 1. It initializes an event listener for `keydown` events on the text field using the `attachEventListener` function from Chapter 13. A `blur` event listener is added as well; this event fires when the text field loses focus (e.g., when the user tabs out of it or clicks elsewhere), and it removes all the elements that are created by the auto-completion functionality.

 ### IE Doesn't Use keypress

Internet Explorer for Windows doesn't trigger a `keypress` event listener when the user presses arrow keys and other control keys. That's why we use a `keydown` event listener for this solution.

When a `keydown` event is registered, `keydownAutoComplete` runs and checks which key was pressed. For keyboard events the event object has a `keyCode` property, which stores the ASCII value of the key that was pressed (you can find the ASCII values of all keys at http://www.lookuptables.com/). For control keys like **Ctrl**, **Alt**, **Shift**, or **Enter**, we don't want to do anything, because the content of the text field won't have changed, but when users press a key that changes the contents of the text field, we want to give them some suitable suggestions.

When users press a subtractive key—**backspace** or **delete**—we don't want the text field auto-complete to kick-in; we just want to enable the suggestions dropdown, otherwise the user would never be able to delete multiple characters. To do this, we call `generateDropdown` with a `false` argument. This means that when `generateDropdown` finishes, it *won't* call the auto-complete function.

The call to `generateDropdown` is made via `setTimeout`, so there won't be rapid flickering as a user types multiple characters. Each time a key is pressed, any existing timer is cancelled and a new one is created, so the drop-down will only be displayed when the user pauses for a moment: 500 milliseconds, to be exact.

For any additive keys (i.e., character keys), `generateDropdown` is still called, but an additional check allows for the auto-complete feature to be enabled if the browser supports it. When that's the case, `generateDropdown` is passed a `true` argument.

The two other keys that require special handling are the up and down arrow keys. These operate the current selection in the suggestions drop-down, so if users press either of them, we check whether the drop-down exists, then move the selection appropriately. Each of the list items in the drop-down is checked to see whether it has the `class` hover, and when the currently selected item is found, either its previous sibling or its next sibling will be selected, depending upon which arrow key was pressed. The value of the text field is then changed to the newly selected drop-down item.

The suggestions drop-down is created by the `generateDropdown` function, and is actually an unordered list with associated items:

File: **auto-complete_text_field.js** (excerpt)

```
function generateDropdown(doAutoComplete)
{
  closeDropdown();

  var input = document.getElementById("email");

  var newUl = document.createElement("ul");
  newUl.setAttribute("id", "autoCompleteDropdown");
  newUl.autoCompleteInput = input;
  newUl.style.position = "absolute";
  newUl.style.left = getPosition(input)[0] + "px";
  newUl.style.top = getPosition(input)[1] + input.offsetHeight -
      2 + "px";
  newUl.style.width = input.offsetWidth - 3 + "px";


  for (var i = 0; i < emailAddresses.length; i++)
  {
    if (emailAddresses[i].indexOf(input.value) ==- 0)
    {
      var newLi = document.createElement("li");
      newLi.appendChild(
          document.createTextNode(emailAddresses[i]));

      if (browserDetected != "ie5mac")
      {
        attachEventListener(newLi, "mouseover", mouseoverDropdown,
            false);
        attachEventListener(newLi, "mouseout", mouseoutDropdown,
```

```
        false);
      attachEventListener(newLi, "mousedown", mousedownDropdown,
        false);
    }

    newUl.appendChild(newLi);
  }
}

if (newUl.firstChild != null)
{
  document.getElementsByTagName("body")[0].appendChild(newUl);
}

if (typeof doAutoComplete != "undefined" && doAutoComplete)
{
  autoComplete();
}

return true;
}
```

generateDropdown first removes the existing drop-down by calling closeDropdown:

File: **auto-complete_text_field.js** (excerpt)

```
function closeDropdown()
{
  var autoCompleteDropdown =
      document.getElementById("autoCompleteDropdown");

  if (autoCompleteDropdown != null)
  {
    autoCompleteDropdown.parentNode.removeChild(
        autoCompleteDropdown);
  }

  return true;
}
```

Then, a new unordered list is created, positioned absolutely, and styled according to the text field's dimensions (with some adjustments for borders), so it has the same width as, and is positioned just below, the text field. The text field's position is calculated using the getPosition function from Chapter 13.

The values inside the drop-down are drawn from our pre-stored array of data. The current value of the text field is compared with each of the array values, and if the text field string is a substring from the start of the array value, then it is added to the drop-down as a list item. As each list item is created, a few event listeners are added to it as well. These handle mouse events and give the user the ability to highlight drop-down items using the mouse cursor, and then to click on them to place the selected value into the text field. We have to do a browser check using `identifyBrowser` (from Chapter 11) because Internet Explorer 5 for Mac has real problems with the mouse events on the newly created list items. That browser won't allow for mouse interaction, but users will still be able to navigate the drop-down using the arrow keys:

File: **auto-complete_text_field.js** (excerpt)

```
function mouseoverDropdown(event)
{
  if (typeof event == "undefined")
  {
    event = window.event;
  }

  var target = getEventTarget(event);

  while (target.nodeName.toLowerCase() != "li")
  {
    target = target.parentNode;
  }

  var childLis = target.parentNode.childNodes;

  for (var i = 0; i < childLis.length; i++)
  {
    childLis[i].className = "";
  }

  target.className = "hover";

  return true;
}

function mouseoutDropdown(event)
{
  if (typeof event == "undefined")
  {
    event = window.event;
  }
```

```
  var target = getEventTarget(event);

  while (target.nodeName.toLowerCase() != "li")
  {
    target = target.parentNode;
  }

  target.className = "";

  return true;
}
function mousedownDropdown(event)
{
  if (typeof event == "undefined")
  {
    event = window.event;
  }

  var target = getEventTarget(event);

  while (target.nodeName.toLowerCase() != "li")
  {
    target = target.parentNode;
  }

  target.parentNode.autoCompleteInput.value =
      target.firstChild.nodeValue;

  closeDropdown();

  return true;
}
```

A mousedown event listener is used instead of an actual click event listener because the blur event on the text field fires before a click event does, and this makes the drop-down disappear before the list item can receive the click.

Each of the listeners uses the getEventTarget function from Chapter 13 to ascertain the precise list item that received the event. To make sure that we have a list item, we iterate upwards until we find an li element, then perform the required operation: changing the class, or copying the value to the text field.

Returning to generateDropdown, the drop-down is added to the page only if it has some valid suggestions. Then, depending upon the *doAutoComplete* argument that was passed to it, it may call autoComplete:

```
function autoComplete()
{
  var input = document.getElementById("email");
  var cursorMidway = false;

  if (typeof document.selection != "undefined")
  {
    var range = document.selection.createRange();

    if (range.move("character", 1) != 0)
    {
      cursorMidway = true;
    }

  }
  else if (typeof input.selectionStart != "undefined" &&
      input.selectionStart < input.value.length)
  {
    cursorMidway = true;
  }

  var originalValue = input.value;
  var autoCompleteDropdown =
      document.getElementById("autoCompleteDropdown");

  if (autoCompleteDropdown != null && !cursorMidway)
  {
    autoCompleteDropdown.firstChild.className = "hover";
    input.value =
        autoCompleteDropdown.firstChild.firstChild.nodeValue;

    if (typeof input.createTextRange != "undefined")
    {
      var range = input.createTextRange();
      range.moveStart("character", originalValue.length);
      range.select();
    }
    else if (typeof input.setSelectionRange != "undefined")
    {
      input.setSelectionRange(originalValue.length,
          input.value.length);
    }
```

```
  if (autoCompleteDropdown.childNodes.length == 1)
  {
    setTimeout("closeDropdown();", 10);
  }
}

return true;
}
```

The auto-complete feature is used only if the cursor inside the text field is situated after the last character, otherwise it will interfere with the user's typing. So, the first thing we need to do is ascertain where the cursor is positioned. In Internet Explorer, we do this by creating a Range from the selection, then trying to move the Range to the right; if the move is successful, we know that the cursor is *not* at the end of the text field. In other browsers, we can simply use the text field's `selectionStart` property. It returns the offset of the selection, which we can compare with the total length of the text field's value to see whether or not the cursor is positioned at the end.

Once we know that the cursor is at the end of the text field, we create a copy of its current value, then copy the first value of the suggestion drop-down into the text field. All that remains is to select the part of the new value that the user *didn't* type. This allows them to continue typing without interference, as the suggested text will automatically be overwritten by their own typing.

In Internet Explorer, we handle the selection of the suggested text by creating a text range from the text field, then moving the start of the range by the length of the text field's original value. Create a selection from the range using `range.select` and: presto! The suggested text is selected.

As most other browsers don't support ranges inside text fields, we have to use a specially supplied method called `setSelectionRange`. It operates on text fields and takes a start index and an end index for the selection to be created. Using the length of the original value as the start index, and the length of the new value as the end index, we end up with the same selection as appears in Internet Explorer.

With the selection completed, the last thing we need to do is to tidy up the suggestion drop-down. The first suggested value has been inserted into the text field, so, if that's the only suggestion in the drop-down, the drop-down becomes redundant. We can close it by calling `closeDropdown`. We need to place it inside a `setTimeout` call because Internet Explorer 5 for Windows crashes when you so quickly create and remove an element (the drop-down). Adding a tiny delay avoids this.

The drop-down, and also its items' hover state, can be styled using CSS, so we not only end up with a really helpful feature, but as illustrated in Figure 18.7, we have a smoothly integrated widget that almost looks like it's native to the browser.

Figure 18.7. A field that allows users to select from a number of suggestions and automatically completes what they're typing

Summary

Online applications are definitely one of the fastest growing segments of the Internet, and as you can see from the examples above, JavaScript will play a pivotal role in their development and use.

Without the interaction provided by JavaScript's "behavior layer," many possible web applications would be unusable, or at the very least, unwieldy. With the techniques that have been outlined in this chapter, you'll be able to create rich, immersive environments that do not suffer from the click-and-wait syndrome of the static web.

The challenge now is to use these capabilities for something that no one has ever imagined.

19

Object Orientation in JavaScript

Object Oriented Programming (OOP) is generally considered to be the best-practice standard for large scale software engineering projects. It differs from traditional procedural programming—where a program is a sequential list of instructions to the computer—by representing a program as a collection of individual units (objects) that process their own data and communicate with other objects.

IMPORTANT

One Size Does not Fit All

OOP is by no means a suitable programming paradigm for every situation. Simple programs often have no need for the structures of OOP, and if they're written in OOP, their size and performance can suffer. However, when it comes to larger projects, OOP offers many valuable benefits including modularity, flexibility, easier maintenance, and more direct correlation with real world processes.

Although JavaScript is most often characterized as an *object based* programming language, it exhibits many of the features that OOP offers, and allows you to benefit from the same advantages. This chapter will show you how to make the most of these features and manage JavaScript as you would any other aspect of a software project.

What's so Good about Object Orientation?

Four main principles form the basis of object oriented programming, and give rise to its main benefits.

Abstraction

The key concept that underpins the very notion of objects is that they **abstract** the details of their own implementation. If we have an object `bird`, it is enough for other objects to know that they can call `bird.moveTo`—they don't need to know any of the details of how that movement will be implemented. By abstracting these details, a standard interface to an object can be created very early in development, and other objects can rely on this interface to remain the same, irrespective of any radical changes that may occur within the object itself.

Encapsulation

Encapsulation ensures that an object's state can only be changed by the object itself, as a result of that object's performing one of the operations (methods) it supports. Encapsulation enforces the advantages of abstraction by ensuring that an object is accessible only by its interface, which makes it impossible for other objects to rely upon the internal representation of an object's behavior.

JavaScript doesn't support a full implementation of encapsulation, as it lacks **private members** (variables that can be accessed only by the object that contains them).

Implementing Private Members

If you wish to implement private members, it is possible to do so using some custom functions,[1] but this will introduce overhead to the object creation process.

---

[1] http://www.crockford.com/javascript/private.html

Class Inheritance

Classes describe the functionality of objects that may be created; thus, each object that a program creates at run time is an **instance** of a class. **Inheritance** allows one class to replicate and extend the functionality of another without having to re-implement the existing class's behavior. This means that several classes can inherit functionality from one **superclass** (or parent class) that contains their shared behavior. The children can then specialize or extend upon the parent class by creating new data and methods, or by overriding those that already exist in the parent. If you think of classes as forming a tree hierarchy, a child class automatically implements every property and method that its parent class supports.

Figure 19.1. A class with three levels of an object hierarchy, including class names and some attributes

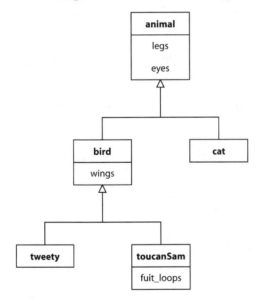

In the class diagram shown in Figure 19.1, the animal class has two properties: eyes and legs. This means that its two **subclasses** (child classes), bird and cat will also have eyes and legs, but bird adds a property that animal and cat won't have: wings. Further down in the hierarchy, both tweety and toucanSam will have eyes, legs, and wings, but only the toucanSam class will have a fruit_loops property.

Although JavaScript doesn't, strictly speaking, implement inheritance, the same advantages can be achieved using its prototype framework.

Polymorphism

Polymorphism literally means the ability to appear in different forms. Where object oriented programming is concerned, polymorphism allows an object of a given class to be treated as if it were an object of its superclass, despite the fact that one or more of the superclass's methods may be defined differently (overridden) in the object's true class.

As an example, if we have a class `animal` that has a method `moveTo`, we can call that method on any object of class `animal` or any of its subclasses, like `cat` or `bird`. If `cats` move differently from other `animals`, the `cat` class can declare its own, alternative implementation of `moveTo`, which will be called for any object of that class, even if the code that calls the method only knows that the object is an `animal`.

The advantage of polymorphism is that, without any additional work, code that's written to make use of simple classes can benefit from the advanced functionality implemented within more complex subclasses. That is, one piece of code can make any `animal` move—but each individual *class* of animal can determine exactly *how* it moves.

Object Based Code vs Object Oriented Code

Although object based programming languages allow for the creation and interaction of objects, they typically lack some of the features that are required in a fully object oriented language. JavaScript, for example, lacks the key features of class-based inheritance and private members.

Inheritance is usually implemented using syntax like this:

```
class Parent
{
    ⋮
}

class Child extends Parent
{
```

```
    ⋮
}
```

However, JavaScript does not support classes, and hence does not support inheritance. JavaScript is a **prototype based** language that uses objects as prototypes for other objects: a new object can replicate the behavior of an existing object by cloning it.

This is very similar to a class based approach, and in fact JavaScript programs *can* utilize centrally defined behavior, and specialize or extend upon it. We'll discuss these capabilities a little later in this chapter.

Writing an Object Oriented Script

Grasping the notion of object orientation is as much about changing the way you think about programming as it is about changing the way you code. However, you'll need to know some new syntax in order to begin object oriented programming in JavaScript.

Solution

If classes are the blueprints for objects in other object oriented languages, functions are the blueprints for objects in JavaScript.

Throughout this book you may have noticed the usage of syntax like this:

```
var tweety = new Bird();
```

For example, we saw the following snippet in Chapter 4:

```
var planets = new Array('mercury', 'venus', 'earth');
```

In that case, we were really creating a new instance of an object. The variable `tweety` was assigned an object based on the function `Bird`. Using the common object oriented programming terminology, `tweety` is an object of class `Bird`. Of course, since JavaScript doesn't *have* classes, `Bird` is simply defined as a function:

File: **construct_object_oriented_script.js (excerpt)**

```
function Bird()
{
    ⋮
  return true;
}
```

As we placed the keyword new before the call to Bird, JavaScript understands that we're creating a new object based on Bird, rather than assigning the output of the function to the variable. Let's check the type of tweety:

```
var tweety = new Bird();

alert(typeof tweety);
```

If you run this code, you'll see that tweety is of type "object", irrespective of the return value of Bird.

Inside the Bird function, we create all the properties that are associated with the object:

File: **construct_object_oriented_script.js** (excerpt)

```
function Bird()
{
  this.feet = 2;
  this.feathers = true;

  return true;
}
```

Bird is a **constructor**—a function designed specifically to create new objects. Within a constructor, this refers to the object that's being created. Any object that's an instance of Bird will automatically acquire all the properties that were assigned to this inside Bird. We can reference these properties immediately after we create tweety:

File: **construct_object_oriented_script.js** (excerpt)

```
var tweety = new bird();
var numFeet = tweety.feet;
```

The value of the variable numFeet is 2.

Direct Referencing of Properties from Outside an Object

Even though the direct referencing of properties from outside an object is possible in JavaScript, it breaks the principles of abstraction and encapsulation, both of which are desirable as software engineering practices. See the next section ("Creating Methods for an Object") for information on how you can provide a maintainable interface to an object.

Creating Methods for an Object

We've discussed how we can create properties for an object by assigning them to this in the constructor. As we're about to see, it's also possible to include methods for an object.

Solution

Object methods are used quite regularly as part of JavaScript. For instance, any text string is actually an instance of String, which has quite a few associated methods that you've probably used already: toLowerCase, replace, indexOf, and so on.

There are two ways in which you can make your own object methods. Because you can assign functions as values for variables in JavaScript, the first approach is to specify a function as a property of an object in that object's constructor:

File: **create_methods.js (excerpt)**

```
function Bird()
{
  this.feet = 2;
  this.feathers = true;
  this.getFeetNum = getFeetNum;

  return true;
}

function getFeetNum()
{
  return this.feet;
}
```

In this listing, Bird assigns to this.getFeetNum a reference to the function getFeetNum, making it a method for the resulting object. Note that we can also use this within the getFeetNum function, again to access properties (and even other methods) of the current object. getFeetNum makes use of this to query the value of the feet property. Therefore, we can call this method whenever we want to find out the number of feet for a Bird object:

File: **create_methods.js (excerpt)**

```
var tweety = new bird();
var numFeet = tweety.getFeetNum();
```

521

The value of the variable numFeet will be 2.

You can even reduce the layers of referencing (and namespace conflicts, as we'll see at the end of this chapter) simply by defining the function explicitly inside the constructor:

```
function Bird()
{
  this.feet = 2;
  this.feathers = true;

  this.getFeetNum = function()
  {
    return this.feet;
  };

  return true;
}
```

Creating a number of methods that can act as the external interface to an object's data is the best way to protect that data. This practice ensures that you see the benefits of encapsulation and abstraction; it provides between objects a stable point of contact that will not change even if the internal representation of data within an object does.

Prototype-based Method Creation

I mentioned previously that JavaScript is a prototype-based programming language. In JavaScript, every constructor has a **prototype object** associated with it. The properties and methods of this prototype object appear as properties and methods of every object that's created using that constructor. Therefore, you can create methods by assigning functions as properties of the prototype object for a constructor.

At first glance, this approach seems exactly the same as defining your methods within the constructor function, but prototype-based method creation offers some important advantages:

❑ Because the functions are only stored once (in the prototype object), rather than in every new object, this approach offers efficiencies over defining methods within the constructor function.

❑ Since you can modify the prototype object at any time, this approach allows you to add methods to classes that you didn't create yourself (e.g., HTML elements).

❑ As changes to the prototype object affect objects that are in existence already, this approach lets you add methods to objects after they're created.

These advantages are particularly important when you're dealing with objects that you don't create yourself, such as HTML elements or simple data values. For instance, you can't modify JavaScript's `String` constructor, which is buried deep within a browser's application code. But by accessing `String`'s prototype object, you can add new methods that will be available to `String` objects throughout your script.

Once a constructor has been declared, the prototype object is available from its `prototype` property:

```
function Bird()
{
  this.feet = 2;
  this.feathers = true;

  return true;
}

Bird.prototype.getFeetNum = getFeetNum;

function getFeetNum()
{
  return this.feet;
}
```

Once `getFeetNum` has been assigned as a property of the prototype object, it can be called as a method of any `Bird` object:

File: **create_methods2.js** (excerpt)

```
var tweety = new Bird();
var numFeet = tweety.getFeetNum();
```

To reduce code clutter, we can create the function directly as a property of the prototype object:

File: **create_methods2.js (excerpt)**

```
function Bird()
{
  this.feet = 2;
  this.feathers = true;

  return true;
}

Bird.prototype.getFeetNum = function()
{
  return this.feet;
};
```

Prototype Methods and Source Order

JavaScript allows you to execute a function with global scope from anywhere inside a source file, irrespective of whether the function is defined before or after the point of execution. That's why code such as this works:

```
init();

function init()
{
    ⋮
}
```

However, when creating object methods using the `prototype` property, you cannot call a method until *after* it has been added to the prototype object. This means that the following code won't work:

```
var tweety = new bird();
var numFeet = tweety.getFeet();

function Bird()
{
    ⋮
}

Bird.prototype.getFeetNum = function()
{
    ⋮
};
```

The call to `tweety.getFeetNum` in the above snippet will cause an error because `getFeetNum` hasn't yet been added to the prototype object for

Bird. That said, you *could* instantiate the object before adding the method to the prototype:

```
var tweety = new Bird();

function Bird()
{
  ⋮
}

Bird.prototype.getFeetNum = function()
{
  ⋮
};

var numFeet = tweety.getFeet();
```

As long as the statement that adds a function to the prototype object comes before any calls to the resulting method, everything will work fine.

This is one advantage of the declaration of methods *inside* an object's constructor—regardless of where you place your constructors in your code file, they will work. For this reason, many developers choose to use prototypes only when they're extending built-in classes and cannot modify the constructor.

Discussion

It's also possible to create methods for built-in objects—such as strings—using the prototype property. For example, we can create a method that automatically converts any underscores in a string's value to spaces:

File: **create_method3.js (excerpt)**

```
String.prototype.convertUnderscores = function()
{
  return this.replace(/_/g, " ");
};
```

Once the above statement is executed, the method convertUnderscores is available for every string (whether newly created or pre existing):

File: **create_method3.js (excerpt)**

```
var underscored = "Are_there_any_spaces_in_here?";
var spaced = underscored.convertUnderscores();
```

The value of the variable spaced will be "Are there any spaces in here?"

Modelling Inheritance

Inheritance is one of the most important principles in object oriented programming. It allows for the specialization and extension of one superclass into many subclasses, with any changes to the superclass propagating through to the subclasses, and is extremely powerful for the creation and maintenance of objects. The way that JavaScript supports inheritance will be unfamiliar to most C++ or Java programmers, but it provides support nonetheless.

Solution

The prototype property allows any JavaScript constructor (or class) to clone the data and methods of another. If we assign a new object instance as the prototype of a constructor, that instance effectively becomes the constructor's superclass:

File: **inheritance.js** (excerpt)

```
function Bird()
{
  this.feet = 2;
  this.feathers = true;

  return true;
}

function Canary()
{
  this.color = "yellow";

  return true;
}

Canary.prototype = new Bird();

var tweety = new Canary();
var tweetyFeet = tweety.feet;
var tweetyColor = tweety.color;
```

The value of the variable tweetyFeet will be 2, even though it's an instance of Canary, which does not contain a feet property. Instead, the property comes from Canary's prototype object, which is a new instance of Bird.

Because of the way prototypes work, it's not a problem that all instances of `Canary` will share a single instance of `Bird` as their prototype object. The methods and properties exposed by a prototype cannot be overwritten by any single object instance. Rather, if you set a new value for the `feet` property of a `Canary` object, that value will be stored as a new property of that instance, hiding the original value that remains stored in the prototype instance of `Bird`. The properties and methods of a prototype effectively act as read-only defaults that may be overridden by instance-specific values at any time.

note

Implementing Multiple Inheritance

If you wish to implement multiple inheritance (where one class may inherit from multiple superclasses), it is possible to do so using some custom functions,[2] but this will introduce overhead to your object creation process.

Discussion

If this business of prototypes is giving you a headache, you'll be pleased to hear that it's possible to mimic inheritance more simply by explicitly executing the constructor of the superclass within the intended subclass's constructor. For this to work, though, you must first assign the superclass's constructor as a method of the subclass:

File: **inheritance2.js (excerpt)**

```
function Bird()
{
  this.feet = 2;
  this.feathers = true;

  return true;
}

function Canary()
{
  this.superclass = Bird;
  this.superclass();

  this.color = "yellow";

  return true;
}
```

---

[2] http://www.sitepoint.com/article/javascript-objects

```
var tweety = new Canary();
var tweetyFeet = tweety.feet;
var tweetyColor = tweety.color;
```

Because the statement `this.superclass();` calls the `Bird` constructor as a method of the new `Canary` object, `this` inside `Bird` will also refer to the new object being created by `Canary`. So `this.feet = 2;` will add the `feet` property to the new `Canary` object.

This technique will work only if all of the superclass's properties and methods are declared *inside* its constructor. Any properties or methods that are assigned to `Bird`'s prototype object will not be available in instances of `Canary`.

Understanding Scope

Have you ever discovered that the value of a variable is coming from a completely unexpected part of your code? It could be caused by an intricacy of variable scoping.

Solution

The **scope** of a variable defines the portion of your script in which it is available. In JavaScript, scope usually is controlled by functions.

If you specify a variable outside any function definition, it automatically has **global scope**. This means that the variable is available from any point within your script:

File: **scope.js (excerpt)**

```
var global = "available";

function availability()
{
  return global;
}

var isAvailable = availability();
```

The value of the variable `isAvailable` is `"available"`.

Global scope is also assigned to any variable that's defined in a function that does not have the keyword `var` before it:

File: **scope2.js** (excerpt)

```
function function1()
{
  global = "available";
}

function function2()
{
  return global;
}

function1();
var isAvailable = function2();
```

The value of the variable `isAvailable` will be `"available"`.

Note this statement inside `function1`:

```
global = "available";
```

This is not a variable declaration, because it does not begin with `var`. Rather, it assigns to the variable `global` a value that JavaScript will implicitly create as a global variable if it does not exist.

If we were to add the `var` keyword that's necessary to turn this statement into a formal variable declaration, `function2` would produce an error, because the scope of the variable `global` does not include `function2`:

File: **scope3.js** (excerpt)

```
function function1()
{
  var global = "available";
}

function function2()
{
  return global;
}

function1();
var isAvailable = function2();
```

In the script above, the variable `isAvailable` would not be initialized, because the script would throw an error when trying to access `global` inside `function2`.

As you can see, variables that are explicitly declared with the var keyword are only accessible inside the function in which they are declared. This limitation is called the variable's scope. A variable declared this way will also override any identically-named variable that would otherwise include the function in its scope:

File: **scope4.js** (excerpt)

```
var global = "available";

function function1()
{
  var global = "unavailable";

  return global;
}

var isAvailable = function1();
```

The value of the variable isAvailable will be "unavailable", because the global variable that was declared within function1 overrides the one declared with global scope.

Discussion

Within nested functions, you can access variables in any of the enclosing functions:

File: **scope5.js** (excerpt)

```
function parentFunction()
{
  var scopedVar = "available";
  var nestedFunction = function()
  {
    return scopedVar;
  }

  return nestedFunction();
}

var isAvailable = parentFunction();
```

The value of the variable isAvailable will be "available".

One useful side effect of these rules of variable scope is that variables in an outer function (e.g., `parentFunction` above) are available from nested functions (e.g., `nestedFunction` above) even after the outer function has finished executing:

File: **scope6.js (excerpt)**

```
function parentFunction()
{
  var scopedVar = "available";
  setTimeout(function() { alert(scopedVar); }, 1000);
  return true;
}
```

One second after `parentFunction` has been executed, an `alert` box will pop up, displaying the message `"available"`.

The ability for a nested function to access the variables in its enclosing environment at any time is called a **closure**. This is a very handy feature of JavaScript, and one we've used several times throughout this book, most notably in "Getting Multiple Scripts to Work on the Same Page" in Chapter 1 (in Chapter 1), where we used a closure in `addLoadListener` for browsers that don't support W3C event listeners.

Implementing Namespaces

As more people around the world create JavaScript that you and I can add to our pages, it becomes more likely that one person's code will overwrite or interfere with the variables and functions in code that's written by someone else. This can be avoided if we provide each piece of code with its own namespace.

Solution

Objects already help us prevent naming conflicts from arising between different scripts. If a function is defined as a method of an object, there is no way that that method can conflict with a function defined elsewhere; the same rule applies to variables defined as properties of an object.

If all of your code is object oriented, the only possible point of conflict lies in the object names. If you declare a constructor for a class named `Bird`, what will happen if someone else declares a class named `Bird`? In most cases, one declaration will silently override the other.

There's no in-built way to prevent name conflicts in JavaScript, so your best bet is to make sure that your classes are named in such a way that other coders are unlikely to use those names for their own classes. Obviously, giving your classes very generic names like `Item` is a bad idea.

One popular method of avoiding naming conflicts is to use the domain name associated with a script, but to reverse the domain hierarchy like so:

File: **namespaces.js (excerpt)**

```
com.sitepoint.Bird = function()
{
    ⋮
}

var tweety = new com.sitepoint.Bird();
```

Of course, you'd need to ensure that both `com` and `com.sitepoint` already exist. So, as well as creating lengthy object names, you'll need to write a little more code to check for object existence (you don't want to overwrite the `com` object that another script might be using for its namespace):

File: **namespaces.js (excerpt)**

```
if (typeof com == "undefined")
{
    com = new Object();
}

if (typeof com.sitepoint == "undefined")
{
    com.sitepoint = new Object();
}

com.sitepoint.Bird = function()
{
    ⋮
}
```

Ajile is a JavaScript module that's designed to improve JavaScript interoperability and reuse through namespacing, so if you're looking for an easy way to control namespaces (in Firefox or Internet Explorer 6, as these are the two browsers with which Ajile is compatible), try it out.[3]

---

[3] http://ajile.sourceforge.net

Summary

JavaScript has long been considered an immature and unstructured programming language, but the techniques discussed in this chapter should demonstrate that it is actually a flexible, powerful, and well-structured language capable of scaling to meet the needs of your largest projects.

If you use the object oriented approach discussed here, your code should benefit from being more maintainable, more modular, and more robust—characteristics that you'll definitely appreciate in the fast-paced world of web development.

20

Keeping up the Pace

This final chapter, like the very first, focuses more on tips than outright solutions. We'll be discussing a range of ideas for improving the efficiency of your scripts—reducing the amount of work they do so that they run faster, and reducing the amount of code required to create them so that they load more quickly.

We'll also look at how to reduce memory usage, and how to avoid or clean up after DOM memory leaks. Although, arguably, these latter problems may be beyond the scope of issues that a JavaScript coder should need to think about, we all have to face them at some point.

Optimization really is the last resort of programming: it's always better to look at the *design* of your code to identify opportunities to make fundamental improvements (maybe a whole chunk of the script is unnecessary, or could be simplified if you took a different approach). A script that's forcibly optimized for speed or file size will invariably lose some degree of readability in the process, and you should give this serious consideration if anyone besides you will look at it in the future.

Nevertheless, if speed is critical to your application and you can't improve the design any further, it's time to look closely at the ideas in this chapter. Most of them will make little or no perceptible difference *by themselves*, but if you apply all of them together in a large and complex script, you can make some very worthwhile optimization improvements.

Making Scripts Run Faster

We obviously want our scripts to run as quickly as possible, all other things being equal, but those last few milliseconds are seldom *that* important. Some optimizations may improve performance in one respect while damaging it in others (for example, one JavaScript construct might be faster to run, but less concise than some other techniques), so as we go through this solution, we'll consider the relative benefits of each idea. You can then make up your own mind as to whether or not it's useful to you.

For General Scripting Only

This solution looks at techniques for general scripting, rather than specifically considering improving the speed of DHTML animation. Although these techniques also apply to that field, animation has its own set of issues and a variety of approaches have evolved to improve its efficiency. These techniques were discussed in detail in Chapter 14.

Solution

To make scripts run faster, we need to have them do less work:

❑ Save references to objects you use frequently.

❑ Use ternary operators and `switch` statements.

❑ Optimize loops.

❑ Avoid using `eval`.

❑ Avoid strict warnings.

❑ Optimize for particular browsers.

Let's have a look at each of these in turn.

Saving References to Objects you Use Frequently

References to elements, collections, properties, and so forth, can be stored so that they're quicker to reference later. Why are they quicker? Because the script interpreter is doing less work. Consider this snippet:

```
document.getElementById('content').getElementsByTagName('p');
```

Here, we're asking the interpreter to start from document, find the element content with getElementById, then find all p elements within that. Every time we use that expression in full, we're making the interpreter do all that work. But we can save the script from performing this operation more than once by creating a variable with its result:

File: **saving-references.js (excerpt)**

```
var p =
    document.getElementById('content').getElementsByTagName('p');
```

The p variable is simply a reference to that node set, which means that it's **dynamic**; if later you add or remove p elements from the content element, the p.length property will reflect the updated length of that set.

The length property is also worthy of inspection, because iterating through a collection by length is a very common process in DHTML:

```
var p =
    document.getElementById('content').getElementsByTagName('p');

for (var i = 0; i < p.length; i++)
{
    ⋮
}
```

The interpreter has to calculate the length of the p collection continually (every time it evaluates the loop condition), and that *might* be unnecessary work. If we stored the length of the p collection in advance, it would only need to be calculated once:

File: **saving-references.js (excerpt)**

```
var p =
    document.getElementById('content').getElementsByTagName('p');
var len = p.length;

for (var i = 0; i < len; i++)
{
    ⋮
}
```

I say "might" because in practice this only makes an appreciable difference in Internet Explorer 5 and 6, for which the approach of referring to a stored length is significantly faster; in other popular browsers this technique makes little or no difference.[1]

Of course, the creation of that `len` variable itself means a slight *increase* in memory usage, so unless you can gain additional benefit from reusing that variable within the loop, this particular optimization is probably not worth it. (It may be worth it if you want the advantage for IE, though; we'll be looking at browser-specific optimizations later in this solution.)

Caveat: Length must not Change

We haven't created a reference here, we've simply copied the value of `p.length` at a single point in time; the value of `len` is *not dynamic*, so we can only do this if we can assert that *the length will not change* within the loop. If the loop were to add or remove members from the collection, then iterating with a stored length would not work correctly; it would either iterate too few times, or too many, resulting in errors. In that situation, a stored value is no good—you have to query the `length` property directly in the loop condition.[2]

You can also save references to properties of DOM nodes and other objects to simplify the use of those properties later on; `style` is an obvious example:

File: **saving-references.js**

```
var p =
    document.getElementById('content').getElementsByTagName('p');
var len = p.length;

for (var i = 0; i < len; i++)
{
  var pstyle = p[i].style;
  pstyle.color = 'red';
  pstyle.fontWeight = 'bold';
}
```

If you create this kind of shortcut for every reference you use more than once, you'll gain a small efficiency improvement; each time you use it, you'll avoid the

---

[1]In a sample benchmark, iterating with a stored length was five times faster than querying the `length` each time in Internet Explorer 6; in Firefox, Safari, and Opera, running the same benchmark, no significant difference was observed.
[2]Incidentally, adding and removing members from a collection will also change the indexes of the other members in the collection, so you'll need to update the value of your loop counter variable (`i`) as well.

work of walking through an object chain, so the overall improvement depends on how often you use that particular shortcut.

Using Ternary Operators and Switch Statements

We've encountered ternary operators a few times in this book. The ternary operator is the only JavaScript operator that takes three operands:

File: **ternary-operators.js** (excerpt)

```
var grade = score >= 40 ? 'pass' : 'fail';
```

That example is equivalent to the following `if-else` statement:

```
if (score >= 40)
{
  var grade = 'pass';
}
else
{
  var grade = 'fail';
}
```

Ternary operators take a lot less code to write, so I recommend you use them wherever practical.

Ternary operators can also be nested as deeply as you like. Consider the code below:

File: **ternary-operators.js** (excerpt)

```
var grade = score >= 70 ? 'merit' : score >= 40 ? 'pass' : 'fail';
```

That script is equivalent to this:

```
if (score >= 70)
{
  var grade = 'merit';
}
else if (score >= 40)
{
  var grade = 'pass';
}
else
{
  var grade = 'fail';
}
```

Keep in mind that the deeper the operators are nested, the harder they are to read! You can improve the situation by wrapping extra parentheses around individual ternary expressions, or by splitting the whole expression into multiple lines with appropriate indentation, something like this:

File: **ternary-operators.js** (excerpt)

```
var grade = score >= 90 ? 'distinction' :
    score >= 70 ? 'merit' :
    score >= 40 ? 'pass' :
    'fail';
```

For very complex sets of conditions, the most useful and efficient construct is a switch statement. Here's one that does the same job as the preceding script:

File: **switch-statements.js** (excerpt)

```
switch (true)
{
  case score >= 90:
    var grade = 'distinction';
    break;

  case score >= 70:
    var grade = 'merit';
    break;

  case score >= 40:
    var grade = 'pass';
    break;

  default:
    var grade = 'fail';
}
```

A switch statement is equivalent to a set of if-else statements. The expression (the value in parentheses) is compared with the value of each case (each outcome that we care about), and the first match dictates the point at which we begin executing the code in the body of the statement. There's also an optional default case, which, if present, is run when no other case is matched (this is equivalent to a final else in a series of if-elses).

The code that follows each case is generally terminated by a break statement, which stops the execution of the switch at that point, and jumps to the code following the closing brace. Without a break, execution would continue through to the code following the next case (or the default), which is not usually desired.

The form of that example might be unfamiliar to you, as it was to me before I wrote this book. The only format I'd used before was this:

File: **switch-statements.js** (excerpt)

```
switch (score)
{
  case 90:
    var grade = 'distinction';
    break;
  case 70:
    grade = 'merit';
    break;
  case 40:
    grade = 'pass';
    break;
  default:
    grade = 'fail';
}
```

Here, the value of the *expression* is a **variable** (score), and each case represents a specific value that it might take. This is a literal interpretation of the specification, which says that each **case** value can *only be tested for equality* against the expression.

But take a look at the generic format of a switch statement:

```
switch (expression)
{
  case value1:
    ⋮
    break;

  case value2:
    ⋮
    break;

  default:
    ⋮
}
```

This allows for greater flexibility than you may think. If the value of the *expression* is **true**, rather than a variable, each **case** value can evaluate a complex expression for a Boolean result (**true** or **false**), and *that* can be tested for equality against the *expression*!

This implies a third way of using `switch`, where the *expression* produces a Boolean result, meaning that only two `case`s are possible (`true` or `false`). In the following example, the `default` branch will never be executed:

File: **switch-statements.js (excerpt)**

```
switch (score >= 40)
{
  case true:
    var grade = 'pass';
    break;

  case false:
    grade = 'fail';
    break;

  default:
    grade = 'infinity plus one';
}
```

I can't think what use that last example might serve, but the three examples together should illustrate the power and flexibility of `switch`. You could say that `switch` is the maestro!

Optimizing Loops

The simplest way to improve the efficiency of a loop is to use a `break` statement to prevent unnecessary iterations.

For example, if we're iterating through p elements in order to find one with a particular `class`, and we're *only interested in finding one*, we can stop the loop as soon as we've found it:

File: **break-continue.js (excerpt)**

```
var p = document.getElementsByTagName('p');
var len = p.length;

for (var i = 0; i < len; i++)
{
  if (p[i].className == 'summary')
  {
    var summary = p[i];
    break;
  }
}
```

continue is similar to break; however, in contrast to break, continue doesn't stop the execution of a loop entirely: it skips the remainder of *the current iteration* of the loop body. Take this example:

File: **break-continue.js (excerpt)**

```
for (var i = 0; i < len; i++)
{
  if (p[i].className != 'summary')
  {
    continue;
  }

  var summary = p[i];
  break;
}
```

Here we're saying, "if the class is not summary, skip the rest of this iteration," which sends execution immediately to the update statement of the for loop (i++). Only if the class *is* summary will the code proceed to the next statement of the loop body, where it creates that summary variable. Remembering that continue doesn't mean "continue this iteration," but "continue the loop with the *next* iteration" can take a little getting used to!

Avoiding eval

The eval function takes a string and attempts to execute it as JavaScript code. eval can be used to create functional code in very powerful and flexible ways, but because of this power it's very expensive to use.[3]

To do its job, eval must first determine whether the argument is a valid string; it will then parse that string looking for JavaScript code. If the string equates to an expression, that expression will be evaluated and its value returned; if it contains statements, each of those will be evaluated and the value of the last one returned. It's a complex business, and usually achieves nothing—most of the more typical uses of eval are uncalled for.

You might have seen it used to create an object reference:

File: **avoiding-eval.js (excerpt)**

```
var ele = eval('document.getElementById("link" + n)');
```

---

[3] In a sample benchmark, creating an object reference using eval was two to three times slower than creating the same reference without it.

It's often used for tasks like testing the stored name of a modifier key against whether that key is pressed:

File: **avoiding-eval.js** (excerpt)

```
var mod = 'shiftKey';
if (eval('e.' + mod))
{
  ⋮ The Shift key is pressed.
}
```

However, both of these are unnecessary uses. The second example could be expressed using square-bracket notation:

File: **avoiding-eval.js** (excerpt)

```
var mod = 'shiftKey';
if (e[mod])
{
  ⋮ The Shift key is pressed.
}
```

The first example just doesn't need `eval` at all:

File: **avoiding-eval.js** (excerpt)

```
var ele = document.getElementById('link' + n);
```

It's almost never necessary to use `eval`, so whenever you come across a situation to which it seems appropriate, look for alternatives first; you might be surprised by how easily you find one!

Avoiding Strict Warnings

We looked at some common causes of strict warnings, like assuming the existence of an object, or re-declaring a variable, in "Strict Warnings" in Chapter 1.

In Mozilla browsers such as Firefox, strict warnings cause the interpreter more work. Although they're not actually errors per se, they're points where an assumption or reliance on a deprecated feature has been used. They force the script interpreter to do "what you mean" rather than "what you say," as it were, and that takes additional processing.

I think it's generally a good idea to avoid strict warnings, because they point to areas of inefficiency or bad coding practice, but in Mozilla browsers we actually gain a significant speed improvement by avoiding them.[4]

Optimizing for a Particular Browser

If you're scripting for only one browser or, conversely, if one browser is performing noticeably worse than others, you may want to optimize your code to suit the foibles of that browser.

We can use **benchmarking** to establish whether a particular code construct could be expressed more efficiently in a different way. The benchmark is a process that runs many times, so that we can time how long the process takes on average, and make comparisons.

For example, let's build a benchmark that compares two ways to find a substring within a string—using `indexOf` and a regular expression `test`. We begin with two test functions, each of which performs one of those operations:

File: **optimizing-browser.js (excerpt)**

```
function test1()
{
  return 'Test string'.indexOf('str') != -1;
}

function test2()
{
  return /str/.test('Test string');
}
```

We then run those functions multiple times:

File: **optimizing-browser.js (excerpt)**

```
var i = 0;

var start1 = new Date();
for (i = 0; i < 200000; i++)
{
  test1();
}
var end1 = new Date();
```

---

[4] In a sample benchmark, testing for the existence of a `navigator` property using `typeof` was ten times faster than relying on automatic type conversion for the check.

```
var start2 = new Date();
for (i = 0; i < 200000; i++)
{
  test2();
}
var end2 = new Date();
```

I'm using 200,000 iterations, which is enough to get useful data, but not so many that it causes a problem for browsers. (For example, Firefox and other Mozilla browsers will optionally time-out a script after a certain amount of continual processing, to avoid a situation where a badly-written script could hang in an infinite iteration or recursion.)

Now that we've run our benchmark, we can query and compare the results (the `getTime` method returns the number of milliseconds in a `Date` object, as we saw in Chapter 9):

File: **optimizing-browser.js (excerpt)**

```
alert('Test 1 = ' + (end1.getTime() - start1.getTime()) + 'ms\n'
    + 'Test 2 = ' + (end2.getTime() - start2.getTime()) + 'ms');
```

For the record, Table 20.1 shows the sample results for four major browsers.

Table 20.1. Substring detection benchmark results

Test	Opera 8	Firefox 1.0	Safari 1.3	IE 6
Test 1: `indexOf`	1562ms	2664ms	6064ms	1302ms
Test 2: `test`	1833ms	1532ms	19656ms	2283ms

Safari and IE 6 prefer `indexOf`, Firefox prefers the regex `test`, and Opera seems to have no preference. So, all other things being equal, you can use the construct that suits your target browser. The "other things" that you might need to consider in this case are the fact that `indexOf` cannot test a regular expression, which might be required, or the fact that you can reuse a regular expression, rather than creating a new one each time it's needed, to save parse time.[5]

That's just a single example, but it illustrates the general point—whenever you want to optimize your code for a particular browser, you can look through your

---

[5] By using the `RegExp` constructor instead of a regex literal, but note that IE 5.0 for Mac has a memory leak with that constructor, which is discussed in "Creating a Regular Expression" in Chapter 3.

code for any constructs you use often, and examine whether there are faster ways of doing the same job.

Remember earlier in this chapter, when we talked about iterating through a node set by length? In Internet Explorer, it was much faster to store the length in advance, than to query it afresh each time.

Let's look at another example. When referring to arguments in a function, is it quicker to use named arguments, or to refer to them using the `arguments` collection? Here's the benchmark:

File: **optimizing-browser.js** (excerpt)

```
function test3(a, b)
{
  return a + b;
}
function test4()
{
  return arguments[0] + arguments[1];
}

start1 = new Date();
for (i = 0; i < 200000; i++)
{
  test3(1, i);
}
end1 = new Date();
start2 = new Date();
for (i = 0; i < 200000; i++)
{
  test4(1, i);
}
end2 = new Date();
```

Table 20.2 shows the results.

Table 20.2. Argument fetching benchmark results

Test	Opera 8	Firefox 1.0	Safari 1.3	IE 6
Test 3: named args	581ms	541ms	4104ms	711ms
Test 4: array	1803ms	571ms	4133ms	1923ms

Opera and IE 6 prefer named arguments, but Firefox and Safari have no preference.

Now obviously the numbers are skewed by factors that are not easy to compare—for example, the CPU speed of the test computer—but that's not actually important, because all we're comparing is the *relative values* of the two numbers (which number is larger), then comparing those differences between browsers. The actual values are not important, nor are they necessarily reflective of the browsers' overall performance; all they tell us is which of those constructs is faster for each browser.

Writing Scripts Using Less Code

Using less code to write your scripts means that those scripts will download more quickly; which is invariably a good thing for a public web site or web-based application, but less significant for an intranet or local application (where the download speed is the speed of the network). However, file size can also make a difference to the time it takes a script to be parsed, since there are fewer actual bytes for the interpreter to read.

However, when we talk about "code," we're talking specifically about *lines of actual code*, not comments. Comments don't count as code, and you shouldn't limit the amount of commenting you do for the sake of file size; comments can always be removed before publishing (as we'll see in the next solution).

Solution

I can make three core recommendations here:

❑ Divide tasks into functions (use OO).

❑ Use arrays and iteration to avoid code repetition.

❑ Write compact conditions and return statements.

Dividing Tasks into Functions (or Using OO)

Whenever you need to perform a set of actions more than once, it's a good idea to abstract them into a function. The more often you need it, the greater the efficiency gains you'll make overall.

Throughout this book we've seen many examples where a single, abstracted function is presented as the solution to a particular problem. For example, here's the `getViewportSize` function that we've used a few times:

```
function getViewportSize()
{
  var size = [0, 0];

  if (typeof window.innerWidth != 'undefined')
  {
    size = [
        window.innerWidth,
        window.innerHeight
    ];
  }
  else if (typeof document.documentElement != 'undefined' &&
      typeof document.documentElement.clientWidth != 'undefined'
      && document.documentElement.clientWidth != 0)
  {
    size = [
        document.documentElement.clientWidth,
        document.documentElement.clientHeight
    ];
  }
  else
  {
    size = [
        document.getElementsByTagName('body')[0].clientWidth,
        document.getElementsByTagName('body')[0].clientHeight
    ];
  }

  return size;
}
```

Imagine we had to reproduce *all that code every time* we wanted to find out the viewport size! That would be ridiculous. If we abstract it into a function, we can simply use its return value:

```
var viewsize = getViewportSize();
```

Object orientated development is naturally geared towards this kind of abstraction, where a script consists of one or more objects, and each of those objects has a number of methods to serve it. Object oriented code is more efficient and reusable by virtue of task separation, and this is one of the reasons why OO is so cool. For more about object oriented development in JavaScript, see Chapter 19.

Using Arrays and Iteration to Avoid Code Repetition

Iteration can be used to express something in fewer lines of code. Here's a simple example:

File: **using-arrays-iteration.js** (excerpt)

```javascript
var p1 = document.getElementById('p1');
p1.style.color = 'red';

var p2 = document.getElementById('p2');
p2.style.color = 'red';

var p3 = document.getElementById('p3');
p3.style.color = 'red';
```

The above script could be expressed fewer lines, like this:

File: **using-arrays-iteration.js** (excerpt)

```javascript
for (var i = 1; i < 4; i++)
{
  var p = document.getElementById('p' + i);
  p.style.color = 'red';
}
```

Obviously, when this approach is used for longer, more complex processes, the gain will be more significant.

If we were setting different values (such as different colors), we could save those values in an array:

File: **using-arrays-iteration.js** (excerpt)

```javascript
var colors = ['red', 'gold', 'green'];
for (var i = 1; i < 4; i++)
{
  var p = document.getElementById('p' + i);
  p.style.color = colors[i - 1];
}
```

Note how the array index is [i - 1], because our i values are 1–3, not 0–2 like the indices of the array.

Compacting Conditions and Return Statements

You can write expressions for evaluation directly inside conditions and return statements, rather than saving the result of the evaluation in a variable and using or returning that. This sounds obvious, but it's a neat trick to implement. Not only does it reduce the amount of code required to evaluate an expression, it also uses less memory, since one less variable has been created.

Here's an example: a short function that returns the first element in a collection, or null if that collection is empty:

File: **compacting-conditions.js** (excerpt)

```
function getFirstElement(root, tag)
{
  var collection = root.getElementsByTagName(tag);
  if (collection.length > 0)
  {
    var first = collection[0];
  }
  else
  {
    var first = null;
  }

  return first;
}
```

We can reduce that script immediately using a ternary operator, which we saw earlier in this chapter:

File: **compacting-conditions.js** (excerpt)

```
function getFirstElement(root, tag)
{
  var collection = root.getElementsByTagName(tag);
  var first = collection.length > 0 ? collection[0] : null;

  return first;
}
```

In fact, we don't need that first variable *at all*. We just need the value of the expression, so let's return that directly:

File: **compacting-conditions.js** (excerpt)

```
function getFirstElement(root, tag)
{
  var collection = root.getElementsByTagName(tag);

  return collection.length > 0 ? collection[0] : null;
}
```

 Tip

Processing Overhead vs Readability

Be careful to weigh the processing savings of your optimized code against its readability; a few bytes' reduction is not worth the trouble of being left with an illegible script!

Optimizing Scripts for the Web

We're no longer looking at your own, development version of a script: we're talking about the one that people actually use. These are optimizations that I strongly recommend you perform on a *separate copy* of your script, so that you're not taking risks with the original. These are all tasks you can complete using the find-and-replace function in your text editor.

Solution

I can recommend two ways to "compress" a script; these can make a dramatic difference to the eventual file size:

❏ Remove comments and unnecessary whitespace.

❏ Compact the names of variables and properties.

Removing Comments and Unnecessary Whitespace

Commenting and whitespace are crucial to good development practice. Line breaks and tabs make a script much easier to read, while comments are there to explain what a script is doing and, more importantly, *why*. Comments are useful both while writing a script, and in the future, when you or others come back to it.

Personally, I comment like it's going out of fashion, using two or three lines of commenting to every line of code. I learnt the hard way how frustrating it is to come back to a script after six months, only to have no idea how it works!

But, critical as they are to development, there's no point leaving comments in the copy that's *actually in use* on your site or application—most users will never read them, and those who are interested can always ask you for a development copy of the script. (And there are obfuscation benefits as well—you *can* say no!)

Terminate your Lines

Before you remove line breaks from a script, you must ensure that *every line is properly terminated* with a semicolon, where necessary. If you don't do this, the lines will run together, generating syntax errors, as in the following example. Consider this snippet:

```
s = document.getElementById(n)
s.style.display = 'block';
```

That code works, but the first line is not terminated, so if it's stripped of line breaks, it will end up like this:

```
s = document.getElementById(n)s.style.display = 'block';
```

This code will generate an error. For more about this particular issue, please see "Using Braces and Semicolons (Consistent Coding Practice)" in Chapter 1.

Table 20.3 shows a sequence of regular expressions that will remove one-line comments, tabs, and line breaks (for more about regular expressions themselves, see Chapter 3).

Table 20.3. Regular expressions to strip comments/whitespace

Replace	With[a]	Description
([a-z]+)://	$1:/	Temporarily convert URL protocols to a single slash
//.*		Remove one-line comments
\t		Remove tabs
\n		Remove line breaks (may need \r on unix systems)
([a-z]+):/	$1://	Restore URL protocols

[a]An empty cell in the "with" column means "replace with nothing."

Removing One-line Comments

If you use the regular expression `"//.*"` (two slashes followed by any number of characters to the end of the line) to remove one-line comments, watch out for points at which that substring might occur within the code, such as in the protocol of a URL, like `http://www.sitepoint.com/`.

To avoid any problems, the above sequence of regular expressions replaces the double slashes in protocols with a single slash before removing comments; it restores the double slashes afterwards.

Now, an additional step you *could* take is to remove spaces between operators and other programmatic special characters. Consider this line:

```
var first = collection.length > 0 ? collection[0] : null;
```

It could be compressed to this:

```
var first=collection.length>0?collection[0]:null;
```

However, *this is dangerous* if it's not done carefully. To remove those spaces with a global replacement we would look for things like `" > "`, to be replaced with `">"`, and `" : "`, to be replaced with `":"`. The risk is that we could end up removing **necessary whitespace**. If the script actually outputs text that includes those character sequences, we'd almost certainly want to preserve the spaces there, to make the output more readable.

Here's another example: I once wasted several hours trying to debug a script for Safari, when it turned out I'd done a global replacement on `", "` (comma followed by space) to reduce the size of argument lists in function declarations. However, that broke the `navigator.vendor` test for `"Apple Computer, Inc."`—the space is part of the value, and without it, the match was failing!

I couldn't recommend performing global replacements on space characters! If you really need the savings, I suggest you replace them one by one, as a manual series of "find next" and "replace" operations, rather than a single "replace all," so that you can check that each one is safe as you go along. You could simply write them like that from the outset, provided you don't mind the consequent loss of readability.

However, there have to be limits on the practicality of code optimization—it's not worth risking the correct functionality of a script for the sake of a few hundreds bytes of processing power.

Tabs and line breaks are not a risk (provided that lines of code are properly terminated with semicolons, as we noted earlier), because even if the script includes those characters, they will be written as literal escape values (such as `"\t"`); our replacement would be looking for actual tabs in the code.

Compacting the Names of Variables and Properties

We have to be careful when naming variables in the global scope if we're scripting on a page or application to which other people will also be contributing script, so as not to choose a name that someone else might use. Two variables with the same name in the same scope will conflict: the variable that's declared second will override the first. Reading the resulting code would involve tedious second-guessing—another reason for reducing the number of global variables you use.

But *within a function* you can safely use the simplest of names, right down to one- or two-letter names (with provisos, which we'll look at in a moment). This is perfectly safe, as the function provides restricted scope for the variables. Take a look at this example:

File: **compacting-names.js** (excerpt)

```
function castSpell(incantation, potion)
{
  if (typeof potion == 'undefined') { potion = 'felix'; }
  var spell = document.getElementById(incantation);
  if (spell)
  {
    spell.style.display = 'block';
    spell.firstChild.nodeValue = 'Potion: ' + potion;
  }
}
```

This script could be compacted like so:

File: **compacting-names.js** (excerpt)

```
function castSpell(n, p)
{
  if (typeof p == 'undefined') { p = 'felix'; }
  var s = document.getElementById(n);
  if (s)
  {
    s.style.display = 'block';
    s.firstChild.nodeValue = 'Potion: ' + p;
```

```
    }
}
```

Notice how I used n, rather than i, for `incantation`? That's one of the provisos I mentioned: i is commonly used as a loop iterator, so I generally avoid using i as a general-purpose variable (and j, for the same reason). I also avoid e, which is commonly used as an event reference.

Avoiding Memory Leaks

JavaScript uses automatic **garbage collection**. Garbage collection is the disposal of (i.e.,the freeing-up of memory used by) objects that are no longer needed. An object is no longer needed when there are no existing references to it. This usually happens when a page unloads.

However, Internet Explorer 5 and 6 cannot garbage-collect certain kinds of objects if they form part of a **circular reference**. A circular reference occurs where two or more objects refer to each other in a circular way—A refers to B, B refers to C, and C refers back to A (we'll see an example in a moment).

What should happen? As soon as the objects are no longer referenced from else-where, the interpreter should recognize that they're only referred to by one an-other, and make them available for garbage collection. But in affected versions of Internet Explorer, if any of those objects is a **DOM node** or an **ActiveX object**, the garbage collector can't see that object's isolated relationship, so it will remain in memory until the browser is closed.

When refreshing a single page, or navigating between pages that use the same script (or another script with the same problem), the amount of memory used by the browser will gradually increase and, in extreme cases, this can result in a user running out of RAM altogether.

Solution

We have two ways to deal with this problem:

❑ Avoid circular references.

❑ Clean up after the fact.

The first solution is not always practical, so the second solution is generally the more useful.

Avoiding Circular References

Circular references are very easy to create without realizing it. Consider this HTML, for example:

```
<h2>Site navigation</h2>
<ul id="menu">
  <li><a href="/">Home</a></li>
  <li><a href="/about/">About us</a></li>
  <li><a href="/contact/">Contact us</a></li>
</ul>
```

The following scripting goes with it:[6]

File: **circular-references.js** (excerpt)

```
function bindListHandler(listid)
{
  var list = document.getElementById(listid);
  list.related = list.previousSibling;
  list.related.related = list;

  list.onclick = function()
  {
    this.related.style.color = 'red';
  };

  list.related.onclick = function()
  {
    this.related.style.color = 'red';
  };
}
```

We've created a related property for the list that refers to the heading, and a related property of the heading that refers back to the list (although this is an oversimplified example, since the heading is not necessarily the previousSibling of the list). This technique can be very useful, as it allows an event handler on either element to refer to the other. But, because they refer to each other, a circular reference has been created.

This problem can be avoided simply by avoiding circular references. Avoid creating objects that refer to each other, and then no circular references will be formed.

---

[6] Based on an example by Peter-Paul Koch [http://www.quirksmode.org/blog/archives/2005/02/javascript_memo.html].

However, that may not be possible, or practical; you may prefer the convenience of this kind of technique. Personally, I think this is really the vendor's problem, and not something we should have to worry about; nonetheless, a client might complain, and we may have no choice but to find a way of fixing it.

I've been in that situation a few times, and fortunately there is an alternative, retrospective solution that can be applied with little or no alteration to the original code.

Cleaning Up After the Fact

If you can't, or don't want to, avoid circular references, they be can be cleaned manually.

Cleaning functions that are written as DOM 0 event handlers (using properties like *element*.onclick, as we discussed in Chapter 13) is as simple as iterating through document.all from the unload event, and "marking" the identified properties for garbage collection by setting them to null. This example is based on a function by Richard Cornford;[7] further handlers can be added to the expandos array as necessary:

File: **dom-cleaners.js (excerpt)**

```
if (typeof window.attachEvent != 'undefined')
{
  window.attachEvent('onunload', function()
  {
    var expandos = ['mouseover', 'click'];

    var elen = expandos.length;
    var dlen = document.all.length;

    for (var i = 0; i < dlen; i++)
    {
      for (var j = 0; j < elen; j++)
      {
        document.all[i]['on' + expandos[j]] = null;
      }
    }
  });
}
```

---

[7] http://groups.google.com/group/comp.lang.javascript/msg/fe9025326f5ae177

But it's equally possible to form circular references with functions that are bound using `attachEvent`; these leak just the same way, but they don't appear in `document.all` or any other collection.

We can only clean them if we already have references to them, and this is where a generic event-binding function can come in extra-handy. Let's look back at the `attachEventListener` function we created in Chapter 13 (here's an excerpt as far as is relevant):

```
function attachEventListener(target, eventType, functionRef,
    capture)
{
  if (typeof target.addEventListener != 'undefined')
  {
    target.addEventListener(eventType, functionRef, capture);
  }
  else if (typeof target.attachEvent != 'undefined')
  {
    target.attachEvent('on' + eventType, functionRef);
  }
  ⋮
```

We simply need to store each reference as it's added:

File: **dom-cleaners.js** (excerpt)

```
var listeners = [];
function attachEventListener(target, eventType, functionRef,
    capture)
{
  if (typeof target.addEventListener != 'undefined')
  {
    target.addEventListener(eventType, functionRef, capture);
  }
  else if (typeof target.attachEvent != 'undefined')
  {
    target.attachEvent('on' + eventType, functionRef);
    listeners[listeners.length] =
        [target, eventType, functionRef];
  }
  ⋮
```

Then, from the `unload` event, we can iterate through our stored listeners, removing them with `detachEvent`:

File: **dom-cleaners.js (excerpt)**

```
if (typeof window.attachEvent != 'undefined')
{
  window.attachEvent('onunload', function()
  {
    var len = listeners.length;

    for (var i = 0; i < len; i++)
    {
      listeners[i][0].detachEvent(
          'on' + listeners[i][1], listeners[i][2]);
    }
  });
}
```

Making Scripts Run Before the Load Event

The load event doesn't fire until a document has completely finished loading, including the loading of all its external dependencies, such as style sheets, scripts and, most significantly, images. It's the same for both event handlers and event listeners that are bound using addEventListener or attachEvent—none of these will be triggered by the load event until the document has completely loaded.

Actually, we don't need to know about external dependencies most of the time. For most DOM scripts, we simply need to know *whether the DOM is ready*, and that occurs irrespective of images and other includes. Unfortunately, there isn't any standard event that tells us when it happens.

Solution

What we can do is use a timer-based solution that continually checks for the existence of the body element, a DOM method (from which we know that DOM scripting is generally safe), and one or more elements that your function may depend upon:

File: **run-before-onload.js**

```
function addDomFunction(fn, dependencies)
{
  var counter = 0, collections = {}, timer = setInterval(
  function()
```

```
{
  var ready = false;
  counter++;

  if (typeof document.getElementsByTagName != 'undefined'
      && (document.getElementsByTagName('body')[0] ||
      document.body))
  {
    ready = true;

    if (typeof dependencies == 'object')
    {
      for (var i in dependencies)
      {
        if (dependencies[i] == 'id' &&
            !document.getElementById(i))
        {
          ready = false;
          break;
        }
        else if (dependencies[i] == 'tag')
        {
          var len = document.getElementsByTagName(i).length;
          if (typeof collections[i] == 'undefined' ||
              collections[i] != len || len < 1)
          {
            collections[i] = len;
            ready = false;
            break;
          }
        }
      }
    }
    if (ready)
    {
      clearInterval(timer);
      fn();
    }
  }

  if (counter >= 40)
  {
    clearInterval(timer);
  }
```

```
  }, 250);
}
```

This helper function can go right at the start of the head of your document, which makes it usable from any other script that's loaded subsequently, in much the same way as were our other encapsulated event-listening functions (such as addLoadListener, which we built way back in Chapter 1). We can use it to call a named function:

```
addDomFunction(function);
```

Or we can use it by writing an anonymous function directly inside the call:

```
addDomFunction(function()
{
  alert('Hello world!');
});
```

When used this way, domFunction can be used to trigger code that creates new elements and adds them to the head or body. However, if the code will manipulate *existing* elements inside the body, we need to take extra steps to ensure that those elements have already loaded. domFunction includes the facility to check for the existence of specific elements or collections; these are defined by passing an object literal as the second argument. Specify either a single element by ID:

```
addDomFunction(function, { 'elementId' : 'id' });
```

Or specify a group of elements by tag name:

```
addDomFunction(function, { 'p' : 'tag' });
```

Specifying an element by ID is a robust approach, because an element either exists or it doesn't, and addDomFunction can hold the execution of your nominated function until an element with the specified ID exists. Waiting for a collection, on the other hand, is shakier ground. Although addDomFunction can check for the *existence* of a collection, it cannot detect *whether that collection has finished loading*, and that might be very significant. For example, if your nominated function iterates through the collection to apply behaviors or properties to all such elements in the document, you want to be sure that all those elements have loaded before it runs. The best addDomFunction can do in this case is recheck the length of the collection every 250ms and, if it remains stable over that period, assume that the collection has finished loading. If that sounds too unreliable for your needs (e.g., if you have a particularly large document in which the elements of a collection might be quite spread out), I recommend you use a single element as the loading "hook"—one which comes later in the source code than the collection in which you're interested—and wait for that element by ID.

Discussion

The fact that scripts don't run until images have loaded can sometimes produce a noticeable difference between the page as it's first seen, and how it looks once the scripting kicks in. The most obvious example of this is a style sheet switcher that applies a user's choice of alternate style sheet from a cookie: if this didn't run until the `load` event, we would see the different styles possibly for several seconds, or even minutes, depending on the number and size of the images involved.

The timer-based solution we have just seen is one way around this, and it's one that offers a good overall level of browser support—the construct works in all modern browsers except Mac IE 5 and Safari 1.0. However, there are other ways to achieve it, and there's a good article and discussion covering the range of possibilities[8] at Web Graphics.

But note that, however it's implemented, this approach won't always be appropriate. We might actually *need* to know about images on the page—to extract properties such as their width and height, for example—and obviously we can't do that until those images have loaded. By the same token, we might be reading data from another external source, such as the DOM of a page in an `iframe`. Likewise, we can't do that until we know the embedded document has loaded: one approach we can use to ascertain this is to wait until the global `load` event. So, while initializing scripts in this independent way will often be a suitable approach (and sometimes is clearly the best one), it's not a direct and interchangeable replacement.

As ever, take care to think through the implications of this, or any script you use.

Summary

In this chapter, we've discussed a range of techniques that aim to improve the efficiency of scripts, and reduce the amount of code they take. The techniques have varied from solid and generally useful ideas, to some that are arguably more trouble than they're worth.

---

[8] http://web-graphics.com/mtarchive/001635.php

We've also seen aggressive techniques for "compressing" a script before publication; distinct from normal coding practice, these should only be applied to the public version of a script, not to your own development copy. And we looked at the dreaded DOM memory leak, and discussed how to avoid it, or clean up after the fact—a task that's almost become a necessity for all but the simplest of scripts!

Finally, we took a peek at an interesting technique for initializing scripts independently of the regular `load` event, and although it may not be something you use a great deal, this idea is gaining popularity as clients demand more sophisticated and seamless user experiences.

Index

Symbols
!= inequality operator, 49
!== non-identity operator, 50
. wildcard character, 56
== equality operator, 48
=== identity operator, 50

A
abs method, Math class, 278
absolute positioning
  browser differences, 248
  CSS clip property and, 305
  drop-down lists, 509
  iframe elements, 357
  menus, IE, 332
  news ticker example, 299
abstraction
  direct referencing and, 520
  object orientation feature, 516, 522, 549
  of tasks as functions, 548
Access Matters web site, 438
accessibility
  (see also keyboard accessibility; screen readers)
  attempted definition of, 386
  automatically initiated scripts, 441
  current sub-branch display, 383
  device-independent event handlers, 393–394
  frames and, 135
  hiding menu elements, 326
  keyboard and mouse, 395–402
  keyboard navigation and, 368
  limitations of menus, 326
  non-programming aspects, 387
  popups and, 129
  screen readers and, 436–456
  slider controls, 428–436
  tooltip display and, 402–411
ActionScript, 461
activate event, IE, 394, 397
:active pseudo-class, 325
ActiveX objects, 3, 468
  (see also Flash; XMLHttpRequest object)
  Flash detection and, 458
  Flash version detection, 460
  FSCommand support and, 461, 463
  memory leaks and, 556
actuate event, 393
addDomFunction function, 562
addEventListener method, 16, 234, 243, 560
addLoadListener function, 15
  accessible tooltip example, 405
  adding a new style sheet, 226
  auto-complete text fields, 507
  clip–based transitions, 306
  custom dialog example, 483
  drag-and-drop effects, 282
  image swapping, 169
  soccer ball animation, 272
  tooltip example, 251
  WYSIWYG editor, 492
addRule method, IE, 221, 226
AJAX (Asynchronous JavaScript and XML), 468
  frameworks, 475
  keyboard accessibility, 401
  screen readers and, 446
Ajile module, 532
alert dialog
  error analysis and, 23
  error messages, 119, 441
  page alternative, 25

accessible slider control, 434
creating iframe elements, 355
menu timers, 339
mouseover event sources, 394, 408, 450
movement (*see* animation; motion effects; mouse movements)
moveObject function, 272–275
Mozilla browsers
(*see also* Firefox)
browser detection, 197
distinguishing Safari from, 196
focus event bubbling, 397
script timeouts, 546
strict warnings and, 545
MSXML parser, 469
multi-dimensional arrays, 66–67, 76
multi-line flag, regular expressions, 55
multiple inheritance, 527
multiple scripts
event handlers and, 14, 230
event listeners and, 233

N

named arguments, 547
namespaces, 88, 531–532
naming conflicts, 531, 555
NaN (Not a Number) value, 41
navigation using lists, 322
(*see also* keyboard navigation; menus)
navigator object properties, 196, 459
browser detection and, 194, 196, 554
nesting
event bubbling and, 243
nested closures, 341
nested divs, 313
nested for loops, 67
nested functions, variable access, 530
nested lists, 323
nested submenus, 412
ternary operators, 539

Netscape, 2, 462
news ticker example (*see* scrolling news ticker)
nextSibling property, 86
nodeName property, 87
nodes, DOM
cloning, 91
iterative change warning, 92
node types, 79
relational properties, 85
whitespace nodes, 86
nodeType property, 87
nodeValue property, 88
non-identity operator, 50
noscript element, 6
Number function, 40
numeric data, 31–44
adding ordinal suffixes, 42
base detection, 41
converting dates to strings, 37
converting numbers to strings, 36–38
converting strings to, 39–42
currency values, 38
random numbers, 35
rounding numbers, 33
sorting and compare function, 75
sorting arrays, 76
sorting in tables, 264
string concatenation risks, 37
testing for, 41, 58
text field validation, 114

O

obfuscation, source code, 18, 553
object based scripting, 71, 518
object detection (*see* feature detection)
object orientation, 515–533
code efficiency and, 549
example script, 519–520
method creation, 521–526

P

round method, Math object, 32, 34–35
rounding numbers, 33, 38
rules property, IE, 217

S

Safari browser
  cancelling link defaults, 237, 483,
    495
  CSS 2 System Colors and, 403, 410
  detection, 197
  distinguishing from Mozilla, 196
  DOM support limitations, 221–223,
    226
  events from text nodes, 344
  href values, 382
  input element problem, 430
  lang pseudo-class, 404
  scroll event problems, 139
  setTimeout support, 344
  stopDefaultAction function and, 368
  stylesheet collection, 217
Safari Enhancer, 20
Sajax JavaScript framework, 476
scope (*see* variable scopes)
screen readers
  accessible scripts for, 436–456
  current sub-branch display, 383
  detection through events, 369–370
  Flash alternative, 455
  form validation, 440
  hiding menu elements, 326
  identification, 449
  link identification by, 439
  menu accessibility, 392
  modal interaction and, 454
  problems with dynamic content,
    390, 442, 444, 453
  products listed, 436
  reading label text, 441
  remote scripting and, 446
  scripting support, 388, 437–449

simulating the user experience, 436
suggested best practice, 453
tricks and hacks, 449
user needs, 385, 388, 454–455
script element, 12, 14
scripts
  anticipating load events, 560–563
  concise coding, 548–552
  faster running, 536–548
  inside iframes, 480
  multiple, and DOM 0 event hand-
    lers, 230
  timing out, 546
  Web version optimization, 552–556
scrollBy method, window object, 140
scrolling
  menu repositioning and, 353
  prevention, accessible menu example,
    428
  scroll position, 137–141, 249
scrolling news ticker, 298–305
  screen readers and, 442, 445
  user control, 302, 305
scrollTo method, window object, 140
scrollTop property, 139
security
  cross-frame scripting, 137
  iframes and, 480
  restrictions on JavaScript, 3
  XMLHttpRequest and, 471
select boxes, 111
select elements, 354, 358, 442
selectedIndex property, 113
selectionStart property, 513
semicolon terminator, 11, 553
send method, XMLHttpRequest object,
    471
separation of content, style, and beha-
    vior, 8–11, 321, 323
  status of navigation arrows, 337
separators
  className property, 100, 102

Books for Web Developers from SitePoint

Visit http://www.sitepoint.com/books/
for sample chapters or to order!

sitepoint

Build Your Own

Database Driven Website

Using PHP & MySQL

By Kevin Yank

A Practical Step-by-Step Guide

The PHP Anthology

Object Oriented PHP Solutions
Volume I

By Harry Fuecks

Practical Solutions to Common Problems

The PHP Anthology

Object Oriented PHP Solutions

Volume II

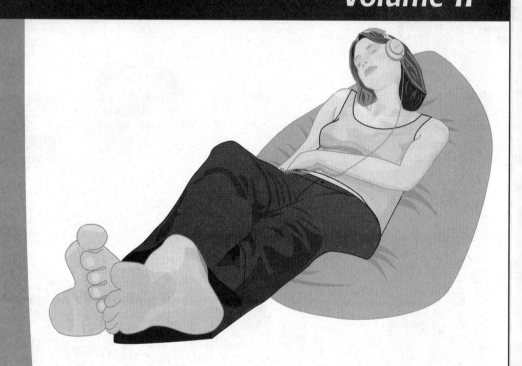

By Harry Fuecks

Practical Solutions to Common Problems

NO NONSENSE
XML WEB
DEVELOPMENT
WITH PHP

BY **THOMAS MYER**

MASTER PHP 5'S POWERFUL NEW XML FUNCTIONALITY

RUN YOUR OWN
WEB SERVER
USING
LINUX & APACHE

BY **STUART LANGRIDGE**
& **TONY STEIDLER-DENNISON**

GET STARTED WITH LINUX AND APACHE — THE EASY WAY!

Build Your Own

ASP.NET Website
Using C# & VB.NET

By Zak Ruvalcaba

A Practical Step-by-Step Guide

HTML Utopia:

Designing Without Tables

Using CSS

By Dan Shafer

A Practical Step-by-Step Guide

THE CSS ANTHOLOGY

101 ESSENTIAL TIPS, TRICKS & HACKS

BY RACHEL ANDREW

DHTML UTOPIA:
MODERN
WEB DESIGN
USING
JAVASCRIPT & DOM

BY STUART LANGRIDGE

PRACTICAL UNOBTRUSIVE JAVASCRIPT TECHNIQUES

BUILD YOUR OWN

STANDARDS
COMPLIANT
WEBSITE
USING
DREAMWEAVER 8

BY **RACHEL ANDREW**

A PRACTICAL STEP-BY-STEP GUIDE TO MASTERING DREAMWEAVER 8

Kits for Web Professionals
from SitePoint

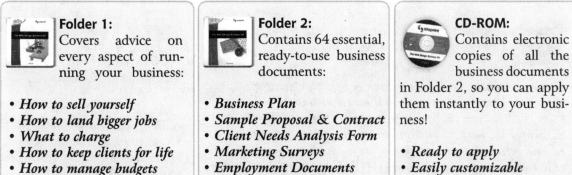